William J. Comley

Comley's History of the State of New York,

embracing a general review of her agricultural and mineralogical resources, her

manufacturing industries, trade and commerce, together with a description of her

great metropolis

William J. Comley

Comley's History of the State of New York,
embracing a general review of her agricultural and mineralogical resources, her manufacturing industries, trade and commerce, together with a description of her great metropolis

ISBN/EAN: 9783337288822

Printed in Europe, USA, Canada, Australia, Japan

Cover: Foto ©ninafisch / pixelio.de

More available books at **www.hansebooks.com**

OF THE

STATE OF NEW YORK,

EMBRACING

A GENERAL REVIEW OF HER AGRICULTURAL AND MINERALOGICAL RESOURCES,
HER MANUFACTURING INDUSTRIES, TRADE AND COMMERCE,
TOGETHER WITH A DESCRIPTION OF

HER GREAT METROPOLIS,

FROM ITS SETTLEMENT BY THE DUTCH, IN 1609.

BY W. J. COMLEY.

ALSO, AN ENCYCLOPÆDIA OF BIOGRAPHY OF SOME OF THE OLD SETTLERS, AND MANY
OF HER MOST PROMINENT PROFESSIONAL AND BUSINESS MEN.

SPLENDIDLY ILLUSTRATED.

NEW YORK:
COMLEY BROTHERS' MANUFACTURING AND PUBLISHING CO., 767 AND 769 BROADWAY.
1877.

DEDICATION.

TO THE INHABITANTS OF THE STATE OF NEW YORK;

TO YOU WHO HAVE DEVELOPED THE RESOURCES AND BUILT UP
THE CITIES AND TOWNS OF THIS STATE; TO YOU WHO
HAVE GIVEN IT ITS WEALTH, ITS FAME, AND ITS
BUSINESS; TO YOU WHO HAVE GIVEN IT
ITS REPUTATION ABROAD AND
PROSPERITY AT HOME,

THIS BOOK IS RESPECTFULLY DEDICATED,

BY

The Author.

PREFACE.

IN laying before the public a new work, designed to present the growth and the importance of the commerce and manufactures, and the development of the agriculture and mineralogy of the Empire State, it is not to be expected that a plan so entirely new, and so ambitious, should be executed with either the precision or the completeness that may be attained by those who travel in a beaten path.

That the task has been adequately performed, is an assertion which is left for other and less deeply interested persons to make. Yet it is not our purpose to offer one word of apology for faulty arrangement, or for imperfections, the causes of which are as patent as the blemishes themselves.

The history of trade, like the history of any other of the transactions in human affairs, can only be intelligently presented to the mass of readers by seizing upon such facts as most fully illustrate its character, and holding up a series of pictures which constitute a congruous whole.

All candid minds must pronounce at once upon the impossibility of elaborating in every detail, in a single volume, the working of the wonderful engine of trade, which is operating continually in our midst. Such a result has not even been attempted; but in its place it has been sought to give a series of outlines, presenting the most prominent features of the relations of the State of New York, with her tributary country, in such manner as to best convey an idea of the magnitude and direction of her commerce, and the requirements it has to supply.

The biographical feature of the work is not new, since biography in some form is inseparable from the relation of any human action; yet, in its treatment in the book the history of men is interwoven with the record of their affairs, in the same intimate connections which they sustain in the daily current of commercial life. Business affairs do not transact themselves; therefore it seemed eminently proper that their history should be blended with the life struggles and triumphs of the men who are charged with the responsibility of their movement.

While not deprecating honest criticism, I will yet express the hope that the difficulties, inherent in such a task as we have undertaken, will meet with due consideration when the value of the work itself is being estimated.

TABLE OF CONTENTS.

	PAGE
TITLE-PAGE....	
DEDICATION....	
PREFACE....	
Ancient Pre-occupants of the Region of Western New York...	33
The Iroquois or Five Nations....	44
New York State....	46
Early Glimpses of Western New York....	64
Observations of Wentworth Greenhalph....	65
Governors of the Colony and State....	70
Great Cities....	71
New York City....	75
Domestic Exports from the Port of New York for the Last Twenty Years....	77
Foreign Exports from the Port of New York for the Last Twenty Years....	77
Foreign Imports at the Port of New York for the Last Twenty Years....	77
Receipts of Domestic Produce at New York for the Year 1876....	78
Exports of Produce from New York for the Year 1876....	78
Manufactures....	79
Finances....	79
Courts....	79
Education....	80
Churches....	83
Charities....	83
Public Buildings....	85
Water-Works....	87
Markets....	87
Fire, Police, and Post-Office Departments....	88
History of New York City....	90
An Historical Summary of the Several Attacks made upon the City of New York, and the Measures that have been adopted for their Defence from 1613 until 1812....	95
Advantages of New York as set forth a Century ago....	109
Mementoes of the Olden Time....	111
A Duel....	111
The Seasons....	111
An Earthquake....	111
The Commercial Marine....	111
Small-Pox....	111
First Fire-Engines....	111
Hard Times....	111
Election....	111
Burning of the Archives of Trinity Church....	112
The Oyster Pasty Battery....	112
Whales in the North River....	112
Wild Pigeons....	112
Sale of Slaves....	112

TABLE OF CONTENTS.

	PAGE
Pillory and Cage	112
King George's Statue	112
The Battery	112
The Dutch Church in the Fort	112
Pirates and Privateers	112
The Windmill on the Commons	113
The City Fathers	113
Beekman's Swamp	113
The First Public Library	113
Negroes and Slaves	113
Office-holders	113
Trinity Church	113
Bolting and Baking Monopoly	113
Watch and Police Regulations	114
Captain Kidd	115
Classical School	116
Road to Harlem	116
Lighting the City	116
Arrival of a Governor	116
Duties of Aldermen	116
Showing Date and Birth of First Female Born in New York	116
Social Amusements in the Olden Time	117
The Battery	117
Ferry to Long Island	117
Mails	118
The Original Mammoth	118
Capture of Pirates	118
The First Presbyterian Church in Wall Street	118
First Daily Newspaper	118
Cold Weather	118
A Nobleman's Mother	118
Estimate of the Support of the City	119
Mild Weather	119
After the Great Fire	119
First Negro Plot in the City of New York	119
Brooklyn	121
Title-page, Biographical Encyclopædia	327
Preface, " "	329
Biographies	331

THE ANCIENT PRE-OCCUPANTS OF THE REGION OF WESTERN NEW YORK.

The local historian of almost our entire continent finds at the threshold of the task he enters upon, difficulties and embarrassments. If for a starting-point the first advent of civilization is chosen, a summary disposition is made of all that preceded it, unsatisfactory to author and reader. Our own race was the successor of others. Here in our own region, when the waters of the Niagara were first disturbed by a craft of European architecture—when the adventurous Frenchman would first pitch a tent upon its banks, there were "lords of the Forests and the Lakes" to be consulted. Where stood that humble primitive "palisade," its site grudgingly and suspiciously granted, in process of time arose strong walls—ramparts, from behind which the armies of successive nations were arranged to repel assailants. The dense forests that for more than a century enshrouded them, unbroken by the woodman's axe, have now disappeared, or but skirt a peaceful and beautiful cultivated landscape. Civilization, improvement, and industry have made an Empire of the region that for a long period was tributary to this nucleus of early events. Cities have been founded—the Arts, Sciences taught; Learning has its temples and its votaries; History its enlightened and earnest inquirers. And yet, with the pre-occupant lingering until even now in our midst, we have but the unsatisfactory knowledge of him and his race which is gathered from dim and obscure tradition. That which is suited to the pages of fiction and romance, but can be incorporated in the pages of history only with suspicion and distrust. The learned and the curious have from time to time inquired of their old men; they have sat down in their wigwams and listened to their recitals; the pages of history have been searched and compared with their imperfect revelations, to discover some faint coincidence or analogy; and yet we know nothing of the origin, and have but unsatisfactory traditions of the people we found here and have almost dispossessed.

If their own history is obscure; if their relations of themselves, after they have gone back but little more than a century beyond the period of the first European emigration, degenerates to fable and obscure tradition, they are but poor revelators of a still greater mystery. We are surrounded by evidences that a race preceded them, farther advanced in civilization and the arts, and far more numerous. Here and there upon the brows of our hills, at the head of our ravines, are their fortifications; their locations selected with skill, adapted to refuge, subsistence, and defence. The uprooted trees of our forest, that are the growth of centuries, expose their mouldering remains; the uncovered mounds, masses of their skeletons promiscuously heaped one upon the other, as if they were the gathered and hurriedly entombed of well-contested fields. In our valleys, upon our hill-sides, the plough and the spade discover their rude implements, adapted to war, the chase, and domestic use. All these are dumb yet eloquent chronicles of by-gone ages. We ask the red man to tell us from whence they came and whither they went? and he either amuses us with wild and extravagant traditionary legends, or acknowledges himself as ignorant as his interrogators. He and his progenitors have gazed upon these ancient relics for centuries, as we do now—wondered and consulted their wise men, and yet he is unable to aid our inquiries. We invoke the aid of revelation, turn over the pages of history, trace the origin and dispersion of the races of mankind from the earliest period of the world's existence, and yet we gather only enough to form the basis of vague surmise and conjecture. The crumbling walls—the "Ruins," overgrown by the gigantic forests of Central America, are not involved in more impenetrable obscurity, than are the more humble but equally interesting mounds and relics that abound in our own region.

We are prone to speak of ourselves as the inhabitants of a *new* world; and yet we are confronted with such evidences of antiquity! We clear away the forests and speak familiarly of subduing a "virgin soil;" and yet the plough up-turns the skulls of those whose history is lost! We say that Columbus discovered a *new* world. Why not that he helped to make two *old* ones acquainted with each other?

Our advent here is but one of the changes of TIME. We are consulting dumb signs, inanimate and unintelligible witnesses, gleaning but unsatisfactory knowledge of races that have preceded us. Who in view of earth's revolutions; the developments that the young but rapidly progressive science of Geology has made; the organic remains that are found in the alluvial deposits in our valleys, deeply embedded under successive strata of rock in our mountain ranges; the impressions in our coal formations; history's emphatic teachings; fails to reflect that our own race may not be exempt from the operations of what may be regarded as general laws? Who shall say that the scholar, the antiquarian, of another far-off century, may not be a Champollion deciphering the inscriptions upon our monuments—or a Stevens, wandering among the ruins of our cities, to gather relics to identify our existence?

> "Since the first sun-light spread itself o'er earth;
> Since Chaos gave a thousand systems birth;
> Since first the morning stars together sung;
> Since first this globe was on its axis hung;
> Untiring CHANGE, with ever-moving hand,
> Has waved o'er earth its more than magic wand." *

Although not peculiar to this region, there is perhaps no portion of the United States where ancient relics are more numerous. Commencing principally near the Oswego River, they extend westwardly over all the western counties of our State, Canada West, the western Lake Region, the valleys of the Ohio and the Mississippi. Either as now, the western portion of our State had attractions and inducements to make it a favorite residence; or these people, assailed from the north and the east, made this a refuge in a war of extermination, fortified the commanding eminences, met the shock of a final issue; were subject to its adverse results. Were their habits and pursuits mixed ones, their residence was well chosen. The Forest invited to the chase; the Lakes and Rivers to local commerce—to the use of the net and the angling-rod; the soil, to agriculture. The evidences that this was one, at least, of their final battle-grounds, predominate. They are the fortifications, intrenchments, and warlike instruments. That here was a war of extermination, we may conclude, from the masses of human skeletons we find indiscriminately thrown together, indicating a common and simultaneous sepulture; from which age, infancy, sex, no condition, was exempt.

In assuming that these are the remains of a people other than the Indian race we found here, the author has the authority of De Witt Clinton—a name scarcely

* "Changes of Time," a Poem by B. B. French.

less identified with our literature than with our achievements in internal improvements. In a discourse delivered before the New York Historical Society in 1811, Mr. Clinton says: " Previous to the occupation of this country by the progenitors of the present race of Indians, it was inhabited by a race of men much more populous, and much farther advanced in civilization." Indeed the abstract position may be regarded as conceded. Who they were, whence they came, and whither they went, have been themes of speculation with learned antiquarians, who have failed to arrive at any satisfactory conclusions. In a field, or historical department, so ably and thoroughly explored, the author would not venture opinions or theories of his own, even were it not a subject of inquiry, in the main, distinct from the objects of his work. It is a topic prolific enough of reflection, inquiry, and speculation, for volumes, rather than an incidental historical chapter. And yet, it is a subject of too much local interest to be wholly passed over.

At the early period at which Mr. Clinton advanced the theory that the Ridge Road was once the southern shore of Lake Ontario—1811—when settlement was but just begun, and a dense forest precluded a close observation, he was quite liable to fall into the error that time and better opportunities for investigation have corrected. The formation, composition, alluvial deposits, etc., of the Ridge Road, with reference to its two sides, present almost an entire uniformity. There is, at least, not the distinction that would be apparent if there had been the action of water, depositing its materials only upon its northern side. By supposing the Mountain Ridge to have once been the southern shore of Lake Ontario, it would follow that the Ridge Road may have been a *Sand bar*. The nature of both, their relative positions, would render this a far more reasonable hypothesis than the other; and when we add the fact that the immediate slope, or falling off, is almost as much generally, upon the south as the north side of the Ridge Road, we are under the necessity of abandoning the precedent theory. There is from the Niagara to the Genesee River, upon the *Mountain* Ridge, a line, or cordon, of these ancient fortifications—none, as the author concludes, from observation and inquiry, between the two.*

But a few of the most prominent of these ancient fortifications will be noticed, enough only to give the reader who has not had an opportunity of seeing them a general idea of their structure, and relics which almost uniformly may be found in and about them.

Upon a slope or offset of the Mountain Ridge three and a half miles from the village of Lewiston, is a marked spot, that the Tuscarora Indians call *Kienuka*.† There is a burial ground, and two elliptic mounds or barrows that have a diameter of 20 feet, and an elevation of from 4 to 5 feet. A mass of detached works, with spaces intervening, seems to have been chosen as a rock citadel; and well chosen—for the mountain fastnesses of Switzerland are but little better adapted to the purposes of a look-out and defence. The sites of habitations are marked by remains of pottery, pipes, and other evidences.

Eight miles east of this, upon one of the most elevated points of the mountain ridge in the town of Cambria, upon the farm until recently owned by Eliakim Hammond, now owned by John Gould, is an ancient fortification and burial-place,

---

* Upon an elevation, on the shore of Lake Ontario near the Eighteen-mile-Creek, there is a mound similar in appearance to some of those that have been termed *ancient ;* though it is unquestionably incident to the early French and Indian wars of this region. And the same conclusion may be formed in reference to other similar ones along the shore of the lake.

† Meaning a fort, or stronghold, that has a commanding position, or from which there is a fine view.

possessing perhaps as great a degree of interest and as distinct characteristics as any that have been discovered in Western New York. The author having been one of a party that made a thorough examination of the spot soon after its first discovery in 1823, he is enabled from memory and some published accounts of his at the time, to state the extent and character of the relics.

The location commands a view of Lake Ontario and the surrounding country. An area of about six acres of level ground appears to have been occupied; fronting which, upon a circular verge of the mountain, were distinct remains of a wall. Nearly in the centre of the area was a depository of the dead. It was a pit excavated to the depth of four or five feet, filled with human bones, over which were slabs of sand stone. Hundreds seem to have been thrown in promiscuously, of both sexes and all ages. Extreme old age was distinctly identified by toothless jaws, and the complete absorption of the alveolar processes; and extreme infancy, by the small skulls and incomplete ossification. Numerous barbs or arrow-points were found among the bones, and in the vicinity. One skull retained the arrow that had pierced it, the aperture it had made on entering being distinctly visible. In the position of the skeletons, there was none of the signs of ordinary Indian burial; but evidences that the bodies were thrown in promiscuously, and at the same time. The conjecture might well be indulged that it had been the theatre of a sanguinary battle, terminating in favor of the assailants, and a general massacre. A thigh-bone of unusual length was preserved for a considerable period by a physician of Lockport, and excited much curiosity. It had been fractured obliquely. In the absence of any surgical skill, or at least any application of it, the bone had strongly reunited, though evidently so as to have left the foot turned out at nearly a right angle. Of course, the natural surfaces of the bone were in contact, and not the fractured surfaces; and yet spurs or ligaments were thrown out by nature, in its healing process, and so firmly knit and interwoven as to form, if not a perfect, a firm reunion! It was by no means a finished piece of surgery, but to all appearances had answered a very good purpose. The medical student will think the patient must have possessed all the fortitude and stoicism of his race, to have kept his fractured limb in a necessarily fixed position, during the long months that the healing process must have been going on, in the absence of splints and gum elastic bands. A tree had been cut down growing directly over the mound, upon the stump of which could be counted 230 concentric circles. Remains of rude specimens of earthen ware, pieces of copper, and iron instruments of rude workmanship were ploughed up within the area; also, charred wood, corn and cobs.

At the head of a deep gorge, a mile west of Lockport (similar to the one that forms the natural canal basin, from which the combined Locks ascend), in the early settlement of the country, a circular raised work, or ring-fort, could be distinctly traced. Leading from the inclosed area, there had been a covered way to a spring of pure cold water that issues from a fissure in the rock, some 50 or 60 feet down

NOTE.—The following passage appears in "Cusick's History of the Six Nations," the extraordinary production of a native Tuscarora, that it will be necessary to notice in another part of the work.

About this time the King of the Five Nations had ordered the Great War chief, Shorihawne (a Mohawk), to march directly with an army of five thousand warriors to aid the Governor of Canandaigua against the Erians, to attack the Fort Kayquatkay and endeavor to extinguish the council-fire of the enemy, which was becoming dangerous to the neighboring nations; but unfortunately during the siege, a shower of arrows was flying from the fort, the great war chief Shorihawne was killed, and his body was conveyed back to the woods and was buried in a solemn manner; but however, the siege continued for several days; the Erians sued for peace; the army immediately ceased from hostilities, and left the Erians in entire possession of the country.

the declivity. Such covered paths, or rather the remains of them, lead from many of these ancient fortifications. Mr. Schoolcraft concludes that they were intended for the emergency of a prolonged siege. They would seem now, to have been but a poor defence for the water-carriers, against the weapons of modern warfare; yet probably sufficient to protect them from arrows, and a foe that had no sappers or miners in their ranks.

There is an ancient battle-field upon the Buffalo Creek six miles from Buffalo, near the Mission Station. There are appearances of an inclosed area, a mound where human bones have been excavated, remains of pottery ware, etc. The Senecas have a tradition that here was a last decisive battle between their people and their inveterate enemies the Kah-Kwahs; though there would seem to be no reason why the fortification should not be classed among those that existed long before the Senecas are supposed to have inhabited this region.

A mile north of Aurora village, in Erie County, there are several small lakes or ponds, around and between which there are knobs or elevations, thickly covered with a tall growth of pine; upon them are several mounds, where many human bones have been excavated. In fact, Aurora and its vicinity seems to have been a favorite resort not only for the ancient people whose works and remains we are noticing, but for the other races that succeeded them. Relics abound there perhaps to a greater extent than in any other locality in Western New York. An area of from three to four miles in extent, embracing the village, the ponds, the fine springs of water at the foot of the bluffs to the north, and the level plain to the south, would seem to have been thickly populated. There are in the village and vicinity few gardens and fields where ancient and Indian relics are not found at each successive ploughing. Few cellars are excavated without discovering them. In digging a cellar a few years since, upon the farm of Charles P. Pierson, a skeleton was exhumed, the thigh-bones of which would indicate great height; exceeding by several inches that of the tallest of our own race. In digging another cellar, a large number of skeletons, or detached bones, were thrown out. Upon the farm of M. B. Crooks, two miles from the village, where a tree had been turned up, several hundred pounds of axes were found; a blacksmith who was working up some axes that were found in Aurora, told the author that most of them were without any steel, but that the iron was of a superior quality. He had one that was *entirely of steel*, out of which he was manufacturing some edge tools.

Near the village, principally upon the farm of the late Horace S. Turner, was an extensive Beaver Dam. It is but a few years since an aged Seneca strolled away from the road, visited the ponds, the springs, and coming to a field once overflowed by the dam, but then reclaimed and cultivated, said these were the haunts of his youth—upon the hills he had chased the deer, at the springs he had slaked his thirst, and in the field he had trapped the beaver.

The ancient works at Fort Hill, Le Roy, are especially worthy of observation in connection with this interesting branch of history, or rather inquiry. The author is principally indebted for an account of them to Mr. Schoolcraft's "Notes on the Iroquois," for which it was communicated by F. Follett, of Batavia. They are three miles north of Le Roy, on an elevated point of land, formed by the junction of a small stream called Fordham's Brook, with Allen's Creek. The better view of Fort Hill is had to the north of it, about a quarter of a mile on the road leading from Bergen to Le Roy. From this point of observation it needs little aid of the imagination to conceive that it was erected as a fortification by a large and powerful army, looking for a permanent and inaccessible bulwark of defence. From the centre of the hill, in a north-westerly course, the country lies quite flat ; more immediately north, and inclining to the east, the land is also level for one hundred rods, where it rises nearly as high as the hill, and continues for several miles quite elevated. In approaching the hill from the north, it stands very prominently before you, rising rather abruptly but not perpendicularly, to the height of eighty or ninety feet, extending about forty rods on a line east and west, the corners being round or truncated, and continuing to the south on the west side for some fifty or sixty rods, and on the east side for about half a mile, maintaining about the same elevation on the sides as in front ; beyond which distance the line of the hill is that of the land around. There are undoubted evidences of its having been resorted to as a fortification, and of its having constituted a valuable point of defence to a rude and half civilized people. Forty years ago, an intrenchment ten feet deep, and some twelve or fifteen feet wide, extended from the west to the east end, along the north or front part, and continued up each side about twenty rods, where it crossed over, and joining, made the circuit of intrenchment complete. At this day a portion of the intrenchment is easily perceived, for fifteen rods along the extreme western half of the north or front part, the cultivation of the soil and other causes having nearly obliterated all other portions. It would seem that this fortification was arranged more for protection against invasion from the north, this direction being evidently its most commanding position. Near the north-west corner, piles of rounded stones have, at different times, been collected of hard consistence, which are supposed to have been used as weapons of defence by the besieged against the besiegers. Such skeletons as have been found in and about this locality, indicate a race of men averaging one third larger than the present race ; so adjudged by anatomists. From the fortification, a trench leads to a spring of water. Arrow-heads, pipes, beads, gouges, pestles, stone hatchets, have been found upon the ground, and excavated, in and about these fortifications. The pipes were of both stone and earthen ware; there was one of baked clay, the bowl of which was in the form of a man's head and face, the nose, the eyes, and other features being depicted in a style resembling some of the figures in Mr. Stevens's plate of the ruins of Central America. Forest trees were standing in the trench and on its sides, in size and age not differing from those in the neighboring forests; and upon the ground, the heart-woods of black-cherry trees of large size, the remains undoubtedly of a growth of timber that preceded the present growth. They were in such a state of soundness as to be used for timber by the first settlers. This last circumstance would establish greater antiquity for these works than has been generally claimed from other evidences. The black cherry of this region attains usually the age of two hundred and seventy-five and three hundred years; the beech and maple groves of Western New York bear evidences of having existed at least two hundred and forty or fifty years. These aggregates would show that these works were over five hundred years old. But this, like other timber growth testimony that has been adduced—that seems to have been relied upon somewhat by Mr. Clinton and others—is far from being satisfactory. We can only determine by this species of evidence, that timber has been growing upon these mounds and fortifications at least a certain length of time—have no warrant for saying how much longer. Take, for instance, the case under immediate consideration : How is it to be determined that there were not more than the two growths, of cherry, and beech and maple ; that other growths did not precede or intervene? These relics are found in our dense and heaviest timbered wood lands, below a deep vegetable mould interspersed with evidences of a long succession of timber growths and decays. We can in truth form but a vague conception of the length of time since these works were constructed; while we are authorized in saying they are of great antiquity, we are not authorized in limiting the period.

The following are among some reflections of Professor Dewey of Rochester, who has reviewed Fort Hill at Le Roy, and furnished Mr. Schoolcraft with his observations. They may aid the reader, who is an antiquarian, in his speculations:

"The forest has been removed. Not a tree remains on the quadrangle, and only a few on the edge of the ravine on the west. By cultivating the land, the trench is nearly filled in some places, though the line of it is clearly seen. On the north side the trench is considerable, and where the bridge crosses it, is three or four feet deep at the sides of the road. It will take only a few years more to obliterate it entirely, as not even a stump remains to mark out its line.

"From this view it may be seen, or inferred,

"1. That a real trench bounded three sides of the quadrangle. On the south side there was not found any trace of trench, palisadoes, blocks, etc.

"2. It was formed long before the whites came into the country. The large trees on the ground and in the trench carry us back to an early era.

"3. The workers must have had some convenient tools for excavation.

"4. The direction of the sides may have had some reference to the four cardinal points, though the situation of the ravines naturally marked out the lines.

"5. It cannot have been designed merely to catch wild animals, to be driven into it from the south. The oblique line down to the spring is opposed to this supposition, as well as the insufficiency of such a trench to confine the animals of the forest.

"6. The same reasons render it improbable that the quadrangle was designed to confine and protect domestic animals.

"7. It was probably a sort of fortified place. There might have been a defence on the south side by a stockade, or some similar means which might have entirely disappeared.

"By what people was this work done?

"The articles found in the burying ground here, offer no certain reply. The axes, chisels, etc., found on the Indian grounds in this part of the State, were evidently made of the green stone or trap of New England, like those found on the Connecticut River in Massachusetts. The pipe of limestone might be from that part of the country. The pipes seem to belong to different eras.

"1. The limestone pipe indicates the work of the savage or aborigines.

"2. The third indicates the age of French influence over the Indians. An intelligent French gentleman says such clay pipes are frequent among the town population in parts of France.

"3. The second, and most curious, seems to indicate an earlier age and people.

"The beads found at Fort Hill are long and coarse, made of baked clay, and may have had the same origin as the third pipe.

"Fort Hill cannot have been formed by the French as one of their posts to aid in the destruction of the English colony of New York; if the French had made Fort Hill a post as early as 1660, or 185 years ago, and then deserted it, the trees could not have grown to the size of the forest generally in 1810, or in 150 years afterwards. The white settlements had extended only twelve miles west of Avon in 1798, and some years after (1800), Fort Hill was covered with a dense forest. A chestnut tree, cut down in 1842, at Rochester, showed 254 concentric circles of wood, and must have been more than 200 years old in 1800. So opposed is the notion that this was a deserted French post.

"Must we not refer Fort Hill to that race which peopled this country before the Indians, who raised so many monuments greatly exceeding the power of the Indians, and who lived at a remote era?"

Upon the upper end of Tonawanda Island, in the Niagara River, near the dwelling house of the late Stephen White, in full view of the village of Tonawanda, and the Buffalo and Niagara Falls Railroad, is an ancient mound, the elevation of which, within the recollection of the early settlers, was at least ten feet. It is now from six to eight feet—circular—twenty-five feet diameter at the base. In the centre, a deep excavation has been made, at different periods, in search of relics. A large number of human bones have been taken from it—arrows, beads, hatchets, etc. The mound occupies a prominent position in the pleasure grounds laid out by Mr. White. How distinctly are different ages marked upon this spot! Here are the mouldering remains of a primitive race—a race whose highest achievements in the arts was the fashioning from flint the rude weapons of war and the chase, the pipe and hatchet of stone; and here, upon the other hand, is a mansion presenting good specimens of modern architecture. Commerce has brought the materials for its chimney-pieces from the quarries of Italy, and skill and genius have chiselled and given to them a mirror-like polish. Here in the midst of relics of another age, and of occupants of whom we know nothing beyond these evidences of their existence, are choice fruits, ornamental shrubbery, and gravelled walks.

Directly opposite this mound upon the point formed by the junction of Tonawanda Creek with the Niagara River there would seem to have been an ancient armory, and upon no small scale. There is intermingled with at least an acre of earth, chips of flint, refuse pieces, and imperfect arrows that were broken in process of manufacture. In the early cultivation of the ground, the plough would occasionally strike spots where these chips and pieces of arrows predominated over the natural soil.

On the north side of the Little Buffalo Creek, in the town of Lancaster, Erie County, there is an ancient work upon a bluff, about thirty feet above the level of the stream. A circular embankment incloses an acre. Thirty years ago, this embankment was nearly breast high to a man of ordinary height. There were five gate-ways distinctly marked. A pine tree of the largest class in our forest, grew directly in one of the gate-ways. It was adjudged (at the period named), by practical lumbermen, to be FIVE HUNDRED YEARS OLD. Nearly opposite, a small stream puts into the Little Buffalo. Upon the point formed by the junction of the two streams, a mound extends across from one to the other, as if to inclose or fortify the point. In modern military practice, strong fortifications are invested sometimes by setting an army down before them and throwing up breast-works. May not this smaller work bear a similar relation to the larger one?

About one and a half miles west of Shelby Centre, Orleans County, is an ancient work. A broad ditch incloses, in a form nearly circular, about three acres of land. The ditch is at this day well defined, several feet deep. Adjoining the spot on the south, is a swamp about one mile in width by two in length. This

NOTE.—The title of this chapter would confine these notices to Holland Purchase. The author has gone a short distance beyond his bounds, to include a well-defined specimen of these ancient works.

swamp was once, doubtless, if not a lake an impassable morass. From the interior of the inclosure made by the ditch, there is what appears to have been a passage-way on the side next to the swamp. No other breach occurs in the entire circuit of the embankment. There are accumulated within and near this fort large piles of small stones of a size convenient to be thrown by the hand or with a sling.* Arrow-heads of flint are found in and near the inclosure, in great abundance, stone axes, etc. Trees of four hundred years' growth stand upon the embankment, and underneath them have been found earthen ware, pieces of plates or dishes, wrought with skill, presenting ornaments in relief, of various patterns. Some skeletons almost entire have been exhumed; many of giant size, not less than seven to eight feet in length. The skulls are large and well developed in the anterior lobe, broad between the ears, and flattened in the coronal region. Half a mile west of the fort is a sand hill. Here a large number of human skeletons have been exhumed, in a perfect state. Great numbers appeared to have been buried in the same grave. Many of the skulls appear to have been broken in with clubs or stones. "This," says S. M. Burroughs, Esq., of Medina (to whom the author is indebted for the description), "was doubtless the spot where a great battle had been fought. Were not these people a branch of the Aztecs? The earthen ware found here seems to indicate a knowledge of the arts known to that once powerful nation."

The Rev. Samuel Kirkland † visited and described several of these remains west of the Genesee River, in the year 1788. At that early period, before they had been disturbed by the antiquarian, the plough, or the harrow, they must have been much more perfect and better defined than now. Mr. Kirkland says in his journal, that after leaving "Kanawageas," ‡ he travelled twenty-six miles and encamped for the night at a place called "Joaki," § on the river "Tonawanda." Six miles from the place of encampment, he rode to the "open fields." ‖ Here he "walked out about half a mile with one of the Seneca chiefs to view" the remains which he thus describes:

"This place is called by the Senecas Tegatainasghque, which imports a doubly fortified town, or a town with a fort at each end. Here are the vestiges of two forts; the one contains about four acres of ground; the other, distant from this

---

* These piles of small stones are frequently spoken of in connection with these works, by those who saw them at an early period of white settlement.

† Mr. K. was the pioneer Protestant Missionary among the Iroquois. The Rev. Dr. Wheelock, of Lebanon, Ct., who was his early tutor, in one of his letters to the Countess of Huntingdon, in 1765, says:—" A young Englishman, whom I sent last fall to winter with the numerous and savage tribes of the Senecas, in order to learn their language, and fit him for a mission among them ; where no missionary has hitherto dared to venture. This bold adventure of his, which under all the circumstances of it is the most extraordinary of the kind I have ever known, has been attended with abundant evidence of a divine blessing." Connected as was the subject of this eulogy with other branches of our local history, he will be frequently referred to in the course of this work.

‡ Avon.

§ Batavia, or the "Great Bend of the Tonnewanta," as it was uniformly called by the early travellers on the trail from Tioga Point to Fort Niagara and Canada. ☞ See account of Indian Trails. Batavia was favored with several Indian names. In Seneca, the one used by Mr. K. would be *Raccoon*.

‖ The openings, as they are termed, in the towns of Elba and Alabama ; lying on either side of the Batavia and Lockport road, but chiefly between that road and the Tonawanda Creek. The antiquarian who goes in search of the ancient *Tegatainasghque*, will be likely to divide his attention between old and new things. It was a part of Tonawanda Indian Reservation. About twenty-five years since, it was sold to the Ogden Company ; and the ancient "open fields" now present a broad expanse of wheat fields, interspersed with farm buildings that give evidence of the elements of wealth that have been found in the soil.

about two miles, and situated at the other extremity of the ancient town, incloses twice that quantity. The ditch around the former (which I particularly examined) is about five or six feet deep. A small stream of living water, with a high bank, circumscribed nearly one third of the inclosed ground. There were traces of six gates, or avenues, around the ditch, and a dug-way near the works to the water. The ground on the opposite side of the water was in some places nearly as high as that on which they built the fort, which might make it necessary for this covered way to the water. A considerable number of large, thrifty oaks have grown up within the inclosed grounds, both in and upon the ditch; some of them, at least, appeared to be two hundred years old, or more. The ground is of a hard gravelly kind, intermixed with loam, and more plentifully at the brow of the hill. In some places, at the bottom of the ditch, I could run my cane a foot or more into the ground; so that probably the ditch was much deeper in its original state than it appears to be now. Near the northern fortification, which is situated on high ground, are the remains of a funeral pile. The earth is raised about six feet above the common surface, and betwixt twenty and thirty feet in diameter. From the best information I can get of the Indian historians, these forts were made previous to the Senecas being admitted into the confederacy of the Mohawks, Onondagas, Oneidas, and Cayugas, and when the former were at war with the Mississaugas and other Indians around the great lakes. This must have been nearly three hundred years ago, if not more, by many concurring accounts which I have obtained from different Indians of several different tribes. Indian tradition says also that these works were raised, and a famous battle fought here, in the pure Indian style and with Indian weapons, long before their knowledge and use of fire-arms or any knowledge of the Europeans. These nations at that time used, in fighting, bows and arrows, the spear or javelin, pointed with bone, and the war-club or death-mall. When the former were expended, they came into close engagement in using the latter. Their warrior's dress or coat of mail for this method of fighting was a short jacket made of willow sticks, or moon wood, and laced tight around the body; the head covered with a cap of the same kind, but commonly worn double for the better security of that part against a stroke from the war-club. In the great battle fought at this place, between the Senecas and Western Indians, some affirm their ancestors have told them there were eight hundred of their enemies slain; others include the killed on both sides to make that number. All their historians agree in this, that the battle was fought here, where the heaps of slain are buried, before the arrival of the Europeans; some say three, some say four, others five ages ago; they reckon an age one hundred winters or colds. I would further remark upon this subject that there are vestiges of ancient fortified towns in various parts, throughout the extensive territory of the Six Nations. I find also, by constant inquiry, that a tradition prevails among the Indians in general that all Indians came from the West. I have wished for an opportunity to pursue this inquiry with the more remote tribes of Indians, to satisfy myself, at least, if it be their universal opinion.

"On the south side of Lake Erie are a series of old fortifications, from Cattaraugus Creek to the Pennsylvania line, a distance of fifty miles. Some are from two to four miles apart, others half a mile only. Some contain five acres. The walls or breastworks are of earth, and are generally on grounds where there are appearances

NOTE.—The traditions given to Mr. Kirkland at so early a period are added to his account of the old forts, to be taken in connection with adverse theories and conclusions upon the same point. As has before been observed, many of the Senecas who have since been consulted, do not pretend to any satisfactory knowledge upon the subjects.

of creeks having flowed into the lake, or where there was a bay. Further south there is said to be another chain parallel with the first, about equi-distant from the lake."

"These remains of art may be viewed as connecting links of a great chain, which extends beyond the confines of our State, and becomes more magnificent and curious as we recede from the northern lakes, pass through Ohio into the great valley of the Mississippi, thence to the Gulf of Mexico through Texas into New Mexico and South America. In this vast range of more than three thousand miles these monuments of ancient skill gradually become more remarkable for their number, magnitude, and interesting variety, until we are lost in admiration and astonishment, to find, as Baron Humboldt informs us, *in a world which we call new*, ancient institutions, religious ideas, and forms of edifices similar to those of Asia, which there seem to go back to the dawn of civilization."

"Over the great secondary region of the Ohio are the ruins of what once were forts, cemeteries, temples, altars, camps, towns, villages; race-grounds and other places of amusement, habitations of chieftains, videttes, watch-towers, and monuments."

"It is," says Mr. Atwater,* "nothing but one vast cemetery of the beings of past ages. Man and his works, the mammoth, tropical animals, the cassia tree and other tropical plants, are here reposing together in the same formation. By what catastrophe they were overwhelmed and buried in the same strata it would be impossible to say, unless it was that of the general deluge."

"In the valley of the Mississippi the monuments of buried nations are unsurpassed in magnitude and melancholy grandeur by any in North America. Here cities have been traced similar to those of Ancient Mexico, once containing hundreds of thousands of souls. Here are to be seen thousands of tumuli, some a hundred feet high, others many hundred feet in circumference, the places of their worship, their sepulchre, and perhaps of their defence. Similar mounds are scattered throughout the continent, from the shores of the Pacific into the interior of our State as far as Black River, and from the Lakes to South America." †

So much for all we can see or know of our ancient predecessors. The whole subject is but incidental to the main purposes of local history. The reader who wishes to pursue it further will be assisted in his inquiries by a perusal of Mr. Schoolcraft's Notes on the Iroquois. But the mystery of this pre-occupancy is far from being satisfactorily explained. It is an interesting, fruitful source of theories, inquiry, and speculation.

* Atwater's Antiquities of the West.
† Yates and Moulton's History of New York.

THE IROQUOIS, OR FIVE NATIONS.*

EMERGING from a region of doubt and conjecture, we arrive at another branch of local history, replete with interest—less obscure—though upon its threshold we feel the want of reliable data, the lights that guide us in tracing the history of those who have written records.

The Seneca Indians were our immediate predecessors—the pre-occupants from whom the title of the Holland Purchase was derived. They were the Fifth Nation of a CONFEDERACY, termed by themselves Mingoes, as inferred by Mr. Clinton, Ho-de-no-sau-nee,† as inferred by other writers; the Confederates, by the English; the Maquaws, by the Dutch; the Massowamacs, by the Southern Indians; the IRO-QUOIS, by the French, by which last name they are now usually designated, in speaking or writing of the distinct branches of the Aborigines of the United States.

The original Confederates were the Mohawks, having their principal abode upon that river; the Oneidas, upon the southern shore of Oneida Lake; the Cayugas, near Cayuga Lake; the Senecas, upon Seneca Lake and the Genesee River. Those localities were their principal seats, or the places of their council-fires. They may be said generally to have occupied in detached towns and villages the whole of this State, from the Hudson to the Niagara River, now embraced in the counties of Schenectady, Schoharie, Montgomery, Fulton, Herkimer, Oneida, Madison, Onondaga, Cayuga, Seneca, Wayne, Ontario, Livingston, Genesee, Wyoming, Monroe, Orleans, Niagara, Erie, Chautauqua, Cattaraugus, Alleghany, Steuben, and Yates. A narrower limit of their dwelling places, the author is aware, has been usually designated; but in reference to the period of the first European advent among them—1678—it is to be inferred that their habitations were thus extended, not only from the traces of their dwellings, and the relics of their rude cultivation of the soil, but from the records of the early Jesuit Missionaries. Their missions were at different periods extended from the Hudson to the Niagara River, and each one of them would seem to have had several villages in its vicinity. Each of the Five Nations undoubtedly had a principal seat. They were as indicated by their names. And each had its tributary villages, extended as has been assumed. It was plainly a coming together from separate localities—a gathering of clansmen—to resist the invasion of De Nonville; and it is to be inferred from the journal of Father Hennepin that there were villages of the "Iroquois Senecas" in the neighborhood of La Salle's ship-yard on the Niagara River, and the primitive garrison, or "palisade," at its mouth. The missionaries who went out from the "place of ship building," and from the "Fort at Niagara," from time to time, upon apparently short excursions, visited different villages. The Jesuit Missions upon the Mohawk, and at Onondaga, would seem to have been visited, each by the inhabitants of several villages. The author rejects the conclusion that the Tonawanda and the Buffalo Indian villages were not founded until after the expedition of General Sullivan; and concludes that these and other settlements of the Iroquois existed prior to the European advent, west of the Genesee River. While some of the Seneca Indians assume the first

---

* The "Five" Nations, at the period of our earliest knowledge of them—the "Six" Nations after they had adopted the Tuscaroras, in 1712.

† "The People of the Long House," from the circumstance that they likened their political structure to a long tenement or dwelling.

position, others, equally intelligent, and as well instructed in their traditions, do not pretend to thus limit the period of settlement at these points.

Their actual dominion had a far wider range. The Five Nations claimed "all the land not sold to the English, from the mouth of Sorrel River, on the south side of Lakes Erie and Ontario, on both sides of the Ohio, till it falls into the Mississippi; and on the north side of these lakes that whole territory between the Ottawa River and Lake Huron, and even beyond the straits between that and Lake Erie."* And in another place the same author says: "When the Dutch began the settlement of this country, all the Indians on Long Island, and the northern shores of the Sound, on the banks of the Connecticut, Hudson, Delaware, and Susquehannah Rivers, were in subjection to the Five Nations, and acknowledged it by paying tribute. The French historians of Canada, both ancient and modern, agree that the more northern Indians were driven before the superior martial prowess of the Confederates." "The Ho-de-no-sau-nee occupied our precise territory, and their council-fires burned continually from the Hudson to the Niagara. Our old forests have rung with their war shouts, and been enlivened with their festivals of peace. Their feathered bands, their eloquence, their deeds of valor, have had their time and place. In their progressive course they had stretched around the half of our republic, and rendered their name a terror nearly from ocean to ocean; when the advent of the Saxon race arrested their career, and prepared the way for the destruction of the Long House, and the final extinguishment of the Council-Fires of the Confederacy." † "At one period we hear the sound of their war-cry along the Straits of the St. Mary's, and at the foot of Lake Superior. At another, under the walls of Quebec, where they finally defeated the Hurons, under the eyes of the French. They put out the fires of the Gah-kwas and Eries. They eradicated the Susquehannocks. They placed the Lenapes, the Nanticokes, and the Munsees under the yoke of subjection. They put the Metoacks and Manhattans under tribute. They spread the terror of their arms over all New England. They traversed the whole length of the Appalachian Chain, and descended like the enraged yagisho and megalonyx, on the Cherokees and Catawbas. Smith encountered their warriors in the settlement of Virginia, and La Salle on the discovery of the Illinois." ‡ "The immediate dominion of the Iroquois—when the Mohawks, Oneidas, Onondagas, Cayugas, and Senecas were first visited by the trader, the missionary, or the war parties of the French—stretched, as we have seen, from the borders of Vermont to Western New York, from the Lakes to the head waters of the Ohio, the Susquehanna and the Delaware. The number of their warriors was declared by the French in 1660, to have been two thousand two hundred; and in 1677, an English agent sent on purpose to ascertain their strength, confirmed the precision of the statement. Their geographical position made them umpires in the contest of the French for dominion in the west. Besides, their political importance was increased by their conquests. Not only did they claim some supremacy in Northern New England as far as the Kennebec, and to the south as far as New Haven, and were acknowledged as absolute lords over the conquered Lenappe—the peninsula of Upper Canada was their hunting field by right of war; they had exterminated the Eries and Andastes, both tribes of their own family, the one dwelling on the south-eastern banks of Lake Erie, the other on the head waters of the Ohio; they had triumphantly invaded the tribes of

---
* Smith's History of New York.
† Letters on the Iroquois, by Shenandoah in American Review.
‡ Schoolcraft.

the west as far as Illinois; their warriors had reached the soil of Kentucky and Western Virginia; and England, to whose alliance they steadily inclined, availed itself of their treaties for the cession of territories, to encroach even on the empire of France in America." *

NEW YORK STATE.

"The Empire State" is one of the Middle States of the Atlantic slope and of the original thirteen of the revolutionary confederation, extending from the parallel of 40° 29' 40" to 45° 0' 42" N. lat., and between the meridians of 71° 51' and 79° 45' 54.4" W. long. from Greenwich. The State is nearly triangular in shape, aside from Long Island, which stretches east for 116 miles. It is bounded on the N. and N. W. by the Dominion of Canada, partly separated from it by the St. Lawrence River, Lake Ontario, Niagara River, and Lake Erie; also on the North by Long Island Sound, which washes the N. shore of Long Island, and the Atlantic Ocean; East by Vermont, from which Lake Champlain partly separates it, by Massachusetts and Connecticut, the Lower New York Bay, and the Atlantic Ocean; S. by the Atlantic, the lower Bay and the States of New Jersey and Pennsylvania; and W. and N. W. by Pennsylvania, Lakes Erie and Ontario, and Niagara River, which divide it from the Dominion of Canada. Its greatest length from N. to S. is 311¾ miles; its greatest breadth from E. to W., including Long Island, is 412 miles. Its area is 47,000 sq. m., or 30,080,000 acres, including its share of the great Lakes—45,658 sq. m. without them.

The surface of New York is greatly diversified. It has numerous chains of hills and mountains, many beautiful valleys, much rolling land, and extended plains. For topographical purposes it is divided into three sections of unequal size by the deep depression of Lakes Champlain and George and the Hudson River, and by the narrower valley at right angles with this, through which the Mohawk flows, which furnishes the natural route for the Erie Canal. These sections are, E of the Hudson, N. and S. of the Mohawk and Erie Canal, designated as E., N., and S. sections. E. of the Hudson is a continuation of the Green and Hoosac ranges southward, reaching the Hudson in Putnam County, opposite West Point, reappearing on the W. side of the river as the Kittatinny Mountains. The northern section has 6 distinct parallel ranges of mountains, besides two ridges of lower altitude. These ranges all trend from N. E. to S. W., and, at their eastern terminii, either on Lake Champlain, Lake George, or St. Lawrence River or its tributaries. They are, beginning at the S. E.: (1) the Palmertown range, from the vicinity of Whitehall S. W. to the lower part of Saratoga County. (2) The Kayaderosseras or Luzerne Mountains, beginning at Ticonderoga, passing along the W. side of Lake George through Warren and Saratoga counties, to Montgomery County. (3) The Clinton or Adirondack range, proper, beginning at Point Trembleau on Lake Champlain, passing through Essex, Warren, Saratoga, Hamilton, Fulton, and Montgomery counties to the Mohawk River. This range contains the highest peaks in the State— Mount Marcy or Tahawas, whose height is variously stated at from 5378 to 5466 feet; Dix Peak, 5200 feet; Mount McIntyre, 5183 feet; Sandanoni and Mount

---

* Bancroft's History of the United States.

McMartin, each about 5000 feet; Dial Mountain, about 4900 feet. It also forms the watershed between the tributaries of the St. Lawrence and those of the Hudson and Mohawk. (4) The Au Sable or Peru range, beginning still higher on Lake Champlain, near the mouth of Au Sable River, and trending S. W. through Essex, Hamilton, and Fulton counties into Montgomery. White Face is the highest mountain of this range, its altitude being 4854 feet, while Mount Pharaoh and Taylor are each about 4500 feet. (5) The Chateaugay range commences near the northern extremity of Lake Champlain in Canada, passes through Clinton, Franklin, and Hamilton counties to Herkimer County and the Mohawk River. It maintains an average height of about 2000 feet through its whole course, while Mount Seward is 5100 feet, and several of its summits approach 4000 feet in height. (6) The St. Lawrence range, parallel with the last, and about 10 or 12 miles N. of it, follows the course of the southern shore of the St. Lawrence. The broad plateau known as the Highlands of Black River is about 60 miles in length and from 1250 to 1650 feet in height.

Between the Highlands and the Mohawk lies a ridge about 20 miles long, nearly 9 miles broad at its base, having a general elevation of 800 or 900 feet, known as Hassencleaver Ridge. The section S. and S. W. of the Mohawk and the Hudson may be divided into two sub-sections—the eastern, which includes three distinct ranges of mountains: viz., (1) the Highlands of Orange and Rockland counties, having a general N. E. direction and coming to the W. shore of the Hudson; (2) back of these, the Shawangunk Mountains, skirting the valley of the Rondout; (3) and most considerable, the Kaatsbergar Catskills, called the Helderberg Mountains near Mohawk. The Catskills are rather a group of mountains than a chain. They cover a region more than 500 square miles, having between 30 and 40 peaks, the most celebrated of which are Round Top, High Peak, Black Head, Overlook, and Pine Orchard, which range from 2900 to 3800 feet in height. The Helderbergs are not so high. The Shawangunk summits do not rise more than 2000 feet, and the Highlands range from 1000 to 1650 feet. S. W. of these, in Sullivan and Delaware counties, the Blue Mountains take their rise. Near their junction with the Kaatsbergs they rise to 2700 or 2800 feet, but elsewhere not above 1400 to 1600 feet. The western sub-section of this southern section is composed of a series of terrace plateaus rising from the shore of Lake Ontario, first, to the Ridge Road—supposed to have been the ancient southern shore of Lake Ontario, now 300 feet above it; this terrace extends from the Genesee to the Niagara above the Falls; second, from the Ridge Road to the falls of the Genesee at Nunda and Portageville, where they meet an abrupt wall of rock about 300 feet in height, and the entire height is over 900 feet; from this point there is a gradual ascent to the summit level from 1500 to 2000 feet in Chautauqua, Cattaraugus, Alleghany, and Steuben counties, the water-courses having eroded the limestones, through which they passed, at numerous points, making picturesque waterfalls, some of them of enormous height—the Taghkanic and Watkins Glen falls, for instance. The greater portion of these terraces are fertile and beautiful plains. The valleys of the Mohawk, of the Upper Hudson, and of the Delaware, Susquehanna, etc., are also very picturesque and fertile.

Rivers, Lakes, Bays, etc.—The Hudson River is the largest river. It is navigable to Troy, nearly 160 miles. It has many tributaries, of which the Mohawk is the most important. The others are Schroon, Hoosick, Battenkill, Kinderhook, and Croton on the E.; Wallkill, Rondout, Esopus, Kaateskill, and Sacandaga on the W. The Chazy and Saranac are the largest streams flowing into Lake Champlain. St. Lawrence River washes the northern boundary of the State for 100 miles, and has several important aids from the State, among which are the Oswegatchie, Indian, Grasse, Racket, St. Regis, and Salmon. Oswego River—the original outlet of the lakes in Central New York, and, in connection with the Oswego Canal and River improvement, navigable for canal-boats and steamers for 118 miles—Black River, and the Genesee flow into Lake Ontario, the last furnishing great water-power and being the outlet of four or five small lakes; Niagara River, connecting Lake Erie and Ontario; the Alleghany, one of the constituents of the Ohio River, has a course of nearly 50 miles in the State; the Susquehanna, with its tributaries, the Tioga and Chenango; and the Delaware, with its E. and W. branches, and its affluents, the Little Delaware, Mongaup, and Neversink, are the more important of the other rivers which drain the State. It is stated that there are 281 miles of river navigation for steam crafts in the State.

Lakes.—The State is somewhat remarkable for its lakes, many of which are navigable, there being 350 miles in length of lake navigation; the eastern end of Lake Erie, one half of Lake Ontario, and one half of Lake Champlain belonging to New York. In the N. E., Lake George, Schroon Lake, and nearly 200 smaller lakes, in Warren, Essex, and Hamilton counties, add beauty to the landscape. In Central New York there are three groups of lakes, the eastern consisting of Otsego, Schuyler, Cazenovia, and Summit. Farther W. commences a chain consisting of Oneida, Onondaga, Otisco, Cross, Skaneateles, Cayuga, Seneca, Crooked or Keuka, and Canandaigua lakes. Still further W. is another chain of lakes, Owasco, Honeoye, Canadice, Conesus, and Silver Lake. In the S. W. corner of the State lies Chautauqua Lake. There are numerous smaller ones in the S. E. counties, and two or three on Long Island. A remarkable feature of the natural scenery of New York is its waterfalls. The Falls of Niagara beggar description, and those of Trenton, the Watkins Glen, the Taghkanic, and the numerous falls near Ithaca are equally noteworthy for their kind. The falls of the Genesee at Rochester, and the High Falls in the same river at Portage, the falls at Ticonderoga, and those in the Adirondacks, are very romantic.

Islands.—The most important islands are Manhattan, Long, and Staten Islands; numerous smaller ones surround these, as Randall's, Ward's, Blackwell's, Governor's, Bedloe's, and David's, around New York; Coney Island, Fire Island, Shelter Island, and a great number of islands in Long Island Sound. There are numerous small islands in the Hudson River; nearly 1500 in the St. Lawrence, one half of which belong to New York; many in Lakes Erie, Ontario, and Champlain; and about 400 in Lake George.

Bays, Sounds, etc.—The bay belonging to Long Island has been described. The lower and upper New York bays form one of the finest approaches to a great harbor in the world. Staten Island Sound is rather a strait than a sound, as is also the East River, but Long Island Sound beyond it is almost an inland sea. The Hudson River forms a broad expanse near Haverstraw, known as the Tappan Zee. There are several small bays and harbors on the New York coast of Lake Ontario, and Buffalo and Black Rock harbors on Lake Erie.

Geology and Mineralogy.—The geology of New York is peculiar. While in some parts of the State nearly every class formation is found, from the lowest Eozoic rocks to the recent alluvium, the whole Carboniferous era, as well as the upper members of the Devonian and the Permian and Jurassic formations, have no place whatever in its geology, and very little of the Lower Tertiary deposits occurs. There are traces of anthracite coal, an inch or two in thickness, found between the strata of older rock, but nowhere is there evidence of the existence of the coal-measures. The following table gives the various formations of the State in their order:

Quaternary	Alluvium, marsh-mud, and sand.
Tertiary	Drift. Pleistocene, boulders, clays, and sand. New red sandstone.
Cretaceous	Lower Cretaceous, mostly on N. shore of Long Island
Devonian	Old red sandstone. Catskill group, conglomerates of the Catskill. Portage group { Portage sandstone. Gardeau flagstone. Coshaqua shales. } Genesee slate. Trully limestone. Hamilton group { Moscow shales. Encrinal limestone. Ludlow shales. } Marcellus shales. Corniferous limestone. Onondaga limestone. Schoharie grit. Cauda-Galli grit. Oriskany sandstone.
Upper Silurian	Upper pentamerous limestone. Delthyris shaly limestone. Pentamerous limestone. Tentaculite limestone. Water-lime group. Onondaga salt group { Gypsum. Green shales. Red shales. }
Middle Silurian	Niagara group, coralline limestone. Clinton group. Median sandstone. Oneida conglomerate, Shawangunk grit. Hudson River group. Utica slate.
Lower Silurian	Trenton limestone. Black River limestone. Birdseye limestone. Chazy limestone. Quebec group, including roofing-slate. Calciferous sandstone. Potsdam sandstone.
Eozoic	Huronian rocks, specular ore beds of St. Lawrence and Jefferson counties. Granite, gneiss, hypersthene. Volcanic and metamorphic rocks, Palisades, etc., trap and porphyry.

With a few words on the distribution of these formations, we must refer our readers to the elaborate treatises on New York geology. The Eozoic rocks are found in the S. E. portion of the State, in a part of Rockland, Putnam, Westchester, and New York counties, and occupy a large tract in the N. E. of the State, including a part of Clinton and Franklin, the whole of Essex, Warren, and Hamilton, the greater part of Herkimer, and a part of Lewis, St. Lawrence, Jefferson, Fulton, Saratoga, and Washington counties. The Potsdam sandstone occupies a narrow belt immediately N. of this Eozoic region, and also a small tract in Jefferson County. The Lower Silurian groups—the Calciferous sandrock, Quebec group, and Chazy limestone—are found along the W. shore of Lake Champlain, the S. shore of the St. Lawrence to a point a few miles above Ogdensburg, and the region E. of the Hudson from Whitehall to Putnam County, and there, crossing the Hudson, reappear in Orange County. The Lower Silurian—Birdseye, Black River, and Trenton limestone—occupy more than one half of Jefferson County, and thence extend in a narrow belt around the lower edge of the great Eozoic tract already described. The Utica and Lorraine slates occupy the region between the last formations and the Mohawk River to Utica, and thence both sides of the Mohawk and the W. side of the Hudson as far N. as Sandy Hill, and S. to a short distance above Poughkeepsie, where they turn W. in a broad belt into Orange County. The Oneida conglomerate and Medina sandstone of the Middle Silurian are found from Oneida Lake on the E., along the S. shore of Lake Ontario to the Canada line, extending in breadth to the Ridge Road. S. of this, and parallel with it in a narrow belt, the Clinton and Niagara groups extend E. to Schoharie, and the Onondaga salt group follows in a more irregular but somewhat wider belt. The four lower groups of Devonian—Lower Helderberg, Oriskany sandstone, Cauda-Galli grit, and Upper Helderberg—are found in a band not more than five miles wide, extending from Buffalo to Albany County, and thence S. W. to Delaware River at Port Jervis; and immediately S of this the Marcellus shales, Hamilton group, and Genesee slate occupy a broader and irregular belt, dipping S. around the shores of the Central New York lakes through Madison, Otsego, and Schoharie counties, and, like the preceding, turning S. W. till they reach the Pennsylvania line. S. of this the whole southern tier of counties belongs to the Portage and Chemung groups, except a few outcrops of the Catskill red sandstone. The New Red sandstone only makes its appearance in the S. part of Rockland County, and as it approaches the Hudson River, the trap porphyry which constitutes the Palisades has forced its way through it. The Cretaceous formations come to the surface only on the northern shore of Long Island, while Drift and Alluvium overlie the other formations in much of the State.

Minerals.—The most important of these is iron, of which there are magnetic, red and brown hematite, specular, and bog-iron ores, and, in Dutchess, Essex, and Clinton counties, carburet of iron or plumbago. Galena or lead ore is found in St. Lawrence and other counties in large quantities. Zinc, copper, arsenic, manganese, barytes, strontian, and alum occur in various parts of the State, but do not possess much economic value. Salt springs, from which a vast amount of salt is made, occur along the line of the Onondaga salt group, especially in Onondaga County. Gypsum and waterlime accompany them.

The State abounds in building material; its granite, white and colored marbles, Potsdam and Medina sandstone, and gray and blue limestone, as well as its excellent clay and sand for brick, furnish a sufficiency of material for its dwellings; but while it exports some of these, it imports more from other States and countries. Its quarries furnish also large quantities of slate, and flagging-stones and trap-rock for paving purposes. Serpentine, soapstone, talc, asbestos, amianthus, magnesia in several forms, are among the minerals of merely scientific value. The State has numerous mineral springs of high repute, the chalybeate and saline at Saratoga, sulphur in Madison and Monroe counties, acid in Genesee and Orleans, those evolving nitrogen gas, as in Columbia, Rensselaer, and Seneca counties, and those possessing magnetic or electrical qualities, as in Tompkins County. In Chautauqua, Dutchess, Oneida, and Monroe counties are illuminating gas-springs. Fredonia, in Chautauqua County, has utilized this gas for lighting its streets and dwellings, and the lighthouse at Barcelona, in the same county, is illuminated by it.

Soil and Vegetation.—Notwithstanding the mountainous and broken character of much of its surface, the greater part of the soil of New York is arable, and some of it very fertile. Most of the mountainous districts are fine grazing lands, and yield the best milk, butter, and cheese. The plains and valleys are adapted to the culture of cereals, and the north and north-western counties to root crops. Oneida, Madison, Otsego, and a part of Chenango are engaged in hop-culture. Tobacco is cultivated in several counties, grapes on the islands of the Hudson, and on the shores of the Central New York lakes, and Indian corn in most every part of the State. Market gardening is extensively practised in the vicinity of the large cities, and great quantities of fruit are grown in the central counties. The forest trees of the State present a great variety, and a few years ago nearly one half the area of the State was covered with forests; but the great demand for timber, lumber, and hemlock and oak bark, for building ships, houses, railroads, and for tanning purposes, has much reduced the forest area. The State has ten genera of the pine family, including the hemlock, balsam, fir, black and white spruce, and tamarack, and the allied species of red and white cedar, arbor vitæ, and Canada yew. There are ten species of oak, of which the white oak is the most valuable and the most abundant, three species of elm, three of ash, five of maple, the sugar maple being the most plentiful; the black walnut and butternut, and four species of hickory, the beach, chestnut, three species of birch, the sycamore, several species of poplar, numerous willows, the robinia or locust, the tulip tree or whitewood, the linden or basswood, the ironwood or hop-hornbeam, the ailantus and its cousins, the sumachs; the *magnolia glauca*, the cornel or dogwood, and various alders, the buttonbush, the shadbush, and spicewood, are the principal other forest growths.

Zoology.—The State, in its geological and natural history survey, ordered in 1836, including the geology, mineralogy, palæontology, agriculture, botany, and zoology of the entire State, and the results were given in a series of magnificent quarto volumes fully illustrated, of which twenty-two have been published, and others are yet to come. The zoology occupies five volumes. According to this work, there are among the mammals one species of opossum, 5 bats, 2 moles, 6 shrews, the black bear, raccoon, wolverine, skunk, fisher, Pennant's marten, pine marten, 2 weasels, the ermine weasel or stoat, the mink, the otter; 30 varieties of dogs, 5 of them native; 2 species of wolf, the gray and black, the panther, Canada lynx, wild cat or bay lynx, the seal, hooded seal, and walrus. Of rodents, there are the gray fox, the red or common fox; four species of squirrel, the woodchuck, the Labrador rat, the beaver, muskrat, porcupine, the Norway or brown rat, two species of black rat, eight species of mice, the gray rabbit, the prairie hare. Of hoofed animals, besides the domestic animals, there are the fallow deer, the elk, moose, stag, and reindeer. There are 9 cetaceans in the waters of the State—6 whales, 2 porpoises, and the grampus. The number of fossil mammals is increasing by frequent discoveries. Three of the elephant family have been found in the State—the original fossil elephant, the American elephant, and the mastodon; of the latter, nearly twenty skeletons, more or less perfect, have been exhumed. Fossil skeletons of several other animals occur. Six orders of birds are found in the State: birds of prey, birds of passage, the cock tribe, waders, lobe-footed birds, and swimmers. Of the birds of prey, there are 3 families and 26 species; of the birds of passage, 20 families and 146 species; of the Gallinæ or cock tribe, 20 families and only 6 species of undomesticated birds; of the waders, 7 families and 57 species; of the lobe-footed tribe, 1 family and 5 species; of the swimmers, 6 families and 65 species. There are 3 orders of reptiles: the turtle, lizard, and serpent tribes. There are 17 species of turtles, tortoises, and terrapins, 2 of lizards, and 2 venomous and 17 or 18 harmless serpents. Of the amphibia or batrachians there are 4 families: the frog tribe, comprising 12 species; the salamander tribe, of which there are also 12 species; the triton tribe, 4 species; and the proteus tribe, 2 species. The number of fishes is very large. The bony and cartilaginous fishes are both represented, the first by 6 orders and the second by 3. Of the first there are 28 families and about 270 species. Of the second, there are 4 families and over 30 species. The crustaceans, including 10 orders, and about 60 species. Of mollusks there are 6 orders, and a large number of species, many of them edible.

The mean temperature of the State, derived from about 1500 observations at 59 localities in the State, is 46° 49'; the mean annual maximum of heat, from the same number of observations, is 92°; the mean annual minimum is —12°; the annual range of the thermometer is 104°. The average date when robins were first seen, from 266 observations, was March 19th; the shadbush commenced blooming May 1st; peaches in bloom (southern and middle portions of the State, only 175 observations) May 2d; currants, plums, cherries, apples, and lilacs in bloom in this order from May 4th to May 15th; strawberries ripe, June 9th to 12th; hay harvest commences (average of the State) July 8th; wheat harvest commences July 25th; first killing frost (471 observations), September 23d; first fall of snow (536 observations), November 5th. The climate is generally healthy; the death-rate even in the large cities, is below the average of the country. Diseases of the throat and lungs, and, in the summer, diseases of the bowels, are most fatal in the eastern counties, while bilious affections are more prevalent in the western counties.

Agricultural Productions.—In the value of her farms, and general farm products, New York is the first State in the Union. The following table gives the statistics of the value of her farms, etc., and the amount of her principal crops and her live stock, according to the United States census of 1870, and the agricultural report of 1874:

CROPS, STOCK, ETC.	Census of 1870.	Report of 1874.
Value of farms..	$1,272,857,766	....
Value of farming implements, etc.............................	45,997,712	....
Value of farm productions for the year.......................	253,526,153	....
Animals slaughtered, or sold for slaughter...................	28,225,720	....
Home manufactures...	1,621,621	....
Forest products..	6,689,179	....
Market garden products..	3,432,354	....
Orchard products...	8,347,417	....
Wages paid for farm labor, including board...................	34,451,362	....
Wheat, for year, bushels..................................	12,178,462	9,161,000
Rye, " "	2,478,125	1,834,000
Indian corn, " "	16,462,825	16,807,000
Oats, " "	35,293,625	30,302,000
Barley, " "	7,434,621	6,463,000
Buckwheat, " "	3,904,030	2,917,000
Flax, " pounds..	3,670,818	....
Wool, " "	10,599,225	....
Hops, " "	17,558,681	....
Hay, " tons..	5,614,205	5,291,800
Tobacco, " pounds..	2,349,789	1,593,000
Maple sugar, " "	6,692,040	....
Sorghum and maple syrup, gallons.............................	53,880	....
Irish potatoes, bushels.......................................	28,547,593	25,423,000
Peas and beans, "	1,152,541	....
Beeswax, pounds...	86,333	....
Honey, "	896,286	....
Value of all live stock.......................................	$175,882,712	$153,006,101
Number of horses..	856,241	665,800
" mules and asses.....................................	4,407	18,500
" milch cows..	1,350,661	1,167,000
" working oxen..	64,141 }	669,900
" other cattle..	671,428 }	
" sheep...	2,181,578	1,996,400
" swine...	518,251	....
Dairy products—Butter, pounds.................................	107,147,526	....
" " Cheese, "	22,769,964	586,300
" " Milk sold, gallons........................	135,775,919	....

Manufactures.—The manufacturing industry of the State is of vast amount, New York being in this the first State in the Union. The statistics of her manufactures in 1875 are not yet revised for the State census of that year; but we give those of 1865 and 1870, and the leading articles in parallel columns in the table below. In 1865 there were 17,525 manufacturing establishments in the State, employing 170,811 persons, using $227,674,187 capital, and $280,690,812 of raw material, and producing goods to the value of $457,133,717. The United States census of 1870 showed a great advance on these figures. There were 36,206 manufacturing establishments, employing 351,800 persons (267,378 men, 63,795 women, and 20,627 children); the amount of capital reported was $366,994,320; wages paid, $142,466,758; raw material, $452,065,452; goods annually produced, $785,194,651.

Railroads and Canals.—(1) *Railroads.* There were on Jan 1, 1875, 164 railroads operated with steam in the State; the total length of these roads was 11,019.47 miles; the length in the State, 9217.69 miles, including sidings. The length of roads in operation in the State was 7615.48 miles; of these 3670.25 were double track. The length of equivalent single track would have been 12,507.77 miles. The total cost of construction and equipment was $598,543,930.24. The amount of capital stock authorized was $611,298,810; the amount of capital stock paid in was $402,365,070.95; the amount of funded debt, $291,681,017.17, and of floating debt, $30,801,657.06; funded and floating debt together, $324,454,408.91. The number of miles run by freight trains was 43,953,254, and the amount of freight transported, 33,555,595 tons. The gross earnings of the year were $97,951,073.94, and the expenditures, except for dividends and surplus, $86,481,988.14; $11,712,066 was paid in dividends, and $3,151,958.62 was carried to surplus fund. Some of the roads earned less than their expenses. There were at the same date 76 street railroads, having a total length of 489.50 miles, the actual length traversed being only 396.57 miles; of this 253.45 was double track. The number of passengers carried on these roads was 228,372,122. The amount of capital stock authorized was $48,861,500; paid in, $22,408,825; funded and floating debt, $16,991,937.06. The total cost of constructing and equipment was $36,600,357.64. The total earnings of the year were $13,195,851.56; the total payments, including dividends, $1,253,073, were $13,237,178.92. (2) *Canals.* There are 11 canals owned by the State. These, with their navigable feeders, have a total length of 906.95 miles, and had cost the State, with their equipment, up to January, 1875, $100,717,995. The receipts from tolls, etc., up to the year 1874 were $2,947,972.91, of which $2,672,787.22 was from the Erie Canal; the expenditure for ordinary and extraordinary repairs, etc., was $2,696,357.30, of which $1,674,889.77 was for the Erie, leaving a surplus of $997,897.45 for the Erie Canal, while all others had expended more than their income, and $773,474.51 was taken from the earnings of the Erie Canal to supply their deficiency. Besides these State Canals there are two others, partly in this State, which belong to corporations, namely, Delaware and Hudson Canal, of which 87 miles are in this State, and the Junction Canal, 18 miles long. The canal debt outstanding September 30, 1874, was $10,230,430, of which $65,430 was not paying interest. There was in the sinking funds $1,561,018.99 for the reduction of this debt.

Finances.—The State debt on September 30, 1875, was $28,328,686.40, less the amounts held by the different sinking funds, which at that date were $13,581,382.14, reducing the actual debt of the State to $14,747,304.26. The bounty debt of $15,054,500 will be extinguished in 1877, and the canal debt much reduced. The State tax of 1875 raised the sum of $14,206,680.61, and the appropriations of the year were $13,172,805.43, leaving a balance in the treasury applicable to the reduction of the debt, of $1,033,875.18. There had been great abuses and frauds in the management of the canals and State Prisons during several years past, but these have mostly been detected and prevented. The building of the new Capitol and of several insane hospitals and a reformatory had been attended with lavish expenditures, the former, though not half finished, having cost more than $6,000,000, and the latter $3,319,547.79; but so vast are the resources of the State that with economy the debt may be entirely extinguished by 1880.

Immigration.—For the statistics of the Commissioners of Emigrations, *see* New York City.

Banks.—There were, January 1st, 1875, 276 national banks doing business in the State; the aggregate capital was $106,004,691; their loans and discounts, $281,459,269.71; the amount of bonds deposited for circulation, $64,414,350; their surplus fund, $32,353,124.47; their undivided profits, $16,681,627.07; specie, $16,118,122.82; their legal-tender notes, $25,099,955; U. S. certificates of deposit, $23,550,000; individual deposits, $269,178,942.51. For the year ending October 1st, 1875, there were 84 State banks in operation, the amount of their capital was about $27,000,000; of their loans and discounts, not quite $70,000,000; and the amount due depositors, $63,000,000. The number of savings banks in July, 1875, was 160; entire number in operation January 1st, 1876, was 150. The aggregate assets of these banks, July 1st, 1875, were $336,308,236.43. They had 891,992 depositors, and the amount of deposits was $316,335,617.82.

Trust, Loan, and Indemnity Companies.—There were, on January 1st, 1876, twelve of these companies doing business in the State; one was organized September, 1875, the other eleven had an aggregate capital paid in of $11,584,475; the total amount of their assets was $69,654,948, and the amount due from them to their depositors was $50,365,569.

Insurance Companies.—On November 19, 1875, there were in the State 102 joint-stock fire insurance companies, 8 mutual fire, 9 marine insurance companies, 22 life insurance companies, and 1 plate-glass insurance company. The balance-sheets of these fire insurance companies for 1875 are not yet reported; for 1874 they were, for joint-stock, fire, and marine insurance companies, total assets, $55,985,676.01; total liabilities, including capital, $41,227,279.20; surplus over liabilities, $14,771,-948.43; amount paid-up capital, $26,307,020; premium received in 1874, $13,398,443.-06; losses paid incurred in 1874, $3,620,564.61; estimated expenses, $4,056,630.77; making a total of $7,677,195.38, and leaving a net profit of $5,721,247.68, and a net loss of $9971.22. The entire amount of risks written was: fire, $1,921,237,417; marine and inland navigation, $49,860,633. The mutual marine insurance companies (not fire and marine nor joint-stock), 9 in number, reported net assets of $21,087,-483.27; gross cash income for the year, $11,209,753.59; gross cash expenditures (including dividends of $3,138,625.10), $9,622,772.86; risk in force, $175,561,504; mutual fire companies, net assets, including premium notes, $2,276,691.13; risks in force, $54,045,208; gross cash income, $137,861.66; gross cash expenditures, $117,-135.66. The assets of the 22 life insurance companies in the State, Gov. Tilden says, amount to nearly $200,000,000, the amount insured by them $1,000,000,000, and their annual receipts to more than $60,000,000.

Commerce.—New York receives and sends from its ports by far the largest part of the foreign commerce of the nation, and by its canals and trunk lines of railroads it also conveys a large portion of the internal commerce of the country. The following table gives the imports and domestic and foreign exports at each of the ports or customs districts of the State for the year ending June 30th, 1874, and for that ending June 30th, 1875, together with the entrances and clearances for the year ending June 30th, 1874:

CUSTOM DISTRICTS AND PORTS.	Imports for year ending June 30, 1874.	Domestic exports for year ending June 30, 1874.	Foreign exports for ports for year ending June 30, 1874.	Imports for year ending Jan. 1, 1875.	Domestic exports for year ending Jan. 1, 1875.	Foreign exports for year ending Jan. 1, 1875.	ENTERED.				CLEARED.			
							Vessels.	Tonnage.	Crews.	Vessels.	Tonnage.	Crews.
Buffalo Creek	$2,016,406	$160,473	$53,046	$2,791,211	$83,288	$7,300	708	241,456	4,888	794	224,179	4,316
Cape Vincent	524,180	113,110		683,230	288,786		735	206,217	8,276	736	202,886	8,151
Champlain	2,171,784	1,041,154	31,957	2,083,015	1,144,263		1,777	196,870	5,743	1,798	145,612	5,346
Dunkirk	8,108			4,530			16	1,258	89	15	957	69
Genesee	429,172	367,527	38	393,074	793,301	38	614	69,945	7,658	580	91,577	7,422
New York	395,133,122	340,361,269	14,633,165	390,936,533	331,447,602	13,561,204	6,773	5,049,618	158,224	6,103	4,837,218	142,062
Niagara	104,570,846	351,078	65,371	3,240,297	412,026	58,013	219	15,220	3,249	215	44,827	3,229
Oswegatchie	1,077,751	605,233	140,264	1,923,601	638,951	13,000	434	86,380	4,877	434	88,356	4,789
Oswego	7,200,952	1,724,651	187	6,686,785	1,684,266	13,629	2,613	438,355	18,462	2,493	373,015	17,528
Totals	$414,947,041	$345,923,495	$14,924,229	$408,565,676	$337,992,243	$13,603,286	13,861	6,185,819	200,753	13,048	5,909,084	192,922

Population.

Census Year.	Total Population.	Male.	Female.	White.	Free, Colored.	Slave.	Native.	Foreign.	Density	Ratio of Increase	Ratio of Illiteracy.	Of School Age, 5-20.	Of Military Age, 18-45.	Of Voting Age, 21, and upward.	Citizen.
1790	340,120	175,597	164,603	314,142	1,654	21,324			7.4						
1800	589,051	312,667	274,692	557,371	10,417	20,903			12.3	72.51					
1810	959,409	493,221	465,228	918,669	25,333	15,017			20.2	65.45					
1820	1,372,812	698,215	674,597	1,332,744	29,279	10,088			29.32	43.14					
1830	1,918,608	975,796	942,812	1,873,663	44,870	75			40.89	39.76					
1840	2,428,921	1,211,966	1,216,955	2,378,890	50,027	4			51.64	26.60					
1850	3,097,394	1,567,194	1,530,453	3,048,325	49,069		2,426,771	655,929	65.90	27.52	78,619	1,052,586	621,904	809,643	598,921
1855	3,466,212	1,729,560	1,736,651	3,415,175	49,037		2,528,444	930,768	73.72	11.90	96,485	1,127,868	739,812	895,064	632,372
1860	3,880,735	1,933,532	1,947,203	3,831,590	49,005		2,870,455	1,001,280	81.58	25.29	72,054	1,235,673	741,850	1,001,326	846,273
1865	3,831,711	1,898,641	1,949,171	3,783,110	44,798		2,860,859	943,157	81.68	21.26	95,865	1,256,914	712,805	937,584	821,484
1870	4,382,759	2,163,229	2,219,539	4,330,210	152,081		3,244,406	1,138,353	93.25	$12.93	239,275	1,230,038	881,500	1,158,901	981,587
1875	4,705,208								100.11	7.36		* 1,579,504			1,138,130

* Ratio of increase for ten years. § 5 to 18. ¶ 5 to 21.
† Also 140 Indians. ∥ Decrease.
‡ Also 439 Indians and 29 Chinese.

Internal Commerce.—This can only be estimated in gross, and at best not very accurately. Many of the smaller and more costly articles of merchandise are transported by express companies or as personal baggage, and their value cannot be determined. The value of the tonnage moved on the canals of the State in 1874 is officially estimated by the auditor as $196,674,322. As the freight transported by the canals in 1874 was but 5,804,588 tons, and that of the railroads of the State (exclusive of express freight) was 33,555,595 tons—which being transported at higher rates may fairly be presumed to be of greater value—we are safe in estimating it as at least six times the value of the canal freight, namely, $1,180,045,932, or an aggregate of $1,376,720,254. This does not include that which passed over the Delaware and Hudson and Junction canals, nor the large amounts conveyed by steamers on Hudson River, Long Island Sound, and the lakes. As most of the costlier freight and all the bullion from the mining-regions is moved by express, the total amount of this internal commerce probably exceeds $2,000,000,000.

Education.—(1) *Common Schools.* The school fund proper, on January 1st, 1875, was $3,054,772.10, and the revenue from it was $178,813.72. The income of the U. S. deposit fund, which in this State amounts to $4,014,520.71, is also applied to educational purposes, a part of it being applied to increase the amount of the capital of the school fund, and a part to increase its revenue; $160,000 was thus applied in 1874, making the entire amount applicable to common schools from these funds in 1874, $392,372.45. But by far the largest part of the expenditure for common schools is raised by taxation, and in some cases this is supplemented by local funds. The entire receipts for school purposes in 1875 were $12,516,362.96, and the entire expenditure, $11,365,377.79. Of this there was paid for teachers' wages, $7,843,231.67; for school-houses, repairs, furniture, etc., $1,844,347.20. The estimated value of school-houses and sites was $36,393,190. The total number of school-houses was 11,787; number of teachers employed at the same time for the full legal term of school, 19,157; number of teachers employed during any portion of the year, 29,977, of whom 7387 were males, and 22,590 females. The average monthly wages was for the cities, $72.28; for the towns, $32.92; for the entire State, $46.68. The difference between the salary of male and female teachers is not given. The number of children attending the common schools was 1,058,846; the average daily attendance, 515,225; the number of persons between five and twenty-one years of age, 1,579,504; the number of persons attending Normal schools, 6207; the number of private schools was 1436. (2) *Academies.* There were in the State, January 1st, 1875, 240 academies and academical departments of Union schools. These are under the care of the Board of Regents of the University of the State of New York, an organization consisting of 23 persons, 4 of them State officers ex officio, and 19 appointed by the governor and senate, which superintends the educational condition of the State, holds examinations at the academies and colleges, and an annual convocation of the heads and professors of colleges and academies, and apportions the income of the literature fund annually. The Board of Regents do not engage in actual teaching, nor perform the usual duties of a university, but they are of great service to the educational interests of the State. They have the power of conferring degrees, but this power is but sparingly exercised. Of the academies, some are of very high grade, and not only prepare students for college, but for business or professional life. The greater part are for pupils of both sexes, but a considerable number are confined exclusively to male or to female pupils. These academies had, about January 1st, 1876, over 1400 teachers, 25,620 pupils, and received from the literature and U. S. deposit funds about $185,000 annually, aside from their tuition and endowment income. Besides the following Normal schools, there are city Normal schools attached to most of the larger city-school systems; 108 academies, etc., in the cities were authorized, in 1874, to instruct teachers' classes. Of these, 92 maintained such classes, instructing 2044 teachers (644 males and 1400 females), for which the State paid $29,337.62; 59 teachers' institutes were conducted during the year, and attended by 11,478 teachers, at a cost to the State for the education of its teachers of nearly $290,000.

NORMAL SCHOOLS.	When opened.	Instructors.	Normal Students.	Academies.	Pupils in low. Dep'ts Intermediate or m'dle.	Primary.	Whole number of Graduates.	Value of School Property.	Annual Receipts.	Annual Expenditures.	Volumes in Library.
Albany	1844	15	544	....	145	63	2,041	$84,000	$21,931.50	$21,519.68	2,500
Brockport	1867	18	291	223	187	170	105	140,000	20,514.74	20,275.21	5,507
Buffalo	1871	16	303	...	7	267	57	127,039	18,510.84	18,481.24	164
Cortland	1869	14	379	27	164	381	120	104,616	20,272.26	17,952.94	6,500
Fredonia	1868	17	237	118	169	239	133	107,750	22,196.31	21,254.45	1,500
Genesee	1871	17	307	157	188	189	26	93,430	21,162.49	20,819.63	2,500
Oswego	1863	15	429	...	238	278	587	84,500	17,861.14	17,861.14	2,941
Potsdam	1869	16	365	173	143	114	59	95,004	19,654.38	19,601.13	....
New York City	1870	32	971	189	....	.	...	390,000	82,000.00	81,500.00	3,000
Totals	....	160	3,846	887	1,241	1,701	3,128	$1,226,339	241,103.66	239,265.42	24,612

COLLEGES AND COLLEGIATE INSTITUTIONS.

COLLEGES, ETC.	Location.	Date of Organization.	Professors and Instructors.	Students in preparatory Dep't	Students in Collegiate Dep't	Value of Buildings, Grounds, Apparatus.	Endowment.	Income from Endowment.	Income from all Sources.	Volumes in Library.
COLLEGES FOR WOMEN										
Vassar College	Poughkeepsie.	1865	35	146	265	$697,347	$331,000	$19,670	$169,894	9,000
Elmira Female College	Elmira	1855	12	81	45	154,800	100,000	7,000	39,500	3,700
Packer Collegiate Ins.	Brooklyn	1845	37	662	96	350,000	40,000	3,000	90,000	5,000
Rutgers Female College	New York	1838	13	84	...	150,000	....	....	17,824	5,000
Wells College	Aurora	1868	12	...	76	300,000	100,000	7,000	22,200	3,000
Ingham University	Le Roy	1835	19	85	71	75,000	....	....	9,000	4,600
COLLEGES FOR BOTH SEXES										
Alfred University	Alfred	1857	22	293	114	80,700	70,000	3,770	9,526	3,400
Cornell University and Lay College for Women	Ithaca	1868	54	...	...	850,000	2,753,999	83,635	135,224	48,000
Syracuse University	Syracuse	1871	11	....	162	300,000	316,187	19,478	23,286	2,500
COLLEGES FOR YOUNG MEN										
St. Bonaventura College	Allegany	1859	20	150	80	....	....	....	....	3,000
St. Stephen's College	Annandale	1860	7	22	42	140,000	....	...	23,000	2,000
St. John's College	Fordham	1840	6	...	120	150,000	....	....	10,000	1,500
St. John's College	Brooklyn	1870	6	....	120	150,000	....	....	....	150
Canisius College	Buffalo	1870	16	...	141	....	....	....	....	5,000
St. Joseph's	Buffalo	1861	23	200	60	75,000	....	....	....	3,500
St. Lawrence University	Canton	1868	9	...	46	38,750	80,472	6,230	6,707	7,108
Hamilton College	Clinton	1812	13	....	150	320,000	300,000	18,300	24,800	18,000
Hobart College	Geneva	1824	7	....	53	67,862	249,814	13,344	13,879	11,970
Madison University	Hamilton	1832	11	....	101	102,500	344,395	20,199	24,942	10,000
College of the City of New York	New York	1847	39	448	316	275,000	....	....	150,000	19,500
College of St. Francis Xavier	New York	1874	42	242	77	428,000	172,000	....	36,084	16,000
Columbia College	New York	1754	10	...	172	787,700	4,581,694	208,502	302,937	16,085
Manhattan College	New York	1863	40	420	222	345,000	....	....	62,343	6,500
University of the City of New York	New York	1830	16	...	146	500,000	100,000	12,000	36,646	4,694
University of Rochester	Rochester	1850	9	....	156	335,274	170,000	10,000	17,000	12,400
Union College	Schenectady.	1795	15	....	157	400,000	665,000	22,000	28,715	18,000
St. Francis College	Brooklyn	....	14	....	215	100,000	....	....	33,796	13,970

SCIENTIFIC AND PROFESSIONAL SCHOOLS.

NAME OF SCIENTIFIC OR PROFESSIONAL SCHOOLS.	Location.	Date of Organization.	Number of Instructors.	Students, Regular Course.	Under what Control.	Value of Buildings, Grounds, and Apparatus.	Amount of Endowment.	Income from Funds.	Total Annual Income.	Vol'mes in Library.
SCHOOLS OF SCIENCE.										
College of Agric. and Mechanic Arts, Cornell University	Ithaca	1868	25	409	State	With University				
Department of Science, University of the City of New York	New York	1871	4	24	Un. N. Y. C.	With University				
Engineering School, Union College	Schenectady	1845	15	47	Union Col.	With Col.				3,000
Rensselaer Polytechnic Institute	Troy	1824	13	190	Private	$76,000	$25,000		$38,000	3,200
Brooklyn Polytechnic Institute, Scientific Dep't	Brooklyn	1855	5	180	Private	164,064			65,089	3,000
Columbia College, School of Mines	New York	1863	14	206	Col. College	With Col.			20,525	5,798
U. S. Military Academy	West Point	1802	46	278	U. S.					25,000
SCHOOLS OF THEOLOGY.										
De Lancey Divinity School	Geneva	1860	4	2	Prot. Epis.		25,796	1,680		100
General Theological Sem. Prot. Episcopal Church	New York	1821	6	69	Prot. Epis.	650,000	138,750	8,600		15,000
Hamilton Theological Sem.	Hamilton	1820	5	42	Baptist	34,000	61,550	1,785	6,000	
Hartwick Seminary	Hartwick	1815	3	4	Lutheran					
Theological Department, Martin Luther College	Buffalo	1854	4	10	Lutheran	13,000				300
Newburg Theological Sem.	Newburg	1822	3	17	Un'td Pres.	25,000	41,600	3,800		3,500
Rochester Theological Sem.	Rochester	1850	6	58	Baptist	75,000	225,000			9,000
St. Joseph's Provincial Sem.	Troy	1864	6	125	R. Catholic					8,000
Seminary of our Lady of Angels	Niagara Falls	1857	17	59	R. Catholic	150,000				3,000
Auburn Theological Sem.	Auburn	1821	5	48	Presbyt'rian	150,000	295,500	20,500		10,000
Theological Department, Lawrence University	Canton	1858	3		Universalist	22,500	92,777	6,494		6,682
Union Theological Sem.	New York City	1836	12	116	Presbyt'rian	200,000	800,000	56,000		33,000
Tabernacle Lay College	Brooklyn	1870	9	230	Non-sectarian	80,000				
SCHOOLS OF LAW.										
Albany Law School, Union University	Albany	1851	5	109	Un. Univ.					5,000
Columbia College Law School	New York	1858	3	522	Col. Col.				41,826	4,100
Department of Law, University of City of New York	New York	1857	5	51	Un. C. N. Y.				3,100	1,200
Law School of Hamilton College	Clinton	1870	2	13	Ham. Col.				780	5,000
SCHOOLS OF MEDICINE.										
Albany Medical College, Union University	Albany	1839	8	117	Union Univ.	25,000			7,202	5,115
Bellevue Hospital Medical College	New York City	1861	18	472	Med. Hos. C. Bellevue				50,000	
College of Physicians and Surgeons	New York City	1807	30	452	Coll. Phys. and Surg.	163,000			31,115	500
College of Physicians and Surgeons, Syracuse Univ.	Syracuse	1872	16	60	Syr. Univ.	16,500			2,000	2,000
Free Medical College for Women	New York	1871	12	48	Free Medical College	26,500				
Long Island College Hospital	Brooklyn	1860	20	97	L. I. Col Hos.					
Medical Department University of Buffalo	Buffalo	1847	9	101	Un. Buffalo	20,000			8,454	
Medical Dep't University of City of New York	New York City	1841	23	360	Un. of N. Y.	50,000			63,000	
Women's Medical College of New York Infirmary	New York City	1864	21	30	N. Y. Infirmary Hos.	2,500		2,500	4,500	
Eclectic Medical College of New York	New York City	1·65	8	55	Trustees	15,000			2,500	400
New York Homœopathic Medical College	New York City	1860	20	131	Trustees	10,000			12,056	
New York Medical College and Hospital for Women	New York City	1863	15	21	Trustees	150,000			3,375	200
New York College of Dentistry	New York City	1866	18	68	Trustees				5,678	
College of Pharmacy of City of New York	New York City	1829	4	137	Trustees		2,000	1,200	7,000	1,000

Special Education.—The institutions for special education in the State are—(1) The New York Institution for the Instruction of the Deaf and Dumb, in New York City, founded in 1817, which had, in January, 1875, 18 teachers and instructors, 584 pupils, of whom 337 were males, and 247 females, and received from the State for the support of its State pupils, 1875, $121,819.97. (2) The New York Institution for the Improved Instruction of Deaf-Mutes, in New York City, intended to teach articulation and lip-reading : it had, in January, 1875, 92 pupils; 103 (55 males and 48 females) had been taught during the year. The State appropriation for 1875 was $18,586.66. (3) Le Couteulx St. Mary's Institution for the Improved Instruction of Deaf-Mutes, at Buffalo, a private institution, but receiving State and county pupils since 1872. It had, January 1st, 1876, 72 pupils (37 males and 35 females), and had 32 State and 20 county pupils at that date, and received from the State $9400, besides the payments from the counties. There are also two private institutions for deaf-mutes, which do not receive State aid: viz., the School of Articulation at Aurora, with 2 teachers and 6 pupils; and St. Joseph's Institution at Fordham, with 6 teachers and 40 pupils. Another institution for deaf-mutes is proposed to be located at Rome, N. Y., for the northern counties, but has not yet been organized. (4) The New York Institution for the Blind at New York City, which had, January 1st, 1875, 173 pupils, of whom 147 were State pupils; it received from the State, in 1875, $43,899.32, and $84,000 from other sources; it had 60 teachers and other employés. (5) The State Institution for the Blind, at Batavia, having 150 pupils and 31 teachers and other employés; it received from the State $52,000, and from other sources $9525. (6) The State Asylum for Idiots at Syracuse, which had in Jan., 1875, 164 pupils, and received from the State, for 1875, $37,500. There are two or three private or city institutions for idiotic, imbecile, feeble-minded, and paralytic children in the State.

Reformatories, Industrial Schools, etc.—With the exception of the State Reformatory at Elmira, now in course of construction, and the Thomas Orphan Asylum for Indian children on the Cattaraugus Reservation near Versailles, none of these are strictly and wholly State institutions. Yet the House of Refuge for Juvenile Delinquents, on Randall's Island, and the Western House of Refuge at Rochester, receive large sums from the State (the former $71,000, and the latter $44,199, in 1877); and nearly all the rest have an appropriation from the educational fund, or some other State aid, each year. There are 25 or 30 reformatories, industrial schools, and mission schools for vagrant children, etc., in New York City (for a fuller account of which *see* New York City). There are four or five institutions within a moderate distance from the city, which receive considerable numbers of these vagrant children from New York City. Brooklyn and Kings County have 9 or 10 of these reformatories and asylums. There are local institutions belonging to this class in all the larger and most of the smaller cities of the State.

Charitable Institutions not Educational.—Of asylums and homes for the aged and infirm there are very many in the State. In the counties of New York, Kings, Richmond, and Suffolk, there are 21, and perhaps more; 2 in Utica, 2 in Rochester, and several in other cities and towns. Of hospitals the number is still larger, some of them city or county institutions, but the greater number endowed by some denomination or nationality, or by individuals. There are 33 in New York, Kings, and Richmond counties, and one or more of the other cities of the State. Of hospitals for the insane the State has 5, namely, the State Lunatic Asylum at Utica, the Willard Asylum for the Insane at Ovid, the Hudson River State Hospital for the Insane at Poughkeepsie, the Buffalo State Asylum for the Insane at Buffalo, the

Homœopathic Asylum for the Insane at Middletown, and in addition, a hospital for insane convicts at Auburn. There are, also, county hospitals for insane in 11 or 12 of the larger counties. There are also corporate institutions, like the Bloomingdale Hospital for the Insane, the Emigrants' Insane Hospital on Ward's Island, and private hospitals for the insane at Flushing, Hyde Park, and elsewhere. The State hospitals received, in 1875, $437,600. The New York State Inebriate Asylum at Binghamton has been under the care of the State since 1868. Its annual expenses, paid by the State, are about $10,000. There are several county inebriate asylums, some of them on a large scale.

Penal Institutions.—There are 3 State Prisons in the State—Auburn, Clinton, and Sing Sing. On Oct. 1, 1875, there were 1312 prisoners in Auburn, 553 in Clinton, and 1616 in Sing Sing—a total of 3481; and their expenditure for the year previous, including the asylum for insane convicts, was $949,510.44, while the earnings of the prisoners amounted to $368,978.51, leaving an excess of expenditures of $580,531.93. Most of the more populous counties have large penitentiaries, and in 4 or 5 of these, State convicts are also placed when the State prisons become too full. The county penitentiaries are usually well conducted, but the county jails—especially in the less populous counties—are often badly managed, and unsafe for the confinement of desperate criminals.

Churches.

DENOMINATIONS.	Ch'ch Organizations. 1870.	Ch'ch Edifices. 1870.	Sittings. 1870.	Church Property. 1870.	Ch'ch Organizations. 1875.	Ch'ch Edifices. 1875.	Clergymen. 1875.	Church Members. 1875.	Adherent Population. 1875.	Church Property. 1875.
All denominations	5,627	5,474	2,282,876	$66,073,755	6,357	6,057	6,115	555,049	3,934,600	$75,924,896
Baptist	817	795	309,311	7,439,350	898	849	776	114,863	570,400	8,772,450
Freewill and 7th-Day Bap't	85	84	23,375	162,925	99	97	86	8,146	40,000	273,300
Christians	95	95	28,175	224,850	107	100	89	9,378	45,000	295,250
Congregationalists	268	246	111,785	2,732,500	259	259	219	29,964	140,400	3,127,500
Protestant Episcopalians	475	465	204,290	7,211,151	596	585	709	72,768	300,000	8,318,000
Evangelical Association	25	25	7,300	228,150	31	30	24	3,215	15,000	207,000
Friends	89	87	24,910	596,300	95	93	....	3,788	17,100	718,500
Jews	47	33	21,400	1,811,950	51	40	46	7,642	35,000	2,167,300
Lutherans	190	182	70,133	1,560,500	257	241	129	21,185	84,000	2,871,500
Methodist Episcopalians	1,745	1,702	606,098	11,768,290	1,676	1,648	1,426	164,853	821,500	17,432,996
Meth. Prots., Free Meths.	....	....	....	....	278	246	267	31,730	150,000	1,157,600
Miscellaneous	4	2	1,000	30,600	4	3	4	350	1,200	35,000
Moravians	6	6	3,000	134,600	7	7	8	750	3,800	160,000
New Jer. Ch. (Swedenbo'n)	4	3	1,950	175,000	6	5	6	600	3,000	237,000
Presbyterian Church	672	656	325,780	12,786,900	....	....	....	....	....	....
Pres. United, Asso. Refor'd.	54	49	24,090	644,140	738	729	987	113,881	566,440	14,580,000
Reformed Ch. (late Dutch)	304	300	147,033	7,070,250	277	278	299	42,545	210,250	7,350,000
Reformed Ch.(late German)	9	8	3,240	134,000	12	10	8	1,000	5,070	181,000
Roman Catholics	455	453	271,285	8,558,750	704	609	791	....	700,000	10,371,500
Second Adventists	17	11	3,120	45,650	19	13	12	1,723	6,800	50,000
Shakers	3	3	2,300	23,000	3	3	....	950	14,000	28,000
Spiritualists	3	2	580	31,000	3	2	....	500	2,500	30,000
Unitarians	22	19	8,850	715,200	24	21	23	2,100	10,000	810,000
United Brethren in Christ.	7	6	1,850	10,200	30	12	26	3,010	12,000	37,000
Universalists	124	120	41,610	1,153,950	89	81	100	4,390	15,000	1,200,000
Local Missions	14	14	2,000	580,900	....	....	....	....	....	....
Union Churches	93	98	32,801	216,050	95	98	80	5,700	20,000	225,000

Newspapers and Periodicals.—In 1870 there were 835 periodicals of all classes published in the State, issuing annually 471,741,744 copies, and having an aggregate circulation of 7,561,497. Of these 87 were dailies, having a circulation of 780,470; 5 tri-weeklies, with 5800 circulation; 22 semi-weeklies, with 114,500 circulation; 518 weeklies, with 3,388,497 circulation; 21 semi-monthlies, with 216,300 circulation; 163 monthlies, with 2,920,810 circulation; 19 quarterlies, with 135,120 circulation; and 6 annuals, with 766,000 circulation. Of the whole number 17 were advertising sheets, 10 agricultural, 12 organs of benevolent or secret societies, 50 commercial or financial, 103 illustrated, literary, or miscellaneous, 6 devoted to nationality, 487 political, 99 religious, 4 sporting, and 56 technical and professional. In 1875 the number of periodicals, according to the *American Newspaper Directory*, had increased to 1086; and while the proportions of the different classes were not greatly changed relatively, there were 100 dailies, 5 tri-weeklies, 15 semi-weeklies, 690 weeklies, 5 bi-weeklies, 27 semi-monthlies, 218 monthlies, and 26 quarterly publications. The number of annuals is not given, but these had increased to 12 or 13. The aggregate circulation of all classes of periodicals was also very largely augmented.

Constitution, Courts, Representatives in Congress, etc.—Under the Constitution of 1846, which, as amended, is the governing law of the State, every male citizen of the age of 21 years (except such as may be idiotic or insane, and such as have been convicted of bribery, larceny, or any infamous crime), who shall have been a citizen for 10 days, an inhabitant of the State for 1 year next preceding any election, and for the last 4 months a resident of the county, and for 30 days of the ward, district, or precinct in which he may offer his vote, shall be entitled to vote for all officers elected by the people. All elections are by ballot. The legislative power of the State is vested in a Senate and Assembly, the former consisting of 32 members, chosen for two years; the latter, of 128 members, chosen for one year. The executive power is vested in a governor, elected for two years. He must be 30 years of age or more, and have been a resident of the State for at least five years next preceding an election. He is chosen at a general State election for the election of members of Assembly, and at the same times and places a lieutenant-governor. In the alternate years a secretary of State, comptroller, treasurer, attorney-general, State engineer, and surveyor are chosen, also for two years; and at the same times and places, 3 canal commissioners and 3 inspectors of State prison, one of each, each year, for the term of three years. The judiciary consists of a court of appeals, composed of a chief judge and 6 associated justices, elected by the people for 14 years, which court has appellate jurisdiction only; of a supreme court in each of the eight judicial districts into which the State is divided, consisting of 5 justices in the New York district, and 4 in each of the others, all elected for 14 years; these courts have general jurisdiction in law and equity. There are, also, county courts, superior courts, surrogates' courts, and in the cities city courts, courts of general sessions, of oyer and terminer, and police courts. In New York City is also a marine court, and a recently established court of arbitration.

Principal Cities and Towns.—Albany, the capital of the State, had in 1875 a population of 86,013; New York, its great metropolis, had the same year 1,046,037;* Brooklyn, 484,616; Buffalo, with 134,593 inhabitants, was the only other city in the State having over 100,000; Rochester had 81,673; Syracuse and Troy not quite 50,000 each; Utica, 32,070; Yonkers, Newburg, Cohoes, Auburn, Poughkeepsie, Elmira, and Oswego ranged between 17,000 and 23,000; 10 cities and towns, viz., Rome, Ogdensburg, Lockport, Schenectady, East New York, Hempstead, Flushing, Binghamton, Long Island City, and Johnstown, range between 12,000 and 16,000; 20 more, including the cities of Kingston and Hudson, and the incorporated villages of Catskill, Plattsburg, Middletown, Newtown, Amsterdam,

---

* Three towns, whose population in 1875 was 36,206, were set off from Westchester, and annexed to New York County, January 1st, 1874.

Oswego, Saratoga Springs, etc., ranged between 8000 and 12,000; and 54 other towns of the State had from 5000 to 8000.

Counties (60).

COUNTIES.	Population. 1870.	Males. 1870.	Females. 1870.	Population. 1875.	Assessed valuation. 1875.	True valuation. Census of 1870.
Albany	133,052	64,775	68,277	147,530	$54,636,234	$152,053,765
Allegany	40,814	20,493	20,321	41,721	9,511,099	23,893,857
Broome	44,103	22,119	22,084	47,913	10,567,500	21,521,822
Cattaraugus	43,909	22,178	21,731	48,477	19,199,817	20,620,578
Cayuga	59,550	29,953	29,597	61,213	20,772,208	65,120,255
Chautauqua	59,327	29,501	29,826	64,869	18,532,112	48,607,170
Chemung	35,281	17,588	17,693	41,879	10,533,677	22,174,820
Chenango	40,564	20,379	20,185	39,937	13,274,437	28,396,584
Clinton	47,947	24,320	23,627	49,701	6,956,450	12,572,960
Columbia	47,044	23,001	24,023	47,756	23,836,835	41,603,545
Cortland	25,173	12,549	12,674	24,500	7,014,354	11,374,829
Delaware	43,972	21,929	21,043	42,149	9,705,049	23,305,734
Dutchess	74,041	36,368	37,673	76,056	35,888,103	99,903,788
Erie	178,699	89,530	89,169	199,317	61,834,512	162,608,496
Essex	29,042	14,719	14,323	34,474	6,568,163	10,262,516
Franklin	30,271	14,991	15,280	31,381	2,826,810	17,403,342
Fulton	27,064	13,349	13,715	31,188	4,076,541	11,714,680
Genesee	31,606	15,703	15,903	32,551	14,829,493	45,354,321
Greene	31,832	15,555	16,277	32,554	6,771,129	25,173,279
Hamilton	2,960	1,638	1,322	3,482	610,187	1,494,320
Herkimer	39,929	20,152	19,777	41,692	11,905,207	30,931,014
Jefferson	65,415	32,434	32,981	65,362	17,518,436	40,019,235
Kings	419,921	202,024	217,897	509,216	217,867,485	700,000,000
Lewis	28,699	14,762	13,937	29,236	4,624,742	11,189,312
Livingston	38,309	18,919	19,390	38,564	15,238,146	44,080,237
Madison	43,522	21,920	21,602	42,490	11,599,189	13,349,705
Monroe	117,868	58,105	59,763	134,534	42,197,964	82,561,640
Montgomery	34,457	17,293	17,164	35,200	10,760,890	19,992,006
New York	942,292	457,117	485,175	1,046,037	1,205,531,580	3,484,268,700
Niagara	50,437	25,010	25,427	51,904	16,076,703	44,959,654
Oneida	110,008	54,022	55,986	113,667	33,665,579	45,912,258
Onondaga	104,183	51,960	52,223	113,223	36,770,451	99,058,400
Ontario	45,108	22,348	22,760	47,730	19,361,602	56,948,816
Orange	80,902	40,146	40,756	85,252	31,936,453	86,267,635
Orleans	27,869	13,752	13,937	29,977	11,255,611	31,132,500
Oswego	77,491	38,907	39,034	78,015	36,773,627	44,094,043
Otsego	48,967	24,432	24,545	49,815	13,865,043	30,474,171
Putnam	15,420	7,652	7,768	15,811	5,965,232	13,192,769
Queens	73,803	36,717	37,086	84,131	32,320,796	26,026,645
Rensselaer	99,549	48,731	50,818	105,051	31,515,813	110,939,120
Richmond	33,029	16,164	16,865	35,241	9,151,590	14,444,276
Rockland	25,213	12,789	12,415	26,951	10,598,851	10,979,456
Saratoga	51,529	25,267	26,262	55,233	14,430,096	36,797,898
Schenectady	21,347	10,481	10,866	22,892	6,501,649	15,057,240
Schoharie	33,340	16,603	16,737	32,419	5,944,824	9,948,844
Schuyler	18,089	9,370	9,619	18,928	4,575,161	9,901,295
Seneca	28,823	13,691	14,132	27,299	10,586,912	33,179,933
Steuben	67,717	34,048	33,669	73,923	14,928,161	36,573,915
St. Lawrence	84,826	42,007	42,819	84,124	16,044,343	51,074,360
Suffolk	46,924	23,295	23,629	52,088	12,642,474	30,317,036
Sullivan	34,550	17,908	16,642	34,935	3,238,077	15,076,043
Tioga	30,572	15,250	15,322	31,744	7,075,284	15,025,923
Tompkins	33,178	16,592	16,586	32,615	9,316,016	19,078,630
Ulster	84,075	42,612	41,463	88,271	13,532,069	45,536,460
Warren	22,592	11,440	11,152	23,295	3,208,040	7,989,885
Washington	49,168	25,068	24,500	48,107	15,080,420	45,345,288
Wayne	47,710	23,715	23,995	49,882	10,706,515	46,081,326
Westchester	131,348	65,739	65,609	100,660	56,167,080	138,410,460
Wyoming	29,164	14,514	14,650	30,595	9,069,807	27,717,538
Yates	19,595	9,726	9,869	19,086	8,382,409	14,858,922
Total	4,382,759	2,163,229	2,219,530	4,705,208	$2,367,780,102	$6,500,841,260

History.—The Bay of New York was first discovered in 1524, by Juan de Verrazano, a Florentine navigator in the service of France. In September, 1609, Hendrik (or Henry) Hudson, a navigator in the service of the States General of Holland, again discovered the bay, and ascended both it and the Hudson River to a point a little below Albany. On his return, landing in England, he dispatched to Holland an account of his discoveries. In 1610, some Amsterdam merchants sent a small vessel to the Hudson River to trade with the Indians for furs, etc. In 1613, two small trading-forts were built on the river, and four houses erected on Manhattan Island. In 1614, an expedition consisting of five vessels was sent out by the States-General to explore this region. These explorers ran along the whole length of Long Island, ascending the strait now known as the East River, entered the Sound, and also passed up the Hudson, and along the Jersey coast to the Delaware River, which they ascended for some distance. In October, 1614, the States-General granted to the explorers the exclusive right to trade between the Delaware and Connecticut rivers for three years from that date. In 1615, a fort and trading-house were erected just below the site of Albany, another on Manhattan Island, and messengers were dispatched to the Indian tribes to induce them to trade with the company which they had organized as the United New Netherlands Company. On the expiration of their grant, the States-General refused to renew it, but they continued to trade thither until about 1623 or 1624, when the Dutch West India Company, a powerful mercantile association chartered in 1621, took possession of the lands temporarily granted to their predecessors. In 1623 they erected Fort Nassau on the Delaware River, and Fort Orange on the site of Albany. In 1624, Peter Minuit was appointed Director of the New Netherlands, and brought over colonists who settled on Long Island. Staten Island and Manhattan Island were purchased from the Indians, the latter for $24. Up to 1629 the settlements were simply trading establishments. In that year the West India Company's Council granted to certain individuals extensive seigniories or tracts of land, with feudal rights over the lives and persons of their subjects. Under this grant Kiliaen Van Rensselaer, a pearl merchant of Amsterdam, secured in 1630 and subsequently, a tract of land 24 by 48 miles in extent, comprising the present counties of Albany, Rensselaer, and part of Columbia; Micheal Paauw purchased Staten Island, Jersey City, and Harsimus; and others, other tracts of great extent. Minuit's administration came to an end in 1632, and he was succeeded by Wouter Van Twiller. Van Twiller extended the colonies, planted a new one on the Connecticut, on the site of Hartford, and erected a fort there and furthered the interests of the company. He was succeeded in 1637 by William Kieft, whose administration of eight years was one of constant turbulence and trouble with the colonists, with the Indians, and with the English settlers on Long Island and in Connecticut. Meanwhile, the colony of the Patroon Van Rensselaer at Rensselaerwyck prospered and extended. In 1645, Petrus Stuyvesant was appointed Director in Kieft's place, and for nineteen years ruled the colony with great ability, though not without many troubles. In September, 1664, the colony of New Netherlands, which, in violation of all national comity, Charles II. had granted to his brother, the Duke of York, was conquered by the capitulation of New Amsterdam, and its name changed to New York, as was that of Beverwyck to Albany. Colonel Nicolls, who had effected the capture, remained governor until 1667, when Colonel Francis Lovelace succeeded him. In August, 1673, the colony was recaptured by the Dutch, and remained in their possession until the following February, when it was restored to the English by treaty. The feudal relations of the patroons or seigneurs and their tenants and subjects, were not materially changed during this period; other manors were granted with similar privileges. Our space does not permit us to go into the details of the 100 years of colonial rule very fully; elsewhere we have given the names and terms of service of the governors who successively ruled the colony. But few of them possessed conspicuous abilities, and of these few the greater part were constantly involved in controversies with the council or assembly. Governors Hunter, Burnet, Montgomerie, Clark, De Lancey, Clinton, Moore, and Colden were deserving of respect, and some of them secured the affection of the people. Governor Tryon, who was governor from 1771 to October, 1775, was an able man, but an intense Royalist. On July 9, 1776, the Provincial Congress, which had been organized in May, 1775, reassembled at White Plains, and took the title of "The Representatives of the State of New York." At the same session they approved the Declaration of Independence, which had just reached them. New York had from the first taken an active part in the movements which led to the Revolution, though there were many Tories in the State. The earliest captures of British forts, as Ticonderoga, Crown Point, and Skenesborough (Whitehall), were within her limits, while the disastrous battle of Long Island (*see* Long Island), the minor actions of Harlem Heights, White Plains, and the capture of forts Washington and Lee, were among the early misfortunes of the New York patriots. New York City and the Hudson below Peekskill, as well as Staten Island and most of Long Island, were occupied by the enemy; the northern border was held by British troops from Canada; and the eastern central counties, along the Mohawk, Schoharie Creek, and the Delaware, were ravaged by Tories and Indians, under the leadership of Sir John and Sir Guy Johnson, the bloodthirsty Butlers, and the Indian chief Brant. Yet occasionally the patriots were cheered by success. Burgoyne, descending upon the State from Quebec with a fine army, was harassed, defeated, and compelled to surrender October 17, 1777, near Schuylerville, Saratoga County. The Indian and Tory raids and massacres continued at intervals, but eventually these cowardly foes suffered so severely that they were glad to be quiet. The frequent incursions of General Lord Howe up the Hudson and on Long Island were not productive of very serious losses, and even the treason of Arnold was discovered too soon to cause serious disaster. Its army quota was kept full through the able management of its governor, George Clinton.

EARLY GLIMPSES OF WESTERN NEW YORK.

A PRIMITIVE glimpse of the western portion of this State has been reserved for insertion here—though not in its order of time. It is by far the earliest notice, of any considerable detail, which we derive from English sources; if in fact it is not the earliest record of any English advent to our region. The author is disposed to conclude that the writer was the first Englishman that saw the country west of the lower valley of the Mohawk. His advent was but three years after the English took final possession of the Province of New York, and ten years previous to the expedition of De Nonville. It is taken from "*Chalmers's Political Annals of the United Colonies,*" a work published in London, in 1780:

"OBSERVATIONS OF WENTWORTH GREENHALPH."

"*In a journey from Albany to the Indians westward [the Five Nations], begun the 28th of May, 1677, and ended the 14th of July following.**

"The Senecas have four towns, viz., Canagorah, Tistehatan, Canoenada, Keint-he. Canagorah and Tistehatan lie within thirty miles of the Lake Frontenac; the other two about four or five miles to the southward of these; they have abundance of corn. None of their towns are stockadoed.

"Canagorah lies on the top of a great hill, and in that as well as in the bigness, much like Onondagoe [which is described as ' situated on a hill that is very large, the bank on each side extending itself at least two miles, all cleared lands, whereon the corn is planted '], containing 150 houses, north-westward of Cayuga 72 miles.

"Here the Indians were very desirous to see us ride our horses, which we did. They made feasts and dancing, and invited us, that, when all the maids were together, both we and our Indians might choose such as liked us to lie with.

"Tistehatan lies on the edge of a hill: not much cleared ground; is near the river Tistehatan, which signifies *bending*.† It lies to the northward of Canagorah about thirty miles; contains about 120 houses, being the largest of all the houses we saw; the ordinary being 50 or 60 feet, and some 130 or 140 feet long, with 13 or 14 fires in one house. They have good store of corn growing about a mile to the northward of the town.

"Being at this place on the 17th of June, there came 50 prisoners from the southwestward, and they were of two nations; some whereof have a few guns, the other none. One nation is about ten days' journey from any Christians, and trade only with one great house,‡ not far from the sea; and the other, as they say, trade only with a black people. This day, of them were burnt two women and a man, and a child killed with a stone. At night we heard a great noise, as if the houses had all fallen; but it was only the inhabitants driving away the ghosts of the murdered.

"The 18th, going to Canagorah, we overtook the prisoners. When the soldiers saw us, they stopped each his prisoner, and made him sing, and cut off their fingers and slashed their bodies with a knife; and, when they had sung, each man confessed how many men he had killed. That day, at Canagorah, there were most cruelly burned 4 men, 4 women, and one boy; the cruelty lasted about seven hours: when they were almost dead, letting them loose to the mercy of the boys, and taking the hearts of such as were dead to feast on.

"Canoenada lies about 4 miles to the southward of Canagorah; contains about 30 houses, well furnished with corn.

"Keint-he lies about 4 or 5 miles to the southward of Tistehatan; contains about 24 houses, well furnished with corn.

"The Senekas are counted to be in all about 1000 fighting men.

```
"Whole force—Maquas.................................................... 300
               Oneydoes..................................................... 200
               Onondagoes................................................... 350
               Cayugas....................................................... 300
               Senekas....................................................... 1000
                                                                          ─────
                                                       2150 fighting men." §
```

* Mr. Chalmers purports to derive the journal "from New York papers," meaning, as is presumed, the manuscripts of the New York "Board of Trade."

[NOTE.—What is said of the " Maquas (Mohawks), Oneydoes, Onondagoes, and Cayugas," is omitted, and the journal commences with the Senecas.]

† The Tistehatan, or bending river, must refer to the Genesee.

‡ Probably among the Swedes on the Delaware—Penn had not yet commenced his settlement.

§ "Among the manuscripts of Sir William Johnson, there is a census of the northern and western

"*Remark.*—During the year 1685 an accurate account was taken by order of the Governor, of the people of Canada (New France); which amounted to 17,000, of whom 3000 were supposed to be able to carry arms. We may thence form a judgment with regard to the comparative strength of the two belligerent powers, whose wars were so long and destructive."—*Chalmers's Annals.*

The Rev. Samuel Kirkland, whose name we have had occasion to introduce in connection with the antiquities of this region, left the mission station at Johnson's Hall, on the Mohawk, January 16th, 1765, in company with two Seneca Indians, upon a mission which embraced all the settlements of the Iroquois, travelling upon snowshoes, carrying "a pack containing his provisions, a few articles of clothing, and a few books, weighing in all about forty pounds." Leaving the last vestige of civilization (Johnson's Hall), his only companions two Indians with whom he had had but a short acquaintance, the young missionary shaped his course to the westward, encamping nights (with his two guides with whom he could hold no conversation except by signs), beneath hemlock boughs, and sleeping upon ground cleared from snow, for his temporary use. Arriving at Onondaga, the central council-fire of the Iroquois, a message from Sir William Johnson secured him a friendly reception. After remaining there one day, the party left, and came on to Kanadasegea, the principal town of the Senecas. Halting at the skirts of the town (a courtesy that his, Mr. K.'s, Indian guides, told him by signs was customary), a messenger came out to inquire "whence they came, whither they were going, and what was their desire." His guides replied: "We are only bound to this place, and wish to be conducted to the house of the chief sachem." The embassy was conducted into the presence of the sachem, to whom, as at Onondaga, a message was delivered from Sir William Johnson. The reception was friendly, except with a few, "whose sullen countenances," Mr. K. says, "he did not quite like." The head sachem treated him with every kindness and attention, and it was, after much deliberation and consultation among the Indians, determined that he should fix his residence with them. Through a Dutch trader, who had preceded him, and located at Kanadasegea, he communicated freely with the Indians. A few weeks after his arrival, he was formally adopted as a member of the family of the head sachem. This adoption was attended with formalities—a council, speeches, etc. The council having assembled, "the head sachem's family being present and sitting apart by themselves," Mr. Kirkland was waited upon and invited to attend. On his entrance, after a short silence, one of the chiefs spoke:

"Brothers, open your ears and your eyes. You see here our white brother who has come from a great distance, recommended to us by our great chief, Sir William Johnson, who has enjoined it upon us to be kind to him, and to make him comfortable and protect him to the utmost of our power. He comes to do us good.

Indians, from the Hudson River to the great lakes and the Mississippi, taken in 1763. The Mohawk warriors were then only 160; the Oneidas, 250; Tuscaroras, 140; Onondagas, 150; Cayugas, 200; Senecas, 1050; total, 1950. According to the calculation of a British agent, several of the tribes must have increased between the close of the French war and beginning of the American Revolution, as it was computed that, during the latter contest, the English had in service 300 Mohawks, 150 Oneidas, 200 Tuscaroras, 300 Onondagas, 230 Cayugas, and 400 Senecas.

[NOTE.—There can be but little doubt that the four villages mentioned by Mr. Greenhalph are those that were ten years afterwards destroyed by De Nonville. The over-estimate of distances made by this early adventurer, may be well attributed to the absence of any means to ascertain them correctly. In the names, as given by De Nonville, and by Mr. Greenhalph, there is sufficient analogy to warrant the identity.

Brothers, this young white brother of ours has left his father's house, and his mother, and all his relations; we must now provide for him a house; I am appointed to you and to our young white brother, that our head sachem adopts him into his family. He will be a father to him, and his wife will be a mother, and his sons and daughters, his brothers and sisters."

The head sachem then rose, called him his son, and led him to his family. Mr. K. thanked him, and told him he hoped the Great Spirit would make him a blessing to his new relations. The zealous and enterprising young missionary says in his journal: "A smile of cheerfulness sat on every countenance, and I could not refrain from tears; tears of joy and gratitude for the kind Providence that had protected me through a long journey, brought me to the place of my desire, and given me so kind a reception among the poor savage Indians."

Mr. K. applied himself diligently to learn the Seneca language, and by the help of two words, "*atkayason*" (what do you call this?), and "*sointaschnagati*" (speak it again), he made rapid progress. He was made very comfortable and treated very kindly.

All things were going on well, but friendly relations were destined to an interruption. The missionary had been assigned a residence with an Indian family, whose head was a man of much influence with his people; "sober, industrious, honest, and telling no lies." Unfortunately, in a few days after Mr. K. had become an inmate of his wigwam, he sickened and died. Such of the Senecas as were jealous of the new-comer seized upon the circumstance to create prejudice against him, even alleging that the death was occasioned by his magic, or if not, that it was an "intimation of the displeasure of the Great Spirit at his visit and residence among them, and that he must be put to death." Councils were convened, there were days of deliberation, touching what disposition should be made of the missionary— the chief sachem proving his fast friend, and opposing all propositions to harm him. During the time, a Dutch trader, a Mr. Womp, on his way from Niagara east, stopped at Kanadasegea, and he was the only medium through which Mr. K. could learn, from day to day, the deliberations of the council. At length his friend, the sachem, informed him joyfully, that "all was peace."

Some proceedings of the council afterward transpired, that Mr. Kirkland was enabled to preserve in his journal. It was opened by an address from the chief sachem:

"Brothers, this is a dark day to us; a heavy cloud has gathered over us. The cheering rays of the sun are obscured; the dim, faint light of the moon *sympathizes with us*. A great and awakening event has called us together, the sudden death of one of our best men; a great breach is made in our Councils, a living example of peace, *sobriety*, and industry is taken from us. Our whole town mourns, for a good man is gone. He is dead. Our white brother had lived with him a few days. Our white brother is a good young man. He loves Indians. He comes recommended to us by Sir William Johnson, who is commissioned by the great king beyond the waters to be our superintendent. Brothers, attend! The Great Spirit has supreme power over life. He, the upholder of the skies, has most certainly brought about this solemn event by his will, and without any other help, or second cause. Brothers, let us deliberate wisely; let us determine with great caution. Let us take counsel under our great loss, with a *tender mind*. This is the best medicine and was the way of our fathers."

A long silence ensued, which was broken by a chief of great influence, who was ambitious of supreme control. He made a long and inflammatory harangue against the missionary. Among other things, he said:

"This white skin, whom we call our brother, has come upon a dark design, or he would not have travelled so many hundred miles. He brings with him the *white people's Book.* They call it *God's Holy Book.* Brothers, attend! You know this book was never made for Indians. The Great Spirit gave us a book for ourselves. He wrote it in our heads. He put it into the minds of our fathers, and gave them rules about worshipping him; and our fathers strictly observed these rules, and the Upholder of the skies was pleased, and gave them success in hunting, and made them victorious over their enemies in war. Brothers, attend! Be assured that if we Senecas receive this white man, and attend to the Book made solely for white people, we shall become miserable. We shall soon lose the spirit of true men. The spirit of the brave warrior and the good hunter will be no more with us. We shall be sunk so low as to hoe corn and squashes in the field, chop wood, stoop down and milk cows, like the negroes among the Dutch people.* Brothers, hear me! I am in earnest, because I love my nation, and the customs and practices of our fathers; and they enjoyed pleasant and prosperous days. If we permit this white skin to remain among us, and finally embrace what is written in his book, it will be the complete subversion of our national character, as true men. Our ancient customs, our religious feasts and offerings, all that our fathers so strictly observed, will be gone. Of this are we not warned by the sudden death of our good brother and wise sachem? Does not the Upholder of the skies plainly say to us in this: 'Hear, attend, ye Senecas! Behold, I have taken one, or permitted one to be taken from among you in an extraordinary manner, which you cannot account for, and thereby to save the nation'? Brothers, listen to what I say. Ought not this white man's life to make satisfaction for our deceased brother's death?"

A long discussion and investigation followed. Mr. Kirkland's papers were carried to the council-house and examined; the widow of the deceased was questioned; she gave a good account of the "young white brother," said "he was always cheerful and pleasant, and they had begun to love him much." Said one of the opponents of Mr. K., "Did he never come to your husband's bedside and whisper in his ears or puff in his face?" "No, never, he always sat, or lay down, on his own bunk, and in the evening after we were in bed, he would see him get down upon his knees and talk with a low voice." This testimony, and the closing speech of the head sachem, brought matters to a favorable issue. The speech was an able reply to Onoongwandeka—not in opposition to his views, as to the effect generally of admitting the white man and his Book, but generally, in reference to the witchcraft and sorcery charged upon Mr. Kirkland, in connection with the sudden death of his host. The speech bore down all opposition, and was followed by shouts and

* The Indian orator had probably been to Schenectady and Albany, and observed the slaves among the Dutch.

NOTE.—The author derives this account of the primitive advent of a Protestant missionary among the Senecas from Sparks's American Biography. The name of the chief sachem of Kanadasegea—Mr. Kirkland's adopted father and friend—does not transpire. The chief who so eloquently spoke for his nation, and ingeniously wrought upon the jealousy and superstition of the council, was Onoongwandeka. The speeches are given (as is what else transpired at the time) as communicated to Mr. Kirkland by Mr. Womp. The reader will bear in mind that in this case, as well as in all reports of the speeches of uneducated Indians, the reporters have but caught the ideas of the native orators, and substituted their own manner of expression. An eloquent idea—a beautiful figure of speech—can, of course, only be faithfully reported in corresponding words and sentences. For instance, we are not to suppose that the Seneca sachem said, "the dim faint light of the moon sympathizes with us," but he did probably make use of a beautiful figure of speech that justified Mr. Kirkland in such an interpretation.

applause, in which only fifteen refused to participate. The chief sachem said, "Our business is done. I rake up the council-fire."

After this, Mr. Kirkland "lived in great harmony, friendship, and sociability." Another trouble ensued in the shape of a famine. The corn crop for the year previous had been short, and game was scarce at that season of the year (March). He wrote to a friend that he had "sold a shirt for four Indian cakes, baked in the ashes, which he could have devoured at one meal, but on the score of prudence had ate only one." He lived for days, on "white-oak acorns, fried in bear's grease." He gives a long detail of suffering and privation, as severe as any of his Jesuit predecessors had endured; which terminated in making a return journey through the wilderness to Johnson Hall, where he procured a supply of provisions.

Mr. Kirkland was a missionary among the Six Nations for eight years previous to the Revolution; during that struggle he was useful in diverting some portions of them from adhering to the British interests; and his name and services are often blended in the Indian treaties that followed after the war, and resulted in the extinguishment of their title to lands in Western New York.

Its first State constitution was adopted April 20th, 1777, and De Witt Clinton was elected its first governor, and continued in office till 1795. The Articles of Confederation for the States were approved by New York in February, 1778. Both in the army and the Continental Congress the State was represented by men of rare ability and patriotism. In the Constitutional Convention which formed the Federal Constitution her delegates were Messrs. Yates, Lansing, and Alexander Hamilton. The Constitution was ratified by New York, July 26th, 1788. John Jay, already illustrious as a statesman, was chosen governor in 1795. The practicability of steam navigation was demonstrated on the Hudson in 1807 by Robert Fulton. In the war with Great Britain (1812-15) New York took an active part, and, aside from the victories gained by her heroes on the ocean, many of the minor conflicts and the important land and naval battle of Plattsburg were fought along its northern and north-western frontier. The battle of Lundy's Lane, one of the most decisive of the war, was fought on the Canada side of Niagara River, less than two miles from the Falls. Soon after the war, the project for a canal from Albany to Buffalo, which had been previously broached, was revived, and in 1817 both the Erie and the Champlain canal were commenced and pushed forward to completion, the latter in 1823, and the former, with great rejoicings, in 1825. A constitutional convention was held in 1821, and a new constitution adopted and ratified by the people. The anti-Masonic excitement in 1826 caused a great commotion and many political changes in the State. The popularity of the Erie and Champlain canals led to a great pressure upon the State for the construction of other canals, unwarranted by the business of the regions through which they were to pass. In an evil hour they were commenced, and have ever since been a constant source of loss to the State. The enlargement of the Erie Canal, begun in 1835, has increased the cost of that great work to $100,000,000, but with advantages perhaps commensurate with its cost. In 1846, another constitutional convention was held, and a new constitution, differing materially from the preceding, adopted and ratified by the people. The interest in public schools continued to increase, and the appropriations voted and taxes levied for their promotion were enlarged every year.

In 1845, the annual expenditure for public schools was $1,240,000; in 1875, as we show elsewhere, $11,365,000, or nearly tenfold. The collection of rate-bills was finally abolished in about 1850, and the schools sustained wholly by tax and appropriations from funds. At the commencement of the late civil war, New York took an active and prominent part in its aid, and her people were to a greater extent than those of most of the States united in sustaining the government. Her immense quotas were promptly filled, and the State paid $40,000,000 in bounties to its volunteers. The so-call "Draft riot" of 1863 in New York City (*see* New York City) was prompted by other causes than fear of the draft, and was promptly suppressed. In her liberality and bountiful care of her own wounded or sick soldiers during the war, and of their suffering families, the State was not surpassed by any other. In 1867, another constitutional convention was held, and a new constitution promulgated, which was, however, rejected by the people, except the articles on the judiciary, which were incorporated into the constitution of 1846, which is yet the governing law of the State, though some further amendments have been adopted.

GOVERNORS OF THE COLONY AND STATE.

(Those marked with a star (*) died in office.)

(1) *Under the Dutch.*

Peter Minuit	1624-33
Wouter Van Twiller	1633-37
Willem Keift	1637-47
Petrus Stuyvesant	1647-64

(2) *Under the English.*

Richard Nicolls	1664-67
Francis Lovelace	1667-73

(3) *Dutch administration resumed.*

Anthony Colve	1673-74

(4) *English administration resumed.*

Edmond Andross	1674-83
Thomas Dongan	1683-88
Edmond Andross	1688-89
Jacob Leisler	1689-91
Henry Sloughter*	1691-91
Richard Ingoldsby	1691-92
Benjamin Fletcher	1692-98
Richard, Earl Bellemont*	1698-1701
John Nanfan	1701-02
Lord Cornbury	1702-08
John, Lord Lovelace*	1708-09
Richard Ingoldsby	1709-10
Gerardus Beekman	1710-10
Robert Hunter	1710-19
Peter Schuyler	1719-20
William Burnet*	1720-28
John Montgomerie*	1728-31
Rip van Dam	1731-32
William Cosby*	1732-36
George Clarke	1736-43
George Clinton	1743-53
Sir Danvers Osborne*	1753-53
James De Lancey	1753-55
Sir Charles Hardy	1755-57
James De Lancey*	1757-60
Cadwallader Colden	1760-61
Robert Markton	1761-61
Cadwallader Colden	1761-65
Sir Henry Moore*	1765-69
Cadwallader Colden	1769-70
John, Lord Dunmore	1770-71
William Tryon	1771-77

(5) *Governors of the State.*

George Clinton	1777-95
John Jay	1795-1801
George Clinton	1801-04
Morgan Lewis	1804-07
Daniel D. Tompkins	1807-17
De Witt Clinton	1817-22
Joseph C. Yates	1822-24
De Witt Clinton*	1824-28
Nathaniel Pitcher	1828-29
Martin Van Buren	1829-29
Enos T. Throop	1829-33
William L. Marcy	1833-38
William H. Seward	1838-42
William C. Bouck	1842-44
Silas Wright, Jr.	1844-46
John Young	1846-49
Hamilton Fish	1849-51
Washington Hunt	1851-53
Horatio Seymour	1853-55
Myron H. Clark	1855-57
John A. King	1857-59
Edwin D. Morgan	1859-63
Horatio Seymour	1863-65
Reuben E. Fenton	1865-69
John T. Hoffman	1869-73
John Adams Dix	1873-75
Samuel J. Tilden	1875-77
Lucius Robinson	1877-

GREAT CITIES.

Great cities grow up in nations and in states as the mature offspring of well-directed civil and commercial agencies, and in their natural development they become vital organs in the world's government and civilization, performing the highest functions of human life on the earth. They grow up where human faculties and natural advantages are most effective. They have a part in the grand march of the human race peculiar to themselves in making the progress of mankind in arts, commerce, and civilization; and they embellish history with its richest pages of learning, and impress on the mind of the scholar and the student the profoundest lessons of the rise and fall of nations. They have formed in all ages the great centres of industrial and intellectual life, from which mighty outgrowths of civilization have expanded. In short, they are the mightiest works of man. And whether we view them wrapped in the flames of the conqueror and surrounded with millions of earnest hearts yielding, in despair, to the wreck of fortune and life at the fading away of expiring glory or the sinking of a nation into oblivion; or whether we contemplate them in the full vigor of prosperity, with steeples piercing the very heavens, with royal palaces, gilded halls, and rich displays of wealth and learning, they are ever wonderful objects of man's creation—ever impressing, with profoundest conviction, lessons of human greatness and human glory. In their greatness they have been able to wrestle with all human time. We have only to go with Volney through the Ruins of Empire, to trace the climbing path of man from his first appearance on the fields of history to the present day, by the evidences we find along his pathway in the ruins of the great cities—the creation of his own hands. The lessons of magnitude and durability which great cities teach may be more clearly realized in the following eloquent passage from a lecture of Louis Kossuth, delivered in New York City:

"How wonderful! What a present and what a future yet! Future? Then let me stop at this mysterious word—the veil of unrevealed eternity. The shadow of that dark word passed across my mind, and amid the bustle of this gigantic beehive, there I stood with meditation alone.

"And the spirit of the immovable past rose before my eyes, unfolding the picture rolls of vanished greatness, and the fragility of human things. And among their dissolving views there I saw the scorched soil of Africa, and upon that soil, Thebes, with its hundred gates, more splendid than the most splendid of all the existing cities of the world—Thebes, the pride of old Egypt, the first metropolis of arts and sciences, and the mysterious cradle of so many doctrines, which still rule mankind in different shapes, though it has long forgotten their source.

"Then I saw Syria, with its hundred cities; every city a nation, every nation with an empire's might. Baalbec, with its gigantic temples, the very ruins of which baffle the imagination of man as they stand, like mountains of carved rocks, in the deserts where, for hundreds of miles, not a stone is to be found, and no river flows, offering its tolerant back to carry a mountain's weight upon. And yet there they stand, those gigantic ruins; and as we glance at them with astonishment, though we have mastered the mysterious elements of nature, and know the combination of levers, and how to catch the lightning, and how to command the power of steam and compressed air, and how to write with the burning fluid out of which the thunderbolt is forged, and how to dive to the bottom of the ocean, and how to rise up to the sky, cities like London and Pekin dwindle to the modest proportion of a child's toy, so that we are tempted to take the nice little thing upon the nail of our thumb, as Microgemas did the man of wax.

"Though we know all this, and many things else, still, looking at the times of Baalbec, we cannot forbear to ask, 'What people of giants was that which could do what neither the puny efforts of our skill nor the ravaging hand of unrelenting time can undo through thousands of years?'

"And then I saw the dissolving picture of Nineveh, with its ramparts now covered with mountains of sand, where Layard has dug up colossal winged bulls, large as a mountain, and yet carved with the nicety of a cameo; and then Babylon, with its beautiful walls; and Jerusalem, with its unequalled temples; Tyrus, with its countless fleets; Arad, with its wharves; and Sidon, with its labyrinth of workshops and factories; and Ascalon, and Gaza, and Beyrout, and, farther off, Persepolis, with its world of palaces."

The first great cities of the world were built by a race of men inferior to those which now form the dominant civilization of the earth, yet there are many ruins of a mould superior, both in greatness and mechanical skill, to those which belong to the cities of our own day, as found in the marble solitudes of Palmyra and the sand-buried cities of Egypt. It is true, however, that ancient grandeur grew out of a system of idolatry and serf-labor, controlled by selfish despot or blind priesthood, which compelled useless display of greatness in most public improvements. In our age, labor is directed more to practical wisdom than of old, which creates the useful more than the ornamental: hence, we have the Crystal Palace instead of the Pyramids.

But, leaving the ancient cities, we are led to inquire, "Where will grow up the future great city of the world?" At the very outset of this inquiry it is necessary to clearly comprehend a few underlying facts connected with the cities of the past and those now in existence, and note the influence of the more important arts and sciences that bear upon man's present intellectual and industrial interests, and, if possible, to determine the tendency of the world's civilization toward the unfolding future.

The first great fact we meet with is, that the inevitable tendency of man upon the earth has been to make the circuit of the globe by going westward, within an isothermal belt or zodiac of equal temperature, which encircles the earth in the north temperate zone. Within this belt has already been embraced more than three fourths of the world's civilization, and now about 950,000,000 people. It is along this belt that the processions of nations, in time, have moved forward, with reason and order, "in a predetermined, a solemn march, in which all have joined; ever moving and ever resistlessly advancing, encountering and enduring an inevitable succession of events."

It is along this axis of the isothermal temperate zone of the northern hemisphere that revealed civilization makes the circuit of the globe. Here the continents expand, the oceans contract. This zone contains the zodiac of empires; along its axis, at distances scarcely varying one hundred leagues, appear the great cities of the world, from Pekin in China to San Francisco in America.

"During antiquity this zodiac was narrow; it never expanded beyond the North African shore, nor beyond the Pontic Sea, the Danube, and the Rhine.

Along this narrow belt civilization planted its system, from Oriental Asia to the western extremity of Europe, with more or less perfect development.

"Modern times have recently seen it widen to embrace the region of the Baltic Sea. In America, it starts with the broad front from Cuba to Hudson Bay. As in all previous times, it advances along a line central to these extremes, in the densest form, and with the greatest celerity. Here are the chief cities of intelligence and power, the greatest intensity of energy and progress. Science has recently very perfectly established, by observation, this axis of the isothermal temperate zone. It reveals to the world this shining fact, that along it civilization has travelled, as by an inevitable instinct of nature, since Creation's dawn. From this line has radiated intelligence of mind to the North and to the South, and toward it all people have struggled to converge. Thus, in harmony with the supreme order of nature, is the mind of man instinctively adjusted to the revolutions of the sun and tempered by its heat."

> "Through the ages one increasing purpose runs,
> And the thoughts of men are widened with the process of the suns."

It is a noteworthy observation of Dr. Draper, in his work on the "Civil War in America," that within a zone, a few degrees wide, having for its axis the January isothermal line of forty-one degrees, all great men in Europe and Asia have appeared. He might have added, with equal truth, that within the same zone have existed all those great cities which have exerted a powerful influence upon the world's history as centres of civilization and intellectual progress. The same inexorable but subtle law of climate which makes greatness in the individual unattainable, in a temperature hotter or colder than a certain golden mean affects in like manner, with even more certainty, the development of those concentrations of the intellect of man which we find in great cities. If the temperature is too cold, the sluggish torpor of the intellectual and physical nature precludes the highest development; if the temperature is too hot, the fiery fickleness of nature, which warm climates produce in the individual, is typical of the swift and tropical growth and sudden and severe decay and decline of cities exposed to the same all-powerful influence. Beyond that zone of moderate temperature the human life resembles more closely that of the animal, as it is forced to combat with extremes of cold or to submit to extremes of heat; but within that zone the highest intellectual activity and culture are displayed. It is not, then, a fact of no little import that the very axis of this zone—the centre of equilibrium between excess of heat and cold—the January isothermal line of forty-one degrees—passes near to the city of New York. Close to that same isothermal line lie London, Paris, Rome, Constantinople, and Pekin, Philadelphia, Chicago, and San Francisco. Thus favored in climate, lying in the very centre of that belt of intellectual activity beyond which neither great man nor great city has yet appeared, New York may, with reason, be expected to attain the higher rank, if other conditions favor.

A second underlying fact that presents itself is, that nearly all the great cities of the world have been built upon rivers, whether in the interior or near the ocean's edge; such as Babylon on the Euphrates; Thebes, on the Nile; Nineveh, on the Tigris; Rome, on the Tiber; Paris, on the Seine; London, on the Thames; New York, on the Hudson; St. Louis, on the Mississippi; Cincinnati, on the Ohio; and Constantinople, on the Bosphorus; while Carthage, St. Petersburg, Chicago, and

Cleveland belong to interior waters, and Palmyra and the City of Mexico to the interior country.

A third fundamental fact is, that the arts and sciences do more to develop cities and multiply population upon the seaboard, than upon interior cities. Steam-engines, labor-saving machines, books, the value and use of metals, government, the enforcement of laws and other means of self-protection all have tended more to make the people of the seaboard more numerous, powerful, and wealthy than those who dwell in the interior.

A fourth fundamental fact is, that to all modern civilization domestic transportation by water and rail is more valuable to nations of large territorial extent than ocean navigation. This fact is founded not only upon the assumption that a nation's interests are of more importance to itself than to any other nation, and it hence necessarily does more business at home than abroad, but also upon the fact that the exchanges of domestic produce within this country, it is estimated, already exceed in value six thousand millions a year.

With every year, as the country advances in population and industry, its domestic exchanges gain upon its foreign.

New York, like ancient Rome, once with its 10,000,000 population, is destined to be flanked and surrounded with a galaxy or cordon of continental cities. Boston, Philadelphia, Brooklyn, Jersey City, Newark, Baltimore, Washington, Albany, Troy, are a few of these satellites, that in the future are to pay tribute to this centre—taking in view the fact of their vast material resources, and these being the centre of the great fruit, agricultural, and wine belt of the continent. The people—the Teutonic and Celtic races—are the pioneer people in all the departments of human industry, politics, culture, theology. We apprehend that the most acute vision, even were that mind in harmony with the spirit of the times, and enabled through that means to look back through the dim geologic history of the past, when the economic laws were piling the iron atom by atom in these iron mountains, growing the dense flora of the coal plants, repleting the veins of lead, zinc, copper, tin, silver, and gold; and at the same time comprehend the ridge, valley, spring, prairie, timber, and river systems; and was enabled to go back in the ethnography and heraldry of these populations, and could fuse these elements or facts in the future, and at the same time realize the grandeur of the empires of the past—the Persian, under Cyrus; the Macedonian, under Alexander the Great; the Roman, under the Republic and the twelve Cæsars—that the truth would be forced upon the mind, that in the future this great valley of the Hudson will include the centre of an empire before which, in wealth, power, and grandeur, all these shall pale; that New York, sitting like a queen on the banks of the great Hudson, will be the central city of this people, the tidal waves of whose civilization will roll to China and Japan on the West, and to the Bosphorus on the East; and with her continental railroad system, her telegraphs over mountains and under oceans, her vast water communications, will radiate law and order, and become the leading national and commercial metropolis of the Western hemisphere.

NEW YORK CITY

[THE *New Amsterdam* of the Dutch], the chief commercial city in the United States, and the most populous, is situated at the junction of the Hudson or North River and the extension of Long Island Sound, familiarly known as the East River. The limits of the city and county (of the same name) are identical, and include the southern portion of the mainland (late part of Westchester County), known as the towns of Morrisania, West Farms, and King's Bridge, together with the islands Manhattan, Blackwell, Ward, Randall, Bedloe, Ellis, and Governor's, of which the three last-named have been ceded for Federal purposes to the Government of the U. S. Its extensive and sheltered harbor, eighteen miles distant from the Atlantic Ocean at Sandy Hook, is known all over the world for its natural beauty and great commercial advantages. An observation taken by the distinguished astronomer, Mr. Lewis M. Rutherfurd, at his observatory, corner of Second avenue and Eleventh street, gives lat. 40° 43′ 48″ + 0.31″ N., lon. W. 4h. 55m. 55.73s. from Greenwich. Its distance from Albany, the capital of the State, is 150 miles.

Area.—The total area of the city before the recent additions from Westchester County was 22 square miles, or 14,000 acres. The additions amount to 13,000 acres. That of Manhattan Island, the seat of population, and divided from the mainland by the Harlem River, is 22 square miles and 20,424 square yards. Of this, 8,712,000 yards are devoted to public parks. The length of the island is 13¼ miles; its width averages 1¾ miles. It is by survey divided into 141,486 lots. The outlying islands are set aside for public purposes, almshouses, penitentiaries, etc. They contain about 300 acres; those ceded to the Government, 100 acres. By Governor Montgomerie's charter, Jan. 15th, 1730, the city was divided into 7 wards, which were, respectively, West, South, Dock, East, North, Montgomerie, and the Outward. It is now divided into 24 wards, which are designated by their numbers—1, 2, etc. The population by decennials is reported by the U. S. census as in

1790	33,131	1840	312,710
1800	60,489	1850	515,547
1810	96,373	1860	813,669
1820	123,706	1870	942,292
1830	197,112	1875	1,046,037

Of the last statement, 426,168 were foreign-born—262,577 British and Irish, and 170,143 German, the rest of other nations

Commerce.—Nearly 60 per cent of the foreign trade of the country passes through this port. Of the total imports for the fiscal year ending June 30th, 1874, amounting to $595,861,248 for all the U. S., $395,133,622 were by New York, against $200,727,626 for all other ports; of the total exports, amounting to $704,463,120 for all the U. S., $340,360,260 were by New York, against $364,102,851 for all other ports; the total aggregate of inward and outward trade being for all the U. S. $1,300,324,368, of which New York had $735,493,882, and all other ports $564,830,477. This foreign trade was in the fiscal year ending June 30th, 1874, divided geographically as follows: Imports from the American continent, $117,524,419; exports to same, $45,999,356; total American foreign trade, $163,523,775. Imports from Europe, $245,130,885; exports to same, $288,581,107; total European trade, $533,711,992.

Imports from Asia, $31,275,679; exports to same, $4,823,683; total Asian trade, $36,099,362. Imports from Africa, $1,202,639; exports to same, $956,123; total African trade, $2,158,762. The importation of sugar at the port of New York for the same fiscal year was valued at $49,293,625; of molasses, at $3,066,551; of coffee, at $33,485,559; of tea, at $15,024,794; imports of wool, raw, $3,956,458, and manufactured, $37,191,046; of silk and silk manufactures, $24,155,711; of manufactures of cotton, $23,709,180; of flax, $14,376,173; of iron and steel, $17,783,924. The principal exports for the same period were of cotton, valued at $41,499,597; of wheat and wheat flour, $77,273,214; of Indian corn and meal, $14,876,603; total breadstuffs, $91,332,669; cheese, $11,624,406; bacon and hams, $23,202,938; beef and pork, $5,366,603; lard and tallow, $20,319,514; of tobacco, $16,117,749; of illuminating oils, $23,121,059. The imports of coin (larger than for some years previous, in consequence of the commercial depression of 1873), $18,401,242, and the exports $50,359,394. Of the total imports, $280,187,426 were of duty-paying articles, and $114,946,196 of articles free of duty; of the duty-paying articles, $276,770,129 were entered for immediate consumption, and $113,351,459 were entered for warehouses. The proportion of imports in cars and vehicles was $70,039; of imports in American vessels, $90,131,181; and in foreign vessels, $304,932,402. Of the total exports, $54,436,965 were exported in American vessels, and $285,923,304 in foreign vessels.

The number of entrances of American and foreign vessels—ocean, steam, and sail—at the port of New York for the year ending June 30th, 1874, was 6723, tonning 5,049,618 tons, and handled by crews amounting in the total to 148,246 men; of the vessels, 4290 were foreign, and 2433 American. Of ocean steam vessels there were entered 1108, tonning 2,792,367, and with crews amounting to 88,042; of these steam vessels, 887 were foreign, and 231 American. The most numerous entrances of vessels were from England, 1087, tonning 1,725,272; from Cuba, 1375, tonning 593,476; from Germany, 412, tonning 678,287; from Scotland, 197, tonning 363,797; and from France, 266, tonning 237,105 tons. Of the 877 entrances of foreign steam vessels, there were 386 from England, tonning 1,275,072 tons; 168 from Germany, of 524,-451; 129 from Scotland, of 332,339; and 33 from France, of 113,449 tons. Of the 231 entrances of American vessels, all, with one exception, were from the West Indies and South America. The registered tonnage of the custom districts of New York was 6630 vessels, of 1,318,523.34 tons, of which 558 were licensed under 20 tons. Of these there were 2810 sailing vessels, with a tonnage of 600,020,421; 788 steam vessels, tonnage 351,686.06; 546 barges, tonnage 123,535.58; 2486 canal boats, tonnage 243,281.18. The coastwise trade engaged 2742 vessels, tonning 1,774,181 tons, of which 1583 were steam vessels, with a tonnage of 1,517,481, and 1159 sailing vessels, tonning 256,700. The ship-building for the year ending June 30th, 1874, comprised 89 sailing vessels, 60 steam vessels (of which 39 were for river purposes and 21 for ocean navigation), 196 canal boats, and 51 barges—a total of 396 of all kinds, tonning 64,-001.55 tons.

The transportation to tide-water on the canals from Western States and the interior of New York State amounted in the year 1874 to 3,323,112 tons, and the returns from tide-water to the interior to 753,981 tons. This transportation has been maintained with moderate fluctuations for many years. The arrivals of immigrants at the port were, in 1874, from all ports, 149,762, against 266,449 in 1873, 294,581 in 1872, 228,962 in 1871, and 209,788 in 1870. Of the arrivals in 1874, 41,368 were from Germany, 41,179 from Ireland, 19,822 from England, and 7723 from Russia. A new feature in American immigration is the religious movement of Mennonites, whose faith forbids their taking military service.

DOMESTIC EXPORTS FROM THE PORT OF NEW YORK FOR THE LAST TWENTY-ONE YEARS.

Year ending June 30th.

Year	Amount	Year	Amount
1856	$98,763,197	1867	$207,382,457
1857	111,029,083	1868	236,031,239
1858	83,403,564	1869	185,384,264
1859	97,461,576	1870	209,972,491
1860	120,630,955	1871	285,530,775
1861	137,379,956	1872	270,413,674
1862	152,377,961	1873	313,129,963
1863	221,917,978	1874	340,360,269
1864	211,237,222	1875	329,201,913
1865	219,379,873	1876	294,705,902
1866	264,510,247		

FOREIGN EXPORTS FROM THE PORT OF NEW YORK FOR THE LAST TWENTY-ONE YEARS.

Year ending June 30th.

Year	Amount	Year	Amount
1856	$6,098,602	1867	
1857	13,360,384	1868	$15,016,273
1858	17,299,097	1869	17,741,836
1859	9,016,853	1870	20,339,410
1860	17,514,689	1871	20,087,211
1861	13,311,495	1872	15,161,218
1862	5,069,953	1873	18,972,099
1863	17,369,353	1874	14,633,463
1864	12,735,640	1875	15,502,056
1865	22,627,018	1876	13,868,321
1866			

NOTE.—The Re-Exports of the Customs Districts for the years 1866 and 1867 were not given.

FOREIGN IMPORTS AT THE PORT OF NEW YORK FOR THE LAST TWENTY-ONE YEARS.

Year ending June 30th.

Year	Amount	Year	Amount
1856	$195,645,515	1867	$277,469,510
1857	222,550,307	1868	242,580,659
1858	170,280,887	1869	295,117,682
1859	218,231,093	1870	293,990,006
1860	233,692,941	1871	357,909,770
1861	189,064,817	1872	418,515,829
1862	142,215,636	1873	426,321,427
1863	177,254,415	1874	395,133,622
1864	229,506,499	1875	368,637,580
1865	154,139,409	1876	311,712,910
1866	302,505,719		

RECEIPTS OF DOMESTIC PRODUCE AT NEW YORK FOR THE YEAR 1876.

ARTICLES.		ARTICLES.	
BREADSTUFFS:		PROVISIONS (*Continued*).	
Flour, bbls................	3,982,707	Lard, bbls................	2,115
Wheat, bush...............	26,411,296	Lard, kegs...............	27,427
Corn, bush................	26,645,599	Lard, cases..............	19,997
Oats, bush................	12,168,809	Bellies, tcs..............	1,077
Barley, bush..............	4,840,095	Bellies, bxs..............	2,701
Barley Malt, bush.........	2,009,824	Middles, tcs.............	12,075
Rye, bush.................	1,753,032	Middles, bxs.............	386,888
Buckwheat, bush...........	18,347	Hams, tcs................	30,677
Peas, bush................	1,177,120	Hams, bbls...............	5,464
Black-Eyed Peas, bags.....	5,378	Hams, bxs................	49,829
Beans, bbls...............	111,253	Tongues, bbls............	12,701
Oat Meal, bbls. and sacks.	92,999	Tongues, kegs...........	578
Corn Meal, bbls...........	178,145	Shoulders, tcs...........	3,159
Corn Meal, sacks..........	158,676	Shoulders, bxs...........	16,633
Buckwheat Flour, sacks....	30,389	Backs, bxs...............	3,786
Hops, bales...............	86,910	Butter, pkgs.............	1,289,889
NAVAL STORES:		Cheese, pkgs.............	2,178,989
Crude Turpentine, bbls....	3,962	Eggs, pkgs...............	500,072
Spirits of Turpentine, bbls.	74,795	Tallow, hhds.............	11,236
Pitch, bbls................	3,357	Tallow, tcs..............	5,547
Tar, bbls..................	18,561	Tallow, bbls.............	58,694
Rosin, bbls................	386,242	Tallow, casks............	4,360
Lard Oil, bbls.............	11,785	Stearine, hhds...........	285
Oil Cake, bags...............	460,303	Stearine, tcs............	19,951
LIVE STOCK:		Stearine, bbls...........	3,439
Beeves, No................	463,671	Stearine, casks..........	1,077
Hogs, Live, No............	1,222,657	Grease, hhds.............	715
Sheep, No.................	1,211,086	Grease, tcs..............	12,449
Calves, No................	110,848	Grease, bbls.............	18,409
Cows, No..................	4,051	Grease, casks............	1,182
PROVISIONS:		Dressed Hogs, No.........	52,287
Pork, bbls................	200,994	SEEDS:	
Beef, tcs.................	52,097	Clover and Timothy, bush.	208,497
Beef, bbls................	37,627	Flax Seed, bags..........	110,885
Beef, cases...............	108,115	Whisky...................	51,434
Beef Hams, bbls...........	10,671	High Wines...............	74,229
Lard, tcs.................	397,245	Alcohol..................	25,784

EXPORTS OF PRODUCE FROM NEW YORK FOR THE YEAR 1876.

ARTICLES.		ARTICLES.	
BREADSTUFFS:		OILS:	
Bread, pkgs...............	143,962	Lard Oil, gals...........	100,621
Flour, Wheat, bbls........	1,947,272	Residuum, gals...........	2,514,870
Flour, Rye, bbls..........	7,634	Naphtha, gals............	9,018,131
Corn Meal, bbls...........	174,608	Benzine, gals............	143,973
Wheat, bush...............	24,945,715	Petroleum, Crude, gals...	10,608,206
Corn, bush................	16,470,935	Petroleum, Refined, gals.	123,665,776
Oats, bush................	683,616	Oil Cake, lbs............	177,005,666
Barley, bush..............	117,815	Oil Meal, lbs............	2,949,320
Rye, bush.................	1,412,673	PROVISIONS:	
Peas, bush................	1,149,970	Pork, bbls...............	201,302
Beans, bush...............	222,400	Beef, bbls...............	157,844
Grass Seeds, bags............	135,475	Bacon, lbs. / Hams, lbs. \	225,945,955
Oatmeal, bbls................	26,724	Butter, lbs..............	14,254,615
Cotton, bales................	456,862	Cheese, lbs..............	106,194,063
Hops, bales..................	41,865	Lard, lbs................	155,662,971
NAVAL STORES:		Stearine, lbs............	307,716
Crude Turpentine, bbls....	232	Grease, lbs..............	3,706,934
Spirits Turpentine, bbls..	20,564	Tallow, lbs..............	60,660,315
Rosin, bbls...............	256,774	Alcohol, bbls............	3,550
Pitch, bbls...............	6,192		
Tar, bbls.................	6,634		

Manufactures.—No returns of the State census of 1875 have been officially given, showing the amount of manufactures of different kinds in the city of New York. The following are taken from the U. S. census of 1870: there were then 7624 establishments, 1261 steam-engines, 16 water-wheels, employing 129,577 hands, at an annual outlay in wages of $63,824,049, and a capital valued at $129,952,262. The value of materials used was $178,696,939, and the annual product, $332,951,520.

Finances.—The official valuation of the property of the city for the purpose of taxation was for 1875, real, $883,643,845; personal, $217,300,154; total, $1,100,943,699. The taxes levied were, for State purposes, $8,012,386; for county and city, $28,159,086.23; for deficiencies, $196,272.52; total, $36,367,744.75. The total expenditures for the city government were, $32,171,472.23; of which the principal items were, for interest on city debt, $9,300,000; for redemption of same, $1,454,763.33; Public Works, $1,582,000; Public Charities and Corrections, $1,183,000; Police Department, $3,387,325; Fire Department, $1,316,000; Board of Education, $3,583,000; Asylums, etc., $825,905; street cleaning, $800,000.

There are 59 banks in the city of New York, with a capital, on December 31st, 1874, of $85,166,100; a circulation of $24,977,300, and deposits to the amount of $165,918,700. These banks are associated in a clearing-house for their daily exchanges. The transactions of this organization from October 1st, 1873, to October 1st, 1874, amounted to $20,850,681,962.82. There is also a gold exchange connected with the clearing-house, the transactions of which amount to the sum of $2,226,832,247.89 for the year 1874. There are also 44 savings banks in New York City, with deposits amounting to $180,010,703, from 494,086 depositors. There 9 marine insurance companies, with assets reported December 31st, 1874, as $25,035,785.62. There are 74 fire insurance companies, with assets reported December 31st, 1874, at $44,696,827.73. There are also 20 life insurance companies, with assets reported December 31st, 1874, at $189,813,949.93; these companies issued 16,197 policies in 1874, for $41,388,349, and had outstanding at the close of the year 99,737 policies for an amount of $279,811,858. The business of Brooklyn companies is not here included, nor that of companies of other States or foreign companies, either fire, marine, or life, the city details of which are not reported.

City Courts.—The United States Circuit Court for the Southern District of New York has ten counties under its jurisdiction, and holds two general terms and one criminal and equity term each year. The United States District Court holds a general term monthly and a special term weekly. Both of these courts occupy rooms in the new Post-office. The courts under State law are elected under a general judiciary law, and are the Supreme Court, the Superior Court, the Court of Common Pleas, the New York Marine Court, Criminal Courts of Oyer and Terminer and of General Sessions. In addition there was established during the year 1874, by act of legislature, the Court of Arbitration of the Chamber of Commerce of the State of New York, the purpose of which is to provide for legal arbitration between all parties making voluntary submission. The cases are heard by the official arbitrator alone, or aided by two other arbitrators selected by the parties in dispute. The Police Courts were remodelled in 1873. They are now under the control of eleven police justices. In the year closing October 31st, 1874, the whole number of cases recorded at special sessions for trial was 5567, of which 4869 were of males, 698 of females. Of these, 3205 were convicted, 869 acquitted, 1366 cases dismissed, 121 transferred or pending. The total number of arrests by the Police Department in 1874 was 90,030, of which 71,260 were for intoxication and disorderly conduct; for crimes of violence, 7860; commitments to the city prisons,

51,466. Of these committed, 41,514 were of intemperate habits. The police furnished 185,124 lodgings at its stations. The cost of the police system is about $4,000,000 a year. The Commissioners of Public Charities and Corrections have made no official report since 1871, but some details are to be found under another head.

Education.—The public instruction of the city of New York is under the charge of a Board of Education, consisting of 21 Commissioners of Common Schools, which has charge of all the common schools and such corporate schools as share in the school money of the State. This board reported the whole number of schools within their jurisdiction December 31st, 1874, as 287, including 57 grammar-schools for males, 45 for females, 11 for mixed sexes, 47 primary schools, and 64 primary departments; there is 1 female normal school, 1 normal school for teachers, and 1 model training school in connection with the Normal College; and there are 13 corporate schools. The public schools are held in 121 buildings, of which 67 are for grammar, 48 for primaries, and 6 for colored. The whole number of scholars taught in 1874 was 251,545, and the average attendance 117,239. The whole number of teachers employed 3215, of which over 3000 are females. The expense of teachers amounted to $2,433,418.08, and the total cost of the system $3,475,313.20. The amount of State school-tax paid by the city of New York in 1874 was $1,381,445.86, and the total amount received from the State for the schools of the county, $554,191.99. The Normal College, the Normal School for teachers, and the Model School, gave instructions to 1996 persons. Of the 512 attendants at the college sessions, 187 were graduated with diplomas. There is also an evening high-school, attended chiefly by adults, at which the highest branches of education are taught. In 1873, the Board of Education was authorized to establish a Nautical School, and in 1874 Congress authorized the Secretary of the Navy to furnish a suitable vessel. A vessel was designated, and the school is now in operation. An act of compulsory education was passed in 1874, and Randall's Island set aside for the reception of delinquents between the ages of 8 and 14. The College of the City of New York, better known as the Free Academy, is a part of the general system of public instruction, an attendance of one year at some one of the public schools being a requisite to admission. It has been in successful operation for twenty-nine years. The Roman Catholics have 20 select schools, averaging 1600 pupils, and about 50 parochial schools, with over 20,000 pupils. Of Jewish education there are no returns made public. They chiefly avail themselves of public schools. The Hebrew Free School Association limits its instruction to the Hebrew language. There are two important literary colleges, both of which make annual reports and are subject to the visitation of the Regents of the University of the State of New York. The older, Columbia College, was established under the name of King's College by royal charter in the year 1754, and its privileges were confirmed by an act of the State, April 13th, 1787, and by subsequent acts of legislature. In the college proper there are 9 professorships and 2 tutorships; in the school of mines there are 8 professorships; in the school of law, 4 professorships, including one of medical jurisprudence. The number of students, under-graduates, in the college in the year 1873, was 123; the number of graduates in the month of June, the same year, 21; the number of graduates in the school of mines, 5; the number of graduates in the school of law (bachelors of law), 138. The charge of tuition in the college and school of law is $100 per annum; in the school of mines, $200 per annum. The old site of King's College was on the beautiful square between Murray, Church, Barclay, and Chapel streets (the latter now known as West Broadway). This college, now known as Columbia, occupies an equally beautiful site at the corner of Forty-ninth street and Fourth avenue. The value of the grounds and buildings now occupied is estimated at $800,000, and the total value of its property at $4,582,000. Its revenues reach the sum of $303,000, and its expenditures $208,000. The second of the literary institutions is the University of the City of New York. It has four departments—arts, sciences, medicine, and law. The first two named are directed by 14 professors; the number of undergraduates in 1873 was 121; of graduates, 10. The third, of medicine, is directed by 14 professors; number of students, 217. The fourth, of law, by a president and four professors; number of students, 35. Instruction is free in the departments of arts and science to all who pass the preliminary examinations, no charge being made beyond an incidental fee of $15 per annum. For the department of medicine the charge is $140; for that of law, $100. The revenue of the University was $36,646.57, and its expenditure $36,646.57. Besides these widely-known institutions there are—the College of St. Francis Xavier, number of professors, 10; number of students in 1873, 80; number of graduates, 21; value of buildings and adjuncts, $228,000; of other property, $172,000; revenue, $36,084; expenditure, $31,084; price of tuition, $60 per annum. Manhattan College: number of professorships, 10; number of students in 1873, 80; in preparatory department, 467; in commercial department, 126; total, 673; no degrees given in the year named; value of buildings and adjuncts, $233,300; other property, $112,000; revenue, $62,343.34; expenditures, $65,357.59; tuition, including board, $600 per annum. The Rutgers Female College: instructors, 12; number of students, undergraduates, in 1873, 68; graduates, 8; no building owned; revenue, various sources, $17,824.45; expenditure, $19,376.14. In addition to these seminaries of general learning there are several medical colleges, first among which is the College of Physicians and Surgeons, medical department of Columbia College (already named above), number of professors, 19; number of students in 1873, 396; number of graduates, 99; value of building and grounds, $154,000; other property, $11,000; revenue, $12,142.50; expenditure, $15,366.59; price of tuition, $140. The Homœopathic Medical College of the State of New York in the City of New York: students, 100; graduates in 1873, 38. The New York Medical College and Hospital for Women, New York City: professorships, 12; number of students in 1873, 25; graduates, 9; value of building and adjuncts, $63,500; of other property, $17,500; revenue, $3375; expenditure, $5740; price of tuition, $70. The Eclectic Medical College, New York City: professorships, 8; number of students, 37; of graduates, 21; value of property (no building), $15,000; revenue, $755; expenditure, $755; price of tuition, $100. The New York College of Dentistry: professorships, 10; number of students, 39; graduates, 10; revenue, $5677.99; expenditure, $6129.76; price of tuition, $100 per annum. New York Free Medical College for Women: professorships, 14; number of students, 43. *Summary.*—Instructors, 3365; number of students, 277,310; cost of instruction, $3,808,381. In addition to these institutions, incorporated by the State or making report to constituted authorities, there are numerous schools for the education of both sexes in the highest departments of knowledge, some of which are as extensive and well known as the colleges. Mr. Peter Cooper has also established an institution for the education of the working classes, which is under the charge of a board of trustees, and to this he has given a building valued at $500,000, and made other munificent donations. The instruction includes engineering, the arts of design, modelling. The tuition and lectures are free.

There are twenty-three libraries of circulation and reference, several of which have reading-rooms attached. The principal is the Astor Library, founded on a bequest of John Jacob Astor, organized under a board of trustees in 1848, with a collection of 70,000 volumes, and made by the distinguished Dr. Joseph G. Cogswell, with a view to the providing of a reference library of works not otherwise of easy access. The original building, 65 feet front by 120 feet deep, is situated on Astor Place. William B. Astor, son of the founder, has since added a second building of similar size, and the number of volumes had increased to 150,306 on January 1st, 1875. The buildings are elegant and commodious. The books are free to the public, for use only in the library. The only other free library is the Lenox, incorporated January 21st, 1870, for which a large and beautiful building has been recently completed, covering the whole front of the block on Fifth avenue, between Seventieth and Seventy-first streets, and commanding a fine view of Central Park. In it the large and valuable collection of the founder, James Lenox, whose munificent gift includes also the real estate and buildings, will be deposited. It is the largest and finest collection of books on early American history ever formed. There will also be a fine-art gallery and a collection of curiosities. The New York Historical Society occupies a fine building on the corner of Eleventh street and Second avenue, the capacity of which it has for some years outgrown. It has a collection of historical works, newspapers from 1704 to the present date, manuscripts, public and private documents of great value, and is the favorite receptacle for family papers of historical importance. The collection of books reaches 60,000; of newspapers bound 2319. It has also a large collection of American antiquities, the famous Abbot Egyptian collection, the Lenox Nineveh marbles, and one of the most extensive and finest art collections in the country. It is supported by a large membership of the leading citizens. The oldest library in the city is the New York Society Library, situated in University Place, between Twelfth and Thirteenth streets. It was organized in 1740, and incorporated in 1754, has a collection of about 70,000 volumes for circulation and reference, and has a reading-room. It is maintained by annual dues. The Mercantile Library Association, Clinton Hall, Astor Place, originally organized for the benefit of merchants' clerks, to whom access is given at a merely nominal charge, has a very large collection of current literature, 158,034 volumes, and a fine and extensively-used reading-room, where both foreign and domestic reviews, magazines, and periodicals are amply supplied. The library is chiefly used for circulation. In addition, there is an admirable system of lectures and classes. The American Geographical Society has rooms in Cooper Institute. It has a good library of books on geography and a valuable collection of charts, maps, and other documents. It is the only institution in the country wholly devoted to geographical science. The Union Theological Seminary has a large and noted collection, chief among which are early American tracts. The Episcopal Theological Seminary has also a large collection. The American Institute is particularly strong in works on mechanics and engineering. The Apprentices' Library, free to this class and female employées, has a large assortment of general literature. The Law Institute has a carefully-selected library, and a reading-room attached for the use of the bar. The Chamber of Commerce has a small but extremely valuable collection of works on finance and subjects of commercial interest. There are several societies for the promotion of the fine arts. The National Academy of Design, instituted in 1826, owns a building on the corner of Twenty-third street and Fourth avenue, and has large and valuable collections. The Metropolitan Musuem of Art, incorporated in 1870, occupies an elegant building on Fourteenth street between Sixth and Seventh avenues. It has a carefully selected and choice collection of antiquities and curiosities, some of great value, chief among which is the Cesnola collection. A building for the accommodation of this museum is now being erected in Central Park. A Studio Art-building Association was organized in 1865, and is located on Tenth street, near Sixth avenue; it is mainly used by artists for studios. There are 444 newspapers and periodicals published in the city of New York. Of these 28 are daily, 8 semi-weekly, 187 weekly, 22 semi-monthly, 180 monthly, 3 bi-monthly, and 16 quarterly; 32 are in foreign languages—16 German, 9 Spanish, 3 French, 2 Scandinavian, 2 Swedish; 99 have a circulation of over 5000 copies. The ten leading newspapers are the *Daily News*, one cent, with a daily circulation of 127,360; the *Sun*, two cents, daily circulation, 119,792, weekly, 73,533; the *Herald*, three cents, daily, 85,000, weekly, 15,000; the *Tribune*, four cents, daily, 43,833, semi-weekly, 10,000, weekly, 48,000, the *Times*, four cents, daily, 42,000, weekly, 30,000; the *Staats-Zeitung* (German), daily, 30,000, weekly, 15,000. Of the illustrated papers, *Harper's Weekly* has a circulation of 100,000; *Frank Leslie's Illustrated News*, weekly, 50,000; the *Graphic*, daily, 11,000. Of the literary papers two are devoted to stories and tales—the *New York Ledger*, with a circulation of 300,000, and the *New York Weekly*, with a circulation of 180,000. Of the religious papers, the *Christian Union*, weekly, has a circulation of 78,333; the *Christian Advocate*, 45,000; the *Catholic Review*, 20,000; the *Sunday-School Journal*, monthly, 75,000; the *Methodist Episcopal Church Missionary Advocate*, 100,000. Of the magazines, *Harper's Monthly* has 130,000; *Scribner's Monthly*, 48,000; *St. Nicholas*, a child's magazine, 40,000; the *Galaxy*, 18,000.

Churches.—New York is largely provided with churches. The total number, together with mission organizations, is 470, of which 334 have edifices of their own, with accommodations for 350,000 persons, and valued at $28,800,000. Of the organizations, 92 are Protestant Episcopal, 70 Presbyterian, 58 Methodist Episcopal, 46 Baptist, 40 Roman Catholic, and 27 Jewish. In the Protestant churches, chapels, etc., there are seats for 250,000 persons, but it is estimated that the average attendance does not exceed 150,000. Of the Protestant churches, 240 are regularly incorporated, with an average membership of 300, giving a total of 72,000 communicants. There are in addition 140 Protestant missions, where religious instruction and service are regularly maintained. The latest census gives 365 Protestant Sabbath-schools, with 88,237 scholars on roll, and an average attendance of 56,187; and of Roman Catholics, Jews, etc., there are 59 Sabbath-schools, having 27,589 scholars on roll, and an average attendance of 18,274. The total number of missionaries is 266, who make 800,000 visits a year, besides hundreds of tract visitors, poor visitors, and other humbler agents.

There are 5 free reading-rooms for seamen and 15 for workingmen, and 10 daily prayer-meetings. The churches most famous for their size, cost, and architectural beauty, are Trinity, Grace, St. George's, the new Fifth avenue Presbyterian, the Reformed Collegiate, and the Jewish Synagogue; a new cathedral is also being erected by the Roman Catholics, which will exceed in size and splendor any church in the city. It is of white marble, covers an entire block, and is in the Gothic order.

Charities.—New York is famous for its munificent and cosmopolitan charities, both at home and abroad. It has never failed to respond to an appeal for aid, and the eyes of suffering nations and communities are first turned to her. Ireland in its famine, France in its floods and desolation, England in its manufacturing distress, even in time of war, found a ready response. And so has every American in its day of distress—witness Portland, Chicago, Boston, etc. The municipal charities of

New York are intrusted to a board of management entitled the Commissioners of Public Charities and Corrections, who have charge of all the criminals, paupers, and public sick of the city.

The prisons, hospitals, asylums, almshouses, nurseries, etc., numbering 27 institutions (viz., the Almshouse, Hospital for Incurables, Asylum for the Blind, Bellevue Hospital, City Prison, Randall's Island Hospitals, Workhouse, Charity Hospital, Fever Hospital, Small Pox Hospital, Infants' Hospital, Inebriate Asylum, Asylum on Ward's Island, Lunatic Asylum, Epileptic and Paralytic Hospitals, Randall's Island Nursery, Free Labor and Intelligence Bureau, Industrial School, Hart's Island, and School Ship Mercury), received last year 153,271 subjects. The department for the outdoor poor gave relief to 22,782. Correct conclusions cannot, however, be drawn from these figures, as the same persons appear more than once upon the register. The money expended in sustaining the board amounted to $1,541,-685.50. The immigrants are under the care of the Commissioners of Emigration; of the 267,901 alien passengers landed in 1874 at the port of New York, 51,871 were relieved, forwarded, or provided with employment by the commission; 12,586 were cared for in the refuge and hospital on Ward's Island—an institution supporting an average of about 2000 persons. The total expenses of the commission were $466,-108.22. Besides these public there are numerous private institutions, endowed by the voluntary benefactions of the citizens, in some cases aided by State or municipal appropriations. The Association for Improving the Condition of the Poor expends about $50,000 annually, and relieves about 5000 families. Last year being a year of extraordinary suffering, aid was given to 24,091 families. The New York City Mission gave aid to 2500 families in 1874. The Howard Mission and the House of Industry disbursed large sums. The Prison Association, the Home for Female Prisoners, and the Midnight Mission are humane reformatories. There are 27 hospitals in the city, of which 15 have large and commodious buildings, the recent erections being admirably adapted to sanitary and curative puposes. The oldest of these institutions is the New York Hospital, founded under a colonial charter in 1771. The large and beautiful site which it occupied for nearly a century has been sold, and this favorite institution has lost its old prestige. The Bloomingdale Asylum for the Insane, located at One Hundred and Seventeenth street, between Tenth and Eleventh avenues, is a branch of the New York Hospital. A farm of 300 acres has been purchased at White Plains, and suitable buildings will shortly be ready for the reception of patients. St. Luke's Hospital occupies spacious buildings on the corner of Fifty-fourth street and Fifth avenue.

The property of this institution was exempted from taxation and assessment by legislative act in 1870. Mt. Sinai Hospital, formerly known as the Jews' Hospital, was established in 1852. It occupies a large building on Lexington Avenue from Sixty-sixth to Sixty-seventh street. The Roosevelt Hospital, a bequest of James H. Roosevelt, who died in 1863, has extensive buildings erecting on Ninth avenue, corner of Fifty-sixth street. There are, besides, the German Hospital, incorporated 1866; St. Francis's Hospital, 1866, under the charge of the Poor of St. Francis; St. Vincent's, 1849, under the Sisters of Charity; the Presbyterian Hospital, 1868; Women's Hospital for Surgical Treatment of Women, 1855; New York Asylum for Lying-in Women, 1822; New York Society for the Relief of Ruptured and Crippled, 1863; New York Infirmary for Women and Children; New York Homœopathic Infirmary for Women; the Hahnemann Hospital; Hospital for Diseases of the Nervous System; Metropolitan Medical and Surgical Institute; Strangers' Hospital. There are four eye and ear infirmaries: the New York Eye and Ear Infirmary, founded 1820; in 1874 there were treated 10,486 patients, of whom 7464 were for diseases of the eye, 2439 of the ear, 583 of the nose and throat. The expenses for the same year were $28,011.70. Manhattan Eye and Ear Hospital; New York Ophthalmic Hospital; New York Ophthalmic and Aural Institute. There are 7 city dispensaries, which supply gratuitously medicines and medical and surgical attendance, and are mainly supported by subscriptions and gifts from the legislature. Besides these, there are several supported by private contributions. The New York Dispensary, corner of Centre and White streets, established 1790, supplies an average of 40,000 patients at an expenditure of $10,000. The Central Dispensary, the Demilt, the Eastern, the Manhattanville, Northern, Northeastern, Northwestern, Western, Harlem, Hoffman, German, Orthopædic, Dispensary for Diseases of the Skin, Bond Street, New York Homœopathic Medical College, Metropolitan Homœopathic, Northwestern Homœopathic, Western Homœopathic, Western Dispensary for Women and Children, Eclectic. There are two institutions for the deaf and dumb: the Institution for the Deaf and Dumb, incorporated in 1817, occupies buildings 650 feet in length, covering two acres, and accommodating 450 pupils; the Institution for the Improved Instruction of Deaf-Mutes. There are three institutions for the blind: the New York Institution for the Blind, which receives pay pupils and others at State charge for $300 per annum; the Blind Mechanics' Association, which secures employment for blind adults; the Holy Light Home for the Blind, for the support of the aged and infirm, without regard to religion or nationality. There are 26 religious, educational, and other Roman Catholic organizations, reformatory and charitable. Of benevolent societies there are 51, of trades' unions about 50, and of secret and benefit societies about the same number. Besides these, there are 75 other charitable institutions. The Society for the Reformation of Juvenile Delinquents, House of Refuge, Randall's Island, occupies two large structures 1000 feet in length, in the Italian order of architecture; the workshops 30 by 100 feet, three stories high; connected therewith a school for seamanship.

The New York Juvenile Asylum receives truant and friendless children; accommodates 500 inmates; the city pays $110 for each child supported. The Children's Aid Society seeks to secure homes for friendless children in country families; schools are attached which educate from 9000 to 10,000 scholars annually. A newsboys' lodging-house is connected with the society, which has provided over 70,000 boys with permanent homes and employment. The New York Catholic Protectory has extensive buildings in Westchester County. The Hebrew Benevolent and Orphan Asylum has a large building, and supports about 200 children annually. There is also an Industrial Home for Jewesses, and the Noah Benevolent Widows' and Orphans' Association. The Colored Orphan Asylum, whose premises were destroyed during the riots in July, 1863, has since erected new buildings; the average number cared for is 260. The Five Points Mission provides food and clothing for the poor, and temporary shelter for the homeless; its school attendance, over 400. There are several institutions for seamen—the American Seamen's Friend Society, the Sailors' Home, etc.; and a Society for the Prevention of Cruelty to Animals.

The foregoing include the best known of these numerous and valuable institutions, all of which draw largely from the private munificence of the charitable community of New York. The organized local charitable societies and institutions receive and disburse annually $2,500,000.

Public Buildings.—The most noted buildings are the City Hall, in the Park, erected in 1803, a graceful and elegant structure. Adjoining is the new Court-House, a large edifice, notorious as the means by which the city treasury was robbed of a large amount of money by William M. Tweed and his followers. They are both in marble, except the rear of the City Hall, which is brown stone, the authorities having then no idea that the city limits would extend any higher. The Custom-House, formerly the Merchants' Exchange, is an immense and massive structure of Quincy granite. The columns are 38 feet in height and 4½ feet in diameter. The Sub-Treasury occupies the old Custom-House, a beautiful and spacious building in white marble. The new Post-Office, the finest public structure in the city, and admirably adapted for its purpose, was begun in 1869 and finished in 1875. It occupies the southern angle of the Park. The Western Union Telegraph Company and the *Evening Post* occupy fine structures of brick, with stone trimmings, upon Broadway, below the Park. The New York *Tribune* Association has lately completed a brick building on Printing-house Square, with a tower of enormous height, which has attracted attention and comments. Of the new buildings in the upper part of the city, the Grand Central Depot, the Windsor Hotel, the Gilsey House, and the Buckingham are the most prominent. The Albany and the Saratoga are large structures of flats on the French plan, now rapidly growing in favor. The Lenox Library has already been noticed. A marked feature of the social life of the city is the prevalence of clubs, of which there are forty, including literary and sporting associations, for friendly intercourse. The most celebrated of these are the Union, limited to 1000 members, with a full membership, and occupying an elegant building on Fifth avenue; the Union League, with a roll even more extensive, and a fine house in Madison Square. The New York, Knickerbocker, Travellers', Century, Lotos, and the German Club on Reservoir Square. These institutions are provided with restaurants, and are daily and numerously attended. The city is admirably provided with parks, which have been aptly termed the "lungs" of the cities. The Central Park is noticed elsewhere. There are also the Battery, Bowling Green, the City Hall Park—all historical ground—Tompkins, Washington, Union, Madison, and Reservoir Squares, and, at the northern end of the island, Mount Morris Square and High Bridge and Morningside Parks. The total area in acres and thousandths is 1007.251. The lower part of the city is quite irregularly built; but from Houston street, about a mile north of the City Hall Park, the construction is regular, with long avenues running to the northern end of the island, and laterally traversed by streets which, like the avenues, are designated by numbers. Broadway, the most famous of the avenues, is an exception to this rule, and in its long extent of six miles crosses five of the avenues in a north-westerly direction. Broadway is lined with shops and hotels, and is one of the gayest streets in the world. Fifth Avenue, with its magnificent private residences, churches, and club-houses, is one unbroken series of architectural display; the natural advantages of this fine avenue, which runs along the ridge of the island, make it the favorite site for residence. Broad and extensive boulevards have been recently laid out in the upper part of the island, which, connecting with the Central Park, offer long and agreeable drives.

The first city railroad was chartered in 1852, since which the system of travel by horse-cars has largely increased. There are now railroads in all the longitudinal avenues except the Fifth avenue and Broadway below Union Square, and there are also numerous transversal lines connecting the ferries of the East and North rivers. The commissioners appointed by the Mayor of the city, under the authority of the legislature, have now under advisement plans for rapid transit to the northern limits, now become indispensable to the growth and prosperity of the metropolis. The New York Central, Hudson River, Harlem, and New Haven Railroads have their terminus in this city at the Grand Central Depot, and bring in and take out a large number of suburban residents who have their place of business in the city. The report of the State engineer and surveyor for 1872 gives the business of the city horse-railroads as follows: horse-car passengers carried, 134,588,871, at fares varying from five to eight cents each; steam elevated roads, 163,153, at a fare of ten cents. There are 23 ferries connecting New York with the west shores of the Hudson, Hoboken, and Jersey City, Staten Island and Long Island. The boats to Brooklyn and Hoboken run every ten minutes by day, and every fifteen minutes by night; fares, from two to four cents each passenger. The number of passengers carried in 1868, the last year of official returns, was 82,321,214. The ferries are all under city supervision, but owing to the policy adopted a few years since of leasing this valuable franchise for terms of years, no returns supplying statistical information are now made. The natural increase would carry the number to 100,000,000 at the lowest estimate. Reviewing the car and ferry traffic, it will be seen that the centre of city travel of New York and its natural suburbs is not far removed from the City Hall Park.

Water-works.—The city is supplied with water by the Croton Water-works, the most extensive and costly in the U. S. The supply is drawn from the Croton River, a clear, pure stream of remarkable quality, in Westchester County, which is conducted to the city by an aqueduct of solid masonry 40½ miles in length, 8 feet 5½ inches in height, 7 feet 5 inches wide at the widest point; and dropping 13 inches to the mile. It has a capacity of 106,000,000 gallons a day. It crosses the Harlem River on the High Bridge, a structure of granite 1450 feet long, 21 feet wide, between parapets 114 feet high; is received in two great basins in Central Park, and is distributed by two reservoirs through 350 miles of pipe. These works are under the supervision of the department of public works, a bureau created under the charter in 1870. Five principal gaslight companies supply the city. The Manhattan Company has two works, which deliver gas through about 170 miles of street-mains to 30,000 private consumers and 7000 street-lamps. The others are the New York, Metropolitan, Mutual, and the Harlem. The mains of these companies are being constantly extended as new avenues and streets are opened.

The system of sewerage is totally unworthy of a metropolitan city with unequalled opportunities for drainage, the rivers surrounding providing ample outlet for all detritus; but there has as yet been no effort to introduce the scientific plans of which Paris presents so excellent an example. The paving of the city is hardly better than the sewerage. For this, however, some excuse may be found in the severity of the winters and the long lay of snow upon the ground. Various tentative experiments have been made; cobblestones have given way to wood; wood, in turn, after having been tried in various forms, has yielded to trap-block, which is now the favorite mode.

Markets.—The market system is absolutely disgraceful, and with hardly any exception, the buildings are rather public nuisances than public benefits. Those owned and rented by the city are 13 in number, of which Washington, Fulton, and Clinton are the most important. With a more bountiful supply of provisions of necessity and luxury than can be had in any city of the world (a remark especially true of its fish, which has developed into a separate trade under the control of a fishmongers' corporation), there is no capital city where the market accommodations for both produce and consumer are so badly managed. The sales of food during the year (1874) for cash are reported by the efficient superintendent, Colonel De Voe, at $130,000,000, of which Washington received $108,000,000; Fulton, $16,000,000; and Clinton, $1,500,000. Besides these for household purposes, it is estimated, by the same competent authority, that 1,350,000 persons dine or lunch every business-day in the city of New York. Not less than 300,000 of these are daily visitors, who leave the city nightly for neighboring towns, and there is an average of 50,000 visitors at the hotels.

The Fire Department, formerly a volunteer organization, has at last passed into the control of a board of commissioners, with salaried employés. The modern system of steam, with engineers and officers, and telegraphic signals, has done away with this formerly prominent feature in the life of the metropolis.

The Police Department is under the control of a board of commissioners, and occupies 34 different stations, which are connected by telegraph wires, and a large, commodious head-quarters. The force numbers 2503. As a system of protection, it can never be thoroughly efficient until withdrawn from the domain of politics, but it is slowly and steadily improving. Its main deficiency, as compared with the European system, is the want of efficiency in the detective force.

Post-Office.—The business of the post-office is enormous. Besides the great building, there are 20 branch stations, of which 12 are on Manhattan Island, A to L, and 8 in the newly-annexed towns of Westchester. The number of superintendents and clerks employed at the general office is 648; at stations, 86; of regular letter-carriers at the general post-office, 100; at stations, 329; of substitutes, 30; total force, 1193. There are 7 daily deliveries by carriers, and 14 collections from 986 street letter-boxes. In the year 1876, the transactions of the New York Post-Office are given below:

TRANSACTIONS OF THE NEW YORK POST-OFFICE, FOR THE YEAR 1876.

The following statement exhibits the transactions of the New York Post-Office for the year 1876. Compiled by direction of Hon. Thomas L. James, Postmaster:

TRANSACTIONS OF MONEY ORDER DIVISION.

International and Domestic Orders issued	$1,062,826 13
Fees on same	12,984 45
International and Domestic Orders paid	6,068,014 74
Deposits received from Postmasters on Money Order account	12,675,514 68
Drafts paid on Money Order letter credit's account	6,691,059 00
Deposited to credit Postmaster General on Money Order account	400,000 00
Postmaster's General checks	565,329 97
International Exchange account	595,320 19
Transfer to Postage account	111,297 29
Revenue account	254,032 68
International Money Orders certified to and from Europe	3,007,999 61
Money Orders issued and paid at Stations in New York City	1,953,712 40
Expense account	58,052 16
Funds advanced to Stations	100,035 00
Total	$33,556,178 30

BRITISH MONEY ORDERS EXCHANGED.

Inwards	$397,027 75	
Outwards	897,457 46	
		$1,294,485 21

GERMAN MONEY ORDERS EXCHANGED.

Inwards	$703,077 61	
Outwards	766,408 37	
		$1,469,485 98

FOREIGN DEPARTMENT.

Letters delivered...	......
Letter and Paper Bags.......................................	26,884
Letters received..	......
Letter and Paper Bags.......................................	22,883
Suplementary Postage.......................................	$14,386 00

REGISTRY DEPARTMENT.

Registered Packages opened.................................	262,533
" " in transit.................................	105,807
" Letters delivered................................	447,582
" " received in Mails for distribution...........	239,652
Letters registered...	175,823
Fees on same..................................... $17,442 40	
Postage Stamp Packages registered	150,823
Stamped Envelope Packages distributed.......................	25,048
Postal Card Packages distributed.............................	8,492
Registered Packages dispatched...............................	161,603
Total..	1,577,363

CARRIERS' DEPARTMENT.

Registered Letters delivered by Carriers......................	248,444
Mail Letters delivered by Carriers............................	37,359,372
Postal Cards " "	10,692,544
Local Letters " "	21,036,945
Local Postal Cards delivered by Carriers......................	6,445,877
Newspapers delivered by Carriers............................	8,892,218
Postal Cards collected by Carriers............................	6,671,795
Local Letters " "	15,530,932
Mail Letters " "	30,614,504
Newspapers " "	5,584,362
Postal Cards deposited in Stations............................	6,356,149
Local Letters " "	14,482,099
Mail Letters " "	31,985,097
Newspapers " "	15,150,761
Letters registered at Stations................................	55,596
Money Orders issued at Stations.............................	46,460
Amount received for the same...............................	$867,209 76
Money Orders paid at Stations...............................	50,712
Amount paid for the same...................................	$702,839 55
Amount of Envelopes, Stamps, etc., sold at Stations,..........	$516,261 85
Postage on Local matter.....................................	$1,009,651 43

AVERAGE QUANTITIES OF MAIL MATTER DISPOSED OF IN ONE DAY DURING THE YEAR 1876.

LETTER MAILS.

	Letters, Number.
Drop Letters for other offices, @ ½ oz........................	272,974
Received in Mails...	20,236
Average weight of Pouch without contents, 7 lbs.	
Whole number of Pouches dispatched for 426 Post-Offices and 95 Routes.....	...

PAPER MAILS.

Average number of Sacks received for distribution, 1620, at average weight of 70 lbs.	
Weight of Sack without contents, 38 ozs.	
Whole number of Sacks dispatched for 322 Post-Offices and 133 Routes.........	..
Number of Sacks of 2d class matter distributed................	..
Number of Sacks of 3d class matter distributed................	..
Total..	293,210

FOREIGN MATTER.
Received per Steamers.

Average number of Letters...	18,150
Contained in Bags...	..
Average number of Bags of Paper Matter........................	..
Total...	18,150

Dispatched per Steamers.

Average number of Letters...	19,264
Contained in Bags...	..
Average number of Bags of Paper Matter........................	..
Total...	19,264

LOCAL MATTER, LETTERS.
Carrier Delivery.

Mail Letters and Postal Cards......................................	153,520
Drop Letters...	67,021
Total...	220,541

Lock-Box Delivery.

Mail Letters...	85,073
Drop Letters..	42,856
Total...	127,929

RECAPITULATION.

Domestic Matter..			293,210
Foreign Matter inward..			18,150
Totals of Matter dispatched over inland Routes................			311,360
Foreign Matter outward..			19,264
	Letters, Number.	Weight, Pounds.	
Carriers' Delivery...	220,541	6,892	
Lock-Box..	127,929	3,996	
			348,470
Total...			679,094
Totals for the year 1876...			254,473,840

History.—Immediately after the discovery of Hudson in 1609, the Dutch undertook the occupation and settlement of Manhattan Island, and in 1614 erected a fort and trading-house at the south-western extremity of the island, to which they gave the name of New Amsterdam. In 1614, an expedition from South Virginia, dispatched by Sir Thomas Dale, took possession of the infant colony, which then consisted of four houses outside the fort; but an amicable settlement was soon made between the respective governments, and the Dutch remained in possession of the Island and neighboring country. In 1652, the city of New Amsterdam was incorporated. In 1656, it had increased to 1000 inhabitants and 120 houses; in 1677, it contained 368 houses. The city remained under the peaceful rule of the Dutch for about a half-century, when Charles II. coming to the English throne, the territory occupied by the Dutch was granted by royal charter to his brother, the Duke of York, March 12th, 1664, and an English fleet took unopposed possession in August of the same year. Colonels Nicoll and Lovelace ruled the settlement for ten years in the name of the duke, and the name of the city was changed in his honor, to New York.

In August, 1673, a Dutch fleet recaptured the city, which it held in the name of the States-General of Holland, and changed the name again to New Orange, in compliment to the Prince of Orange. It was again restored to English rule by treaty in 1674, and resumed its name. In 1686, the municipal rights of the free city were confirmed and enlarged to cover all vacant land on Manhattan Island to low-water mark, by charter from Gov. Dongan. In 1708, certain ancient rights of ferry were also confirmed by new charter from Gov. Cornbury, but the charter upon the foundation of which, as Chancellor Kent remarks, the city of New York is at present governed, was that of 1730, as granted by Governor Montgomerie. This charter recites the former charters, confirms the privileges of the city, and defines the water-boundary as extending to low-water mark on the opposite shores of Long Island and New Jersey. This claim of New York gave occasion to long litigation with the State of New Jersey, until the boundary-line was happily settled by commissioners mutually appointed by the each State in 1833. This settlement leaves the exclusive jurisdiction of the waters to the State, and consequently to the city of New York, while the right to the land under water and the wharves which may be built thereon, on the Jersey shore, is vested in New Jersey, subject only to the quarantine and health laws of the city. An act of confirmation was passed by the assembly October 14th, 1732. Under these royal charters the mayor, sheriff, recorder, and other officers were appointed by the governor of the colony. This mode of appointment continued until the Revolution, when the power of appointment was, by the constitution of 1777, vested in the governor and council until otherwise ordered by the legislature. Under the amended constitution of 1821, the mayor was directed to be appointed annually by the common council, and the other officers to be chosen triennially by the electors of the city. This mode continued until the act of March 3d, 1834, directed that the mayor be annually chosen by the electors of the city. In 1849, important alterations were made in the creation of executive departments, the chief officers of which to be elected by the people. The police department, however, was continued, the mayor being designated as its head, but a bureau established under the control of a chief of police. In 1852, a further amendment instituted a board of 60 councilmen, to be chosen from 60 districts of the city, in place of the board of assistant aldermen of the wards. In 1857, a further radical change was made. The act of this year repealed all the amendments of 1830, 1849, 1851, 1853, only continuing in force the ancient Dongan and Montgomerie charters. The amended charter divided the city into seventeen aldermanic districts, from each of which an alderman was to be chosen, to serve two years; the board of council to be composed of six members elected annually from each of the senatorial districts of the city; the mayor, comptroller, and counsel to the corporation to be elected by the people, the mayor for two, the counsel for three, the comptroller for four years, all three removable by the governor for cause; and the heads of departments were made removable by the board of aldermen without consent of the mayor. The powers of the street department were increased, and a number of executive departments abolished. This act, restricting the powers of the mayor, was resisted by him as unconstitutional, and popular disturbances ensued. The same legislature had placed the police force of the city and the neighboring counties under a metropolitan commission. The forces met in violent struggle; resort was finally had to the Court of Appeals, which fully sustained the constitutionality of the new charter. By an amendment passed in 1863, the term of office of the several heads of departments was extended to four years. The board of councilmen was abolished after 1869. On April 5th, 1870, further and thoroughly radical changes took place, the city government being essentially withdrawn from any control of the State authorities, and the executive power vested in a mayor and eleven departments, the mayor to be elected for two years, heads of departments to be appointed by the mayor. The police was withdrawn from the metropolitan commission, and became one of the new departments. Earnest protest had been made against the passage of the charter of 1870, but few alterations were consented to, a few modifications only being made by the act of April 18th, 1871, with regard to the school officers and Central Park commission. The abuses and reckless expenditure which followed this change in municipal rule became so enormous and flagrant that there was a great reaction in public opinion. The amendment again reorganizing the local government was passed June 13th, 1873, and is now in force. It abolished the board of assistant aldermen, constituted a new common council of twenty-one aldermen, to be elected at the general State election the next year; three members to be elected in each senatorial district; six alderman at large, to hold office for one year; and the mayor to be elected for two years.

In reviewing these changes in the form of administration of the city government, it is interesting to notice the tentative process by which a solution has been diligently sought for the problem of a city government where a population is subject to such increase—a population at once uneducated and unaccustomed to self-government. And it is not too much to say that only with a constitution and manners as free and liberal as those which prevail in the State of New York, could the principle of universal suffrage have endured the severity of the strain. The most important events in the history of the city since the English occupation have been the usurpation of the government by Leisler in 1689, and his trial and execution by Gov. Sloughter in 1691. The same year the laws of the Duke of York and provincial laws were framed. The first assembly met in the city April 9th. In 1696, the first Trinity Church was built. In 1712, the negroes rose in insurrection, set fire to the city, and killed several persons; nineteen of the negroes were subsequently executed. (*See* First Negro Plot.) In 1725, Bradford established the New York *Gazette*. In 1729, a city library was founded; in 1740 the New York Society Library was organized. In 1741, the famous delusion known as the "Negro Plot" occurred; the city was in the greatest consternation, and a large number of negroes were executed, and together with them a Catholic priest: when reason was asserted itself, no real grounds could be discovered for any alarm. In 1750, a theatre was established. In 1754, King's (now Columbia) College was chartered. In May, 1763, the Sandy Hook lighthouse was first lighted. In 1765, the famous Congress known as the Stamp Act Congress, met in the city; delegates were present, and grievances were adopted. The Sons of Liberty were organized, with affiliations throughout the colonies. The Stamp Act was burned, and an agreement not to import goods from Great Britain until the repeal of the obnoxious act signed by a large concourse of merchants. On the 1st of November, amid great excitement, the effigies of Gov. Colden and the devil holding the Stamp Act were burned on the Bowling Green. On the 5th, the excitement continuing, and the citizens threatening to storm the fort and seize the stamps, the paper was delivered by the governor to the mayor, John Cruger, and taken to the city hall for safe keeping.

On May 20th, 1766, the news of the repeal of the act reached the city, and the assembly was petitioned to erect a statue to William Pitt. In 1768, the Chamber of Commerce was organized at the Queen's Head Tavern, kept by Bolton & Sigel—a building better known later as Frances' Tavern, and which is still standing at the corner of Pearl and Broad streets, and now called Washington's Headquarters, this being the spot where he bade adieu to his officers at the close of the Revolution. On May 14th, 1770, a statue to William Pitt was erected in Wall street at the intersection of William, then Smith street. On April 18th, 1774, the Nancy arrived with a cargo of tea; the vessel was not permitted to land her cargo, nor to make entry at the Custom-House. News reached the city of the closing of the port of Boston in May, 1774; a committee of correspondence was organized. The non-importation agreement was again proposed, but declined, and a "Congress of the Colonies" insisted upon by the merchants. To their persistent adherence to this scheme the first Congress was mainly due. In the same month, strong resolutions of resistance were adopted by a great meeting on the Common, now the Park. The colonial assembly finally adjourned April 3d, 1775. Delegates were elected to the Continental Congress, July 25th, same year. On August 22d, Congress having ordered the withdrawal of cannon to the interior, the Asia, man-of-war, fired upon the city. In January, 1776, a detachment of militia took possession of the city, and in the spring the American army followed. On the 8th of July, the Declaration of Independence was proclaimed, and read to the army. On the 26th of August, after the battle of Long Island, the city fell into the hands of the British. On the 21st of September, a destructive fire consumed an eighth of the city, destroying 492 houses. On November 25th, 1783, the British evacuated the city, and Gen. Washington entered at the head of the American army. In January, 1785, Congress removed from Philadelphia to New York, and met in the City Hall, corner of Wall and Nassau streets, now the site of the United States Sub-treasury. The Bank of New York was organized this year, and a manumission society was established. On July 26th, 1788, the new Constitution of the United States was adopted by the legislature, and celebrated by a grand procession. On April 30th, 1789, Gen. Washington was inaugurated President of the United States, on the gallery in front of the old City Hall, facing Broad street. On December 4th, the adoption of the new Federal Constitution was ratified by an immense procession, in which all the professions and trades were represented. In 1792, the Tontine Coffee-House was built; June 1st, 1795, the Park Theatre was erected. In 1799, the Manhattan Company was chartered to supply the city with water; the Bronx River was proposed as the source of supply, and was surveyed. In 1801, the total valuation of the real and personal estate of the city and county was $21,964,037, and a tax laid of one mill on the dollar. In 1804, hackney coaches were first licensed. July 11th, of this year, Alexander Hamilton fell in a duel with Aaron Burr. In 1805, the winter was one of intense severity. This year the New York Free School was incorporated, and also the Tammany Society or Columbian Order. In 1806, steam navigation was first successfully inaugurated on the Hudson River, by Robert Fulton. In 1807, the city was surveyed and laid out by a commission of the legislature, consisting of Gouverneur Morris, De Witt Clinton, and others. Their plan has been substantially adhered to, with the exception of the late new improvements. In June, 1812, on the declaration of war against Great Britain, a large number of privateers left the city, and became the terror of British traders till the peace. This year the first steam-ferry was established to Jersey City. On August 31st, 1814, the scarcity of specie and the drain upon the banks brought about a suspension of specie payments, which lasted till July, 1817. On February 12th, 1815, the first news of the treaty of peace was received at New York with enthusiasm. In 1824, the House of Refuge for the Reformation of Juvenile Delinquents, was established, and a building erected by private subscription. This was the beginning of a new order of correction of the vices of the young. On August 15th, 1824, Gen. La Fayette arrived in the city, and was welcomed with great rejoicings as the guest of the city and nation. The quintal of 100 instead of 112 pounds was voluntarily adopted by the merchants as the new measure for purchase and sale after January 1st, 1825. Gas was first introduced in this year, and mains laid in Broadway. On October 26th, 1826, the sound of cannon, commencing at Buffalo, and repeated from point to point, announced the completion of the Erie Canal, and the final union of the lakes with the Atlantic—the presage of the coming power and wealth of the city as the great gateway between the Western and Eastern hemispheres. On November 11th, the arrival of the first canal-boat was the occasion of a grand aquatic and civic pageant, in which the "commingling of the waters" was typically illustrated by the pouring, by Gov. Clinton, the father of the canal, of a keg of fresh water of Lake Erie into the Atlantic Ocean at the Narrows. In 1832, the Asiatic cholera ravaged the city. Hardly had its effects been recovered from when the city was prostrated, December 16th, 1835, by a terrible and disastrous conflagration, which raged three days, and destroyed more than 600 buildings, and property to the value of over $20,000,000. Close upon this calamity followed the commercial distress and financial panic of 1836-37, which spread over the whole country, and swept countless prosperous firms out of existence. The banks suspended specie payments under authority of the legislature, and resumption was only effected with great difficulty in 1839. The Croton Aqueduct was completed in 1842, and the health and comfort of the city assured by the colossal and beneficent monument of the enterprise and foresight of the citizens. In the year 1844 began the enormous immigration—first from Ireland, in consequence of the famine, and, later, from other parts of the continent, consequent on political disturbance—a movement which, mainly passing through New York, has greatly added to her wealth and population. On July 19th, 1845, another disastrous fire destroyed several million dollars' worth of property. In 1849, a disturbance, known as the Astor Place Riot, springing from a quarrel between theatrical partisans, cost the lives of several citizens, and was only suppressed by the interference of the militia. In the month of December, 1851, Kossuth, the Hungarian patriot, received an enthusiastic public welcome. On July 14th, 1853, an exhibition of the industry of all nations was opened in a building of extreme beauty, of iron and glass, on Reservoir Square. The building was soon after destroyed by fire. On July 2d, 1855, the Central Park was selected by the commissioners appointed by the supreme court. (*See* Central Park.) In the summer of 1857, a financial crisis swept over the commercial world of both hemispheres. The business of the city was prostrated, the banks suspended specie payments, all enterprises were stopped, and the working classes thrown into a state of destitution, to which a severe winter soon added fresh terrors. Relief was provided by the municipal authorities, by labor on public works, and distribution of food. In August, 1858, the successful laying of the Atlantic cable was announced, and, on September 1st, was celebrated by a holiday and a grand public demonstration.

During the display of fireworks, the City Hall was badly injured by a conflagration. In 1860, the city was visited by the Japanese embassy, which was entertained with great splendor by the municipal authorities. The Prince of Wales was officially received the same year with a military display and welcome, by an immense concourse of citizens. In the fall of this year, the secession of South Carolina arrested business. The winter of 1860-61 was one of unquiet and distress. The attack upon Fort Sumter, in April, 1861, aroused the spirit of the people, and was responded to by a spontaneous uprising of the loyal element, which resulted in a meeting upon Union Square, and a demonstration surpassing in magnitude and enthusiasm any public assemblage in this country. Its effects were instantly felt in every part of the Union. The work of organizing regiments was at once undertaken, the banks pledged enormous sums for the support of the government, and the whole city set itself to the stern repression of the Southern revolt. In 1861, the banks, which had already loaned $150,000,000 in coin to the government, suspended specie payments. On July 13th, 1863, the militia of the city having been sent to Pennsylvania, and the United States authorities undertaking to enforce the draft, an insurrection took place, no doubt instigated by agents of the Southern rebels, which turned almost immediately into a furious attack upon the negro population of the city. The elements of disorder and crime common to large cities were combined in this movement. For a few days there was universal consternation. The courageous action of the police, supported by the United States troops, soon restored order. During each year of the war, repeated large outdoor manifestations were made in support of the government, of which those in Union Square, July 15th, 1862, and April 11th, 1863, were the most conspicuous. In 1865, upon the news of the capture of Lee, and the overthrow of the rebellion, great preparations were undertaken for the celebration of peace; but the assassination of the President turned the universal joy into mourning. The body was brought to the city on its way to the West, and lay in state in the City Hall, where it was visited by a continuous stream of mourning citizens. On the 25th of April, the remains were escorted to the Hudson River depot, by an enormous and imposing procession, through streets densely lined with sorrowing spectators. Such a spectacle had never been seen in New York. During the war, the city furnished 116,382 troops to the government. On July 12th, 1871, the Orangemen, an association of Protestant Irishmen, undertaking to celebrate the "battle of the Boyne," were attacked by the opposite party, the Ribbonmen, a Roman Catholic association, and a riot ensued, which was only put down by the use of military force. This disgraceful occurrence ended in the loss of numerous lives. In 1872, the citizens combined against the public plunderers who had for years controlled the city government; a committee of seventy was appointed, and the leaders of the "Ring" brought to justice. In 1873, the business of the city was again paralyzed by a panic of unusual length and severity. Great corporations closed their doors, and went into bankruptcy. So universal was the want of confidence that the Stock Exchange, for the first time in its history, suspended all transactions. The effects of this panic are still evident, and the present depression of business may be rather considered as its continuation than its result; nor can any improvement be looked for until the currency of the country be arranged on a permanent and stable basis.

AN HISTORICAL SUMMARY OF THE SEVERAL ATTACKS THAT HAVE BEEN MADE UPON THE CITY OF NEW YORK, AND OF THE MEASURES THAT HAVE BEEN ADOPTED FOR ITS DEFENCE FROM 1613 UNTIL 1812. By SAMUEL L. MITCHELL, M.D., LL.D.

1st.—*Capture of New York by Captain Argal in* 1613.

We have been informed that Verrazano discovered New York about the year 1524. Hudson visited it in 1609; and the Dutch sent vessels in 1610 to open trade with the natives.

In 1613, we have the first instance of invasion by an army force. Argal, the Governor of Virginia, after having destroyed the French settlements in Acadia, attacked the Dutch at New York, on his way homeward. Hedrick Christiaensen, the Dutch governor, submitted himself and his people to the governor of Virginia, and, through him, to the king of England.

2d.—*Restoration of the Dutch authority in 1614, and continuance of it until 1664, when the English took it.*

In 1614, Elkens, a new governor, came out from Amsterdam with a reinforcement. He threw off all dependence on the English and bade them defiance. He built the fort at the south-western extremity of the island, where the Custom-House and parade-grounds are now. The States-General of Holland made a grant of it under the title of New Netherland; under this possession it was long held and known.

No important occurrence took place until the reign of Charles II., King of England. In 1664, this sovereign, disregarding the rights, claims, and settlements of the Dutch, granted all New Netherland to his brother James, Duke of York and Albany. This grantee was afterward the noted James II. of England, who was declared to have abdicated the throne; who was thereafter hospitably received by Louis XIV., and whose successor was William III., the Dutch stadtholder. The patent was dated the 12th of March, pursuant to which Colonel Richard Nichols and his associates proceeded with four frigates and three hundred soldiers directly to Manhattan, for the conquest of the Dutch. On the 27th of August, in that year, the city of New Amsterdam capitulated to the English; and on the 24th of September, Fort Orange (Albany) made a similar submission. In commemoration of the titles of their ancient lord, the former has since been called New York and the latter Albany. The same year the duke conveyed New Jersey to Berkeley, Carteret, and their associates.

3d.—*Extinction of the English power and restoration of the Dutch in 1673.*

In 1665, a code of laws was compiled called the Duke's laws. They were transmitted to England, and confirmed by the duke in 1666.

In 1667, the Treaty of Breda was ratified. By this, New Netherland was confirmed to the English; and as an equivalent therefor, Surinam was ceded to the Dutch. This year Nichols retired and was succeeded by Lovelace, whose most remarkable act was the purchase of Staten Island from the natives. In 1673, a Dutch war having broken out, a small squadron under the command of Benckes and Evertsen, after having committed ravages in Virginia for the annoyance of the English commerce, came to New York for the purpose of regaining some of their lost possessions. On the 13th of July, the Dutch ships moored under the fort, landing their men, and entered the garrison without giving or receiving a shot. The city and all New Netherland immediately assented to the same humble concession.

4th.—*Restoration of the English authority in 1674, and the continuance of it until the abdication of King James II. in 1688.*

In 1674, peace was made between England and the States-General of Holland, by the Treaty of Westminster. In the sixth article of this instrument, New Netherland was restored to the English, and the English territories in Guiana to the Dutch. On this occasion the Duke of York confirmed his title by a new patent, and appointed Major Andros to be his governor. To his authority the Dutch submitted as far westward as Delaware River.

In 1682, the Duke of York released to William Penn his rights west of the Delaware, and especially his territories since called "the three lower counties on the Delaware," now the State of Delaware.

In 1683, the first legislative assembly was held under Governor Dongan, who, on his arrival, issued a proclamation to the sheriffs for choosing representatives to meet him on the 17th of December in that year.

In 1685, the Duke of York succeeded his brother, Charles II., as King of England. He was the last male of the Stuarts who reigned, and was called James II. of England. By this event the proprietary government was changed to a royal government. Dongan was restored to the administration of affairs in New York in 1686. New York, among the other colonies, though favored with charters of incorporation for its two principal cities, experienced the effects of that prince's arbitrary rule by being deprived of legislative assemblies, the printing-press, and by being annexed, with the Jerseys, to the jurisdiction of the four New England colonies, under Gov. Andros, as captain-general and admiral of the whole, in 1688. In the month of December of that year, James abdicated, and went to France; and his daughter, Mary, and William, Prince of Orange, succeeded him in February, 1689. At this time Jacob Leisler seized the fort at New York, took command of the garrison, and ruled New York by a committee of safety, until William and Mary were proclaimed there.

5*th.*—*Proceedings relative to Fortifications at New York, from the Protestant Revolution, in 1688, to t.e Treaty of Utrecht, in 1713.*

William was entering upon the great continental war in Europe when he died, in 1701.

The first governor he appointed for New York was Henry Sloughter, who reached his government (3 W. & M.), and called the assembly together, in April, 1691. The war into which William was plunging the nation was continued with great vigor under his successor, Queen Anne.

Sloughter, in his speech of the 17th August, 1692, mentions to the assembly, that "the fortifications are out of repair." He was succeeded by Benjamin Fletcher, who, in his speech to the legislature on the 12th September, 1693, recommends that "a fort be built in this city." The Earl of Bellemont took the administration (10 W. & M.) in 1698. On meeting the legislature, on the 19th of May, he uses these words: "I cannot but observe to you what a legacy my predecessor ha left me, and what difficulties to struggle with: a few miserable naked, half-starved soldiers, not half the number the king allowed pay for; the fortifications, and even the governor's house, very much out of repair, and, in a word, the whole government out of frame. It hath been represented to the government in England that this province hath been a noted receptacle of pirates, and the trade of it under no restrictions," etc. The governor died toward the end of 1700. Colonel Smith, senior councillor, administered the government until the arrival of John Nanfan (13 W.), in 1701. Lieutenant-Governor Nanfan, on meeting the legislature on the 22d of April, 1702 (1 Anne), recommended, among other things, "that the payments of the soldiers be more certain, and fortifications put in a good posture of defence." This same year Governor Cornbury recommended, in his speech of the 20th of October, "to provide for the defence of the city and port of New York, which seemed to him to be very much exposed, and, likewise, for the defence of the frontiers," etc. This was the year the session was held at Jamaica, in Queens County, on account of the yellow fever. The great warfare concerning the succession of a grandson of Louis XIV. to the crown of Spain was carried on. England, Holland, and their allies, were leagued against France. The British Colonies in North America trembled lest a French navy should assail them on the oceanic side. An attack from the French was also dreaded from the Canadian frontier, and from the savages in their alliance.

Under these impressions, excited by the formidable conflicts of Marlborough and Villars, Governor Cornbury, in his speech of the 13th of April, 1703, employs these words: "Gentlemen, I must acquaint you that since your adjournment, I have received information that the French intend to attack this place, by sea, this summer. I think the best way to prevent their design will be to erect two batteries of guns at the Narrows, one on each side, which I believe is the only way to make this port safe."

In his speech of the 29th of May, 1706, Governor Cornbury says: "The repeated advices our merchants here have received from their correspondents in the West Indies, of the design the French have of attempting this colony, has made me think it of absolute necessity to call you together at this time, that all proper measures may be taken for the defence of this place, which, as yet, lies very open, naked, and defenceless. There are two things, therefore, which I shall chiefly recommend to your care; one is the providing a fund for the fortifying of this city; the other is the providing a fund for the repairing of her Majesty's fort, which is extremely out of order, and for mounting the guns, most of the carriages being rotten and unserviceable. These two things are of absolute necessity, and without which, it is to be feared, this place will become a prey to a powerful enemy, who can design no less than to lay waste and destroy it, as they have done the Islands of Nevis and St. Christopher, etc. Gentlemen, I must take notice to you that the last assembly did pass an act for the raising of £1500 towards erecting batteries at the Narrows, which would have been of very great use at this time, had the money been collected, but it has not. I am sensible that some malicious, ill-minded people have reported that I had taken that money into my hands. That truth hereof may be known and I justified, I recommend to you to make strict inquiry into that tax."

The same Governor in his speech of the 27th of September, 1706, observes: "I must again recommend to you the providing a fund for repairing and maintaining her Majesty's fort in this city, which yet wants several things to put it in a posture to resist an enemy, if we should be attacked, which we very narrowly escaped this summer. Whether you will not think fit to fortify the Narrows, to prevent any attempt of like nature for the future, I leave to your consideration; but in my judgment, I look upon that to be the best way to cover this city from any attempt the French may intend to make upon us: and I choose to mention it to you at this time, the rather because Captain Reid Knap, whom the Queen has been pleased to appoint to be her engineer in these parts, is now here, and will, if you desire it, give you an account of what he thinks proper to be done to answer that end."

After all these urgent calls on the part of the executive, the legislature, which seems to have been uniformly hard to move, passed an act for raising £3000 toward defraying the expense of fortifying the city of New York, on the 21st of October, 1706.

In his speech of the 7th of April, 1709, Governor Cornbury again says: "I must in particular desire you to provide for the necessary repairs of the fortifications of the province."

Governor Robert Hunter, in his speech of the first of May, 1712, remarks that these letters from the Governor of Bermuda, as well as other good advices which I have received, will convince you of the necessity I lie under of calling for one more of the independent companies from Albany for the security of this place (New York), not being very sure what parts this storm is to break.

From all which it appears that it was the fashion a century ago to express great apprehension, to form grand objects, and to do very little.

6th.—The series of events relative to fortifying New York, from the death of Queen Anne, in 1714, to the arrival of Lord Loudoun with a fleet in 1756.

In his speech of the 5th June, 1716 (2 George I.), Governor Hunter observes, "that the vast preparations of France, etc., justify my apprehensions, and I hope will be sufficient to induce you to put yourselves in a better state of defence against the evil day to come. The strength of this fort is very little proportioned to its use, which I take to be not only the security of this province, but in a great measure that of the continent."

Afterward, Governor Burnet (10 Geo. I.), in his speech of the 15th of May, 1724, addressed the assembly thus: "When you are informed of the ruinous condition of the buildings of this fort (which is the only strength of this town and harbor), you will agree with me, that an immediate and sufficient provision to repair it is the most frugal method to go about so necessary a work; what you have formerly provided, has been fully employed by me for that service; and I will order an estimate of the extraordinary repairs now wanting, to be laid before you."

In a message to the assembly, of the 4th of November, 1725, in his speech at the opening of the session on the 6th of April, 1726, Governor Burnet urges the importance of making repairs to the fort and buildings. This he repeats in his speeches of the 27th of September, 1726, and the 13th of September, 1727.

A thorough repair of the barracks in the fort is earnestly requested by Governor Crosby in his speech of the 16th of October, 1733 (6 Geo. II.). In his speech of the 25th of April, 1734, Governor Crosby recommends to the assembly, "the safety and protection of the harbor of New York, and of the frontiers, no time being so fit to guard against our future enemies as a time of peace, the duration of the present peace being uncertain. I therefore earnestly recommend to you to make use of the present time and to give a sufficient sum for the erecting of a battery at the point of rocks by Whitehall, and of new forts at Albany and Schenectady. I will cause to be drawn such plans for these purposes as I think will best answer the end, and make an estimate of the expense."

On the 21st of November, 1736, an order of corporation of the city of New York was made out under the signature of Robert Curting, then mayor, giving the assembly their consent to the insertion of a clause in a bill now under commitment, for erecting a battery on Copsee Rocks, saving to the corporation the undoubted right they have to the soil, to high-water mark, to low-water mark, from Whitehall to Elds corner.

In the speech of the 14th of October, 1736, Governor Crosby again urges attention to the fortifications, and reiterates it in the speech of the 5th of April, 1737.

Governor Clark, in his speech of the 5th of September, 1738, recommends fortifications and measures of defence. In his speech of the 15th of April, 1741, he addresses the legislature in these terms (14 Geo. II.): "There is great cause to apprehend a speedy rupture with France: your situation ought, therefore, to awaken you to a timely provision against that event in fortifying this town in a better manner than it is at present, by erecting batteries, in proper places, upon some of the wharves facing the harbor, others upon the side of the Hudson River, adjoining the town, and one at Red Hook, upon Long Island, to prevent the enemy landing upon Nutten Island." Then follows a list of ordnance and stores for New York, prepared in consequence of an order of Lords for Plantations, etc.

Governor Clinton, in his speech of the 17th of April, 1744 (17 Geo. II.), expresses apprehensions of a French war, and calls attention to fortifying the city. The battery on Copsee Rocks appears to have been a very popular subject, and to have excited great interest at that time. In Lott's Journal of Assembly, II. 25, is a long enumeration of what Governor Clinton judged expedient to be done for the security of New York, Albany, Oswego, and Ticonderoga. On the 31st, he assured them, by a special message, that it was absolutely necessary there should be a battery of six guns at Red Hook, on Nassau Island, which would effectually prevent the enemy's lying there to bombard the city, or their landing any force or artillery on Nutten Island. In case of any such attack upon us, this battery might be easily supplied and maintained by force of the country. It would likewise be proper to raise another battery on the front of the Great Dock of this city, in order to flank the east side of Copsee Battery as the Flat Rock Battery does the westward.

In the speech of June 25th, 1745, the same governor observes, that " in order to put the province into a proper posture of defence, it is necessary that such other fortifications be erected about this city, with all possible dispatch, as may be sufficient to enable us to repel any force that may attack us on this quarter. For this purpose a strong battery of twenty guns, at the east end of the town, in the harbor, and some other batteries in other parts of the city, should be forthwith erected; of which I will direct plans to be laid before you. It is worth considering whether, as matters are now circumstanced, this city may not have a considerable share of the war."

In his speech of the 24th of October, 1752, fortifications are seriously recommended once more. By reason of the prevalence of the small-pox in the city of New York, in 1753, the legislature met at Jamaica, on the 13th of May, and received in Governor Clinton's speech another hint upon fortifications.

In a message from Lieutenant-Governor De Lancey, of the 31st of October, 1753, more money is asked for Copsee Battery. And in his speech of 9th April, 1754, he observes, that Copsee Battery in this city is in a ruinous condition; and I am persuaded you will think it absolutely necessary to put it into good repair. In his speech of 20th August, 1754, Governor De Lancey tells the council and assembly, that schemes have been formed to attack Albany and New York at the same time; the former by a land force from Canada, and the latter by naval armament. Let me therefore earnestly solicit you to provide in time for your security. In the speech of 28th November, he complains heavily "of the ruinous condition of the fortifications, and of the necessity of repairing them, and erecting others." In the speech of 4th February, 1755 (28 Geo. II.), the fortifications of New York are again recommended to be repaired, altered, or other works made.

In 1756, Lord Loudoun came to New York with a large fleet, and quieted all apprehensions. We find but little more on the subject of fortifications in the metropolis, during the continuance of the Canadian war, which terminated in 1759.

7th.—A summary of the proceedings from the arrival of the friendly British fleet, in 1756, to the extinction of the royal authority, by the meeting of the Continental Congress, on the 5th of September, 1774.

The presence of this fleet and the success of provincial and British arms on the side of Canada, Illinois, and Louisiana, rendered the people easy as to their situation; nor did Governor Hardy, whose administration terminated in 1757 (31 Geo. II.), nor Lieutenant-Governor De Lancey, during his second administration, which lasted till 1760, nor Colden, who ruled until 1764, trouble the legislature much about fortification. And the like stillness on that subject seems to creep through the administration of Governor Moore and of his successors, Dunmore and Tryon, up to the time of the Revolution, which may be dated from the 5th of September, 1774, when the Continental Congress first assembled at Philadelphia.

After the dangers from the French and Indians were past, difficulties arose between the colonies and the mother country, in which New York fully participated. As a civil war began, the next efforts of the colonists were to fortify, not against their old enemies, but against their late friends and fellow-subjects; and this new posture of affairs rendered it necessary to take additional precautions for defence and security.

8th.—The means used to defend New York, from the commencement of the Revolutionary War, to its termination by the peace signed at Paris, in 1783.

As early as May, 1775, the Continental Congress was consulted by the city and county of New York, through their delegates, how they ought to conduct themselves with regard to British troops expected there. Congress took the matter under consideration, and recommended, among other things, for the present, a defensive conduct as long as that should be consistent with their safety; but if they invade private property or commit hostilities, to repel force by force. They advised the removal of warlike stores from the city, and procuring of places of retreat for women and children, and the keeping in constant readiness a force for repelling insult and injury.

On the 26th of that month, Congress exhorted the Provincial Convention of New York to proceed the more vigorously in preparing for their defence, inasmuch as it was very uncertain whether the differences could be accommodated; and that the militia be in readiness to act at a moment's warning.

George Washington, a delegate from Virginia, accepted the appointment of general and commander-in-chief of the American armies, on the 16th of June, 1775. On the 6th of October, Congress decreed that the Provincial Convention of New York be directed immediately to render Hudson River defensible; that in doing this, they be particularly attentive to form such works as may be finished before the winter sets in; and that the Convention be directed to inquire whether there are not some other places where small batteries might be erected, so as to annoy the enemy on their passage, particularly a few heavy cannon at, or near Moorehouse, and at a point on the shore a little above Verplanck's Point.

On the 5th of January, 1776, Congress passed this Resolution: That having conferred with the gentlemen sent by the Convention of New York, and resumed the consideration of the report on the state of that colony, they decreed that no further fortifications be erected on Martless Rock on Hudson's River, and that a point of land on Puplopenskill on the said river, be without delay effectually fortified.

Congress, on the 9th of January, passed a resolve in these memorable words: "That it recommended to the Committee of Safety of the Province of New York to appoint proper persons to inquire into the propriety and practicability of obstructing or lessening the depth of water in the Narrows, or in any other place at the entrance of New York, or of any way of fortifying that pass, so as to prevent the entrance of the enemy;" and also to inquire whether the depth of water in Hudson's River, below the Battery, may not easily be lessened so as to prevent large ships passing up, and to make an estimate of the expense, and report their proceedings in the premises immediately to Congress.

On the 26th of the same month, a committee of three members of Congress, consisting of Messrs. Harrison, Va.; Lynch, S. C.; and Allen, Pa., was appointed to repair directly to New York to consult and advise with the Council of Safety of that colony, and with General Lee, respecting the immediate defence of the city of New York; and that General Lee be allowed to follow the determination of the said committee thereon. And the said committee was further instructed to consult with General Lee and the Committee of Safety about the fortifications on Hudson's River, and about fortifying the pass at Hell Gate. In case the city cannot be defended, the inhabitants are recommended immediately to remove their most valuable effects to a place of safety.

Eight thousand men were voted for the defence of New York on the 14th of March, 1776; and on the 15th, the Governors of Connecticut and New Jersey were requested to hold their militia in readiness for that service, to be paid, when on duty, as continental troops; and on the 9th of April, two hundred thousand dollars were ordered to be sent to New York, for the continental troops there.

Congress, on the 16th of May, 1776, directed their President to write to General Washington, requesting him to repair to Philadelphia, so soon as he conveniently could, in order to consult with Congress upon such measures as may be necessary for carrying on the ensuing campaign.

In consequence of a conference held with Generals Washington, Gates, and Mifflin, Congress, on the 13th of May, authorized the commander-in-chief to direct the building of as many fire-rafts, row-galleys, armed boats, and floating batteries as may be necessary and suitable for the immediate defence of the port of New York and Hudson's River.

On the 23d of July, Congress informed General Washington that they had such entire confidence in his judgment that they gave him no particular directions about the disposition of the troops, but desired he would dispose of those at New York, the Flying-Camp, and Ticonderoga as to him shall seem most conducive to the public good.

The Convention of New York having represented, on the 20th of August, that for want of blacksmiths they were greatly delayed in obstructing the passage of Hudson's River in the Highlands, which is an object of great importance, Congress ordered that the Convention of New York be empowered to employ for the purpose aforesaid the blacksmiths that are now engaged in building the continental frigates at Poughkeepsie.

General Washington's letter of the 31st of August reached Congress on the 2d of September, inclosing the determination of a council of war, and the reasons for quitting Long Island. In consequence of that decision, the city, with all its fortifications and appurtenances, was given up to the British fleet and army, under Admiral and General Howe. They fortified it and its environs strongly, to secure themselves against the American forces.

On the 20th of September, 1776, Congress appointed a committee of its own body, consisting of Mr. Sherman (Ct.), Mr. Gerry (Mass.), and Mr. Lewis (N. Y.), to repair to headquarters, and inquire into the state of the army, and the best means of supplying their wants. During this season, the commander-in-chief was zealously employed in providing the means of safety to New York. Between April and August, he undertook various tours and expeditions to accomplish this object. The historian records with pleasure the exertions of Washington for the security of New York. His biographers ought to give him credit for the pains he took to guard so important a station from an invading enemy. The public will peruse, with interest, the following extract from his own book accounts and vouchers, now to be seen in the office of the Register of the Treasury.

These official papers are among the most memorable that exist. After the general had resigned his commission, he made a statement of his accounts with his own pen, and presented himself with them in his hands at the Treasury. There he continued personally to attend until they were passed. In this honorable manner he underwent the ordeal of fiscal examination. This remarkable collection of documents exists in the Treasury, as an example to all public agents, of the correctness and fidelity of George Washington. They are contained in a box by themselves, and are marked on the outside by a suitable inscription.

The extract from a book in his proper handwriting was copied in the course of these inquiries concerning the general defence:

```
            1776.
April  25th. To the expenses of myself and party reconnoitring the several
               landing places, etc., on Staten Island.................... £16 10 0
May    11th. To expenses of a tour, and reconnoitring Long Island.........  26  8 6
June   26th. To expenses in reconnoitring the channel and landings on
               both sides the North River, as high as Tarrytown, to fix
               the defences thereof.........................            10 18 0
             To reconnoitre of the East River and along the Sound as far
               as Mamaroneck..............................................  16  9 4
July   15th. To my own and party's expenses laying out Fort Lee on the
               Jersey side of the North River..............................   8 15 0
July   23d.  To the expenses of reconnoitring the country as far as Perth
               Amboy.....................................................   19 10 0
```

Oct. 29th, 1748. At night we took up our lodgings at Elizabeth-town Point, an inn about two English miles distant from the town, and the last house on this road belonging to New Jersey. The man who had taken the lease of it, together with that of the ferry near it, told us that he paid a hundred and ten pounds of Pennsylvania currency to the owner.

Oct. 30th. We were ready to proceed on our journey at sunrise. Near the inn where we had passed the night, we were to cross a river, and we were brought over, together with our horses, in a wretched, half-rotten ferry; this river came a considerable way out of the country, and small vessels could easily sail up it. This was an advantage to the inhabitants of the neighboring country, giving them an opportunity of sending their goods to New York with great ease; and they even made use of it for trading to the West Indies. The country was low on both sides of the river, and consisted of meadows. But there was no other hay to be got than such as commonly grows in swampy ground; for as the tide comes up in this river, these low plains were sometimes overflowed when the water was high. The people hereabouts are said to be troubled in summer with immense swarms of gnats or mosquitoes, which sting them and their cattle. This was ascribed to the low swampy meadows, on which these insects deposit their eggs, which are afterwards hatched by the heat.

As soon as we were over the river, we were upon Staten Island, which is quite surrounded with salt water. This is the beginning of the province of New York. Most of the people settled here were Dutchmen, or such as came hither whilst the Dutch were yet in possession of the place. But at present they were scattered among the English and other European inhabitants, and spoke English for the greatest part. The prospect of the country here is extremely pleasing, as it is not so much intercepted by woods, but offers more cultivated fields to view. Hills and valleys still continued, as usual, to change alternately.

The farms were near each other. Most of the houses were wooden; however, some were built of stone. Near every farm-house was an orchard with apple-trees. Here and on the whole journey before, I observed a press for cider at every farm-house, made in different manners, by which the people had already pressed the juice out of the apples or were just busied with that work. Some people made use of a wheel made of thick oak planks which turned upon a wooden axis, by means of a horse drawing it, much in the same manner as the people do with wood; except that here the wheel runs upon a plank. Cherry-trees stood along the inclosures round the corn-fields.

The corn-fields were excellently situated, either sown with wheat or rye. They had no ditches on their sides, but (as is usual in England) only furrows, drawn at greater or lesser distances from each other.

In one place we observed a water-mill, so situated that, when the tide flowed, the water ran into a pond; but when it ebbed, the flood-gate was drawn up, and the mill driven by the water flowing out of the pond.

About eight o'clock in the morning, we arrived at the place where we were to cross the water, in order to come to the town of New York. We left our horses here, and went on board of the yacht: we were to go eight English miles by sea; however, we landed about eleven o'clock in the morning at New York.

We saw a kind of wild ducks in immense quantities upon the water: the people called them blue-bills, and they seemed to be the same with our pintal ducks or Linnæus's Anas acuta; but they were very shy. On the shore of the continent we saw some very fine sloping corn-fields which at present looked quite green; the corn already had come up. We saw many boats, in which the fishermen were busy catching oysters: to this purpose they make use of a kind of rake with long teeth bent inwards; these they used either single or two tied together in such a manner that the teeth were turned toward each other.

October 31st. About New York they find innumerable quantities of excellent oysters, and there are few places which have oysters of such exquisite taste and of so great a size: they are pickled and sent to the West Indies and other places; which is done in the following manner: As soon as the oysters are caught, their shells are opened, and the fish washed clean; some water is then poured into a pot, the oysters are put into it, and they must boil for a while; the pot is then taken off from the fire again, the oysters taken out and put upon a dish till they are somewhat dry: then you take some mace, allspice, black pepper, and as much vinegar as you think sufficient to give a sourish taste. All this is mixed with half the liquor in which the oysters were boiled and put over the fire again. While you boil it, great care is to be taken in scumming off the thick scum; at the last the whole pickle is poured into a glass or earthen vessel, the oysters are put into it, and the vessel is well stopped to keep out the air. In this manner oysters will keep for years together, and may be sent to the most distant parts of the world.

The merchants here buy up great quantities of oysters about this time, pickle them in the above-mentioned manner, and send them to the West Indies: by which they frequently make a considerable profit; for the oysters which cost them five shillings of their currency, they commonly sell for a pistole, or about six times as much as they give for them; and sometimes they get even more: the oysters which are thus pickled have a very fine flavor. The following is another way of preserving oysters: They are taken out of the shells, fried with butter, put into a glass or earthen vessel with the melted butter over them, so that they are quite covered with it and no air can get to them. Oysters prepared in this manner have likewise an agreeable taste, and are exported to the West Indies and other parts.

Oysters are here considered very wholesome. Some people assured us that they have not felt the least inconvenience after eating a considerable quantity of them. It is likewise a common rule here, that oysters are best in those months which have an " r " in their name, such as September, October, etc., but that they are not so good in other months. However, there are poor people who live all the year long upon nothing but oysters and bread.

The sea near New York affords annually the greatest quantities of oysters. They are found chiefly in a muddy ground, where they lie in the slime, and are not so frequent in a sandy bottom : a rocky and a stony bottom is seldom found here. The oyster-shells are gathered in great heaps, and burnt into a lime, which by some people is made use of in building houses, but is not reckoned so good as that made of limestone. On our journey to New York we saw high heaps of oyster-shells near the farm-houses upon the sea-shore, and about New York we observed the people had carried them upon the fields, which were sown with wheat. However, they were entire and not crushed.

The Indians who inhabited the coast before the arrival of the Europeans have made oysters and other shell-fish their chief food; and at present, whenever they come to a salt water where oysters are to be got, they are very active in catching them and selling them in great quantities to other Indians who live higher up in the country: for this reason you see immense numbers of oyster and muscle-shells piled up near such places where you are certain that the Indians formerly built their huts.

This circumstance ought to make us cautious in maintaining that in all places on the sea-shore, or higher up in the country, where such heaps of shells are to be met with, the latter have lain there ever since the time that those places were overflowed by the sea.

Lobsters are likewise plentifully hereabouts pickled much the same way as oysters, and sent to several places. I was told of a very remarkable circumstance about these lobsters, and I have afterward frequently heard it mentioned. The coast of New York had already European inhabitants for a considerable time; yet no lobsters were to be met with on that coast; and though the people fished ever so often, they could never find any signs of lobsters being in this part of the sea: they were therefore continually brought in great well-boats from New England, where they are plentiful; but it happened that one of these well-boats broke in pieces near Hell-gate, about ten English miles from New York, and all the lobsters in it got off. Since that time they have so multiplied in that part of the sea, that they are now caught in the greatest abundance.

Nov. 1st. A kind of cold fever, which the English in this country call fever and ague, is very common in several parts of the English colonies. There are, however, other parts where the people have never felt it. I will in the sequel describe the symptoms of this disease at large. Several of the most considerable inhabitants of this town assured me that the disease was not near so common in New York as it is in Pennsylvania, where ten were seized by it to one in the former province; therefore they were of opinion that this disease was occasioned by the vapors arising from stagnant fresh water, from marshes, and from rivers, for which reason those provinces situated on the sea-shore could not be so much affected by it. However, the carelessness with which people eat quantities of melons, peaches, and other juicy fruit, in summer, was reckoned to contribute much toward the progress of this fever, and repeated examples confirmed the truth in this opinion. The Jesuits bark was reckoned a good remedy against it. It has, however, been found to have operated contrary to expectation, though I am ignorant whether it was adulterated, or whether some mistake had been committed in the manner of taking it.

Mr. Davis Van Horne, a merchant, told me that he cured himself and several other people of this fever, by the leaves of the common garden sage, or Salvia officinalis of Linnæus. The leaves are crushed or pounded in a mortar, and the juice is pressed out of them: this is continued till they get a spoonful of the liquid, which is mixed with lemon-juice. This draught is taken about the time the cold fit comes on, and after taking it three or four times, the fever does not come on again.

The bark of the white oak was reckoned the best remedy which had as yet been found against the dysentery. It is reduced to a powder, and then taken. Some people assured me that in cases where nothing would help, this remedy had given a certain and speedy relief.

The people in this place likewise make use of this bark (as is usually done in the English colonies) to dye wool a brown color, which looks like that of bohea tea, and does not fade by being exposed to the sun. Among the numerous shells which are found on the sea-shore, there are some which by the English are called clams, and which bear some resemblance to the human ear. They have a considerable thickness, and are chiefly white, excepting the pointed end, which both without and within has a blue color, between purple and violet. They are met with in vast numbers on the sea-shore of New York, Long Island, and other places.

A considerable commerce is carried on in this article, with such Indians as live further up the country. When these people inhabited the coast, they were able to catch their own clams, which at that time made a great part of their food; but at present this is the business of the Dutch and English, who live on Long Island and other maritime provinces. As soon as the shells are caught, the fish are taken out of them, drawn upon a wire, and hung up in the open air, in order to dry by the heat of the sun. When this is done, the fish is put in proper vessels, and carried to Albany upon the river Hudson; there the Indians buy them, and reckon them one of their best dishes. Besides the Europeans, many of the native Indians come annually down to the sea-shore in order to catch clams, proceeding with them afterwards in the manner I have just described.

The shells of these clams are used by the Indians as money, and make what they call their wampum; they likewise serve their women for an ornament, when they intend to appear in full dress. These wampum are properly made of the purple parts of the shells, which the Indians value more than the white parts. A traveller, who goes to trade with the Indians and is well stocked with them, may become a considerable gainer; but if he take gold coin or bullion, he will undoubtedly be a loser; for the Indians who live further up in the country put little or no value upon these metals, which we reckon so precious, as I have frequently observed in the course of my travels. The Indians formerly made their own wampum, though not without a deal of trouble; but at present the Europeans employ themselves that way; especially the inhabitants of Albany, who get a considerable profit by it.

November 2d. Besides the different sects of Christians, there are many Jews settled in New York, who possess great privileges. They have a synagogue and houses, and great country-seats of their own property, and are allowed to keep shops in town. They have likewise several ships, which they freight and send out with their own goods. In fine, they enjoy all the privileges common to the other inhabitants of this town and province.

During my residence at New York this time, and in the next ten years, I was frequently in company with the Jews. I was informed, among other things, that people never boiled any meat for themselves on Saturday, but they always did it the day before; and that in winter they kept a fire during the whole Saturday. They commonly eat no pork; yet I have been told by several men of credit that many of them (especially among the young Jews), when travelling, did not make the least difficulty about eating this or any other meat that was put before them, even though they were in company with Christians. I was in their synagogue last evening, for the first time, and this day at noon I visited it again; and each time I was put in a particular seat, which was set apart for strangers or Christians. A young Rabbi read the divine service, which was partly in Hebrew and partly in the rabbinical dialect. Both men and women were dressed entirely in the English fashion; the former had all of them their hats on, and did not once take them off during service. The galleries, I observed, were appropriated to the ladies, while the men sat below. During prayers, the men spread a white cloth over their heads; which perhaps is to represent sackcloth. But I observed the wealthier sort of people had a much richer cloth than the poorer ones. Many of the men had Hebrew books, in which they sang and read alternately. The Rabbi stood in the middle of the synagogue, and read with his face toward the east; he spoke, however, so fast as to make it most impossible for any one to understand what he said.

New York, the capital of a province of the same name, is situated under forty degs. and forty min. north lat. and seventy-four degs. and four min. of western long., from London; and is about ninety-seven English miles distant from Philadelphia. The situation of it is extremely advantageous for trade; for the town stands upon a point which is formed by two bays, into one of which the river Hudson discharges itself not far from the town. New York is therefore on three sides surrounded with water; the ground it is built on is level in some parts, and hilly in others: the place is generally reckoned very wholesome.

The town was first founded by the Dutch. This, it is said, was done in the year 1623, when they were yet masters. They called it New Amsterdam, and the country itself New Holland. The English, toward the end of the year 1664, taking possession of it under the conduct of Des Cartes, and keeping it by the virtue of the next treaty of peace, gave the name of New York to both the town and province belonging to it. In size it comes nearest to Boston and Philadelphia. But with regard to its fine buildings, its opulence and extensive commerce, it disputes the preference with them; at present it is about half again as large as Gottenburgh in Sweden.

The streets do not run so straight as those of Philadelphia, and have sometimes considerable bendings; however, they are very spacious and well built, and most of them are paved, except in high places, where it has been found useless. In the chief streets there are trees planted, which in summer afford a cooling shade. I found it extremely pleasant to walk in the town, for it seemed quite like a garden. The trees which are planted for this purpose are chiefly of two kinds. The waterbeech, Linnæus's Plantanus occidentalis, are the most numerous, and give an agreeable shade in summer by their great and numerous leaves. The locust-tree, or Linnæus's Robinia pseudacacia, is likewise frequent; its fine leaves and the odoriferous scent which exhales from its flowers make it very proper for being planted in the streets, near the houses and in gardens. There are likewise lime-trees and elms in these walks; but they are not by far so frequent as the others. One seldom met with trees of the same sort next to each other, they being planted in general alternately.

Besides number of birds of all kinds, which make these their abode, there is likewise a kind of a frog which frequents them in great numbers in summer; they are Dr. Linnæus's Rana arborea, and especially the American variety of this animal. They are very clamorous in the evening and in the nights (especially when the days had been hot and a rain was expected), and in a manner drown the singing of the birds. They frequently made such a noise that it is difficult for a person to make himself heard.

Most of the houses are built of brick, and are generally strong and neat, and several stories high. Some have, according to old architecture, turned the gable-end toward the streets; but the new houses were altered in this respect. Many houses had a balcony on the roof, on which the people used to sit in the evening in the summer season, and from thence they had a pleasant view of a great part of the town, and likewise of part of the adjacent water, and of the opposite shore. The roofs are commonly covered with tiles or shingles; the latter of which are made of white fir-trees, or Pinus Strobus (Linn. sp plant.), which grows high up in the country. The inhabitants are of opinion that a roof made of these shingles is as durable as one made in Pennsylvania of the white cedar or Cupressus thyordes (Linn. sp. plant.). The walls were whitewashed within; and I did not anywhere see hangings, with which the people in this country seem in general to be but little acquainted. The walls were quite covered with all sorts of drawings and pictures in small frames. On each side of the chimneys they had usual sort of alcove, and the wall under the windows was wainscoted, and had benches placed near it. The alcoves and all wood-work were painted with a bluish-gray color.

There are several churches in the town which deserve some attention. 1. The English, built in the year 1695, at the west end of the town, consisting of stone, and has a steeple with a bell. 2. The new Dutch church, which is likewise built of stone, is pretty large, and is provided with a steeple; it also has a clock, which is the only one in the town. This church stands almost due from north to south. No particular point of the compass has here been, in general, attended to in erecting sacred buildings. Some churches stand, as is usual, from east to west, others from south to north, and others in different positions. In the Dutch church there is neither altar, vestry, choir, sconces, nor paintings. Some trees are planted round it, which make it look as if it were built in a wood. 3. The old Dutch church, which is also built of stone. It is not so large as the new one. It was painted in the inside, though without any images, and adorned with a small organ, of which Governor Burnet made them a present. The men, for the most part, sit in the gallery, and the women below. 4. The Presbyterian church, which is pretty large, and was built but lately. It is of stone, and has a steeple and a bell in it. 5. The German Lutheran church. 6. The German Reformed church. 7. The French church, for Protestant refugees. 8. The Quaker meeting-house. 9. To these may be added the Jewish synagogue, which I mentioned before.

Toward the sea, on the extremity of the promontory, is a pretty good fort, named George, which entirely commands the port and can defend the town at least from a sudden attack on the sea side. Besides, it is likewise secure on the north or towards the shore by a palisade, which, however (as for a considerable time the people have had nothing to fear from an enemy), is in many places in a very bad state of defence.

There is no good water to be met with in the town itself; but at a little distance there is a large spring of good water, which the inhabitants take for their tea and for the uses of the kitchen. Those, however, who are less delicate in this point make use of the water from the wells in town, though it be very bad. This want of good water lies very heavy on the horses of the stranger that comes to this place; for they do not like to drink the water from the wells in the town.

The port is a good one; ships of the greatest burthen can lie in it quite close up to the bridge; but its water is very salt, as the sea comes continually in upon it, and therefore is never frozen except in extraordinary cold weather. This is of great advantage to the city and its commerce; for many ships either come in or go out of the port at any time of the year, unless the winds be contrary—a convenience which, as I have before observed, is wanting at Philadelphia. It is secured from violent hurricanes from south-east by Long Island, which is situated just before the town; therefore only the storms from the south-west are dangerous to the ships which ride at anchor here, because the port is open only on that side. The entrance, however, has its faults. One of them is, that no man-of-war can pass through it; for though the water is pretty deep, yet it is not sufficiently so for great ships. Sometimes even merchant-ships of a large size have, by the rolling of the waves and by sinking down between them, slightly touched the bottom, though without any bad consequence. Besides this, the canal is narrow; and for this reason many ships have been lost here because they may be easily cast upon a sand-bar, if the ship is not well piloted. Some old people, who had constantly been upon the canal, assured me that it was neither deeper nor shallower at present than in their youth.

The common difference between high and low water at New York amounts to about six feet, English measure. But at a certain time in every month, when the tide flows more than commonly, the difference in the height of the water is seven feet.

New York carries on a more extensive commerce than any town in the English-American provinces; at least it may be said to equal them. Boston and Philadelphia, however, come very nearly up to it. The trade of New York extends to many places, and it is said they send more ships from thence to London than they do from Philadelphia. They export to that capital all the various sorts.

Advantages of New York, as set forth a Century Ago.—About the middle of last century, the attention of the different sections of the country became especially directed to the encouragement of colonization from Europe, and a competition arose between the different cities of Boston, New York, and Philadelphia, in respect to the advantages afforded to settlers by the situation and commerce of the cities, and the climate and soil of the country adjacent to them. The leading minds of the colonies engaged in the publications, to further the views of their respective localities, and the newspapers devoted considerable space to articles designed for the information of the European public. We copy one of these publications, dated 1753, which perhaps will give to the people of the present day as novel an idea of the olden time as it was new to the people of the old countries at the time of its publication:

"A Brief Consideration of New York with respect to its Natural Advantages; its Superiority in several Instances over some of the Neighboring Colonies.

"O fortunatos nimium,
Bona si sua norint."

"Awake the Muse, bid industry rejoice,
And the rough sons of lowest labor smile."—*Thos. Brit.*

With respect to what nature has done for us, there is not a happier people in the world than the inhabitants of this province. I hope the assigning of a few instances from whence this happiness is derived, will not be displeasing to them, as it tends to inflame them with a love of their country and at the same time excite their gratitude for the happiness they enjoy.

The necessaries of life, which for that reason are its most substantial blessings, we possess with the richest affluence. The natural strength and fertility of the soil we live upon will, by grazing and tillage, always continue to us the inexhaustible source of profuse abundance. There is nothing we possess that mankind can well be without and scarce any thing they really want but we either enjoy or can easily procure in luxuriant plenty. Provisions, in short, are our staple, and whatever country sufficiently abounds with so necessary a commodity can never fail of wealth—a sure magazine! which will always be attended with power and plenty, and many other springs of social happiness, as its natural concomitants. The want of such an unfailing staple is a fountain of misery to a province on the East of more show than substance, pomp than riches. By constant supplies from our exuberance, we hold them in debt, and annually increase it; while we are so happy as to taste the sweets of the truth of what they have remarked, that there are fewer poor men in this than in any one of the plantations of this continent. I have myself spent a month in their metropolis, the most splendid town of North America, not without some pleasure in reflecting that I had not a morsel of bread, even at their common tables, that was not the produce of this colony. Nor has the prettiest beau in the town so easy an access to their ladies, as a certain baker of ours universally celebrated there for the goodness of his biskets.

But this opulence is not our only advantage for raising the trade of this Province and enlarging its extent: every thing in it conspires to make New York the best mart in the continent. Our coasts are regular, and navigation up to the city from the sea, short and bold, and, by a good lighthouse, might be rendered safe and easy.

The publication then goes on to show to the people the vast advantages of the North River and the immense extent of water frontage; and goes on to show the disadvantages of Philadelphia, where all the product of the surrounding country has to be brought in carts and wagons; and thus the author shows to the people an advantage of 30 per cent in farming in the country surrounding New York over that round about Philadelphia. Also shows the expense of transporting a bushel of wheat 100 miles in this province to be about one sixth of that in Pennsylvania.

The article then explains the many disadvantages of Massachusetts and Connecticut by showing that the many towns are always a mischievous consequence to new settlements. After treating on the many drawbacks to the surrounding provinces, the author describes the city as follows:

The city of New York consists of about two thousand five hundred buildings. It is a mile in length, and at a medium not above half that in breadth. On the south it forms a point into a large bay. The east side lies on a strait which at eighteen or twenty miles eastward opens to the sound. It adjoins to Hudson River on the west; and such is its figure, its centre of business, and the situation of its buildings that the cartage in town from one part to another does not at a medium exceed one quarter of a mile. The prodigious advantage of which to a trading city is more easily conceived than expressed. It facilitates and expedites the loading and unloading of ships, saves time and labor, and is attended with innumerable conveniences to the inhabitants.

MEMENTOES OF THE OLDEN TIME.

A Duel.—September, 1713. A duel was fought near New York by Dr. John Livingston and Mr. Thomas Dongan, which resulted in the death of the former. Mr. Dongan was tried for murder, and found guilty of manslaughter.

The Seasons.—1718, January 15th. The ice from the rivers had disappeared, and the frost was out of the ground. For three weeks previously, the weather had been like the spring, and peas, beans, etc., were planted. But a week had scarcely elapsed ere severe cold weather set in, and the rivers were filled with ice.

An Earthquake.—November, 1727. Two shocks of earthquake were felt in New York in one day. Crockery fell from shelves, and the clocks in all parts of the town ceased the vibration of their pendulums.

The Commercial Marine.—1730. The number of vessels that entered the port of New York were 211, viz.: From Jamaica 30, from Boston 28, from Barbadoes 14, from Bermuda 13, from Curaçoa 12, from Antigua 11, from London 7, from Rhode Island 7, from North Carolina 6, from Bristol 5, from Dover 5, from South Carolina 5, from Newfoundland 4, from Philadelphia 3, from Surinam 3, from Madeira 3.

Small-Pox.—1731. This disease raged fearfully in New York. Inoculation, which was then a novelty, was tried with success. But the safest course was believed to be to retire from the locality where it prevailed. The trade of New York suffered greatly from this cause, at this as well as other periods when the epidemic prevailed. In one place fifty persons died of small-pox. The disease set in about midsummer, and continued its ravages until Christmas, during which period about six hundred persons fell victims to its ravages.

First Fire-Engines.—December, 1732. The first fire occurred at which fire-engines were used. Two fire-engines had recently been imported from England, and companies were formed which became the foundation of the New York fire department. Their efficiency was found greatly to exceed the former method of lines of bucket-men, passing the water from hand to hand from the nearest wells or from the river.

Hard Times.—1735. Political troubles, and high taxes and *imposts* drove many people from the city to seek more advantageous places of residence. No less than 158 dwellings were to be let at one period. The wealth of the people was freely drawn upon to sustain the merchants of the *mother* country and her officials in this province. Philadelphia was a favorite residence, the more especially as it was a free port.

Election.—1735. A vigorously-contested election for representative of New York City in the Provincial Assembly took place. At no period had party spirit run so high. The candidates were two leading merchants, Adolph Philipse and Cornelius Van Horne. The electors appeared in the fields (now the park), about 9 o'clock, with colors flying and drums beating. Apparently, by the show, the friends of Mr. Philipse, who were the principal merchants and gentlemen, were in the majority; but a poll was demanded, and thereupon the candidates and electors repaired to the City Hall, where the poll was carried on all day till about 9 o'clock at night, with the greatest warmth on both sides, the drums and music going about during the time. Between 9 and 10 at night the polls closed, and the votes were for Philipse 413, for Horne 399. It was agreed that a scrutiny should be had on the following Monday. The zeal of the friends of the candidates was so great that it was supposed every voter in the city was brought out. One gentleman used his chariot in bringing up voters of all sorts, so that the poor women cried out: "These are fine times when carmen and chimney-sweeps ride in coaches."

Burning of the Archives of Trinity Church.—February, 1750. A fire broke out in the new Free School-house, kept by Joseph Hildreth, clerk of Trinity Church. The church was frequently in danger, but was saved. All the records of the church were consumed.

The Oyster Pasty Battery.—In May, 1751, some workmen, digging down the bank of the North River, in the rear of Trinity Church, discovered a stone wall, four or five feet thick, and nearly eight feet under ground. It was supposed at the time to be the breastwork of a battery, but the oldest person then living could give no account of it. We are more familiar with the city antiquities than the residents a century ago, and know from the records which have been published that this was at or near the locality of the fortification at the North River end of the city wall, called "Oyster Pasty Mount."

Whales in the North River.—December, 1755, two whales were struck south of the Highlands.

Wild Pigeons.—April, 1759. In one day 75,000 wild pigeons were brought to the market in the city, selling at fifty for one shilling.

Sale of Slaves.—November, 1762. "To be sold at Cruger's Wharf, on board the sloops Rebecca and Joseph, just arrived from Arrambo, in Guinea, a parcel of likely young slaves, men, women, and boys."

Pillory and Cage.—September, 1764. The new pillory, with a large wooden cage behind it, was erected between the new jail (the present Hall of Records) and the workhouse (the site of the City Hall), the cage being for disorderly boys who publicly broke the Sabbath.

King George's Statue.—August, 1770. An elegant equestrian statue, the first of the kind in this city of his Majesty George III., was erected in the Bowling Green, in presence of a large concourse of persons, and amid music and a discharge of ordnance. It remained six years, but was destroyed by the Liberty Boys, in 1776, and its material (lead) cast into bullets.

The Battery.—July, 1735. The first stone of the platform of the new battery on Whitehall rocks was laid by his Excellency, the Governor (Cosby), who named the battery, after his son-in-law, the "George Augustus Royal Battery." At the close of the ceremonies one of the cannon burst, by which three persons were killed, namely, John Symes, Esq., High Sheriff; Miss Courtland, daughter of Colonel Courtland, one of the members of his Majesty's Council; and a son-in-law of Alderman Romer.

The Dutch Church in the Fort.—June, 1790. While engaged in the work at the Government house, on the site of the old fort, a flat stone was taken up from under the ruins of the chapel which formerly stood there, on which was found to be the tablet of the Dutch church erected within that inclosure in 1642. It had upon it the following inscription:

"An. Do. M. D. C. X. L. I. I. N.
Kieft, Dr. Gl. Heeft
de Gemeenten Deese
Temple doen Bouwen."

Translation: "Anno Domini 1642, N. Kieft, Director-General, hath caused the congregation to erect this temple."

Pirates and Privateers.—July, 1723. Captain Peter Solgard, commander of

H. M. ship Greyhound, the station-ship of this province, on a cruise on the coast, on intelligence given him, pursued and overhauled two pirate sloops, commanded by one Low, a "notorious inhuman pirate," after much resistance capturing one and shattering the other, who, however, escaped in the night, whereupon the freedom of the city was presented to the gallant officer.

The Windmill on the Commons.—December, 1723. The land lying near the windmill formerly of Jasper Nessepot, near the commons of the city, was surveyed, with the view of laying out a regular width the high road now known as Chatham street.

The City Fathers.—1728. The members of the city government generally personally attended to the laying out of public lands, and on such occasions a fine collation was served at the public expense.

Beekman's Swamp.—1728. Ten lots sold by the city, 25 x 120, for £100.

The First Public Library.—July, 1729. The Rev. Dr. Millington, Rector of Newington, in England, bequeathed to the Society for Propagating the Gospel 1642 volumes of miscellaneous works, which became the foundation of the present Society Library.

Negroes and Slaves.—1731. The law for regulating required that no negro or Indian slave above fourteen years should appear in the streets south of Fresh Water Brook (Pearl and Chatham streets), in the night, after an hour succeeding sunset, without a lantern, by the light of which they could be plainly seen, or else to be in company with a white person.

Office holders.—1732. William Sharpas had been city clerk for over forty years, and continued to hold the office some years subsequently, when he died. At the time above stated he petitioned for an increase of salary.

Trinity Church.—1696. During this year Trinity Church was begun; it was opened for worship by the Rev. Mr. Vesey in the year 1697. This building was enlarged in 1735-6, and burnt down in 1776, and another building erected in 1788. It was consecrated by Bishop Provoost, in 1791. The last has, in its turn (1839), been demolished, with the intention of erecting a third Trinity. The cemetery of this church was granted by the Common Council gratuitously to the vestry in 1703, on condition that it be neatly fenced, and that the fees for burial be limited to 3s. 6d. for grown persons, and 1s. 6d. for those under twelve years of age. By the records it appears that this cemetery had received more than 160,000 bodies before the conflagration of 1776.

Bolting and Baking Monopoly.—1696. Upon inquiry, it is found that there is not more than seven hundred bushels of corn within the city, and the number of inhabitants being computed six thousand or more, therefore found that the stock of corn would not be sufficient for a week's maintenance. The cause assigned by the Common Council for this scarcity is "the liberty and latitude that every planter had lately taken, of making his house or farm a market for his wheat, or converting the same into flour by bolting of it, and that under pretence of a privilege they conceived they have obtained, by virtue of a law of the General Assembly, entitled an act against unlawful by-laws," which had deprived the city of the monopoly formerly enjoyed.

The Mayor craves advice to remove this intolerable grievance, that the city may be restored to its rights and privileges; they recommend an address to his majesty for the repeal of said law, and a committee is accordingly appointed. An assize of rye bread agreed on—a loaf weighing five pounds for 4½d., rye being at 3s. 3d. the bushel.

Watch and Police Regulations.—1676. "Ordered that the watch be set every night by eight o'clock; immediately after the ringing of the bell. That the city gates be locked up by the constable or deputy, before nine of the clock, and opened in the morning presently after daylight, at the dismission of the watch, and if any person goes from, or absents himself without consent, he, or they, shall forfeit for every such default ten guilders." That the sergeant or corporal of the watch, shall at all times succeed the deputy constables on the watch for the execution thereof. That if any one come upon the watch overcharged with drink, he shall pay two guilders; but if abusive or quite drunk, he is to pay the same as if he absented himself, four guilders. If any person shall quarrel upon the watch on account of being of different nations or other pretence, he shall pay four guilders. Any sentinel leaving his post before he is relieved, shall pay twenty guilders, and suffer three days' imprisonment. The sentinel to stand on his post one hour. That frequent rounds about the city be made, especially toward the bridge. No cursing and swearing shall be allowed upon the watch, nor any gaming at dice or cards, nor any exercise of drinkinges upon the penalty of four guilders. That a list of fines be brought by the provost unto the mayor. The sergeant belonging to every watch shall come with his halbert; and see that every one of the watch brings his armes, that is to say, his sword and good half pike. Every head of a family to have one good musket or firelock, with six charges of powder and six of ball at least, on penalty of four guilders for the first offence, eight for the second, and twelve for the third; and the officers of each county are to search four times a yeare. The citizen soldiers are to appear with good arms before their captain's coullers, at the first beating of the drum. Penalty for non-appearance, thirty guilders—for defficient armes, ten.

January 20th. Ordered, by the mayor and aldermen, that all masters of vessels arriving at New York, as soon as they shall come ashore, give an account to the mayor of all and every passenger; penalty for neglect, a merchandable beaver. Ordered, that no person shall sell any goods, wares, etc., by retail, on pain of forfeiture, unless he be a freeman, or made free, or burgher of this city, settled housekeeper; unless by special licence from the mayor, etc., with approbation from the governor. Any person departing from the city, unless he keep fire and candle light, and pay scott and lott, shall lose his freedom; and every merchant hereafter to be made free shall pay for the same six bevers—and handicraft trades and others to pay two bevers for being made free. Ordered, that all persons that keep public houses shall sell beer, as well as wine and other liquors, and keep lodging for strangers; dated 20th January. Samuel Leeth Clarke.

April 14th. Proclaimed, that every merchant trading at this place, before the new docke or wharfe (intending to be built) shall be finished and paid for, shall pay proportionably for his estate, the same as the inhabitants and other traders here, towards the building of the same. 15th April, allowed by the governor, and forthwith to be put in execution.

Proposals by the mayor and aldermen, presented to his honor, the governor. That there be six houses appointed to sell all sorts of wine, brandy, and rum, and lodging. That there be eight houses appointed to sell beer, cider, mum, and rum, and to provide for strangers as the law directs, to sell brandy, rum, and strong waters, and tobacco. That two of the wine-houses be *ordinaryves*: and four of the beer-houses. The prices of wines and other liquors as they are to be sold by the trappers: French wines, 1s. 3d. per quart; Fayal wines and St. Georges, 1s. 6d.; Madera wines, and portapont, 1s. 10d.; Canaryes, Bresadoes, and Malagoes, 2s. per quart; Brandy, 6d. per gill; Rum, 3d. per gill; Syder, 4d. per quart; Double beer, 3d. per quart; Mum, 6d. per quart. The ordinary at wine-houses, 1s. per meal; at beer-houses, 8d. per meal. Lodging at wine-house, 4d. per night; at the beer-house, 3d. per night.

Proclamation was made by the governor, Edward Andros, February 3d, that a weekly market should be held every Saturday at the houses built for that purpose by the water side, near the bridge, *i.e.*, at the foot of Broad street, the first market to be held March 24th, and a fair to be held at Breukly for cattle, grain, and country produce, the first Monday, Tuesday, and Wednesday in November; and in the city at the market-house and plain before the fort the Thursday, Friday, and Saturday following. All persons coming thereto are to be free from any arrest or debt coming or returning from said market or fair. This Proclamation to remain in force three years from the 24th of March next.

Matthew Hillyer petitions the common council, and says that he hath kept school for children of both sexes, for two years past, to the satisfaction of their parents; but as he understands complaints have been made to the Mayor, etc., and to be trobled with so often removals. But your petitioner understanding of an obstruction, by a person lately arrived, who endeavours the circumventing of your petitioner, and reaps the fruits of his labors, of which likewise your petitioner has fully informed your honor, who is by the petitioner's humble request pleased to ordering of a school and master to your worship's pleasure, giving your petitioner hopes and encouragement that by your worship's wisdom things may be better regulated; and he requests that he may be established in his employ, in which, with the help of God, he doubts not he shall give your worships satisfaction.

August 25th. Upon the petitions of Ebenezer Kirtland and Matthew Hillyer, it is ordered that Matthew Hillyer continue in the same—the school-master's office, in behaving himself for the future better than the time past, and instead of £12 the annum, according to the former order, is only to have a room provided for him.

The court choose two tanners, and forbid all others to exercise the trade; and Peter Pangborne is chosen the currier of the city. Also ordered that no butcher be permitted to be currier, or shoemaker, or tanner; nor shall any tanner be either currier, shoemaker, or butcher, it being consonant to the laws of England, and practice in the neighboring colonies of Massachusetts and Connecticut. Further, it is ordered that if any Indians shall be seen coming out drunk of any house, that it shall be a sufficient conviction; and if seen drunk in the street, and the house not found out, or known where he or she were made drunk, the whole street to be finable. Likewise ordered that no person distill any grain unless it be unfit to grind and boalt.

Captain Kidd.—*Assembly Journal*, Saturday, the 18th of April, 1691. Gabriel Monville, Esq., and Thomas Willett, Esq., are appointed to attend the House of Representatives, and acquaint them of the many good services done to this province by Capt. William Kidd in his attending here with his vessels before his Excellency's arrived, and that it would be acceptable to his Excellency and this Board that they consider of some suitable reward to him for his good services.

Per order,
DAVID JAMISON, *Clerk*
Of the Council.

Ordered, Thursday, 8 o'clock A.M., May 14th, '91, That his Excellency be addressed unto, to order the Receiver General to pay to Captain William Kidd one hundred and fifty pounds, current money of this Province, as a suitable reward for the many good services done to this Province.

Classical School.—Assembly Journal, October 3d, 1732. Ordered, That care be given to bring in a bill for encouraging a public school, to teach Latin, Greek, arithmetic, and the mathematics, in the city of New York; and that for the encouragement of a school-master for that purpose, the unappropriated money, to rise by the act for licensing hawkers and peddlers, until the first day of December, 1737, be applied for that end; and that the said city make up the income of that fund annually, during that time, to the sum of —— pounds; and that in consideration thereof, the said school-master shall be obliged to teach gratis the number of —— children.

Road to Harlem.—Assembly Journal, October 4th, 1740. A petition of several inhabitants and freeholders, of the Out ward of the city of New York, was presented to the house, and read, setting forth,

That the King's Road or Highway is laid out to Adrian Hogland's house, and no farther, so that those who live or reside thereabouts are obliged to go about eleven rounds in going to Harlem; whereas, if the King's Road or Highway be laid out from Adrian Hogland's house to the King's Road or Highway, at Harlem, it will be no more than three quarters of a mile, and therefore, pray that a King's Road or Highway may be laid out from Hogland's house to the said King's Road at Harlem, which will be of great ease to the inhabitants there settled, as well as to travellers; Ordered, that the petitioners serve the owners of such land who may be affected by the prayer of the said petitioner with a copy of this petition; after which, both parties may attend if they think fit.

Lighting the City.—December, 1697. Resolved, that the mode of lighting the city be that, during the dark time of the moon, until the 25th of March next, every seventh householder cause a lantern and candle to be hung out on a pole every night. The expense to be divided equally between the seven. The aldermen are charged to see this done.

Arrival of a Governor.—Resolved, that a dinner be proposed at the charge of the corporation, for the entertainment of his Excellency, Richard, Earl of Bellomont, Captain-General, etc., etc., and a committee appointed to make a bill of fare (two aldermen and two assistants), and that for the effectual doing thereof, they call to their assistance such cooks as they shall think necessary to advise.

Duties of Aldermen.—1700. Alderman Provoost and Mr. Duykink appointed to take care that the public house or office on the dock be cleaned and put in repair, and a person appointed daily to keep the same clean.

Showing Date of Birth of the First Female Born in New York.—The ship New Netherland, which brought to the new world the first colony of families, arrived at the bay of the Hudson River in the year 1623. The colonists commenced at once to erect cabins for their temporary accommodation on the southerly point of Manhattan Island, their cattle being turned out upon the island in the harbor, now known as Governor's Island. Among these colonists were Jons Jansen de Rapelje, and the young woman who was then, or soon after became, his wife, a young couple whose first child was born in June, 1625. This child is alluded to in the public records, at a period when she had herself become a mother, and a favor was granted her of a public nature, one of the inducements to which was that she was "the first born Christian daughter" born in the colony of the New Netherlands.

Under these circumstances, the family record of the Rapeljes is of peculiar interest; and fortunately, it has been preserved in perfect form during the intervening centuries. We give the translation of the original record:

The names and family register of the children of George Jansen de Rappelje, and Cataline his wife.

1625, the 9th of June, is born the first daughter of George Jansen de Rappelje, named Sara.
1627, the 11th of March, is born the second daughter, named Marratis.
1629, the 18th of August, is born the third daughter, named Jannetie.
1635, the 5th of July, is born the fourth daughter, named Judick.
1637, the 28th of August, is born the first son, named Jan.
1639, the 28th of May, is born the second son, named Jacob.
1641, the 28th of March, is born the fifth daughter, named Catalyna.
1643, the 27th of June, is born the third son, named Jeronimus.
1646, the 8th of February, is born the sixth daughter, named Annetie.
1648, the 28th of March, is born the seventh daughter, named Elizabeth.
1650, the 29th of December, is born the fourth son, named Daniel.

Social Amusements in the Olden Time in New York.—The amusements in bygone days partook, much more than at present, of local gatherings, such as supper-parties at the public gardens and "tea-houses," dancing-parties, etc. Public exhibitions, such as might attract amusement-seekers to an evening entertainment, were comparatively rare, although a house for theatrical performances was erected as early as 1751, and a regular company was for many subsequent years established in the city. Itinerant performers of various sorts also travelled through the city and erected temporary places for their exhibitions; but these failed to take the place of the social entertainments with which the descendants of the old Dutch stock delighted to pass away their festive hours, of which dancing-parties were the leading feature. For a long time prior to the Revolution, the dances in vogue were mostly those introduced from English sources, with others of American production; and they were, all of them, of a lively character, involving swift motions of the feet and aerial movements upon the toes; the "double-shuffle," the "pigeon-wing," being steps which marked the proficiency and grace of the performer. It was not alone, however, by individual agility, that these dances were characterized; the graceful evolutions, in which the ease of the dancers might be indulged; but on the contrary, they were of such a nature as to require constant movement and vigorous action. This period dates back to about the middle of the present century.

The Battery.—1695, October. The governor and council, in consequence of actual war between the King and Queen on one part, and the French, and the knowledge that a squadron of ships are ordered to invade this city, ordered that a platform be made upon the outmost point of the rocks, under the fort. Whereupon, as the Governor says, "I intend to build a battery to command both rivers;" therefore he requires the corporation to order the inhabitants of the Out ward part of the city, and Manning and Barnes's Island, to cut down eighty-six cords of stockades of twelve feet in length, and to have them in readiness at the water-side, to be conveyed to New York at the charge of the city and county."

1694, January 15th. The common council addressed the governor. They thanked him for ordering the platform and battery on the point of the rocks under the fort—"a work absolutely needful, and of so great a contrivance, that no doubt (by the assistance of God, your excellency's indefatigable diligence, etc.) the province for the future will be in perfect security, and the rumor thereof make the enemy change his measure, and not attack the city.

Ferry to Long Island.—1699, February. The ferry is let for seven years, on condition of security for payment given. The former to provide two great boats or scows for cattle, etc., and two small boats for passengers, one of each to be kept on each side. That the city build a ferry-house within the first year of the lease. The fare for a single person is fixed at eight stivers in wampum, or a silver twopence.

If a company cross together, each is to pay four stivers in wampum, or a silver penny; but after sunset, double ferriage. A single horse, 1s.; several in company, 9d.; a colt, 3d.; a hog the same as a single person; a sheep, half; a barrel of liquid, 3d.; an empty barrel, four stivers in wampum, or a silver penny; a beast's hide, do.; a firkin or tub of butter, two stivers in wampum; a bushel of corn, half; a hogshead of tobacco, 9d.

The rent per year is £165.

Mails.—1705, May 14th. "The Pennsylvania postman has not yet come in, and it is supposed the three days of rainy weather last week has hindered him."

The Original Mammoth.—1705, July. "There is a prodigious tooth brought here, supposed to be the tooth of a man," from the shop. "It weighs 4¾ lbs." It was dug up on the side of a hill, thirty or forty feet under ground, "near a place called Clovarack, about thirty miles this side of Albany; it is looked upon here as a mighty wonder, whether the tooth of a man or beast." Other bones were dug up, which crumbled away from exposure to the air; "they say one of them, which is thought to be a thigh-bone, was seventeen feet long."

Capture of Pirates.—1723, July 25th. The Common Council, in consideration of the services done by Captain Peter Solgard, of his Majesty's ship Greyhound, in seeking and engaging two pirate sloops, commanded by one Low, "a notorious and inhuman pirate," one of which sloops he took, after a desperate resistance, and very much shattered the other, which, by the favor of the night, escaped—" Twenty-six of the pirates were lately executed at Rhode Island; therefore, ordered that the freedom of the city, in a gold box, be presented to him—the arms of this corporation to be engraved on one side thereof, and a representation of the engagement on the other, with this motto, "*Quæsitos Humani Generis Hostes debellare superbum*, 10th Junii, 1723." Charles Le Roux, goldsmith, is paid, the 6th of August, £23 19s. for the above box and engraving the same. (This Charles Le Roux appeared, at this time, as an artist in New York.) The corporation waited upon Captain Peter Solgard, and presented said box, which he "accepted with great satisfaction, and invited the corporation to a collation to-morrow night." The pirates thus taken were captured off the east part of Long Island.

The First Presbyterian Church in Wall Street.—1718, April 16th. Gilbert Livingston, Thomas Grant, Patrick Macknight, and John Nicholls, in behalf of themselves and the congregation of dissenting Protestants, called Presbyterians, represent that they have bought a piece of ground continuous to the City Hall, or near thereunto, with intent, speedily, to erect a meeting-house for public worship, and they pay for the use of the City Hall for the same purpose, until their meeting-house is finished.

First Daily Newspaper in New York.—1785. The Daily Advertiser was started.

Cold Weather.—1780, January 29th. Eighty sleighs, with provisions, escorted by one hundred soldiers, crossed the harbor on the ice from Staten Island to New York.

A Nobleman's Mother.—1760, April. Mrs. Mary Alexander died. She had kept a store in New York for many years. Her husband was a distinguished lawyer, who acquired wealth and distinction here. Her son was educated in England, and after his father's death visited that country, where he attempted to procure recognition of his claim to the title of the Earl of Stirling. Her relationship to the late Earl was so far established as to secure the indorsement of a jury, though not under forms which were recognized by the House of Peers. He assumed the title, but was specially enjoined from its use. He returned to America, where by courtesy he was addressed by his title. He became a distinguished American general.

Estimate for the Support of the City.—1800.

Almshouse	$30,000
Bridewell	5,000
Roads	7,550
Streets	5,000
Support of Prisoners	3,000
Contingencies	29,450
Watch	25,000
Lamps	15,000
Wells and Pumps	2,500
City Contingencies	7,500
Total	$130,000

Mild Weather.—1755. The winter was so mild that navigation was open on the Hudson to Albany during the whole season.

After the Great Fire of 1776.—*Proclamation by Major-General James Robertson.* Whereas, there is ground to believe that the rebels, not satisfied with the destruction of part of the city, entertain designs of burning the rest. And it is thought that a watch, to inspect all the parts of the city, to apprehend incendiaries, and to stifle fires before they rise to a dangerous height, might be a necessary and a proper means to prevent such a calamity. Many of the principal inhabitants have applied to me to form such a watch, and have all offered to watch in person. I do therefore require and direct that all persons may take a part in this matter and turn out to watch when called for. A sense of duty and interest will lead all good subjects and citizens cheerfully to give their attendance; and any who refuse to take part in preserving the city will be judged unworthy to inhabit it. I have appointed persons to summon and superintend the Watch of each Ward, and the number of men to be given by each is subjoined. Signed, James Robertson, Major-General, Commander in New York.

The Out Ward to furnish 14 men each night.
Montgomerie Ward to furnish 15 men each night.
North Ward to furnish 15 men each night.
These to meet at the Guard-Room near Cuyler's Sugar-House.
West Ward to furnish 6 men each night.
South Ward to furnish 4 men each night.
Dock Ward to furnish 10 men each night.
East Ward to furnish 16 men each night.
These to meet at the Guard-House in Hanover Square.

The First Negro Plot in the City of New York.—The institution of slavery, as it existed in early times in New York, was a source of constant anxiety to the inhabitants of this city, arising from the turbulent character of that class of the population. This arose partly from the fact that the slave-trade was then in active operation, and New York City was the mart from whence the other parts of the colony were supplied. A slave-market was established, where the imported negroes were exposed for sale, and where other slaves stood for hire. The negroes, when newly arrived, were ill at ease, and differed greatly from the same class who had been born on the soil. Ignorant of the language of the country, and unused to labor in the fields, and to the restraint under which they were held, the imported negroes were disposed to deeds of desperate outrage, reckless of the fact that no good result to them could arise from their wild endeavors to rid themselves of thraldom. Their known dispositions, however, excited fear, which was kept alive by the occasional murders in different parts of the country, and especially by various plots of still more serious nature.

Among these was one in the spring of 1712. At this time a combination of from thirty to fifty newly-imported negroes was formed with the intention to make a general assault upon the town. Their plans were laid with secrecy, and do not appear to have been suspected before they were ripe for execution. The design appears to have been simply to murder the people and burn the town; and the time selected for beginning their bloody work was midnight of the 6th of April, 1712. The method adopted was to set fire to a house and await the coming forth of the inmates, when they, as well as others who came to quench the flames, were to be killed. The negroes were well armed, while it might reasonably be expected that citizens aroused from their slumbers by the cry of fire would be defenceless. The alarm took place about two o'clock, and the whole town was at once in uproar. Upon reaching the burning house, one citizen after another was dispatched, until the number killed and mortally wounded amounted to about twenty persons. The cry of murder, added to the general din, soon changed the character of the affray. The citizens speedily armed and charged upon the blacks, who, after a brief resistance, fled to the woods, pursued by the excited crowd of whites. Meantime, as morning broke, the whole town was placed under arms, under apprehension that the conspiracy was more widely diffused, and that there was danger of a general uprising of the slave population.

This state of things continued several days, in the course of which a large number of suspected negroes were arrested in the town, while the hunt was being continued throughout the forest, with which nearly all the upper part of Manhattan Island was then covered. These wild fastnesses offered peculiar facilities for concealment, as their rocks and caves were almost unapproachable. The negroes, however, had no friends to whom they could fly for ultimate safety, and starvation brought them forth from their hiding-places.

Some of these misguided persons committed suicide in the woods, using for that purpose the arms that they had brought with them. Others were taken and were brought to summary punishment in the most tormenting manner; some by burning at the stake; others by being broken at the wheel; others by being hung up alive. No leniency was shown to any who were known to have been any way cognizant of the plot. Self-preservation was felt to exist in putting the abject race in fear; thus extreme measures were resorted to without stint.

The horrors of that event long dwelt as a cause of disquiet to the townspeople, and occasioned a morbid subject of household gossip, until the minds of the inhabitants became infected with one ever-existing apprehension—that of a negro plot. The influence of this state of feeling affected even the best classes of the population, so that in the course of a generation afterward, upon the happening of some suspicious circumstances, as to which the proof in the light of history appears entirely inadequate to sustain the grave accusations, hundreds of the negro race were visited with terrible punishment.

BROOKLYN,

A CITY, seaport, and capital of Kings County, N. Y., situated at the west end of Long Island, on New York Bay and the East River, an arm of the sea which divides it from New York City and connects Long Island Sound with the Atlantic Ocean. Brooklyn is the third city of the Union in population. Its latitude (at the navy-yard) is 40° 51' 30" north; longitude, 73° 59' 30" west from Greenwich. Its area is about 14,000 acres, which is nearly 22 square miles.

Population.—In 1698, Breuckelen had 509 inhabitants; in 1800, 3298; in 1810, 4402; in 1820, 7545; in 1825, 8800; in 1830, 15,292; in 1835, 24,310; in 1840, 36,233; in 1845, 59,574; in 1850, 96,850; in 1855, 205,250; in 1860, 226,661; in 1865, 296,112; in 1870, 396,350. In 1877 its population is estimated, on the basis of school censuses and directory returns, at 600,000.

Commerce.—Brooklyn is a commercial port of great and constantly increasing importance. The city of New York, naturally desirous of concentrating on its own shores and at its own docks, slips, and piers, its vast commerce so long as it could find room for it, discouraged all efforts for the erection of wharves, piers, docks, or warehouses on the Brooklyn side for many years. There had been a government navy-yard in the city limits since 1801, and it had ranked as first-class since 1824, but the commerce of the city had no existence beyond a moderate coasting-trade prior to about 1844. In that year, the Atlantic Docks Company, incorporated in 1840, completed their first warehouse. This company, after passing through many discouragements, has now three miles of wharf accommodation, 40 acres of water-area, warehouse covering 20 acres, 9 steam elevators, and every facility for shipping and storing cargoes. There have been in this dock at one time 130 sea-going vessels. The Erie Basin, south of this, has a water-area of 60 acres, and the Brooklyn Basin, still further south, a surface of 40 acres. Both are surrounded with warehouses, and are thoroughly equipped for accommodating shipping of the largest class. Since 1844, there has been invested in docks and warehouses a private capital of more than $125,000,000 on the shore line of Brooklyn, which extends 8¼ miles, and has 25 miles of dockage, with vast warehouses, piers, slips, docks, and basins along the whole distance. The following statistics, gathered by careful examination in 1876, will give some idea of the extent of this commerce: In the warehouse of the Atlantic Dock Company, and others south therefrom to Red Hook Point, there is stored—grain, $26,000,000; sugar and molasses, $18,000,000; provisions, $3,300,000; flour, $1,700,000; lumber and stone, $1,800,000; cotton, $2,700,000; guano, $1,900,000; rags, $970,000; saltpetre and brimstone, $220,000; salt, $700,000; iron, $4,000,000; miscellaneous, including resin, turpentine, etc., $11,000,000; in the section north from Atlantic Docks to South Ferry, $80,000,000. That which diverges to the Gowanus Canal, comprising coal, building and other material, valued at $6,000,000; from South to Fulton Ferry, $140,000,000; from Fulton Ferry to Main street, $27,000,000; making an aggregate to this point of over $309,000,000 annually stored. These figures seem enormous, but are borne out by facts. The warehouses from Red Hook to Main street are full of merchandise, and literally overflowing. A number of other large warehouses are now in process of erection. From Main street, north-east to the bridge over Newtown Creek, a distance of four miles, there is an extensive commerce. Many ship-yards, gas-works, lumber-yards, coal-yards, sugar refineries, and most of the vast petroleum refineries and shipping-houses, are on this part of the coast-line. The annual commerce from this section, aside from the navy-yard, is somewhat more than $49,000,000. All through the year, with more or less activity, the business of loading and unloading vessels is going on. It is estimated that 2500 vessels are unloaded every year between Red Hook and Main street. In the business of warehousing alone some 5000 men are engaged along the shore-line. Brooklyn is already the largest grain depot in the world. Immense steam elevators are employed to lift and deliver the grain. The stores of E. C. Lockwood & Co. have storage for 3,000,000 bushels at a time, employ 1000 hands, and pay to the city a tax of $50,000. The flour-mills of F. E. Smith & Co. deliver 1200 barrels a day. During the receiving season, from October to December, canal-boats arrive by the hundred to be discharged. On the closing of navigation, as many as 600 canal-boats loaded with grain lie up for the winter in the basins, in many cases, with the captains and their families on board, until the cargoes can be sold. The value of the boats engaged in the grain-carrying trade is estimated at $18,000,000. The bulk of grain afloat seeking port frequently amounts to 5,000,000 bushels at one time.

Continuing the shore line from Main street to the navy-yard, and beyond to the north-eastern boundary, including the large interior dockage made by the Wallabout improvements, on the Newtown Creek, and at Gowanus Creek and Canal, it is apparent that the capacities of the city for extensive commerce can hardly be over-estimated. These are likely to be greatly aided by the removal of the obstacles at Hell Gate, at the confluence of the East River with the Sound. Five lines of steamships now ply between Brooklyn and their respective ports: the State line, to and from Glasgow; the North American line, to and from London, Newcastle, Christiania, and Bergen; the South American line, with U. S. mail, to and from Rio and other ports; the White Cross line, to and from Antwerp; the Netherlands and Rotterdam line, to and from Rotterdam. The Brooklyn *Eagle* now gives daily reports of arrivals and departures to and from this port.

The census gives, as the true valuation of Kings County in 1870, $700,000,000. The valuation of the other towns of the county in 1873 was $11,626,043. The assessed valuation of 1872 was $207,952,332.

Brooklyn has four daily papers, nine weeklies, and several monthlies, mostly advertising journals. There are, however, two monthly magazines, not very large circulation. The morning newspapers of New York City circulate almost as largely in Brooklyn as in New York, but the Brooklyn evening papers have a very large circulation.

History.—Brooklyn was named from Breuckelen ("marshy land"), in the province of Utrecht in Holland, six miles from the city of Utrecht, from which some of its earliest settlers came. The first step toward its settlement was the purchase from the Indians in 1636, by Willem Arianse Bennet and Jaques Bentyn, of a tract of 630 acres, lying at Gowanus, between Twenty-seventh street and the New Utrecht line; the second step, the purchase by Joris (George) Jansen de Rapalje of 325 acres at the Wallabout Bay, June 16th, 1637.

At the time of the discovery of Long Island shores, in 1609, by Hendrik Hudson, several tribes or settlements occupied Long Island, one of which was at Canarsie, and another, the Mareckawick tribe, at Brooklyn, which, from the spot where they were located (sandy place or shore) at the Wallabout, gave the name *Mareckawick* to that locality. Brooklyn Heights, overlooking the East River, was called in the Indian dialect *Ihpetonge* (highlands).

Families of these were at New Utrecht and Gowanus, in 1680, on the visit of the Labadists to those places in that year. The first ferry was established by license in 1642, running from Peck Slip to a point near the present Fulton ferry, from this period named "The Ferry." There were at that time five hamlets—"The Ferry," "Breuckelen," near present Hoyt on Fulton street, where stood the church; "Gowanus," around Gowanus Bay; "Bedford," inland; and "the Wallabout," around Wallabout Bay. The first house known to have been built in Brooklyn was that of Willem Arianse Bennet, located on his purchase with Jaques Bentyn, from the Indians, prior to 1643, as in that year it was burnt by the Indians in the Indian wars, and replaced by the Schermerhorn House, on or near the same site; and the second, probably that yet standing, and known as the De Hart or Bergen House, which was existing and visited by the Labadists in 1680, being then occupied by Simon Aertsen de Hart, grantee of Bennet. George Jansen de Rapalje did not come over from New Amsterdam to occupy his farm till about 1654. Later history has entirely exploded the story that his daughter, Sarah Rapalje, was the first Christian born child in New Netherlands, and also that her birthplace was Brooklyn, at the Wallabout. The Labadist manuscript, published by the Long Island Historical Society, shows that this distinction of first birth in the colony probably belongs to a male person, Jean Vigne, who was born in New Amsterdam in 1614, eleven years before the birth of Sarah, who was born in 1625. Besides, it is clear that Sarah, instead of being born at the Wallabout, as often asserted by early historians, was born in Albany (Fort Orange) in 1625, removed with her parents to New Amsterdam in 1626, lived there till after her marriage, between the age of fourteen and fifteen, was a church member in New York, and united with the Brooklyn church by certificate in 1661; was twice married in the Wallabout, gave birth to fourteen children, and died in 1685, age about sixty. There is no proof than any white person lived upon Long Island prior to 1636. Immediately upon the establishment of the ferry in 1642, grants of building lots at that point began, and that locality, as well as the other hamlets, increased. The union of all the hamlets into one incorporated jurisdiction named Breuckelen, took place in 1646, under Director-General Kieft. The Labadists, who crossed this ferry in September, 1679, speak of it as "a considerable thoroughfare," and say, " A considerable number of Indians live upon Long Island, who gained their subsistence by hunting and fishing; and they, as well as others, must carry their articles to market over this ferry, or boat themselves over, as it is free to every one to use his own boat if he have one, or to hire one for the purpose. The fare over the ferry is three stuivers in German (less than half a cent English) for each person."

In 1665, Breuckelen had attained the leading position among the towns in point of population and wealth, and was granted the privilege yearly of " a fayre and market near the ferry for all graine, cattle, or other produce of the country." Whatever the increase of population, it must have been very gradual, as (to skip a long period) the canvasser for the " New York and Brooklyn Directory" in 1796, passing up " the old road " (Fulton street), and down " New Ferry" (Main street), and through the intervening streets, gives but 125 names. The statistics of population, and the picture painted by Francis Guy of its condition up to 1820, also show that, up to this time, it held but the rank of an inconsiderable village, without institutions, commerce, or manufactures.

Over the space now occupied by Prospect Park, Washington Park, Greenwood Cemetery, Evergreen and Cypress Hills Cemeteries, was fought, on the 27th of August, 1776, the important battle which has been properly designated "the battle of Brooklyn," the first great battle of the Revolution after the Declaration of Independence. The British army was under the command of Lord Howe, the Hessians under

General von Heister. Gen. Greene being ill, Gen. Putnam was in command of the American forces. The result is well known. An important pass was left unguarded in Howard's Hills, just beyond Bedford, by which the English troops gained the rear of the American army, and defeated it with heavy loss. Those who escaped within the lines were rescued by the masterly retreat effected by General Washington on the 28th to New York, by means of boats, and under cover of a heavy fog, by which their movements were concealed. A memorable incident of this battle was the death of Gen. Nathaniel Woodhull, of Suffolk County, Long Island, while engaged on the 28th, the day after the battle, in driving the cattle eastward. He had entered the "Increased Carpenter house," two miles east of Jamaica. While there, a body of horsemen rode up, commanded by Captain Oliver de Lancey, who struck the general several times with his sword, and wounded him so severely that he died a few days after at New Utrecht, where he had been conveyed as a prisoner. The Brooklyn navy-yard was begun with the purchase, by the United States government, of forty acres in 1801, which were converted into a navy-yard, and which was designated in 1824, by the secretary of the navy, as one of the first-class navy-yards of the nation. It has since added largely to its domain by other valuable purchases, upon which are placed the United States hospital, a dry dock, and costly buildings for the repair and construction of the largest vessels.

The War of 1812.—On August 9th 1814, the patriotic citizens of Brooklyn and the surrounding country flocked to Fort Greene, and aided in rehabilitating that old fortification and following out the line of earthworks across the island, conformably to the plans of Gen. Joseph G. Swift, after whom one of the forts which cornered on Atlantic street (the "Cobble Hill Fort" of 1776) was named "Fort Swift." Every preparation was made to meet the dangers to which New York was liable from her exposed situation by sea and land. By these precautions or otherwise, Brooklyn did not, as in the Revolution, bear the brunt of the first systematic strategic conflict.

The Civil War of 1861-65.—In this emergency the city of Brooklyn was not exceeded by any other city in raising regiments and supplying material aid. Her Sanitary Fair of February 22d, 1864, was extraordinary as an effort of local unity and successful effort, the pecuniary realization reaching the magnificent sum of $402,-943.74. This was aptly characterized as the first great act of self-assertion ever made by the city of Brooklyn, and did much to bring her citizens together for other efforts.

The village charter of Brooklyn is dated April 12th, 1816; the city charter was passed April 8th, 1834; the consolidation-act uniting Williamsburg and Greenpoint with it passed April 17th, 1854, and took effect January 1st, 1855.

The new charter was passed in 1873, and went into effect the same year. The institutions which have had the greatest influence upon the social organization and material progress of the city have been the Apprentices' Library and Graham Institute (founded July 4th, 1825), the Academy of Music (open January 15th, 1861), the Mercantile Library Association, the Atlantic Docks, and the Long Island Historical Society. (*Alden J. Spooner, late Editor of " The Long Island Star."*)

BIOGRAPHICAL ENCYCLOPÆDIA,

COMPRISING

THE LIVES AND RECORDS

OF MANY OF

THE LEADING PROFESSIONAL AND BUSINESS MEN OF NEW YORK STATE.

ARRANGED IN ALPHABETICAL ORDER.

WRITTEN AND COMPILED EXPRESSLY FOR

COMLEY'S HISTORY OF THE STATE OF NEW YORK,

AND

ILLUSTRATED

WITH NUMEROUS PORTRAIT-ENGRAVINGS ON STEEL AND STONE, FROM PHOTOGRAPHS TAKEN FROM LIFE, AND ENGRAVED BY OUR FIRST ARTISTS.

———•———

NEW YORK:
COMLEY BROTHERS, 767 AND 769 BROADWAY.
1877.

BIOGRAPHIES.

BIOGRAPHY is the most important feature of history, for the record of lives of individuals appears to be invested with more vitality and interest than the dry details of general historical narrative. In biography, the attention is not distracted by a multiplicity of leading and disconnected events, but every incident that is related serves to illustrate the character of some eminent person, and is another light by which we can see more clearly the elements which form their being.

The gentlemen whose biographies make so large a portion of the work have not been selected on account of their wealth, their social position, or their particular avocation, but from other and more worthy motives. In the number are embraced the professions and most of the other callings of life, and they find a place in this book from the circumstance that they excel in their respective vocations, are men of sterling virtue, and in their efforts to establish position and fortune they have given wealth, stamina, and character to the State of New York. We have no favorites to support, no political or sectarian interest to advance, but in choosing the subjects of these biographies have been guided by a sense of duty, and a wish to pay some tribute to well-deserved merit.

Biographies of those who have become identified with the progress of the great State—who have guided and directed its business currents year by year, swelling with the elements of prosperity, and who have left the impress of their genius and judgment upon the legislative enactments of our State—must be sought after with avidity, and must be fraught with useful information.

It will be a source of satisfaction to the reader to know that the biographies of individuals who adorn this work are not drawn by the flighty imagination from airy nothingless, but represent the lineaments of men, nearly all of whom are living, have achieved lofty positions, are still active in the busy, bustling world, and afford sterling examples of business excellence and moral and social virtues.

In writing the lives of these men, the author has not attempted to swell facts beyond their proper magnitude, for the incidents which make up the biographies are of sufficient importance in themselves to vest them with interest, without the adventitious aid of the imagination.

Biographical Encyclopædia.

Allen, Lewis F., of Buffalo, N. Y., descended from Pilgrim ancestry, who emigrated from England during the seventeenth century, and settled in the colony of Massachusetts. He was born at Westfield in that State, on the first day of January, 1800, and there received most of his early education.

He came to Buffalo in April, 1827, and took charge of "The Western Insurance Company of the Village of Buffalo," as its secretary, in which he remained until the expiration of its charter, about the year 1830. He then entered the office of "The Buffalo Fire and Marine Insurance Company," recently incorporated by the State legislature, as its first secretary, about the year 1831, and had the principal charge of its affairs for nearly or quite three years.

Becoming interested in real estate operations soon after coming to Buffalo, in connection with Col. Ira A. Blossom, then agent for the Holland Land Company at its Buffalo office, they erected, in 1830–31 and 1832, several of the largest blocks of brick stores, warehouses, and dwellings on Main and other streets, which then existed in the village.

In the year 1833–4, in conjunction with a few capitalists in Boston, Mass., they purchased about 16,000 acres of land on Grand Island, in the Niagara River, then a dense forest, and built a large steam saw-mill for working up the extensive growths of white oak and other timbers with which the soil was clothed; and sent considerable quantities of it, for ship-building purposes, through the Erie Canal to New York and Boston—the first timber of the kind ever transported from the Western part of the State, and of such superior quality as to stand for many years at the head of the market quotations, as "Grand Island white oak." The timber finally becoming exhausted, the land, fertile in quality, was sold out in farms, and soon afterward became incorporated into a town under its original name, and is now populated by a substantial body of farmers; with two commodious steam-ferries, one near the south end or head of the island, and the other opposite Tonawanda, connecting with the main shore. A portion of the lower or northerly end of the island is celebrated for its valuable and productive apple, peach, and other fruit orchards.

This island, soon after its survey into farm-lots by its then proprietor, the State of New York, was selected as the proposed foundation for a Jewish colony, in the year 1825, though the scheme fell through and was abandoned.

In the year 1836, Mr. Allen became associated with several prominent business men in Buffalo and elsewhere, in purchasing and developing a large portion of the lands in the village of Black Rock, immediately adjoining the northerly side of the city, fronting the Niagara River. Its streets and extensive water-power were soon afterward thoroughly planned, and several large flouring-mills and other valuable manufacturing establishments have been since erected. Its territory is now incorporated with the city, and become an important part of its industries. In these developments, Col. William A. Bird, also an extensive land proprietor there, and other citizens, have been large and influential participators.

Possessing a decided taste for agricultural improvement and the finer breeds of farm stock, Mr. Allen has devoted much attention to those interests at his farm on Grand Island. He was one of the founders of the State Agricultural Society, in the year 1841, and its President in 1848. In the year 1838, he was a member of the State Legislature for the county of Erie.

In the year 1846, he founded and edited the "American Short-Horn Herd-Book," since continued through sixteen large octavo volumes, now annually issued, of about 1000 pages each, comprising altogether more than 70,000 pedigrees of that noble race of cattle, the most numerous and valuable of all "improved" breeds in the United States.

In several of the useful institutions and associations of the city, he has also been associated with their founders and managers down to the present time.

Allen, Orlando, was born in New Hartford, Oneida Co., N. Y., in 1803, and came to this city in 1818, and proved himself to be one of the most useful and enterprising citizens of Buffalo. He was widely known throughout the western portion of New York State as a man of uncommon talent. In many prominent public positions he displayed great executive ability, rare industry, and inflexible integrity. He made an admirable Mayor of the city in 1848, and his discharge of the responsible duties of the station won the approbation of all classes. He was for three years member of Assembly. The all-important lake and canal commerce was especially cared for and materially advanced by him. He was also for several years member of the Board of Supervisors, and twice chairman of the board. He was also Alderman from the twenty-second ward, Trustee of the Western Savings Bank, Chairman of the Building Committee which superintended and controlled the erection of the splendid edifice on the corner of Main and Court streets, Trustee of the Insane Asylum Board. As President of the Buffalo Historical Society, he displayed his characteristic ability and public spirit. Indeed, in all the stations which he ever filled, Orlando Allen proved himself fully equal to their responsibilities and requirements. Deceased was a member of the First Presbyterian church for upward of forty-eight years. He died Sept. 4th, 1874, much respected by all who knew him.

Ames, Leonard.—The subject of this sketch was born February 8th, 1818, at Mexico, Oswego County, N. Y., and was the tenth child of a family of thirteen. His parents moved to Oswego County in 1804, from Litchfield, Ct. Mr. Ames's early life consisted of being raised on the farm. At the age of twenty-three he commenced life himself by purchasing 150 acres of land, well stocked with cows. He soon became tired of farming. Being ambitious to attain business and social position, he sold his farm and commenced a small manufacturing business. Shortly after

this, he went into beef and pork packing at Syracuse, N. Y., and Delphi, Ind., which he continued nine or ten years; when he sold out, returned to his native village, and commenced a private banking establishment. He has held several positions of trust and honor; among them we may mention supervisor of the town of Syracuse. In 1857 he was a member of the State Assembly. He was also delegate to the National Convention held in Chicago, that nominated Abraham Lincoln. He afterward received the appointment of United States Assessor for the Twenty-second Congressional District, having twenty-two assistants. This position he occupied until removed by Andrew Johnson, for political reasons. In 1864, he started the Second National Bank of Oswego, was its first and only President. In 1870, he purchased one half interest in the Ames Iron-Works, which he still retains, operating the works successfully, and turning out annually 200 to 300 engines. He is just in the prime of active manhood, eminent for his public enterprise, and popular with all classes of citizens.

Amsdell Brothers—George I. and Theodore M. They who have reaped a plenteous harvest in the fields where they have labored, and have won honorable names in the community where they have resided, well deserve an honorable record in the history of their native State, and the events of their lives furnish a useful lesson to posterity. The subjects of this sketch are George I. and Theodore M. Amsdell. The former was born at Kinderhook, N. Y., and the latter at Troy. Their father, William Amsdell, was born in the county of Cambridge, England, and belonged to the honest yeomanry of that country, who brought up his children to habits of industry, and early instilled into them the love and practice of moral attributes. Their mother, Abigail Millard, was born in 1803, in Ulster County, N. Y., and could trace her ancestry back to the Pilgrims, who landed at Plymouth Rock, on the May Flower. They gave their children a practical education, and then set them to work at suitable business. The subjects of this sketch moved to Albany when quite young, and, in 1845. entered their father's brewery, learning from him all that was practical in this important branch of industry, and in which he had served a lifetime. In 1851, they went into business for themselves, taking their father's brewery, then a diminutive concern, and no more like their present structure than a pigmy is like a giant. In 1856, they commenced building their present premises, which now cover an area of 350 feet each on Jay and Lancaster streets, by 150 on Dove street. The main building is five stories high, fitted up with all the modern improvements for turning out the best material at the minimum of cost. The capacity of this colossal establishment is 200 barrels of ale per diem, and 125,000 bushels of malt per annum. Their ales have become such general favorites that they supply an enormous trade all along the Hudson River, and the country tributary to it; and in New York City they have a large distributing depot, from which they serve their products to their numerous customers in the city. The great reputation their establishment has made has been due to the fact that up till 1870, Mr. George I. Amsdell personally superintended the malting, and Theodore M. personally did the brewing for the whole establishment. This, together with the location; for there is none better in the State than Albany for brewing ale, it being the great central mart for barley and hops raised in the west, which, by the way of the Erie Canal, are brought to market at a cheaper rate than they could be by any other conveyance. The water, too, which is used, is particularly adapted by its purity and softness for making the best ales. Albany may well feel proud of her enterprising citizens, and especially of such men as George I. and Theodore M. Amsdell, who, by the erection and working of their immense brewery and malt-house, give employment to a large number of men, and indirectly add largely to the value of the agricultural portion of the State. Besides attending to the daily duties imposed by this large concern, and its business details, George I. Amsdell has for four years represented the Ninth Ward in the aldermanic board, and is also a director in the Capitol City Insurance Company. Theodore M. Amsdell is a director in the Albany Horse Railroad Company, and the Brewers and Maltsters' Insurance Company, also one of the Governors in the Albany City Hospital; positions they have both served with marked distinction and fidelity. George I. Amsdell was married September 5th, 1847, to Miss Esther J. White, of Albany, by whom he has had six children, five still living.

Theodore M. Amsdell was joined in wedlock in 1855, to Miss Ella E. Zeh, also of Albany; of this marriage five children have been born to them, only one of whom survives. The business capacity of the Amsdell Brothers is second to none. They have combined judgment that never errs in its calculation and an industry that is untiring in its pursuit of business. They commenced in the world without the gifts of fortune or the aid of auspicious patronage, but made their way to wealth and influence by their own efforts, and are indebted to no extraneous aid for their possessions. They are retiring in disposition, domestic in habits, warm in each other's friendship, and pass life chiefly in giving attention to their business, and in the serene enjoyments which nestle around their family hearthstones. They have also extensive and valuable libraries, embracing the standard works on science, history, and letters, with all of which they are familiar, and devote much of their leisure time in arduous study to keep pace with the rapid advance made by the intelligent investigations of modern science, which knowledge they have a ready aptitude to apply in the improvement of their already excellent product.

Armstrong, E. B.—A man who, from a humble position and by his own efforts, has risen to affluence and social position, and through all the events of a checkered life has preserved his integrity unimpeached, well deserves the pen of the historian and to be held up as a model to posterity. E. B. Armstrong was born in the town of Lee, Oneida County, January 10th, 1809. His father, Oliver Armstrong, moved to that locality previous to 1800. The subject of this sketch attended the school of his native town till eighteen years of age, after which he attended the private school of Oliver C. Grosvener for nearly one year. His education finished, he entered the store of his brother, General J. Armstrong, as clerk, and after two or three years of strict business training, during which time he proved himself to be the possessor of excellent business qualities, he became a partner in the business, the firm continuing until his brother's death, which occurred in August, 1852. His brother's place was filled by young members of the family for some time; finally he became sole proprietor, remaining so till 1870, when he virtually retired from active business duties. Since that time he has found his time well employed looking after his own private affairs, and in the management of his estate, which is very extensive, and includes large interests in the manufacture of iron. He has been engaged in the manufacture of pig iron, more or less, for over thirty-five years, and at one time was manager of the Talberg Furnace. During the past twelve years, he has been a Director in the Franklin Iron-Works. He is also Vice-President and Director of the Rome Iron-Works, with a capital of $400,000; and President of the Rome Merchants' Iron Mill, capital $150,000. Mr. Armstrong is also a Director of the Fort Stanwix and Central National Banks.

He was joined in wedlock in 1837 to a daughter of Henry Tibbets, Esq., an old resident of Rome, by whom he had four children; none of them, however, are living.

Mr. Armstrong has always been thoroughly identified with the interests of Rome and Oneida County, being a large real estate holder and the owner of many valuable farms in the county. He is to-day, with one or two exceptions, the oldest " Roman of them all," and has gained his position and influence by personal exertion, proving himself to be an indefatigable worker.

A history of Mr. Armstrong's life is useful for its practical instruction. He has amassed a fortune that would content the extravagant requirements of royalty. Yet he has never risked a dollar in the precarious investment of wild speculation, but day by day added to his little commencement. Attending wholly to his own business, he has become honored for his integrity and known as one of the most influential citizens of Oneida County.

Arnot, John, was born in Doune, Scotland, September 25th, 1793. When he was eight or ten years of age, his family came to this country and settled in Albany, where they resided for a short time, and then moved to Catskill on the Hudson. Subsequently they moved back to Albany, where Mr. Arnot engaged in mercantile pursuits on a small scale. In company with Egbert Egbert, Mr. Arnot moved to Elmira, N. Y., and opened his first stock of goods in a store located on Water street. He continued in business at this point ten or eleven years, and was very successful. In 1824, he was married to Miss Harriet, daughter of Stephen Tuttle. In 1830, Mr. Arnot built the brick block on the corner of Water and Lake streets, which was the first brick store built in Elmira. In 1829, he built the old foundry on the site of the Opera-House block. In 1833, the Chemung Canal Bank was organized, and he became stockholder. In 1842, he became cashier of the bank. In 1843, he became president, and held the position until his death, which occurred November 17th, 1873. In 1854, he took an active part in the construction of the Junction Canal, and became its president. In 1862, he became largely interested in mining. He was one of the projectors of the Chemung Railroad. He was a man of marvellous business sagacity and perseverance. For honesty and integrity he had no superior. Mr. Arnot was very benevolent, but it was unaccompanied by ostentation or display. He was universally loved and respected, and mourned by all classes of citizens; and during his life did more to further the interests of his beautiful town than any other of its citizens.

Astor, John Jacob.—Born at Waldorf, near Heidelberg, in Germany, July 17th,

1763, emigrated to the United States in 1783, and invested his capital in furs, which he took to London and sold with much profit. He next settled at New York, and engaged extensively in the fur trade. He exported furs to Europe in his own vessels, which returned with cargoes of foreign commodities, and thus rapidly amassed a large fortune. In 1811, he founded Astoria on the western coast of North America, near the mouth of the Columbia, as a depot for the fur trade, for the promotion of which he sent two expeditions to the Pacific Ocean. He was remarkable for his sagacity and diligence in business. He purchased in New York a large amount of real estate, the value of which increased enormously. At his death (March 29th, 1848), his fortune was estimated at $20,000,000. He left $400,000 to found a public library in New York.

Austin, Stephen Goodwin, was born at Suffield, in the State of Connecticut, on the 28th day of October, A.D. 1791. His father was Joseph Austin, Esq., of Suffield, and his mother was Sarah, daughter of Capt. Goodwin, of Goshen, in the same State.

Stephen G. was the youngest of three sons. His studies preparatory to entering college were pursued at the academy in Westfield, Mass. In 1811, he entered as freshman at Yale College, and, completing the full regular course of studies, graduated with honor on the 13th day of September, 1815, under the presidency of Dr. Dwight.

Immediately after graduating, Mr. Austin entered upon the study of the law in the office and under the guidance of Daniel W. Lewis, in Geneva, N. Y., and remained there until fully prepared for practice; and on the 15th of January, A.D. 1819, he received at the hands of Hon. Ambrose Spencer, at that time Senior Justice of the Supreme Court of the State of New York, his license to practise in that court. He remained in Geneva but a short time after his admission. During the year 1819, he removed to Buffalo, N. Y., and entered upon the practice of his profession.

His license to practise in the Court of Chancery for the State of New York is dated February 22d, 1822. Kent, Chancellor.

Mr. Austin established himself at Buffalo at a time when there were great and exciting public questions under consideration and discussion in regard to the welfare of the town, and it became evident to observing men that the then village held in its position all the elements of a great and thriving city. The subject of this notice was not slow to perceive the bearing of these questions and the advantages of the location, and never from that time wavered in his determination to make Buffalo, as it ever after was, his home.

He held for a time the office of justice of the peace, the duties of which his studies had fitted him to perform with ability; but in after-life he steadily declined public office, although often solicited to permit his name to be used in candidacy for high and responsible positions.

On the 1st day of October, 1829, Mr. Austin was married, at Middle Haddam, Ct., to Miss Lavinia, daughter of Jesse Hurd, Esq., of that place.

In 1831, the degree of Master of Arts was received by him from his Alma Mater.

Mr. Austin was a man of quick perception and acute intellect. As a man of business his judgment was sound, and as a lawyer his opinions were based on the closest analysis of the principles of law as applicable to the case in hand. He was in no sense a "case lawyer," although not averse to strengthening a cause by decisions in point.

These traits, supplemented by unwavering industry and untiring pertinacity, rendered him a formidable opponent in his profession, and secured for him the rewards of success as a lawyer; and later in life, the same characteristics enabled him to conduct his business operations and shape his investments to the best advantage and with ultimate success.

Exemplary in his character, conversation, and deportment as a gentleman, faithful to all trusts as a citizen and a patriot, kind and generous in his relations as husband and father, true to his family, his friends, and to society, prompt and practical in all business affairs, of unimpeachable integrity and sound judgment, Mr. Austin lived a laborious, useful, and earnest life, and on the 19th of June, A.D. 1872, died a peaceful death at a ripe age, with judgment, memory, and all his faculties not only not in the least impaired, but growing more and more perfect.

Babcock, Hon. George R., was born in Gorham, Ontario County, N. Y., on the 20th day of September, 1806; and his education was such only as the common schools afforded him. He taught school for a time, and came to Buffalo in 1824. Shortly after arriving here, he entered the law office of the late Heman B. Potter, where he prosecuted his studies until admitted to the bar, when he entered into partnership with General Potter. For some time the firm name was Potter & Babcock; but by the admission of E. G. Spaulding into the firm in 1836, it became and continued for several years the firm of Potter, Babcock & Spaulding. In 1835, Mr. Babcock was married to Miss Mary B., daughter of General Potter, who bore him two children: Emily, the wife of D. R. Alward, of Auburn, and Dr. H. P. Babcock, now residing in Oakland, Cal. Both mother and children survive him. About 1841, he was appointed by Governor Seward Supreme Court Commissioner, which office he held for several years. In 1842, he was in partnership with Hon. James O. Putnam, the firm name being Babcock & Putnam, and his subsequent partnerships prior to the last were with the late Thomas C. Welch, Esq., and E. C. Sprague, Esq. Although not in active practice, his partnership relations for some years past have been with Mark B. Moore, Esq. He was elected Member of Assembly in 1845; in 1850 he was elected to the State Senate, and in 1852 he was re-elected, serving two terms with distinguished ability. In the winter of 1875-76, he was appointed a member of the Commission whose duties he was giving his attention to when taken with his final illness. He was a member of the First Presbyterian church for forty years, and at the time of his death was the oldest member of the Bar of Erie County.

We have thus sketched in merest outline the career of one of the most remarkable men Buffalo has ever been able to boast of—a man altogether more remarkable for what the general public did not know of him than for what was outwardly manifest in his daily life and conversation; and the sacred duty of presenting to the world an analysis of his character must remain to some of those who knew him most intimately, and who loved him sincerely for the strength and profundity of his intellect and the depth and beauty of his heart. He was a man of great ability. His mind was not of the brilliant, flashy order, but was broad, serene, and sound to the core. Endowed with rare common sense, remarkable powers of observation, a prodigious memory, great reasoning powers, and an instinctive idea of the right in all cases, he was always thoroughly reliable in counsel, always singularly exact in his history of a law case, a person, or a locality; and a wonderfully honest, direct, and accurate thinker. He knew the history of Buffalo better than any other man, and his knowledge of men here and elsewhere in the country was simply astonishing. He was a veritable encyclopædia, with never a hint of pedantry or superior knowledge in his intercourse with men. While severely close in his reasoning and eminently practical in all things, his mind had a most agreeable flexibility, and those who were privileged to draw upon his intellectual resources found him well read and wise beyond most men of the age. He was in no sense a superficial man; he must be master of any particular subject with which he assumed to deal, or he would express no opinion about it. He was temperamentally the victim of inertia; he was modest and unobtrusive almost to the last degree, and self-assertion was an attribute entirely foreign to his nature. Apparently stiff and cold in his manner, wanting in ambition, caring only for the appreciation of a few friends, he was not, in the generally accepted sense, a public man, and never would have made a politician; but he was the idol of those who knew him for the wealth and honesty of his mind and the simplicity and purity of his life. He was a lover of any thing that was genuine, whether it was a man or a book, but he had no sympathy with any thing that wanted honesty. He was a conservative; he believed in the ancient ways; he rode his hobbies, and never gave his assent to any thing that he did not consider right. He was deliberate and methodical, and although he worked slowly, his work was faultlessly complete when it received the last touch at his hand. An able lawyer, in whose hands for many years large and important trusts have rested, a profound scholar, a benevolent, undemonstrative gentleman, a loyal, self-sacrificing friend, and an honorable citizen departed from among us when George R. Babcock died.

Bacon, Jared G., was born near Fort Ann, Washington County, September 6th, 1805. He first embarked in business with his brother in Buffalo in 1822, where he remained for several years. Subsequently he moved to Albany, and in 1829 to Troy, where he was one of our pioneer collar manufacturers, and notwithstanding the fact that it was before the invention of sewing-machines. At one time he had in his employ a great number of hands in the manufacture of shirts alone. He was one of the founders of the State National Bank, and was also prominently connected with the old Commercial Bank of this city. In the year 1854, he started in the lumber business with the late Lorenzo D. Baker, and continued in the same up to the time of the great fire in 1854, which destroyed their yard. A short time afterward he engaged in the insurance business, and was one of the first representatives appointed in this country by the Liverpool and London Fire and Life Insurance Company. He remained in the insurance business up to the time of his death, which occurred December 18th, 1872, and was one of the most successful underwriters in this section of the State. His wife, who was the daughter of Mr. Leavens, a wealthy farmer of Grant's Junction, died a few years ago. He leaves a son, Jared L., who was associated with him, and now conducts the business, together with W. J. Kelly, under the old firm style of J. G. Bacon & Son.

Troy could ill afford to lose such a man as Jared G. Bacon. He was missed both in social circles and in the banking house. He had always taken a decided interest in the

welfare of their city, and was blessed with what always ennobles its possessor, a generous heart. His absence caused a void which will not soon be filled. His demise was universally mourned, for he was a man of many friends.

Barnum, Stephen Ostrom, was born at Utica, Oneida County, N. Y., January 14th, 1816, and is a son of Ezra S. Barnum, formerly of Danbury, Ct., now of Utica, N. Y., and who is about the oldest living inhabitant of that place. He was in the United States army, and present at the taking of Fort Erie in the old war of 1812. The Barnum family in this country, from information given us by Mrs. David Barnum, of Baltimore, Md., sprang from three brothers, who emigrated from England long before the Revolution. One settled in Massachusetts, one in Vermont, and the ancestor of the subject of this sketch settled at Danbury, Ct. The original family in England was named Van Barnum, the Massachusetts branch adopting the name of Varnum.

Mr. S. O. Barnum in his early days entered the Utica post-office as clerk, then afterward accepted the position of discount clerk in the Oneida Bank. This sedentary life not agreeing with his health, he entered into co-partnership with his father in the fancy goods business, and finally struck out for himself, and removed to Buffalo, N. Y., in 1845, and opened a variety store on a very limited scale in a small wooden building on the same spot now owned and occupied by him. He at first met many discouragements from lack of capital and being an entire stranger; but he had experience and determination, which finally succeeded, and after gradual progress, he can now boast of one of the largest variety stores extant, and his reputation is as broad as the country. He is still active, attending to his business duties daily, and in the full tide of success.

Bearns, James S., was born in the city of New York, August 28th, 1816. His father, Capt. Henry Bearns, came from Holland in the early part of the present century, and was for about twenty-five years captain of a merchant-vessel plying mostly between New York port and Ireland.

The subject of this sketch received a good academic education in the city of his birth. When seventeen, he engaged himself to Thomas Morrell, wholesale grocer, with whom he remained eleven years. In January, 1845, on account of failing health, he was compelled to resign his position and go South. During the long course of his business connection with Mr. Morrell, he, by his energy and business tact, had so gained the esteem of his employer that the last year of his connection with him he was given an interest in the business as a reward for fidelity to his trust. After remaining South several months, he had so far recovered his health that he returned to New York, and, in company with John F. Fisher, commenced the wholesale grocery business, the firm style being James S. Bearns & Co. It continued as such until 1853, at which time Mr. B. bought his partner's interest, and continued alone until 1866. At this time he admitted his nephew, Joseph H. Bearns, into the firm, and it resumed the old style of James S. Bearns & Co. In 1874, Mr. James S. Bearns, determined to retire from the cares of business life, sold his interest to his nephew, who still continues the business. In 1848, he moved his residence to Brooklyn, N. Y., which he has since made his permanent home, becoming thoroughly identified with

3

her interests and institutions. In 1860, on the organization of the Kings County Savings Institution, he became its secretary, a position he filled with credit and ability till March, 1865, when he was elected its president, in which capacity he still serves, having *declined any compensation* for his services. On the 1st of June, 1854, Mr. Bearns was joined in wedlock to Miss Elizabeth J., daughter of Thomas Cosgrove, Esq., of New York City, by whom he has had five children, two sons and three daughters, all of whom survive. In his manners he is affable and genial, and his disposition frank and generous. In business matters he has always been prompt and attentive, and has made it a principle through life never to break his word when once given; and to these traits of character, together with unswerving integrity and honorable dealings, does he owe his success through life.

Belden, J. J.—This subject was born in September, 1825, at Fabius, Onondaga County, N. Y., where he resided until eighteen years old, receiving a common school education. In the humble capacity of clerk was his first experience in the affairs and tides of business. Being ambitious of distinction and notoriety, which he found impossible to attain in the country home, he in 1853 moved to Syracuse, and boldly entered into the noble calling of contractor, which has made his name so famous in the Empire State. The success that has, in a measure, attended his exertions and shrewd management are apodictical to all; for there are probably few among our readers who do not know this gentleman by reputation and his connection with several large public contracts. Like the famous Murphy, he has been a leading mover in the temperance cause. In the spring of 1877, he was elected Mayor of Syracuse, which must have been very gratifying to him after the little annoyances he was put to by some of the State dignitaries, who attempted to seize his property, including his palatial mansion, familiarly known as the "State House," for his alleged connection with the great Canal Ring frauds, by which the State was swindled out of hundreds of thousands of dollars.

In 1853, he was married to Miss Anna Gere, daughter of Robert Gere, of Syracuse.

We intended to present with this sketch a steel portrait of J. J. Belden, and had the promise of a photograph from that gentleman, though something caused him to suddenly change his mind—probably his extreme modesty. He holds several prominent positions in Syracuse banks and railroads, and continues to conduct the business of contracting on a large scale.

Benjamin, Simeon, was born in the town of Riverhead, in what was called Upper Aquebogue, Long Island, May 29th, 1792. His father was a plain substantial farmer, highly respected, and an earnest, active Christian.

Simeon Benjamin was the third son in a family of six sons and two daughters. He was accounted rather of feeble physical constitution and was allowed some special advantages for an education, which in those days consisted chiefly of extra time from farm-work for attending district-school, and an early initiation into a clerkship in a plain country store in his native town, which remains and is kept as a store at the present time. At the early age of sixteen, he came to the city of New York, and was a clerk in the store of Mr. Kipp, in Broadway.

After about two years of city experience, he returned to his native town—Upper Aque-

ELMIRA FEMALE COLLEGE, ELMIRA, N. Y.

bogue, and went into business for himself. This was in 1812, just at the beginning of the war.

This was the beginning of his success as a business man. His favorable location and the favor of a kind Providence centred at his store the trade of an extensive section. It was also greatly in his favor that other portions of Long Island found their trade greatly disturbed by the British cruisers, who intercepted the goods on their way from New York. This rendered prices and the demand such that the young merchant soon found himself with a handsome capital, and few men have ever been more intelligently and successfully cautious in preventing losses. Like the seafaring men of his native town, he could not endure a leaky ship, nor would he abide a losing business, even if the loss seemed small. It was a business crime in his eyes to have the income fall short of the expenses and outlay for a single year.

After a few years, he gathered up his capital and went to the city of New York. With long-practised economy and caution, willing to avoid ostentation, having no taste for hasty, perilous speculation, he steadily and surely added to his wealth and enlarged his business only as fast as actual gains and the soundest credit would allow. In this he was slowly but surely successful.

Passing over the subsequent period of his business history in New York City, in which he trained several clerks who have since become very distinguished business men, we next find him investing a considerable portion of his amassed capital in Elmira, with a sagacious forecast of the future growth of that place. He moved to that place in the spring of 1835, and purchased considerable real estate. The bulk of his large fortune was derived from the rising value of his village property, the erection of buildings, and the constant growth of improvements. His early habits of caution and watchfulness against all losses, small as well as great, still characterized him. Both a sound and honorable policy, and the dictates of a generous public spirit, led him to take a deep and liberal interest in public improvements, in building churches, school-houses, hotels, and especially in connecting Elmira with Seneca Lake by railroad. He was the first President of the Chemung Railroad, and perhaps it is not too much to say that he was its chief manager, and its success was chiefly owing to him. He was also somewhat largely engaged in banking, for which his peculiar style of business in some respects eminently fitted him.

He was the son of pious parents and had the covenant blessing of a godly ancestry. He was first a communicant in the church at Aquebogue. In the city of New York, he united with the Presbyterian church in Vandewater street, then under the ministry of the too celebrated Hooper Cummings.

He resided for a time in Newtown, Long Island, where he was an elder in the church of Rev. John Goldsmith, who was an uncle to Mrs. Benjamin. His next church relation was with the first Presbyterian church of Brooklyn, under Mr. John Sanford, and afterward Dr. Carroll.

From Brooklyn he came to Elmira in 1835. The next year he was chosen trustee of the First Presbyterian church, and continued by re-election to hold that office until his death, which occurred September 1st, 1868. In November, 1836, he was elected an elder, and was always an efficient member of the session—able in counsel and fully identified with the prosperity and progress of the church.

He began early a system of beneficence

but he never gave ostentatiously. Probably no man in Southern New York has, during the past thirty-five years, given so large an amount to religious, charitable, and educational objects, even besides his large gifts to the College. He was for many years a trustee of Auburn Theological Seminary. He was also for a number of years a trustee of Hamilton College. To both these institutions he made liberal donations, and freely expressed the intentions of making some further addition by bequests. For more than ten years he was a corporate member of the American Board of Commissioners for Foreign Missions, and took a deep but quiet interest in the great missionary work.

But the last and crowning object of his Christian liberality was the Elmira Female College, a fine view of which we give.

From the first he was the financial manager, as Treasurer and President of the Board of Trustees. His donation of $5000, the largest amount then subscribed by any one, fixed the location, changing it from Auburn, where it had been located, and for which a charter had been granted as the Auburn Female University. By act of the Legislature the charter was amended, the name changed, and the institution removed to Elmira.

The college opened with a debt of nearly forty thousand dollars, more than half of which was owed to Mr. Benjamin himself, and a considerable portion of the remainder to personal friends in New York and on Long Island.

After a few years, Mr. Benjamin proposed to give to the college $25,000, by releasing so much of the amount due him, on condition that the college be placed under the supervision of the Synod of Geneva, with the provision that the evangelical denominations be represented in the Board, and also with the condition that the interest of the sum so released should be every year paid into an endowment fund, for the endowment, first, of the presidency, and then of professorships, and the increase of the library.

The college accepted the proposal, and has been from that time under the care of the Synod of Geneva. Yet Mr. B. never designed to narrow its boundaries or diminish its liberal catholicity. In the recent effort to raise $50,000 by subscription to improve and endow the college and meet the conditions of the State appropriation, Mr. B. at once subscribed $25,000, in addition to his previous gift, making a total of $55,000.*

Bennett, James Gordon—A journalist, born in Banffshire, Scotland, September 1st, 1795, and educated for the Roman Catholic priesthood, emigrated to the United States in 1819, was connected with several journals published in the city of New York, and was chief editor in 1833 of the *Pennsylvanian*, a daily paper of Philadelphia. In 1835, he founded the *New York Herald*, which was very successful. He died June 1st, 1872.

Bills, Alfonzo, was born in Jamaica, Windham County, Vermont, July 9th, 1815, where he lived and worked on his father's mountain farm until seventeen years old, with the exception of the summer of 1829, when he worked for Judge Taft, of the same town, whose son Alphonso was then home on his summer college vacation, and assisted in gathering the farm crops. Young Bills little thought he was working in the hay-field with a future Secretary of War and Attorney-General of the United States.

* This was still further increased by legacy to $80,000.

Mr. Bills's early educational advantages were very poor, being obliged to work hard for his daily bread (as the injunction, "In the sweat of thy face shalt thou eat thy bread," was particularly applicable to that hard, sterile soil)—brown bread at that, except on state occasions, such as the visitation of the minister, general training-day, etc., when a wheaten loaf would be made and a general feast enjoyed.

In the summer of 1832, the subject of our sketch entered the employ of Captain Daniel Read, of Wardsboro, an adjoining town, where he worked three years, learning the tanner and currier's trade. When his apprenticeship was completed, he took his first job of finishing a lot of leather, under the coveted and exalted title of journeyman; and right here happened one of those strange freaks of chance, or, from a higher standpoint, one of those providential orderings which change the whole course of one's life. Our journeyman being ambitious to complete his job and count his first money, was in the habit of rising early in the morning. One cold Monday morning, he went to the shop between four and five o'clock, and found the stove quite full of ashes. Under the finishing-table was a wooden box, in which cold ashes were kept; he scooped out a hollow in the middle of the old, to deposit the new ashes, and in cleaning out the stove he found considerable heat, and on examination found occasionally a small coal of fire. The proprietor also saw it, and remarked, it might do mischief. Nothing more was thought of it until Tuesday night, when the whole family were startled by the crackling of fire. The house and shop were not far apart. The works were burned to the ground. The journeyman was out of a job, and the owner was out of a place of business. It is needless to say, as the burned child dreads the fire, so Mr. Bills has ever since been very suspicious of wood-ashes. Luckily for our young friend, J. & S. Newell, the merchants of the village, were just then in want of a clerk. They offered the situation to the journeyman, who gladly accepted it, and proudly exchanged the title of journeyman for that of clerk. He then began to dream that perhaps his fondest wishes might be realized. For when a mere child, he would tell his mother he intended to be a merchant, and if he could find a boy to play "store," calling sand, sugar; muddy water, molasses; and clover-heads, tea; and buy and sell, using chips as the circulating medium, he was happy. He remained with the Newells two years, occasionally driving their four-horse team to Boston, Brattleboro, and Troy, exchanging country produce for merchandise. On one of these trips to Troy, another pivot presented itself, on which hung still another important change, and which undoubtedly altered his subsequent career. He took a package of money from a neighboring merchant to A. & J. Howland, flour-merchants, River street, Troy; and while it was being counted, and a receipt prepared, he got into conversation with the senior partner, who said to him, "We are looking for a Yankee boy to enter our office, as our book-keeper is about leaving us."

The young man replied, "Guess I am the boy you are looking for, as I certainly am a Yankee, and would like to get a situation in your office."

A hurried engagement was at once entered into, and the following April our Yankee was on hand to carry out the arrangement; but as there was some misunderstanding as to the situation he was expected to fill, he declined going with Messrs. Howland, and found a vacancy in the post-office under

Judge Isaac McConihe, Postmaster, at $15 per month and board himself.

He immediately accepted it in hopes of doing better some time, and remained there about three months, when Mr. Howland again appeared and asked if he was satisfied with his situation? Mr. Bills promptly replied, "No, sir!" A new arrangement was immediately made, and the young man entered Messrs. Howland's employ in July during the height of the panic of 1837, where he remained a book-keeper until the spring of 1841, when Mr. James Howland retired from the firm, and Mr. Bills became a partner in the new firm of Howland, Loveland & Co. This firm lasted but one year, when Mr. Loveland retired, and the firm became Howland & Bills, which remained the same until 1846, when Mr. Howland died; which caused great distress of mind to Mr. Bills, as he had learned to love and respect him, and look up to him as a father. He was a noble man, honest and true.

A new firm of Howland, Sage & Bills was soon formed, consisting of James Howland, William F. Sage, and A. Bills, which was dissolved in a year or two. That firm was succeeded by Howland, Bills & Thayer; then Bills & Thayer; then by Bills, Thayer & Usher; then Bills, Thayer & Knight. Then Mr. Bills retired from the old concern and entered into business with William F. Sage again, under the firm of Sage & Bills, which remained a year or two, when, at the death of Mr. Knight, in 1867, he took his place again in the old concern under the firm of Bills & Thayer, where he remained until the spring of 1873, when he sold his interest in the mill and business to Mr. Thayer, and has done but very little since, although he yet keeps an office near the old spot, having spent the last forty years within a few hundred feet of the place he now occupies. He bought the house he now lives in, near Washington Park, nearly a quarter of a century ago. Mr. Bills has had perhaps more than his share of disasters by fire. His store was burned on River street in 1844, which was immediately rebuilt; it was again burned and rebuilt in 1846; the large down-town fire of 1855 burned the back part of his house and outbuildings. The old Merritt & Hart mill, at the nail-works, was burned while owned by his firm; also a cooper-shop burned in West Troy, in which he was interested. He also lost a barn by fire in the alley between First and Second streets.

He often speaks with much interest of a land operation he was engaged in in Illinois, with two brothers-in-law, about twenty-three years ago. They bought nearly two thousand acres choice prairie land near Geneseo, Henry County, Ill., at a low price. They then induced relatives and friends from the old Vermont hills to emigrate to the newly-purchased Illinois land. To-day there are sixteen families of their own kith and kin located within a short distance of each other, and mostly well-to-do farmers; they have all vastly improved their condition by the change. Another experience he often relates to his friends with much gusto: It was hard times with him from the time he first entered business until 1846. He had a family on his hands, and was obliged to practise the strictest industry and economy in order to keep the wolf from the door; but in 1846 a foreign war broke out, which caused a large export demand for breadstuffs. His firm, Howland, Sage & Bills, bought largely of wheat early in the fall of that year; very soon the market commenced advancing, whereat, of course, the partners felt somewhat elated. After the business of the day was over, they would get together in their office and compare notes. One Saturday evening, after getting very favorable market reports, Mr. Sage remarked he wanted a good horse; Mr. Howland said he wanted a rifle that would kill a crow as far as he could be seen; Mr. Bills said he wanted a good watch. They finally agreed to gratify these wants providing the market kept on advancing another week. The market did advance. Mr. Howland bought his rifle, Mr. Sage his horse, and Mr. Bills his gold watch, which he carries to this day, a memento of his first extravagance, also of his first successful speculation.

He has never mingled to any extent in politics; was alderman one year; received the nomination for mayor from the American party when that party was in its glory. He declined to run. Was interviewed once or twice as to taking the nomination for member of Assembly. He always said No! He was satisfied that he had neither taste nor ability to make a successful politician and retain his self-respect. He preferred to give his strict attention to the manufacture of flour, and let others more willing and capable attend to making laws. He never could get rid of his early Vermont training, that it was not quite the thing for a man to work for his own political preferment by buying his nomination, then buying his election, electioneering, and voting for himself. He thinks the office should seek the man, and not the man the office.

Mr. Bills has for many years spent a good deal of his time in working for others, and is yet doing the same thing. He has been a governor of the Marshall Infirmary for nearly twenty years, and for about ten years one of its committee of management, and for a number of years its secretary. He was a director in the old Bank of Troy until it was merged in the United National Bank; has since been a director and one of the executive committee in the last-named bank; was one of the incorporators of the Free Library and Reading-Room; was executor of three of his old partners' estates; was a member of the vestry of St. John's church for a number of years, and took quite an active part there during the rectorship of Rev. Dr. Potter, now of Grace Church, New York, for whom he formed a very strong attachment; was also one of the incorporators of the Troy Board of Trade, and its president one year; also one of the advisory committee of the Day Home in the early days of that most excellent charity.

He was married, in 1840, to a daughter of Peter Hammond, of Wardsboro, Vt. One child, now Mrs. Knight, was born in 1842.

The venerable father Hammond is yet living at Geneseo, Ill., and will be one hundred and two years old at his next birthday.

Bird, William A.—Descended in a direct line from Thomas Bird, of Hartford, in 1642. His great grandfather, John Bird, was sergeant-at-law, settled early in Litchfield, Ct., and was a large landed proprietor. His grandfather, Seth Bird, was a physician of distinguished ability in Litchfield. His father, John Bird, was a graduate of Yale College, studied law with Tappan Reeve, and settled in Troy, N. Y., in 1791. He was a member of the Legislature in New York City in 1796 and 1797, and at Albany in 1798, the first year the Legislature met at that place. He was a member of Congress in 1800 and 1801. William A. was born in Salisbury, Ct., March 23d, 1797, at the residence of his maternal grandfather, Colonel Joshua Porter, his father being then in the Legislature in New York City. He was fitted for college at Lenox Academy, and entered Yale College in 1813; but left the next year on account of his mother's sickness, and did not return. He was a clerk in a store in New York in 1815–16. In 1817, he was appointed Assistant Surveyor with the Commission for running the boundary-line, under the sixth and seventh Articles of the Treaty of Peace at Ghent. He served as such in 1817 and 1818, and in 1819 was made principal surveyor, and had charge of the survey, until, having completed the surveys and maps from St. Regis, on the St. Lawrence, through the lakes and rivers to the Nebish Rapids in the St. Mary's River (the terminus of the sixth Article), in 1822, he resigned and soon after settled permanently at Black Rock.

In 1824–25 and 1826, he was employed in the construction of the piers and harbor of Black Rock. In 1827, in company with General Porter and Robert McPherson, they built the *first flouring-mill* at Black Rock. In 1835 and 1836, he superintended the building of the Buffalo and Niagara Falls Railroad, and was director, superintendent, and treasurer of that road until it was leased to the New York Central Railroad Company in 1823–24. In 1852, he was appointed Supervising Inspector of Steamboats, and with the first Board assisted in forming a code of rules, which, with little variation, have continued to this time. He was several years supervisor of the town, and was twice elected and served in the Legislature in 1842 and 1851. In 1854, he was elected President of the Erie County Savings Bank, when first organized, and has continued in that situation to this time.

He early became a large owner of real estate at Black Rock, and was deeply interested in the growth of the place. In 1836, he was associated with L. F. Allen, H. Pratt, and others in the purchase of a large part of the lands in the village plot, and for many years was an active agent in the construction of basins, flumes, and other facilities for the mills and machinery being erected on the water-power, and in the laying out and opening of streets and other improvements.

Blossom, Colonel Ira A.—Colonel Blossom was born in Monmouth, Kennebec County, Maine, December 24th, 1789. His early education was from the common schools, though later he attended the academy of his native town. Early in the year 1810, at the age of twenty, he went to Erie, Pa., and took charge of an academy, continuing in that employment a year or two, after which he studied medicine and practised that profession for a time in Erie; from thence he removed to Meadville, Pa., and was employed by the Holland Land Company in the sale of their lands in that State, with Harm. Jan Huidokoper, Esq., where he continued several years till 1826, when the company employed him to take the local agency for the sale of their lands in Niagara and Erie counties, N. Y., his office being in Buffalo.

In 1828, he was espoused to Miss E. J. Hubbard. Their only child, a daughter, is still living.

He was interested with large interests of a public nature, such as the settlement of the affairs of the late United States Branch Bank; also another State bank located in Buffalo.

Though frequently solicited by his fellow-citizens to become a candidate for important and responsible civil trusts, he always preferred the tranquil satisfaction of a life of private benevolence to the enjoyment of public honors.

He was called from this transitory life October 22d, 1856, and his loss was sincerely felt, not only by the immediate circle of his intimate friends, who lost in him a quiet, genial, and most attractive gentleman, but also by the destitute, whose wants his liberal hand was ever ready and open to relieve, by the sufferers whose sorrows have been soothed by prompt and feeling sympathy, and by the numerous young men whom he assisted with his credit and his means, and who were indebted to him for the beginning of their prosperity.

He was a man of marked character, combining great business capacity with singular suavity of manner and great firmness and decision, and he illustrated a long life by the most unblemished integrity and the faithful discharge of every public and private duty.

Bowen, Judge Levi Fowler. — This distinguished jurist was born November 11th, 1808, at Homer, Cortland County, N. Y., where his parents, Levi and Anna Bowen, had for some time lived, though they were originally from Woodstock, Ct. Levi Fowler Bowen, the subject of this sketch, was sent early to school, and afterward received a preparatory education at the Academy at Homer. He then entered Union College at Schenectady, from which institution he graduated with honors during 1830. He then, for a short season, attended law school at Lexington, Ky. After which, he read law with Joseph C. Morse and Judge Woods, at Lockport, N. Y., and in due season was admitted to the practice of his profession. Soon after this eventful period, he became a partner with his former preceptors, continuing as such five years, when J. C. Morse retired from the firm. The copartnership with Judge Woods continued for some time after this. It, however, was ultimately dissolved, when he took into partnership his nephew, G. W. Bowen, who had been prepared for the law by and read under him. After being admitted to the bar, Levi Fowler Bowen used all his industry, for which he is now remarkable, to qualify himself thoroughly in his profession. In 1845, he was elected a member of the State Assembly, and in 1867 a member of the Constitutional Convention. During his professional career, he has been Judge of the Supreme Court, member of the Court of Appeals, County Judge, a position he still holds, besides being President of the National Exchange Bank of Lockport. In 1840, he was joined in wedlock to Miss Sylvia M. De Long, who departed this life in 1867. As a member of the Niagara County bar, by the consent of his professional brethren, he stands proudly eminent. He is profound as a lawyer, as a judge, and as a speaker before court and jury. Judge Bowen is now seventy years of age, with a mind matured by experience, a constitution that is hale and vigorous. Without injuring any one, he has accomplished much; and as a judge, lawyer, a citizen, and a man he deserves the esteem of posterity.

Brand, John, was born in Germany, January 1st, 1821, received a common-school education, and at the age of thirteen was apprenticed to the soap-and-candle making business, at which he worked till he was twenty-nine years of age, when he came to this country, working on a farm and at many other laborious occupations. In 1853, he owned a brick-yard, with which, together with a garden for raising vegetables, he occupied himself till 1860, when he engaged in the retail grocery and provision business, at which he remained ten years, when he sold out with the intention of retiring from business life. But in 1872 he embarked in the leaf-tobacco business, at which he is still engaged. Though of a retiring disposition, he has been compelled to accept several local official positions, such as supervisor, city treasurer, police commissioner, etc., all of which he has filled with honor.

Bradley, George B.—This distinguished jurist was born at Greene, Chenango County, N. Y., February 25th, 1825. His education included common-school and academic training. In May, 1848, he was admitted to the bar at Oswego, N. Y., when he immediately moved to Steuben County, where he has practised law ever since, residing at Corning since 1852. Filled with honorable emulation and a fair field before him, it was not long before he became known as a rising man in his profession. In 1871, he was nominated in the twenty-seventh district for State Senator, though defeated by a small majority. In 1872, he was appointed by Governor Hoffman a member of the Constitutional Commission. In 1873, he was again nominated for the State Senate, and elected by over 2800 majority. In 1875, he was again nominated and elected, filling the positions each time with distinction and ability. He has been a stirring practical man, both in his public and his private life. He has done much and all honorably. He is a polished, ready, eloquent, and most effective speaker, and takes a prominent part in all important debates. He signalized his entrance into the Senate by his minority report from the Committee on Privileges and Elections on the Abbott-Madden contested election case. He favored the retention of Abbott as sitting member until all the evidence in the case had been offered and reported on by the committee. His speech in support of his report was the most able and eloquent presentation of Mr. Abbott's claims that was addressed to the Senate. In the community in which he lives he enjoys the entire confidence of all who know him, regardless of party or condition, as one of the purest of men, reliable in every respect, though modest and retiring, passing for less than his real worth; a man of great attainments, which are sound and substantial.

Burrell, Harry, was born in Sheffield, Berkshire Co., Mass., November 28th, 1797. When six years old, he moved with his parents to Salisbury, Herkimer Co., N. Y., and there received all his education from the public schools of that locality. At an early age he commenced to help his father on the farm. Afterward he embarked in farming for himself, besides dealing largely in cheese, which he collected from the farmers, sending it to New York, and from there shipped it to European markets, he being among the first who ever sent cheese to England. He now owns twelve large dairy-farms, which are all sub-let, his farmers receiving two fifths of the proceeds, and he the remaining three fifths.

Mr. Burrell has been married three times: first to Miss Charlotte Waterman, who died April 10th, 1821; next to Miss Ormenda Carr, who died January 17th, 1839, and by whom he had seven children, four sons and three daughters. His third marriage took place September 17th, 1839, to Miss Sarah M. Hamlin, by whom he has had two sons.

The principal cause of success has been active attention to business; and though now eighty, he is in the full bloom of manhood. One of the effective attributes of his popularity is the purity of his character. It is this which has given him the esteem of all men. He will leave as a heritage to his children wealth, honor, and position—and all has been his own work.

Burrill, T. N., was born at Elbridge, Onondaga County, N. Y., March 2d, 1832. His father's and mother's names were Lyman and Electa Burrill. His early education was confined to the opportunities afforded by the schools of his native town, which he attended until he was seventeen, when he moved to Vernon, Oneida County, N. Y., and filled the position of clerk for one year, when he moved to Penn Yan, Yates County, N. Y., and clerked there for two years, when he went into business for himself. In 1862, he sold out and entered the army; returning in 1866, he for some time made Rochester his home, and finally moved to Buffalo, and engaged himself in the furniture business. The firm he is now a member of is the well-known house of Burrill, McEwen & Co.

Mr. Burrill was married November 1st, 1859, to Miss Julia A. Robbins, of Penn Yan, the issue of which has been two children, only one of whom survives. No man really occupies a more enviable position in the community of which he is a member, nor more clearly exemplifies the legitimate result of well-directed energy, industry, and thoroughness of purpose.

Carryl, Lorenzo, was born January 15th, 1816, in Schoharie County, N. Y., and was the oldest son of N. F. Carryl, a native and merchant of that county. The subject of this sketch received a good common school and academical education, after which he served in his father's store till twenty years of age. In this way he obtained a good business training. In 1836, he moved to Herkimer County, continuing to act as clerk for four years, when, stimulated by honorable business emulation, he commenced for himself as a country merchant. This proving successful, he became largely identified with the cheese interest, for which Herkimer County is so justly noted, and in this branch he was engaged over twenty-five years, after which he went into dairy-farming and banking. Virtually retiring from business, he in 1867 removed to Little Falls, where he has since resided. In 1842, he was joined in wedlock to the eldest daughter of William Burrell, Esq., of Salisbury, by whom he has had eight children, three of whom survive, one daughter and two sons. The latter are lawyers practising at Little Falls. Mr. Carryl has been the architect of his own fortune. He has always followed the golden maxim, "Attend to your own business, and it will attend to you." As far as worldly wealth is concerned, he has accomplished a sufficiency, and now is retired. In review of his life he does not have to mourn over an ill-spent youth. He has filled many important positions in life, among which we may enumerate many trusty offices, and in 1852 he was elected sheriff of the county. In 1870 he was appointed by Gov. Hoffman, as one of the State Assessors. He was also delegate from his district to the famous "Charleston Convention," and was for a number of years a member of the State Democratic Committee. In the fall of 1860, he was a Democratic candidate for Congress. The district being largely Republican, he suffered honorable defeat. Mr. Carryl is now director in the Herkimer County National Bank and Warrior Mower Company. His life is a bright example to the living and to posterity.

Case, George M.—In speaking of the commercial interests and developments of New York by her prominent citizens, it is with pleasure we produce a brief notice of George M. Case, of Fulton, Oswego County, N. Y., one of her well-known and successful operators. He was born at Fulton, N. Y.,

August 29th, 1827, to which place his parents removed from Oneida County, N. Y., two years before. Here he received his early schooling and training, and when seventeen, he taught school one winter. After this, he acted as clerk in a general store, where he remained until of age. At this time he entered into partnership with his father and brother, continuing in trade until 1861, when he commenced business for himself as contractor. This particular branch had been a specialty with his family for many years. In it he proved successful, and so continued until 1870, when he was elected cashier in the Citizens' National Bank of Fulton, a position he still holds. He was also a director for fifteen years in the Oswego River, now First National Bank, a position he filled with great benefit to the institution. In 1872 and 1876, Mr. Case represented his congressional district in the Republican State Committees. In the last legislature he represented the Second Assembly district of Oswego County. In September, 1850, he was joined in wedlock to Miss French, also of Fulton, by whom he has one son and one daughter.

Thus he has added to his interests, and through his shrewd business management, observation, and extensive knowledge, has managed to make his investments profitable. His tastes are elegant and refined, and since his virtual retirement from the pressing duties of business, he has found enjoyment in the cultivation of those tastes. In manners he is affable and genial, and his disposition frank and generous. In business matters he has always been prompt, and has never allowed his engagements to be unfulfilled or postponed.

Chatfield, Thomas I., was born at Great Barrington, Berkshire County, Mass., September 16th, 1818, where he resided until he was twenty years of age, during which time he was brought up on the farm, receiving, during the winter months, the advantages of the common schools of his locality, until eighteen years old. He then apprenticed himself to a baker, with whom he remained two years, when he left home for the then called "West," and landed at Owego, Tioga County, N. Y., March, 1839, where he has since resided. For the first six months he lived out as a journeyman baker; after which, he bought the business and connected the grocery trade with it. Three years later, he sold the bakery and moved his grocery business on to Front street, which he has since continued. In 1849, he was visited by fire, and lost every thing, even his insurance. Stimulated by ambition, he on the same day of his loss made a fresh start, and had a stock of goods on sale before nightfall, proving successful. In 1853, he built a large block on Main street, occupying the corner store himself, where he remained about five years. His great and growing business requiring more room, he moved on to his present site, and here in 1870 the fiery element paid him another visit, destroying every thing. He immediately rebuilt, during which time he occupied the adjoining store. Aside from giving his close attention to his large business, he has held the positions of president, trustee, and supervisor of the village of Owego on various occasions; he has also been vice-president of the National Union Bank of Owego, and director in the Bank of Owego. In 1853, he represented the county of Tioga in the State Assembly. In 1872 and 1873, he served in the State Senate, with distinction and honor.

Mr. Chatfield was twice married, the first time in 1841. His second marriage occurred in 1858, when he was joined in wedlock to

Lucy B. Goodrich, of Owego. By this marriage one son was born, October 4th, 1871.

He has amassed a large estate; but we are happy to say his charities have always increased in the ratio of his growing fortune, and few men have lived who have been of more substantial benefit to society than Thomas I. Chatfield.

Childs, Henry, the subject of this sketch, was born in Deerfield, Franklin County, Mass., on the 18th day of July, 1819, and is descended from ancient American stock. His great great great grandfather, Deacon Richard Childs, settled in Barnstable, Mass., about the middle of the seventeenth century. His son, Deacon Samuel Childs, settled in Deerfield, Mass., as early as 1709. His son, Deacon Samuel Childs, Jr.; grandson, Amzi Childs; and great-grandson, Henry Childs, were all born, died, and are buried in the town of Deerfield, Mass.

Henry Childs, first above mentioned, was sent to school when young, and had all the advantages of early mental culture. When twenty years of age, he commenced a course preparatory for college at Phillips Academy, Andover, Mass., entering Yale in 1842, and graduating in 1846 with full honors. The same year he located in Cleveland, O., where he remained eleven years, engaged during this time in teaching and in book business.

Mr. Childs was always remarkable for perseverance and ambition to excel in business pursuits; and having faith in the future of Buffalo, N. Y., he moved to that city in 1857, an opening being afforded to engage in the business of iron manufacture in a forge. This vocation he has since then successfully pursued, being at present sole proprietor of works known by the name of Buffalo Steam Forge.

On the 19th of August, 1847, Mr. Childs joined in wedlock to née Miss Elizabeth Hitchcock, also of Deerfield, Mass. (whose ancestors sleep in the same cemetery as his); and of their marriage have been born four children, the three youngest of whom survive. Mr. Childs is a member of the La Fayette street Presbyterian church, and through his liberality and devotion has been appointed to some of the most responsible positions of the church.

In manners he is affable and genial; his disposition frank and generous.

In business matters he is always prompt, never allowing his engagements to be unfulfilled or postponed.

In the community in which he lives he enjoys the entire confidence of all who know him, as one of the purest of men, reliable in every respect, though modest and retiring, and passing for less than his real worth. A man of large attainments, which are sound and substantial.

Clarke, Freeman, was born in Troy, N. Y., March 22d, 1809. At an early age he began business for himself as grocer and dealer in country produce. In 1829. when but eighteen years old, he went to Albion, Orleans County, with a large stock of goods bought on credit, where he engaged in mercantile pursuits, the manufacture of flour, and other successful enterprises. In 1837, he was elected cashier of the Bank of Orleans, at which he served eight years, when he removed to Rochester, where he conducted a large and successful banking business for many years, and where he has held office in several large companies.

Mr. Clarke has always taken more or less interest in politics. Up to 1837, he was identified with the Democratic, and subsequently with the Whig and Republican parties. He was vice-president of the Whig State Convention, in 1850, in which Washington Hunt was nominated for governor. The president, Hon. Francis Granger, seceded with a portion of the delegates, and organized as the Silver Gray and Know-Nothing party. Mr. Clarke acted as president of the convention after Mr. Granger retired.

In 1852, he was a delegate to the Whig National Convention which nominated General Scott for the presidency. He was vice-president of the first Republican Convention of New York, in which Myron H. Clark was nominated for governor, and Henry J. Raymond for lieutenant-governor. In 1856, he was chosen presidential elector on the Fremont and Dayton ticket. In 1862, he was elected a representative from New York to the Thirty-eighth Congress, at the expiration of which he declined a re-election. In 1865, he was appointed Comptroller of the Currency. During the administration of this office, the State banks were nearly all reorganized under the National Currency act. In 1867, he was elected a member of the New York State Constitutional Convention, of which he was one of the leading members.

In 1870, he was re-elected a representative from New York to the Forty-second Congress, in which he served on the Committee on Appropriations.

In 1872, was re-elected to the Forty-third Congress, in which he served on the Committee of Foreign Affairs. In 1876, was candidate from his district for presidential elector.

As a business man Mr. Clarke has been uniformly successful, and has discharged the duties of every public position he has held with great credit and with the approval of his constituents.

Comstock, George Franklin.—The subject of this sketch was born of revolutionary ancestry, at Williamstown, in the county of Oswego, August 24th, 1811. His parents emigrated from Connecticut before the commencement of the present century. His father was a soldier and non-commissioned officer in the revolutionary army. Having entered the service when very young, he continued through the war, and was at the siege and surrender of Yorktown. He died in the boyhood or early youth of his son, who was left without means of acquiring a liberal education. The latter was distinguished at a very early age by the love of study and books, and he enjoyed some of the advantages of the common schools of that day. Thrown upon his own resources, he resolved to achieve a liberal and classical education. He taught in the common schools, and receiving aid from liberal friends, he entered Union College at Schenectady, from which he graduated with high honors in the year 1834. After graduating, he taught for a year or two the Greek and Latin languages in a classical school at Utica, of high reputation, pursuing at the same time the study of the law in that city. In 1835, he removed to Syracuse, where he has since resided. He finished his preparatory law studies in the office of the late B. Davis Noxon, a lawyer of great distinction at the bar of Central New York, and was admitted to practice in the year 1837. In 1839, he was joined in wedlock with Cornelia, the daughter of Mr. Noxon. After admission to the bar, he entered at once upon a large practice, to which he applied himself with extraordinary industry, while continuing his professional reading.

In 1874, after ten years of practice, he received from the Governor the appointment of Reporter to the decisions of the Court of Appeals, which was the tribunal of last resort in the State. This appointment might be deemed flattering to a young lawyer, because the position had usually been filled by the best legal talent in the State. The names of Judge Denio and Nicholas Hill, who had preceded him in the same position, are familiar to the profession. During the three years for which he held this appointment, he prepared and published four volumes of the decisions of that court, practising during the same period actively as counsel, and mainly at the bar of that court. In 1852, he was invited by President Fillmore to fill the office of Solicitor of the Treasury of the United States. He accepted this appointment, and retired from the office with the administration of Mr. Fillmore, on the 4th of March, 1853, resuming immediately his professional practice in the higher courts. In 1855, he was elected by the Conservative Whigs and Americans as judge of the Court of Appeals, and remained on the bench for six years, during two of which he was the Chief-Justice. He was nominated for re-election by the Democratic party in 1861, but was defeated with all the other candidates for State officers nominated by the same party. This event was deemed by him most fortunate. He wisely chose to resume his career at the bar. Having become widely known as a lawyer, his decisions as a judge had enhanced his reputation, and opened a field of practice in causes of the first importance. Soon after leaving the bench, he found time to annotate and edit for the heirs of the late Chancellor Kent a new edition of his celebrated commentaries.

In 1867, he was elected a delegate for the State at large to a convention called for the purpose of revising the State Constitution. Prominent among the causes for calling this convention was the necessity for reorganizing the judicial system of the State, especially in respect to the Court of Appeals. To that branch of the work of the convention Judge Comstock gave his particular attention, and a new judiciary article was framed, which was accepted by the people of the State, on a separate submission to the popular vote, while the residue of the work of the convention was rejected. To his efforts in the convention, and in securing the approval of the public, the important changes in the judicial organization of the State are, in a very important sense, due.

In politics he belonged to the Whig party, while it existed. When it went out of existence, he joined the Democratic party, to which he has steadily adhered ever since. He mingled somewhat actively in political discussion before and during the war of the rebellion, and his speeches and addresses commanded the public attention, especially in the constitutional aspects which the cast of his mind imparted to them. His views were considered decided and pronounced in opposition to the measures and policy of the Republican party in power. He is still actively as ever engaged in his profession, but only in its higher walks. Upon his private life no stain has ever rested, and as a citizen he is distinguished for the prominent part he has taken in the foundation and care of public institutions of learning and charity.

Cooke, C. W., was born at Preston, New London County, Ct., in the year 1800. During his youth, he had all the education afforded by the schools in the locality of his home. After which, he entered his father's factory, where he received his early business training. In 1820, he, in company with two brothers, moved to North Hampton, and there started a woollen factory, which they continued for ten years. In 1830, he and his brother James moved to Lowell,* Mass., and took charge of the Middlesex Woollen Mills. In 1845, the subject of this sketch moved to Seneca Falls, where he remained some time as superintendent of woollen mills, and finally moved to Waterloo, N. Y., to take entire charge of the large woollen mills there, continuing in that position until his death, which occurred February 15th, 1873, surrounded by his wife, family, and friends, deeply mourned and beloved as a faithful Christian. During his life's pilgrimage, he was very much interested in Sunday-schools, and during his residence both in Lowell and Waterloo was superintendent of the Episcopal Sunday-schools, and in them a great worker.

Through all the vicissitudes of a long business life, he maintained a character of the most perfect integrity, and died amidst the love and respect of zealous, admiring friends; and hundreds of young hearts who are religiously educated by his bounty breathe his name with gratitude.

Cooke, William Warren, was born August 23d, 1804, at Fort Ann, Washington County, N. Y., where he resided until he was twenty-six years of age, during which time he received a good education.

In 1831, he removed to Peru, Clinton County, N. Y., and in company with his elder brother, Calvin Cooke, went into the lumber and iron business. This continued until 1845, when the copartnership was dissolved. In 1836, Mr. W. W. Cooke removed to Whitehall, and in 1838 formed a copartnership with a younger brother in the lumber business, which continued until 1846, when it was terminated by the decease of his brother.

W. W. Cooke carried on the lumber trade at Whitehall alone until 1862, when one of his sons, Mr. W. H. Cooke, was admitted to a partnership in it, the firm name being W. W. Cooke & Son, which firm exists at the present time.

During his connection with the lumber business, he has built six steam planing-mills, of which one was in Canada, and was finally abandoned in consequence of the effect on the business of the Reciprocity Treaty between the United States and Canada.

During an experience of upward of forty-five years, steady and increasing prosperity has attended him.

He was among the first to import lumber from the Ottawa and lower St. Lawrence into the United States, a trade since grown to enormous proportions between the two countries.

He established a reputation for strict integrity and fair dealing in all transactions with individuals and the two governments, to which his large operations made him commercially responsible.

Besides the care bestowed upon his large business operations, he was one of the organizers and directors of the Commercial Bank of Whitehall, also a director in the old National Bank since its organization; director in the New York and Canada Railroad, Saratoga and Whitehall Railroad; director and president of the Whitehall and Rutland Railroad—positions he filled with distinction and ability.

He was joined in wedlock June 5th, 1832, to Miss Hearty C. Clark, of Middletown, Vt., by whom he has living six children. She was one of the family of Enos Clark and

---

* The two brothers had charge of the Middlesex together.

Electa Colver, and was born at Middletown, September 6th, 1805. She possessed in an eminent degree superior traits characteristic of both her paternal and maternal families, and through life demonstrated the real use of woman's peculiar and extraordinary power without ostentatious display. She exerted a positive and salutary influence over her family in the home circle, where all woman's virtues shine the brightest. She died June 3d, 1874, deeply mourned by her family and friends.

Mr. Cooke has been a staunch member of the Baptist Church since 1823, and one of the finest edifices erected for Christian worship at Whitehall was built mainly by his assistance.

Mr. Cooke is now in his seventy-third year, and has virtually retired from active business life. He lives at his mansion on a farm of 500 acres at Whitehall.

He has always been a working man; in fact, still works, enjoying a green old age. He has not frittered away his time in visionary impossibilities or slothful inaction, but "honorable labor" has been the maxim of his life, and to it he is indebted for the worldly comfort he possesses in the decline of life.

To his industry, integrity, philanthropy, and domestic virtues he owes the tribute of respect that is paid to his character.

Cornell, Ezra, was born at Westchester Landing, N. Y., January 11th, 1807. Soon after the invention of the telegraph, he devoted his attention to that enterprise, became very wealthy, and in 1865 founded the Cornell University. Died December 9th, 1874, at Ithaca, N. Y.

Crocker, Leonard, was born at Argyle, Vermont, March 17th, 1805. His father, Rev. Lemuel Crocker, was a Congregational clergyman.

While Leonard was an infant, his parents removed to Whitehall, New York. His father died suddenly March 20th, 1820. In 1825, the subject of our sketch was married to Miss Penelope Parks, of Albany, who still survives him. During the next thirty years after his marriage, he was engaged in the business of transportation, residing a part of the time in New York City, and afterward at Kenosha, Wisconsin.

In the spring of 1856, Mr. Crocker came to Buffalo, and purchased a portion of the track known as the Tifft farm, lying on the lake shore south-east of the city. He at once took the superintendency of the cattle yards.

In the early part of the year 1865, the extensive stock-yards of the New York Central Railroad were opened at East Buffalo, and to them the business was transferred, Mr. Crocker continuing in charge till his death, which occurred January 2d, 1870. We believe it can truly be said that during this long period he never made an enemy.

During all the time of his devotion to the duties of a business so complicated and absorbing, Mr. Crocker was distinguished as a public-spirited and prominent citizen, and an active and earnest Christian. The Methodist Episcopal church of St. Mark's was built up and sustained in a large degree by his contributions.

Cushman, Paul.—The subject of this sketch was born at Albany, N. Y., December 25th, 1822. His father, P. Cushman, was originally from New Hampshire, and his mother, Margaret McDonald, was a native of New York State. From 1833 until 1840, Paul Cushman attended the Albany Academy.

After finishing his education, he entered the employ of Isaac Newton, as clerk, a position he filled two years, when he moved to Oswego for one year, where he acted as agent for a house at Albany. He then returned to Albany, and in 1849 commenced the produce and commission business for himself. In 1853, he formed a copartnership with his brother, Robert S. Cushman (deceased); they continuing together until 1869, when, on account of declining health, his brother retired. Mr. Cushman still continues the business, as importer of wines, brandies, and mineral waters, under the firm style of Cushman & Co.

In 1845, he was joined in wedlock to Miss Mary Jane Taylor, daughter of Captain I. I. Taylor, of Oswego, N. Y., who died in 1854. The issue of this marriage was two children. He was married a second time, 21st January, 1856, to Miss Julia A. C. Blackwell, of Richmond, Va., by whom he has had three children.

Mr. Cushman's life has been one of great activity, and besides attending to his usual business duties he has held the position of school commissioner; director in the Capitol City Insurance Company; trustee in the National Savings Bank; trustee of the Albany Analine and Chemical Works, besides having interests in railroads and such other projects that have aided to develop the business industries of Albany. He is now in the full vigor of manhood, and has already accomplished what many men lay out as the work of a protracted life—"wealth, honor, and the goodwill of all men."

Cuyler, George W., born at Palmyra, February 17th, 1809. Died at Palmyra, July 20th, 1876. He was the eldest son of Major William Howe Cuyler, who was killed by the enemy at Black Rock, during the war of 1812.

Mr. Cuyler was educated at Middlebury, N. Y.; was two years in the National Academy at West Point, but, leaving for the study of law, did not graduate. He studied law with his guardian, the late Heman Bogert, of Geneva, and practised his profession at Palmyra until 1840, engaged during portions of the same time in mercantile business, and also owned and edited the *Wayne Sentinel*, in conjunction with the late Judge Theron R. Strong. About 1840, he gave up his profession and entered the banking business, in which, during the balance of his life, he continued actively engaged. He was president of "Cuyler's Bank" from 1839 till 1864, when it became the "First National Bank of Palmyra," of which institution he continued president until his death.

During the whole of his life he was an active Democrat, with an influence largely recognized in the councils of his party and the politics of the State. In financial circles he was regarded as a conservative financier of distinguished ability. He was a vestryman and warden of the Episcopal Church for more than forty years. With the general material interests of that church his name is intimately connected, and it was the object of his constant care and generous and repeated liberality. He was of quiet and unobtrusive tastes —of remarkable industry and scrupulous integrity—and he was led to decline frequent offers of large place and emolument, because of his devotion to his family and his care for the interests of the village in which he was born, lived, and died.

Dakin, George, was born January 10th, 1815, at Concord, Mass. His father was Amos Dakin, and his mother a Miss Barritt, of the same place, and he can date his ancestors back to the early arrivals at Plymouth Rock, who reached these shores soon after

the May Flower. During his early life, he attended the common schools of his native town, and in 1834 moved to Geneva, N. Y., where his brother Eldridge was in the forwarding business, and connected himself with him. In the spring of 1837, he was engaged as captain to ply on the Seneca Lake, and for the next fifteen years commanded in turn all the new steamers built by the company he was with, including the famous steamer Ben Loder, named after the then president of the Erie Railroad Company, and in whose interests she was running. During this time, Mr. Dakin was married to Miss Charlotte Brown, of Albany, N. Y., in August, 1841, the issue of which has been seven children. After the railroads killed the lake business, Mr. Dakin engaged in the coal trade at Geneva, receiving the first load of coal that came into that town from Scranton, after the Delaware, Lackawanna, and Western Railroad was opened. In this business he continued successfully for three or four years, when he sold out, and commenced farming. This vocation did not agree with him, and in 1859 he accepted the position of travelling agent for the Delaware, Lackawanna, and Western Railroad Company's coal interests, with headquarters at Syracuse. In the winter of 1861, he was sent to Buffalo to locate yards for receiving and shipping their coal, and was appointed their local agent. At that time, 5000 tons of anthracite coal overstocked a market that now consumes over 500,000 tons per year.

The association is now composed of the Delaware, Lackawanna, and Western Railroad Company, J. Langdon & Co., the Delaware and Hudson Canal Company, and W. L. Scott & Co. of Erie. Mr. Dakin has remained connected with the association ever since its formation, and now has charge of the retail and shipping business at Buffalo. The position is one full of onerous responsibility, and the manner in which the duties are performed is best attested by the results that have followed.

Dart, Joseph, was born at Middle Haddam, Ct., April 30th, 1799, and was the third son of Joseph and Sarah Dart, whose family consisted of fourteen children.

During his youth, he received a common-school education, and was also for a time a pupil of the Rev. David Selden, a graduate of Yale.

When seventeen years old, the subject of this sketch moved to Woodbury, Ct., where he served an apprenticeship of three years in a hat-factory. In December, 1819, he moved to Utica, N. Y., and took charge of a similar establishment. In 1821, he moved to Buffalo, then a village of 1800 inhabitants, and, in company with Joseph Stocking, commenced the hat and fur business, continuing the same till the death of his partner in 1835. In 1836, Mr. Dart disposed of his interest to the son of his former partner, Thomas R. Stocking.

On the first of December, 1830, he was married to Miss Dotha Denison, daughter of E. H. Denison, Esq. They have had seven children, two sons and five daughters.

From 1836 to 1842, Mr. Dart was occupied in looking after his interests in real estate, in which his partner and himself had been heavily interested.

In the fall of 1842, he commenced building a grain elevator for the transfer and storage of grain, which was completed and in operation the following June. In the interesting history of this elevator, read before the Buffalo Historical Society, it appears that Mr. Dart was the pioneer in this business, being the first person to put the elevator into practical use for commercial purposes. They are now in use in most of the leading grain depots of the globe. At the single port of Buffalo, there are twenty-seven at this time (1877), not including two floating elevators, with an aggregate storing capacity of six millions of bushels. It is thus seen that to Mr. Dart the world is indebted for the introduction of this great and indispensable convenience of modern commerce, by which is effected a saving of more than half of the tonnage and expense in the transportation of grain. By the old method, two weeks were required to accomplish what can now be done in seven hours, and to the elevator, in a great measure, may be attributed the rapid growth and prosperity of the Queen City of the Lakes.

Mr. Dart remained identified with the elevator till 1852, when he rented it to other parties, and in 1855 sold his interest.

In 1852, in company with his brother, E. D. Dart, and his brother-in-law, William H. Ovington, he embarked in the lumber business, and built a planing-mill on the Ohio Basin. The firm name of Dart & Bros., on the withdrawal of Mr. Ovington in 1862, became Dart & Bro., which is the present style.

Although well advanced in years, Mr. Dart is still actively engaged in business, and maintains a lively interest in all that affects the public welfare.

Judging from the longevity of his ancestors, he will continue to be hale and hearty for some time to come.

Of Mr. Dart's parents the following record is preserved: "On the fifth of October, 1792, Joseph Dart, aged twenty-two, and Sarah Hurd, aged nineteen, both of Middle Haddam, Ct., were united in marriage. After a pleasant pilgrimage together, passed in the same parish on the banks of the Connecticut, another festal group gathered around them at the old home, and celebrated the sixty-second anniversary of their espousals. In this gathering were thirteen of their fourteen children, with an average age of forty-six years. At the same meeting were present a brother and sister of Mrs. Dart, aged ninety-two and ninety-nine."

De Laney, C. D., was born in Westmoreland County, Pa., August 9th, 1811.

Losing his father during early childhood, he was obliged to begin the hard struggle of life at twelve, and was apprenticed at this age to a man in Pittsburg, and while there underwent hardships that the apprentice lad of to-day would think almost impossible to endure. At sixteen, Mr. De Laney entered the machine-shop of Warden & Arthur, in Pittsburg.

From there he moved to Cincinnati, and worked with John B. Greene, during which time a desire for knowledge made him eager to form a night-school; and he with other companions tried hard to learn higher mathematics, in order that he might apply it to his business as a machinist. Unfortunately, their teacher knew but little more than the scholars, and they soon came to a stand-still.

From Cincinnati he returned to Pittsburg as a machinist for a Mr. Gibson, and it was while in his employ (1831) that Mr. De Laney came to Black Rock, to superintend the construction of the engines for the steamboats Pennsylvania, New York, and Gen. Porter, the one put in the Pennsylvania being the first marine engine ever built on the lakes.

In 1832, Mr. De Laney went to Niagara, where he superintended the iron work for a dry-dock at that point. Thence, in 1835, he

went to New York, and engaged in the Novelty Works, then owned by the late Dr. Nott and F. B. Stillman, where he worked most of the time until 1837, when he came back to Buffalo and bought out a man named Buttrick.

While occupying that shop, he built a low-pressure engine, ten-foot stroke, for the steamboat New England.

In 1841, he was burned out, and in 1842 built the Fulton Foundry, now Vulcan Works, on Water street. In that shop he built two passenger and a number of freight cars for the B. & A. R.R. The wheels, axles, and in fact every part complete were manufactured by him. This was the first attempt at car-building in Buffalo. The same year Mr. De Laney built the locomotive engine (excepting the boiler) "Tecumseh," which is yet in use. This is believed to be the first locomotive built in Buffalo. About this time reverses came, and Mr. De Laney was submerged with others in the iron line in a general crash.

He, however, started again in a small shop, employing only a boy, the two doing all the work offered until 1853, when he purchased the site on which the De Laney Forge and Iron-Works now stand. Here is where the first steam forge in Buffalo was erected. During the war, there were forged at this establishment six monitor turrets complete, and parts of seven others, which were sent to New York for iron-clads.

The iron rollers in the Union Iron-Works were also forged at these works, and are the largest in diameter of any forged work in the United States.

In one year this establishment turned out $240,000 worth of work. The large hammer used in the forging department was built by Mr. De Laney, and is considered the most effective of any tool of the kind in the United States, and a blow of 100 tons can be obtained with ease.

Mr. De Laney was the first to use anthracite and bituminous coal in Buffalo.

Always working to educate boys and men mechanically inclined and showing ability, some of the best smiths and hammersmen in the country served more or less of their apprenticeship with him. Now, having acquired a competency, he is gradually withdrawing from active work, but has the pleasure of knowing that the present firm is an assured success, and will ultimately be managed and owned by his son and others whom he has educated to the work himself while in his prime. He has done much, and all honorably; and now, dwelling in the affluence and honor gained by his industry and talents, he can look upon the past unsullied carrier of his somewhat checkered life with conscious pride and satisfaction.

Douglas, Asa W., was born at Stephentown, New York, June 17th, 1794, and died at Lockport, Niagara County, New York, June 4th, 1875, and was a cousin of the late Stephen A. Douglas, the eminent Democratic statesman, and a lineal descendant of William Douglas, who landed at Plymouth, in 1630. The following is copied from the Lockport *Daily Journal*, issued on June 4th, 1875, the date of his death :

"Asa W. Douglas came to this county in 1814—sixty-one years since. He resided at Olcott two years, being extensively engaged in the lumber business, and also having a store in the same place. He came to this city, or what was then little else than a wilderness, in 1816, having lost every thing by shipwreck and commercial ventures on Lake Ontario. He was at first a clerk with Darius Comstock; but gradually, by untiring industry, worked into positions of power and trust. He had the contract for and built the present canal locks in this city, after which the city of Lockport was named. He was the first canal collector at this point. He was subsequently largely engaged in the lumber and stave business here. About the year 1846, he went into the milling business with the late Gen. John Jackson, under the firm name of Douglas & Jackson. The mill was burned about 1855, but rebuilt the next year, and the business continued until sold to Saxton & Thompson, in August, 1867. Since that time, Mr. Douglas has not been in any business. He bought his present elegant residence in the southern part of the city in the fall of 1872. As was his right, he has of late enjoyed exemption from labor and care. Travel with his only surviving son, Mr. W. Bruce Douglas, through the West Indies; the hospitable and courteous entertainment of friends; the quiet pleasures of ease and comfort, have of late years been his.

"The death of a man like Asa W. Douglas naturally prompts sincere mourning. One of the pioneers of this county and city, his interests have been its interests. Always a public-spirited citizen, the present prosperity of Lockport is largely due to his wise counsels, his directing hand and indomitable energy. What he found to do, he did with his might. He amassed wealth by sturdy blows and well-matured efforts. He won success because he forced it. And nobody was ever jealous of that success. But the other day we heard two of our older citizens joining in the remark that they never knew Asa W. Douglas to be spoken ill of. A gentleman of the olden school; naturally humane and kind; deliberate and wise in judgment, he formed his opinions with judicious care and defended them with tenacious zeal. No man's opinion was more widely sought in this section at the full tide of his life than Mr. Douglas's. Never an office-seeker (although often honored with the place of supervisor, and perhaps others of local significance), his judgment was sought and heavily leaned upon by those anxious for official position. His was the silent power that conquered because born of justice, tact, and skilled observation. Another feature of Mr. Douglas's long and useful life was his disinterested benevolence. When convinced that a cause or an applicant was worthy, he bestowed with generous and warm appreciation. He could not do too much where his judgment and his feelings were enlisted. Impostors, on the contrary, he could not and would not endure. He brooked no shams. The death of such a one, we repeat, calls for sorrow in this vicinity, and for a more detailed newspaper notice than we have facts at our disposal at this time to write. His noble and busy life, however, is treasured up among the sunny memories of our older inhabitants, and has passed as a sort of heirloom to the keeping of a later generation."

Du Bois, Cornelius, son of Koert Du Bois, descended from a Huguenot settler in Ulster County, N. Y., was born in the town of Pleasant Valley, Dutchess County, N. Y., the 9th of July, 1802. His mother was a member of the society of Friends. His father was a farmer, and in that pursuit Cornelius was educated, and has been engaged in it all his life. In his earlier years, the common school furnished him with the best education it could then afford.

At the age of twenty-four, Mr. Du Bois married Julia, daughter of William A. Moore, of Fort Anne, Washington County, N. Y., who is still his life-companion. They have had eight children, seven of whom are living.

From boyhood he has been distinguished for integrity, sobriety, industry, thrift, and common sense. At the age of twenty-six, he was chosen foreman of the Grand-Jury of Dutchess County, by Judge James Emott, Senior, and served in the same capacity many times afterward. So trustworthy has he always been that, in the course of his busy life, he has settled twenty-four estates as executor, and four as administrator, mostly without the assistance of associates or attorneys.

Mr. Du Bois pursued farming practically and successfully until 1840, when, without disposing of his land, he engaged in the freighting and forwarding business in the then thriving village of Poughkeepsie, which contained 10,000 inhabitants. The firm name was Du Bois & Co. In this business he was engaged successfully for six years, when he exchanged his property in the village for a farm of 163 acres, lying on the borders of the corporate limits of Poughkeepsie. There, with his family, he remained twenty years, during which time he served four years as supervisor of the village and township of Poughkeepsie. These have since been divided. The village was incorporated a city in 1854, and now contains over 20,000 inhabitants. For four years, Mr. Du Bois was President of the Dutchess County Agricultural Society. In 1861, he was chosen by the late Matthew Vassar to be one of the corporators of Vassar College, and has been an active member of its Board of Trustees from the beginning. For six years, he was superintendent of the building, and has ever been one of the most judicious members of the Executive Committee of Vassar College Board of Trustees, enjoying the unbounded confidence of the founder while he lived.

For four years, Mr. Du Bois was one of the managers of the Hudson River State Hospital for the Insane, near Poughkeepsie, and was one year a member of the Assembly of the State of New York. He was one of the founders of the First National Bank of Poughkeepsie, and was president of the institution eleven years from its organization.

Mr. Du Bois is now seventy-five years of age, and full of mental and bodily vigor; for he has ever been active and temperate; and during his long business life of fifty five years he never had a suit at law on his own account, but he has been compelled to defend three estates against loss by lawsuits. He says, "All the knowledge I want about law is to know enough to keep out of lawsuits;" and the highest title to which he aspires is that of a skilful *Dutchess County Farmer.*

Dunbar, Robert, was born in Carubee, Fifeshire, Scotland, in the year 1813, received a common school education, learned the trade of millwright with his father, and moved to Canada with his parents in 1831. The subject of this sketch worked at his trade in Toronto for two years; from there he moved to Guelph, Ontario, and worked at his trade between two and three years; afterward moved to the village of Black Rock, now Buffalo. After moving to several places, helping to complete mills, he returned to Black Rock in 1839, and took charge of building the Niagara Flour Mills. From that time he continued to live there, building mills there and elsewhere. In 1847, he formed a copartnership with C. W. Evans, of Buffalo, and built and ran a grain elevator, now the Evans elevator, in the Ship-Canal, until 1853. During the time he was connected with Mr. Evans, he made plans and sent the machinery from Buffalo for the first grain elevator ever built in New York City. In 1861, the Messrs. Follett and Jewett and Root retired from the company, and S. W. Howell, of Black Rock, became a partner with him, changing the name to the Eagle Iron-Works, Dunbar & Howell proprietors, which partnership continued until 1874, when Howell retired, leaving him alone in the business. In 1875, he associated with him in the business his son, George H. Dunbar, under the style of Robert Dunbar & Son, which is the firm at the present time.

Dutton, Edward Holmes, was born December 12th, 1805, at East Haddam, Middlesex County, Ct., and was the fourth child of Amasa Dutton and Mary Mather, a descendant of Cotton Mather. The subject of this sketch moved to Ogden, Monroe County, New York, September, 1810, that section being at that time little better than a wilderness, effecting a crossing of the Genesee River at Avon, the only bridge over the river in those days. He attended the district-school at Ogden, also the Henrietta and Rochester high-schools, and afterward studied under Ebenezer Everett, a graduate of Yale, from whom he received most of his education. After three years' hard study, with that end in view, he took a district-school in the town of Gates, now part of Rochester. This was in November, 1824. For the next seven years, he taught in various schools in that section, during which time he was school inspector for the town of Ogden three years.

In April, 1831, he moved to Lockport, where he entered the stave and lumber business, and added to his enterprise a country store. In 1835, he was joined in wedlock to Miss Lovinda Legge. In 1838, he commenced the stave business at Buffalo, continuing his residence at Lockport until 1846, when he moved to Buffalo, where he has since resided. In 1862, he opened an office in New York City, and in this branch took John P. Townsend in as partner. For many years he has had an extensive stave business throughout the West and all the wine-making countries of Europe, proving himself an able and conscientious business man. He is well known to the citizens of Buffalo, and in connection with his acknowledged business qualifications he is highly esteemed for his social and moral attributes.

Ethridge, Alfred, was born at Little Falls, Herkimer County, N. Y., July 29th, 1817.

When the subject of this sketch was between five and six years old, he left his native town in company with his parents, who moved to Herkimer village; and when between nine and ten years old, Mr. Ethridge left home and commenced to carve his own way in the world. His first four years were spent on a farm, after which he returned to his parents, who then lived at Frankfort, Herkimer County, where he remained thirteen or fourteen years, except one year spent in Utica, N. Y.

Two years before leaving Frankfort, Mr. E., in company with W. Northup, started the grocery and provision business, previous to which he had been a clerk with Mr. Northup and other parties, besides teaching school part of one year. In 1844, Mr. Ethridge moved to Rome, N. Y., to start a branch business, and the partnership of Northup & Ethridge continued until the winter of 1856, when fire consumed the whole of their premises: after this, this firm was dissolved, and the subject of this sketch commenced again for himself, running the business for three years successfully, when he gave a former clerk, A. P. Tuller, an interest in the business. In 1862 and 1863,

Mr. Ethridge built their present building, especially adapted for the wholesale grocery and provision business, a fine brick building, covering an area of 42 feet front by 144 deep, running from Dominick street back to the Erie Canal. The building is fitted up with every convenience, including a steam elevator, for handling their goods cheaply and with dispatch; and their annual sales reach about one million dollars. The firm is now Ethridge, Tuller & Co., and is among the heaviest and most respectable firms in Central New York. Mr. E., by his close attention to business, good judgment, and honorable dealing, has won the confidence, respect, and esteem of all who know him.

Eustaphieve, Alexander A., was born in Boston, Mass., March 25th, 1812; his father being for a long time well known as the Russian Consul-General to the United States. The subject of this sketch received his education mainly in the city of his birth, during which period he attended the Boston Latin School four years. His first business experience was in George Douglas & Co.'s commission house, New York City. In 1830, he moved to Detroit, and accepted the position of teller in the Farmers and Mechanics' Bank. In 1832, he moved to Buffalo, and accepted a similar position in the Bank of Buffalo; in 1834, was teller in the Commercial Bank of Buffalo; and after that, held various positions of trust in banks as teller and cashier, until 1842, when he moved to New York and went into the commission business; though in 1847 returned to Buffalo, and was appointed secretary of the Buffalo Mutual Insurance Company, which he occupied until 1863, when he took up the insurance agency business with H. C. Walker, they remaining as partners till 1877, when H. C. Walker retired. The business is now conducted by A. A. Eustaphieve, who has always proved himself a capable and thorough business man.

Farthing, George, was born in Somersetshire, England, April 21st, 1831, and removed to Buffalo with his parents during 1835. His father has been dead twenty-five years, and his mother twenty years, and both are buried in Niagara County, N. Y.

The subject of this sketch commenced business for himself in 1849, feeding cattle at Clark's distillery, and later at Tonawanda. At the commencement of the war, he, together with his brother James, began the distilling business at Tonawanda; three years later they were burned out; after which, George removed to Buffalo, and did business in cattle-yards with his brother Thomas Farthing. In 1872, they bought out Moore's distillery, which they are now running successfully in connection with cattle-trade, malt-house, etc.; the style of the firm being George and Thomas Farthing, the latter attending to the cattle department of the business. George Farthing was married in April, 1850, to Miss Matilda Kelly, the issue of which has been eight children, seven of whom are living.

Mr. Farthing has always proved himself a capable business man, and under his able management has, from a small beginning, placed himself high in the community in which he lives.

Ferguson, A. W., was born in Springfield, Otsego County, N. Y., May 13th, 1819. In early life he received only a common-school education, after which he was for four years apprenticed to the trade of saddle and harness maker. In 1840, he moved to Jefferson County, and commenced working at his trade as a journeyman, continuing for eighteen months, when he commenced business for himself in a very small way, doing a more or less successful business for three or four years, during which time he was married to Miss Electa Francis, by whom he has had four children; two only survive. In 1848, he, stimulated by ambition to benefit his position, moved to Malone, N. Y., and opened a saddlery and harness store, which proved very successful until 1860, when he disposed of his business that he might give his whole time and attention to hop-growing, a branch of agriculture he started in 1850 with a very few acres of land; little by little has he added to his first possessions, until he now has under culture one hundred and fifteen acres of the finest hops, and his productions are as well known throughout our country among the brewers as "household words." This enviable reputation he has achieved by proper care of the details of hop-raising, watching their progress, and giving them every attention, to insure for his products nothing but first quality; and generally his crops are engaged by the best brewers in the country long before picking time, so anxious are they to secure what they know to be the great essential ingredient for the production of the finest ales. His hop-yard, during the growth of the crop, presents pictures of agricultural perfection, each vine receiving such care and treatment as to secure good and permanent results; and in this has he ever been successful, and when others have found themselves with short and blighted crops, his kilns have been full and his customers happy.

In 1854, he was elected to the State Assembly, a position he filled with dignity and honor. In 1853, he was elected and served a four years term as justice of the peace. He, feeling a pride in the future welfare of the home of his adoption, became one of the organizers of the Malone Hotel Company, which built the Ferguson House, and he is a one half owner of the property, by far the handsomest block in Malone. Fully intending to pass his life in this beautiful town, he erected the finest residence in Northern New York. It is built of Milwaukee brick, and is fitted up inside with all modern conveniences to the ends of happiness and comfort. The woodwork throughout the house is of beautiful black-walnut and ash (native wood), highly polished, fit for the requirements and luxury of royalty itself. Mr. Ferguson owes his success in life to close application to the details of his business, by which, together with his natural business habits, he has amassed a large fortune. Though he has been frugal, he has never been parsimonious in his manner of life, and with a liberal hand has he dispensed his charities. Without injuring any one, he has accomplished much, and as a citizen and man he deserves the esteem of posterity.

Field, Joseph, the subject of this brief sketch, was born in Taunton, Mass., March 29th, 1787. When seventeen years of age, he partially served an apprenticeship at the carpenter's trade, but followed the occupation only a short time. At the age of twenty-one, he married Miss Lydia Glover, of Dorchester, Mass. Of this his only marriage, he has had five daughters, three of whom survive—Mrs. Eliza A. Staunton, Mrs. Caroline Ely, and Mrs. Almira Beers. Of the remaining two, one died in infancy, the other, Mrs. Emeline Cobb, died a few months since.

From Dorchester he removed to Walpole, New Hampshire, where he remained for several years. But having a great desire to

Joseph Field

visit the western and south-western parts of the United States, he, while here, explored much of the southern and south-western parts of our country, visiting New Orleans twice, once having had the fever of the country while there. He also visited most of the cities south, and nearly all the inland cities from Pittsburg to St. Louis—travelling most of the way on horseback and by boats on rivers, this being the only way of journeying of that time.

After these travels, having great faith of the future of Western New York, he removed in 1827 to Rochester, and soon after entered into the auction and commission business with Derick Sibley. Added to this, the firm engaged in the buying and selling real estate, and purchased one hundred acres or more of land adjoining the city on the west, buying Town Lot No 63, which lay on both sides of Genesee street and along the line of Buffalo street. This land they cut up into city lots, laid out streets, made maps, etc. This purchase was called the "Sibley and Field Tract." They erected the once famous and large (for those times) stone building on the corner of Buffalo and Genesee streets, called "The Bull's Head," which was opened and occupied for several years as a hotel. On this purchase, also, they reserved on Genesee street a lot of ten acres, called "The College Square," dedicating its use, as a gift, to any parties who should take it and put up educational buildings in accordance with the views of the donors. It was never so taken, and after twenty years it reverted back to the original owners.

During this time, Mr. Field attended a government sale of lands at Green Bay. He procured a horse at Chicago—then a small, insignificant village—and in company with the government agent, went to Green Bay on horseback, the party finding their way by "*blazed trees*," and camping at night in the forest. This journey resulted in a purchase of some lands by Mr. Field, and in his prospecting in the West, which he was anxious to do, that he might judge of the extent and state of the country, which was then called "The Great West;" and though impressed with its prospective greatness, it did not wean him from his interests in Rochester.

Leaving the auction and commission business after about four years, he entered into the milling business, operating for the first two years in the "Genesee Falls Mills," at the brink of the "High Falls," on the east side of the river. The mills were then known as the "Palmer Cleveland Mills." In this first enterprise he was successful, though occupants before and after him were not as much so.

From this beginning he came to the west side, and opened business on the lower, or Brown's Race, making a flouring mill out of what had been a woollen mill; and afterward he built the upper mill on that race. Here he continued business until he sold out and withdrew, continuing altogether as a merchant miller about fifteen years; and it is believed that at the time of his retiring, he was one of the few who had continued to be prosperous in that business which has engaged so many men and so much capital from the beginning of Rochester.

Mr. Field was one of the originators of the "Rochester City Bank," was its president for many years, and at its close. His mind next turned to railroad interests, he being connected with the old Tonawanda Railroad west, which was afterward built from Batavia to Buffalo. He was Superintendent of Construction, and afterward President of the Buffalo and Rochester Railroad, which now is part of New York Central. Being thoroughly interested in steam highways, he turned his attention to roads west of Buffalo, and was a member of the meeting at Fredonia that first advocated a Lake Shore road, which was afterward built. He was also more or less interested in all the railroads from Buffalo to Chicago, and was a Director of the first Board after the consolidation of the roads which now form the New York Central.

In this connection it may be stated that, less than two years ago, he attended the annual meeting of the stockholders of the Lake Shore and Michigan Southern Railroad in Cleveland, Ohio, and was made chairman of that meeting, though then nearly ninety years of age!

Having always an interest in the city where he lived, he consented, in former years, to be a candidate for Mayor of Rochester, was elected, and served with honor and efficiency one term; but respectfully declined the second nomination, though pressed to accept it by many citizens.

He has also been a large owner of real estate in Rochester, and only five years ago erected a fine large block of stores on State street, corner of Market.

The subject of this short sketch is now in the 91st year of his age, and—as will be seen by the accompanying engraving—is still vigorous and well-preserved for a man of his years. He has already passed the age allotted to man, and in the course of a long and active business life, has been brought in contact with very many men of wealth and mind, of the best standing and business capacity in the different enterprises of life. This has led him through numerous transactions, requiring labor, caution, and energy, as well as executive ability; and it may be added as a marvel, exceptionally strange, that he has been successful in all his varied pursuits, never having been forced to succumb to financial embarrassments.

It may be said too, with perfect truth, that there is not a word of reproach against his good name—nothing to sully his honor or character—nothing to dim the lustre of his life, now so near its close. And when his spirit shall calmly and hopefully glide from earth into the great unknown beyond, his honored name will not be forgotten as one of those efficient pioneers who helped to lay the foundations of civil and religious society in Rochester and Western New York, and who did their work so well.

April, 1877.

Forman, Joshua, was born at Pleasant Valley, Dutchess County, N. Y., September 6th, 1777. His parents were Joseph and Hannah Forman, who previous to the Revolution resided in the city of New York. Upon the breaking out of the war and the approach of the British to that city, Mr. Joseph Forman with his family retired to Pleasant Valley, where the subject of this sketch was born. At an early age he evinced a strong desire for learning, in which he was encouraged by his friends. In the fall of 1793, he entered Union College at Schenectady, and in due time graduated with honor. Directly after his collegiate course was completed, he entered the law office of Peter W. Radcliffe, Esq., of Poughkeepsie, where he remained about two years. He then went to the city of New York, and completed his law studies in the office of Samuel Miles Hopkins, Esq. Soon after the close of his

professional course, he was married to Miss Margaret Alexander, a daughter of the Hon. Boyd Alexander, M.P. for Glasgow, Scotland. In the spring of 1800, Mr. Forman removed to Onondaga Hollow, and opened a law office, where he began early to manifest his public spirit and enterprise. By his integrity and straightforward course in the practice of his profession, he soon became distinguished as a lawyer, and by his talents and gentlemanly deportment became familiarly known throughout the country. In 1803, William H. Sabin joined him as a partner in the practice of the law. In 1807, he was elected to the legislature, where he became prominent as the first projector of the Erie Canal. In 1813, he was appointed Judge of the Onondaga County Common Pleas Court, a station he filled with credit and ability ten years. In 1807, he erected the first grist-mill on the Oswego River, which greatly facilitated the settlement of that region. In 1808, he founded the celebrated Plaster Company at Camillus. In 1821, Judge Forman obtained the passage of a law authorizing the lowering of Onondaga Lake, and subsequently the lake was lowered about two feet, draining the unwholesome marshes and improving the lands about the lake. In 1822, he embarked in salt manufacturing, introducing the manufacture of solar salt. Judge Forman was emphatically the founder of the city of Syracuse. He laid out the centre of the city in 1818, and moved to that place in the year 1819, where he persisted in his efforts until he had laid the broad and deep foundations of this flourishing city. After his work was accomplished, he in 1826 removed to New Jersey, near New Brunswick, where he superintended the opening and working of a copper mine. Soon after his departure, the State of New York became sadly deranged in its financial affairs. The banking system was extremely defective. At this crisis Judge Forman came forward with a plan for relief. At the request of Mr. Van Buren, then Governor, he spent the winter at Albany, drew up and perfected his bill, which was the Safety Fund act passed that winter. In 1829–30, Judge Forman and others bought from the State of North Carolina some 300,000 acres of land in Rutherfordton and other counties. He took up his residence at the village of Rutherfordton, where he made great improvements, besides improving the mental and moral condition of the inhabitants. In 1831, after an absence of five years, Judge Forman visited Onondaga, where he received a public dinner tendered by all the leading gentlemen of Syracuse. He was welcomed with unqualified demonstrations of joy and respect. On his return to his home in North Carolina, while his health permitted, his business was principally that of making sales of the lands he had purchased. After visiting Syracuse once more in 1846, he retired to his mountain home, where he looked back upon a well-spent life, much of which was devoted to the service of his country, without regret. He died at the village of Rutherfordton, August 4th, 1848, and his remains were removed to Syracuse, where they rest in the beautiful rural cemetery, Oakwood.

For a fuller account of Judge Forman, see Clark's "Onondaga," "The Leavenworth Genealogy," and "Hosack's "Life of De Witt Clinton."

Francis, John M., editor of the Troy *Times*, was born March 7th, 1823. His father was a native of Wales, and a man of extensive reading and great force of character. In 1798, he emigrated to the

United States, and settled near Utica, from whence he removed to Prattsburg, Steuben County, then almost a wilderness region, and became one of the pioneers of Western New York. Here he engaged in agricultural pursuits, and here the son, John M., was born. Young Francis enjoyed in his early years the limited advantages of the district-school, and was permitted to spend one winter at the village academy—this last privilege constituting all the academic instruction he ever received. At the age of fourteen years, he became an apprentice to the trade of a printer, in the office of the Ontario *Messenger*, published at Canandaigua. This town was then the seat of considerable political influence, and the young apprentice soon became not only an interested observer of events as they occurred, but a close student of political economy and a patient listener at the earnest discussions which took place between the many distinguished men of the village. At the age of nineteen, having completed his apprenticeship, he removed to Palmyra, in Wayne County, and began his first experience as an editorial writer in the columns of the Wayne *Sentinel*. In 1845, he became the associate editor of the Rochester *Daily Advertiser*, and in 1846 took up his residence in Troy, where he connected himself with the Troy *Budget* as its editor, and subsequently as one of its proprietors. In the Hunker and Barnburner campaigns which succeeded, he distinguished himself as an advocate of free soil, free speech, and free men. He was the first editor to establish the home or city department—a feature which has since become so prominent in all journals. Brief connections with the Troy *Whig* and *Post* ensued; and in 1852 Mr. Francis began his great life-work in establishing his present journal—THE TROY DAILY TIMES—a paper of pre-eminent enterprise, ability, and influence, and which has been correspondingly successful in the material elements of prosperity. From 1852 to 1856, Mr. Francis was city clerk of Troy; in 1867, he was elected from the district composed of Rensselaer and Washington counties, to serve in the convention to revise the constitution of New York State. While in that body, he delivered one speech evincing elaborate preparation (upon the government of cities), and took part in several debates. In 1869, he travelled extensively in Europe, and in 1871 was appointed United States Minister to Greece by President Grant. He made a popular and able representative abroad; and his resignation, two years later, was accepted with reluctance by the government. In 1875-6, Mr. Francis made a tour of the globe, writing a series of letters for his paper descriptive of his travels and of the foreign countries he visited, which were widely read and extensively copied by the press. As the editor of THE TIMES, Mr. Francis has a national reputation. Few men are so well versed in public affairs or wield a readier and more skilful pen. His observations abroad, combined with his extensive reading, have enriched his mind, and given him broad and comprehensive views of subjects as they arise and require treatment at his hands. He is practically a self-made man; and being still in the prime of life, with mental powers increasing rather than diminishing, of a strong and robust constitution, and a judgment upon men and things that rarely errs, it may be predicted of him that, both as a journalist and as a public man, he can, if he shall choose, make for himself a conspicuous and honorable figure in the history of the times.

Yours truly Wm H Frear

Frear, William H., was born in Coxsackie, N. Y., March 29th, 1841. His parents were in somewhat straitened circumstances, but they afforded William fair educational advantages, which he zealously improved. He secured a situation in a country store in his native village when sixteen years of age, and at the expiration of two years of faithful clerkship, entered into the service of John Flagg, then the leading merchant of Troy, N. Y. Young Frear continued a salesman in Mr. Flagg's store for six years, during which period he mastered every detail of the dry goods trade, developed astonishing aptitude for business, and won the unlimited confidence of his employer. In 1865, the ambitious subject of this sketch, restive under the restraints incident to a subordinate position, took the few hundred dollars he had saved from his earnings by an economy approaching hardship, and embarked in mercantile life as the partner of Mr. Haverly, under the firm name of Haverly & Frear. They opened a small store in an unfavorable location; but the extraordinary energy of Mr. Frear bore fruit in sales aggregating $300,000 during the three years' existence of the firm. In 1868, the firm of Haverly & Frear changed into Flagg, Haverly & Frear, with Mr. Frear as the managing partner; and the three rented the most central store in Troy, situated in the Cannon Place building. Mr. Haverly retired in 1869; in the following year a large cloak, shawl, and suit apartment was added; and in 1874 Mr. Frear became the sole proprietor—a distinction he still maintains. As a practical illustration of the remarkable augmentation of his transactions since that time, it is only necessary to mention that he added a contiguous store to his dry goods house in April, 1875, and still another one, with an entrance on an adjoining street, just one year later. Mr. Frear now controls a corps of fifty of the most expert clerks in the city, all of whom are the fast friends of their employer. His annual sales approximate a million dollars, and it is no exaggeration to say that his mammoth place of business is the head centre of trade in Northern New York. In that entire section of the State there is no name seen or spoken so often as that of Frear. The advertising columns of the newspapers teem with flaring announcements of Frear's bargains; ferry-boats, street cars, ice-wagons, fences, bill-boards, stages, cards, circulars, posters, transparencies, and a multiplying army of patrons, unite in one grand chorus to proclaim Frear's low prices; tremendous piles of dress-goods lining the sidewalk, and reaching heavenward, give ocular demonstrations of the magnitude of Frear's stock; lavish liberality and praiseworthy public-spiritedness tell the story of Frear's flattering financial foundation; and yet the busiest, most unassuming and genial man in Frear's famous store, is William H. Frear. His undaunted genius, prodigious enterprise, and brilliant success compel universal admiration. He has no bad habits to block the pathway of prosperity, and his life presents to the struggling youth a striking example of what brains, self-denial, honesty, and enterprise may accomplish. Although he has yet to reach the meridian of his career, William H. Frear is, to-day, the most powerful name in commercial circles north of the city of New York.

Ganson, John, was born in Le Roy, Genesee County, N. Y., January 1st, 1819, and was of Dutch and Scotch descent.

At the age of two, he lost his father, thus being left entirely to the care of his mother

How well she discharged her duties, the career of the lamented son bears witness. His early education was looked after by her, and in 1838, at the age of nineteen, he was a graduate of Harvard University, and soon after commenced the study of law in the office of the distinguished firm of Sibley & Worden, of Canandaigua, and was admitted to the bar in 1842.

He was married to the daughter of M. H. Sibley, who still survives him.

He continued the practice of law in the office in which he had prosecuted his studies till 1846, in which year he came to Buffalo, where he resided till the time of his death. Immediately on arriving here, he went into partnership with E. G. Spaulding, with whom he remained associated about three years. From that time till January 1st, 1862, he practised his profession alone, when he formed a copartnership with James M. Smith, which continued till June, 1873, when Judge Smith was called to the bench. His last partnership was with E. R. Bacon, Esq.

In 1862, Mr. Ganson was elected to the State Senate. In 1863, he was elected to Congress, and refused the nomination for a second term. In 1873, he was again elected to the State Senate, and was a member of the same at the time of his death, which occurred the 28th of September, 1874.

He was a man of magnificent physique and noble bearing, a nobleman of nature, and a kindly, courteous gentleman always. And the loss of no one has been more severely felt through the whole community of this city for many years than that of John Ganson.

Gardner, Hon. Hiram.—This eminent and distinguished jurist was born in Dutchess County, N. Y., February 9th, 1800. His parents were farmers of excellent character and intelligence, belonging to the society of Friends. While they felt a deep interest in the welfare of their son, and watched his early years with the utmost care, yet they unfortunately could afford him but little financial help in the pursuit of his studies. Consequently, thrown upon his own resources from the beginning to the end of his noble career, he was self-made. After pursuing an academical course as far as circumstances would permit, he entered himself as a student of law, and studied for about two years, when he removed to New York, and finished the course. In 1821, he was admitted to the bar, and a year later commenced practice in the Supreme Court. In October (1822), he moved to Lockport, N. Y., where he resided till his death, which occurred March 13th, 1874. In 1823, he was appointed to the office of Justice of the Peace; in 1825, Associate Judge of the Court of Common Pleas; in 1827, Supreme Court Commissioner, and was admitted as a Master in Chancery. In 1831, he was appointed Surrogate, which office he resigned in 1836, that he might represent his district in the State Legislature, to which position he had already been elected. In 1845, he was elected a member of the Constitutional Convention which revised the second and framed the third State Constitution. In 1847, he was elected County Judge and Surrogate under the constitution he helped to frame. In 1858, he was elected Canal Commissioner. In the fall of 1868, he was appointed to the office of County Judge, to supply a vacancy, and in the following November (1869), he was elected to the same position for the term of four years.

In enumerating these facts, the reader may realize how large a portion of his professional life was employed in the execution of duties

connected with public trusts, and how constantly and entirely he was confided in by his fellow-citizens. His conspicuous ability and talent were uniformly and successfully directed to the elevation of the judicial office and of the legal profession. He was not a politician, but never shrank from what he considered his duty as an American citizen. His ideas of political purity, integrity, and honor were of the most elevated character, and though twenty-five of the fifty years spent as a practitioner he held public office, we can conscientiously say he never sought, by word, act, or deed, any favors of this character.

In December, 1873, the members of the bar of Niagara County held a meeting for the purpose of taking suitable action in reference to the final retirement of Hon. Hiram Gardner from the bench. Appropriate resolutions were adopted, and upon retiring they proceeded in a body to his residence, and were received by the judge in a most cordial manner. After a brief pause, the chairman of the meeting arose, and in a few touching remarks presented an engrossed copy of the same to the judge, who replied with deep emotion, thanking them for such a testimonial of confidence and esteem. The affair throughout was one which will linger long in the memory of those present. Few men ever retired from public life with so honorable and satisfactory a record as Judge Gardner. The ermine dropped from his shoulders as spotless as when its folds first graced the wearer.

In his family his influence was delightful and all-pervading. In the church of God he was an ornament and a pillar of strength, reflecting in his life the beauty and power of Christianity. He was untiring in his labors for the welfare of the place where he resided, an ardent lover of his country, and did what he could for the elevation and purification of humanity in its largest and most extended sense.

"He towered above his fellow-men as a majestic tree
In some primeval forest rears its topmost branches free;
Raised up of God in kingly strength above the storm and strife,
A landmark to the race, a type of Christian life."

Greeley, Horace, was born in Amherst, N. H., February 3d, 1811. His father was a farmer in humble circumstances, and while yet a child Horace took an active part in the labor of the farm. It was his task to ride the horses to plough, to assist in the spring planting, to pick up stones from the field, and in the frosty autumn mornings to watch the oxen as they fed on the grass beside the corn-field before they were yoked up for their day's work. At an early age he gave tokens of remarkable intelligence and a singular love of learning. He could read before he was two years old, and had scarcely reached the age of ten before he had devoured every book that he could borrow within seven miles of his father's house.

His third winter was spent at the house of his maternal grandfather in Londonderry, where he attended a district-school for the first time. He at once attracted notice by the excellence of his recitations, and especially by his skill in spelling. When he was about ten years old, his father removed with the family to West Haven, Vt., where for about five years he was assisted by Horace in clearing up wild land and other severe manual labor. At the end of that time, in the spring of 1826, he became an apprentice to the printer of a weekly newspaper in East Poultney, Vt. This was a position which he had long coveted, having early set his heart on following the trade of Benjamin Franklin.

He soon learned the art of setting type, and even before the first week was over, his skill was superior to that of many an apprentice who had been in practice a month. After remaining in this situation about four years, he had become master of the trade, and rendered valuable assistance in conducting the newspaper. In June, 1830, the paper was discontinued, and young Greeley, after spending a few weeks with his parents, who had removed to Erie Co., Pa., obtained employment in some of the printing-offices in that vicinity. The work was hard and the pay poor, and he at length made up his mind to seek his fortune in New York. He arrived in that city on August 17th, 1831, with only ten dollars in his pocket, and a scanty stock of clothing in his bundle. After much difficulty, he found employment as a journeyman printer. In this capacity he worked in several different offices until January 1st, 1833, when he entered into partnership with Francis Story, and commenced the publication of the *Morning Post*, the first daily penny paper ever printed. The enterprise was unsuccessful, and the paper failed in about three weeks. The partnership, however, went on in the job-printing business until July, when it was dissolved by the sudden death of Mr. Story. His place was supplied by Mr. Jonas Winchester, and on March 22d, 1834, the new firm issued the first number of the *New Yorker*, a weekly journal devoted to literature, politics, and news. This was edited almost exclusively by Mr. Greeley, and published under his immediate supervision. It was considered at that time the best newspaper of its kind ever attempted in this country. In spite of its high character, it never gained financial success, and Mr. Greeley was obliged to engage his labors. He supplied the *Daily Whig* with its leading articles for some months, and in 1838 undertook the editorial charge of the *Jeffersonian*, a political weekly newspaper, devoted to the interests of the Whig party, and published in the city of Albany. This journal, according to its original plan, continued in existence but one year, and in May, 1840, Mr. Greeley devoted himself to the editorship of the *Log Cabin*, a campaign journal established in the interest of Gen. W. H. Harrison, the Whig candidate for the presidency. It obtained a large circulation, but in the autumn of 1841, was merged, together with the *New Yorker*, in the *Tribune*, with which Mr. Greeley's name is completely identified, and for which his previous newspaper enterprises had served as a preparation.

The first number of this celebrated journal was issued on April 10th, 1841. It was a small sheet, retailing for one cent, with no presses, no capital, and with only 500 subscribers. For the first week, the expenses exceeded the income, but in the course of six months it was established on a sound financial basis, when Mr. Thomas McElrath became a partner and undertook the sole charge of the business of publication, leaving Mr. Greeley the exclusive care of the editorial department. In 1848, Mr. Greeley was elected to fill a vacancy as a member of the House of Representatives in the National Congress, and served in that body from December 1st of that year to March 4th, 1849. He took an active part against the abuses of the mileage system and in favor of the establishment of homesteads in the public lands. In 1851, he visited Europe and served as one of the jurors of the World's Fair in the Crystal Palace in London. He also appeared before the parliamentary committee on newspaper taxes, and gave full and important details concerning the newspaper press of this country. His letters during his absence are among his most interesting productions. In 1855, he made a second visit to Europe, chiefly for the purpose of attending the French Exhibition, remaining abroad about three months. In 1859, he made a journey across the plains to California, and was honored with a public reception at Sacramento and San Francisco. After having exerted himself for the prevention of civil war between the South and the North, at the National Republican Convention which met in Chicago in May, 1860, he took a decided stand in favor of its vigorous prosecution subsequent to the actual commencement of hostilities. In 1864, he made an attempt at reconciliation on a plan of adjustment proposed to President Lincoln, which proved unsuccessful. In the same year, Mr. Greeley was a presidential elector for the State of New York, and a delegate to the Loyalist Convention at Philadelphia. Upon the close of the war in the spring of 1865, Mr. Greeley became a strenuous advocate for complete pacification based on the conditions of impartial suffrage and universal amnesty. In pursuance of this end, he consented to be one of the bondsmen for Mr. Jefferson Davis, the late President of the Confederacy, who was imprisoned by the Federal Government on the charge of treason. In 1867, Mr. Greeley was a delegate to the New York State Convention for the revision of the Constitution, and in 1869 was brought forward as a candidate for the office of State Comptroller, but was defeated in the canvass. In 1870, he stood for Congress as a candidate for the Sixth New York district, and was again defeated, though receiving an exceptionally large number of votes. The Liberal Convention for the nomination of a candidate for the presidency, which met in Cincinnati on May 1st, 1872, after the fifth ballot, gave a majority of votes for Mr. Greeley. He accepted the nomination, and in the month of July following was nominated for the same office by the Democratic Convention at Baltimore. He was thus presented to the country as the candidate of two great parties for the highest office in the government, and an impassioned contest ensued; and he lost the election by a large majority. During the canvass, Mr. Greeley performed an incredible amount of mental and physical labor. He constantly spoke, and in all parts of the country, to numerous and eager audiences, frankly discussing the great questions at issue, and expressing his conviction with equal boldness and candor. His strong constitution at length became impaired by excessive toil and intense excitement. The loss of his wife, who had been a hopeless invalid for many years, and upon whose death-bed he attended during the last week of the canvass, served to complete the fatal work. He was attacked with inflammation of the brain, and sinking under the disease, died on November 29th, at the residence of his physician, two or three miles from his own country-home at Chappaqua.

In addition to his labors as a journalist and public speaker, Mr. Greeley was the author of several works, the principal of which are the following: "Hints towards Reforms" (1850); "Glances at Europe" (1851); "History of the Struggle for Slavery Extension" (1856); "Overland Journey to San Francisco" (1860); "The American Conflict" (1864); "Recollections of a Busy Life" (1869). Mr. Greeley was also the writer of the sketch of Henry Clay and of other articles in the New American Cyclopædia, and of the Confederate States, and several other valuable papers in "Johnson's Cyclopædia," of which he was one of the original editors. The life of Mr. Greeley has been written by

James Parton (Boston, 1855; reviewed, 1868), and a memorial volume was issued by the Tribune Association in 1873. (*George Ripley*.)

Green, Robert, was born in Londonderry, Ireland, May 12th, 1821. His parents removed with him to Canada in his infancy and remained there three years. They then removed to Troy, N. Y., where he received a common-school education. At the age of twelve, he commenced to earn his own living at the trade of cabinet-making. At twenty-three, with a capital of not more than $100, saved from his wages and over-work, he commenced business for himself in a small way. At first only a dealer in chairs, he enlarged his business by degrees to include general furniture and cabinet-making. In 1851, his place of business was burned with a loss that exceeded his insurance. He suffered loss by fire on two other occasions and in the great fire of 1862, lost store, factory, and home. Notwithstanding these repeated and severe discouragements, he continued business with great courage and energy. While his store was rebuilding, he occupied a small store on Congress street, and subsequently bought the premises on River street, still occupied by his business. In 1863, he built his fine residence, No. 72 Fifth street, where his family still reside.

His death occurred in February, 1877. Those who live to lament him may well find comfort and satisfaction in the memory of his manly, worthy, and blameless life, and the patient fortitude and resolution with which he met and overcame checks and hardships before which a weaker nature would have lost heart and given way.

The charities of Mr. Green were as large as they were unostentatious. He had a kind heart, a liberal hand, and a genial temper, and has left behind him a name for excellence and honor in all the relations of life which will prove his enduring monument.

Greene, W. K., was born at Woodstock, Ct., July 18th, 1816. He removed to Hagaman's Mills in 1838, and commenced the manufacture of carpets. In 1841, he moved to Amsterdam, where he continued the same business until 1847. He then went to Astoria, Long Island, where for one year he had charge of Higgins's carpet-mills. In 1848, he moved to Schenectady, where he also remained one year, having charge of a carpet-mill owned by a stock company of which he was a member. In 1849, he sold out his interest there, and returned to Amsterdam, where he continued to reside until his death. On his return there, he again embarked in the manufacture of carpets, and carried on the same successfully until the year 1860, when he sold his carpet looms and machinery, and instead put in knitting machinery for the manufacture of knit wrappers, drawers, and jackets. He continued in this branch of manufacture until his death, at which time he was running 13 sets of cards and employing some 300 hands. He was always a successful business man, and amassed a large fortune. In July, 1869, he went to Europe, hoping to regain his health, which had become seriously impaired. His family consulted the best of foreign physicians, but they were unable to do any thing for him, and he finally died at Rome, Italy, Jan. 23d, 1870, in the 54th year of his age. His remains were embalmed and brought to his home in Amsterdam, and now rest there among his kindred in the beautiful Green Hill Cemetery. His virtues were many. Few personal pleas for help fell upon his ear unheard or unanswered. He dispensed his charities with liberality while living, and without ostentation. His position in life and his fortune were of his

own creation. By untiring industry, strict economy, and close attention to business, he attained reputation and social position, which will live as a monument to his proud character.

Haberstro, Joseph Lambert.—Whoever achieves fortune and social position by his own efforts, and preserves at the same time an unblemished reputation, is a credit to any community, and is a safe example and guide to succeeding generations. The subject of this sketch was born in Buffalo, on the 27th of July, 1831. His parents, Joseph and Catharine M. Haberstro, were natives of Alsace, and came to this country in 1828. His father was a gunsmith by trade, and followed this occupation in Buffalo till 1845, when he commenced merchandising, which he carried on successfully for many years, and died much respected in 1862, his wife surviving him twelve years.

Joseph Lambert Haberstro received only a common-school education, and at the age of thirteen left his studies to learn his father's trade, continuing at the same till 1847, when he joined his father in the mercantile business, following the same till 1859. At the age of twenty-two, in 1853, and while in merchandising, Mr. Haberstro was married to Miss Barbara Scheu, daughter of Philip Scheu, by whom he has had ten children. In 1859, Mr. Haberstro commenced the business of brewer and maltster, which he still follows. The business career of Mr. Haberstro in this city has been a most successful one. His business talents, industry, and energy, which have never wavered from the proper direction, would have made him partially successful in any place; but in Buffalo, where there was such an ample field for their development, Mr. Haberstro has reached a position in the business world which must satisfy all his aspirations, and in said career he has made many friends, the result of successful enterprise and exalted merit. In 1864, he was elected to his first political office, that of alderman; and in 1866 was re-elected, thus serving four years in that capacity. During the second term of his service, he was president of the council, and was also acting mayor of the city. How well he filled these positions, was best acknowledged by the fact that, in 1867, he was elected City Treasurer, and, in reward for his faithful services, was again elected in 1869, thus having the honor of being the first gentleman who held the office for four years since Buffalo became a city. This did not end his official career and usefulness, for his name was a tower of strength to his party in the election of 1876; and at that time he was chosen sheriff, which position he now holds, and his devotion to his official trusts has won for him the general respect of the community in which he lives.

No man occupies a more enviable position in the community of which he is a member, nor more clearly exemplifies the legitimate result of well-directed energy, industry, and thoroughness of purpose.

Agan, Patrick H.—The subject of this sketch was born at Watertown, N. Y., in the year 1817. In 1826, both his parents died, leaving a large family of children without adequate means of support. The household was consequently broken up and scattered—Patrick finding a refuge and home in a good family a few miles distant. Here he remained seven years, attending a country school in winter for three years, and a village school the remaining four winters. His studies were confined to the rudimentary branches. At sixteen, he was offered a clerkship in a store at Liverpool, Onondaga County, and gladly accepted the situation. In 1836, he went to Detroit, Mich., intending to remain there, but returned in 1837. Soon afterward he engaged in trade in a small way, and continued in business for six years. In 1846, he purchased a half interest in the *Onondaga Standard*, and then moved to Syracuse. This paper remained under his editorial management for more than twenty years. In 1850, the *Syracuse Daily Standard* was established, under his management also. In 1856, he sold his interest in these two papers, but continued his editorial work ten years longer. During these twenty years, the slavery question became the paramount issue in our politics. Although the *Standard* was the Democratic "organ" of the county, Mr. Agan earnestly advocated the adoption of the "Wilmot Proviso," opposing the election of General Cass in 1848, by reason of the party's hostility to that measure. For the same reason he refused to support Mr. Buchanan in 1856. In 1860-64, he favored Mr. Lincoln's election to the presidency. Mr. Agan was always the foe of legislative subsidies and of governmental aid to internal improvements. He also earnestly advocated free-trade doctrines, believing "Protection" to be grounded in selfishness and a device for robbery. In State affairs he was for confining legislation to general objects and within constitutional limitations, favoring the repeal of the usury and inspection laws, and opposing all attempts to enforce morality through legal restraints and penalties. He likewise urged the sale of the Canals and their relinquishment by the State, as a measure of relief to the treasury, and as the only sure method of eradicating corruption in their management. In 1866, differing from the Republican party in its Southern policy, Mr. Agan withdrew from the *Standard* and from editorial life. In 1855, Mr. Agan was nominated on the Democratic ticket for the office of Inspector of State Prisons, but was defeated with all his associates. In 1857, he was elected County Treasurer, and served one term. In 1861, he was appointed Postmaster at Syracuse, and served four years in that office. From 1850 to 1856, he was clerk of the Board of Supervisors of Onondaga County. Mr. Agan was the earliest advocate of the Syracuse Northern Railway enterprise, and devoted much time and labor in promoting its success, having been secretary of the company from the outset until after the road was completed. He was also the first to suggest the conversion of the Adirondack wilderness into a State Park—a measure that has received the public sanction, and although still delayed in its consummation, is in a fair way of ultimate accomplishment.

Hardin, George A.—This distinguished jurist, the son of Col. Joseph and Amanda Backus Hardin, was born August 17th, 1832, in the town of Winfield, Herkimer County, N. Y. He received a preparatory education at Cazenovia and Whitestone seminaries before entering Union College, from which place he graduated with honors in 1852. He completed his law studies with J. N. Lake and the late Judge Nolton, pre-eminent in that part of the State for their great learning in the law, of which they gave their student the benefit, inspiring him with a portion of their zeal for the profession. He was admitted to the bar at Watertown, N. Y., July 4th, 1854, and soon after formed a law partnership with Judge Nolton. Filled with honorable emulation and a fair field before him, it was not long before he became known as a rising man in his profession. Fortunately he received all the adventitious assistance of thorough train-

ing in mental exercise previous to commencing the study of the law; and when he had mastered his profession, he possessed an untold advantage over those who had been deprived of a suitable preparatory education.

In 1858, he was appointed by Governor King district-attorney of Herkimer County, elected the same year, and filled the position until January 1st, 1862; when, having been elected by the Union Republican party, he took his position and entered the State Senate, representing the Twentieth district, Herkimer and Otsego counties. At the close of the session in 1863, he returned to the practice of the law, which he continued until 1871, when he was, by both Republican and Democratic parties, nominated and elected Justice of the Supreme Court for the Fifth Judicial District for the term of fourteen years. The nomination by both political parties was a marked testimonial to his standing, and he has ever endeavored to discharge the judicial duties so as to merit the partiality and kindness shown him by the people and the very able bar of his district.* He has been a stirring, practical man both in his public and his private life. He has done much, and all honorably, and studiously endeavored to discharge the duties imposed on him in every public position he has held. In the community in which he lives, he enjoys the entire confidence of all who know him, regardless of party or condition, as one of the purest of men, reliable in every respect, though modest and retiring, passing for less than his real worth. A man of good attainments, which are sound and substantial.

Harper, Fletcher, senior member of the firm of Harper & Brothers, publishers, died May 29th, 1877. He was the youngest of the four

*In 1876, Hamilton College conferred on him the degree of LL.D.

brothers who founded and brought to great and deserved eminence the publishing house of Harper & Brothers, and was the last survivor of the four. James, the oldest of the four, was born in 1795; John, in 1797; Wesley, in 1801; and Fletcher, in 1806. Wesley Harper was apprenticed to his brothers after they had set up in business; and some years later, Fletcher also became an apprentice. When the two younger brothers had "worked out their time," they purchased a share in the business, Wesley in 1823, and Fletcher in 1826. Thereupon the firm became Harper & Brothers. For some years, and while the business was growing, Wesley, who had a cultivated literary taste and wrote all his life remarkably pure and vigorous English, was the proof-reader of the firm, and Fletcher was foreman of the composing-room; and tradition relates that he was a very energetic and driving foreman.

The four brothers worked together all their lives with singular unanimity. They adopted a rule early in life never to enter on any enterprise unless all four were agreed to it, and to this they adhered constantly, and to it they doubtless owed their safety in many instances as business men. It is related that the establishment of *Harper's Magazine* was due to him.

The success of the *Magazine*, which is one of the greatest known in literary annals, so completely justified his judgment that his predominant influence in the firm was established from that time. This was in 1850. In 1853, the great fire consumed, in a day, their whole stock, and inflicted on them a loss of over a million of dollars. Then the energy of these printers was shown. They held, on the evening of the fire, a family council, to decide whether or not they should rebuild their business. They had already so great wealth that their loss, so far from crippling them, left them with a competence for themselves and their children. But the claims of authors, of workmen who had been long with them, and the desire to leave a well-established business to their children, induced them to determine to go on. An order on Adams, of South Boston, for twenty of his new power presses, to replace those destroyed by the fire, was telegraphed the same day, thus anticipating by a few hours applications by mail from other enterprising printers for a similar number of presses. By this prompt and characteristic action the Harpers were enabled to furnish their new office with presses several months sooner than they could have done had they sent their order by mail instead of telegraph. It is said that the whole question was discussed and decided at this family council the evening after the fire, and the next week already plans began to be considered by the firm for a new building. Of course, the business was temporarily carried on in another place. The new building, it was determined, should be fireproof, as it is.

Fletcher Harper was for many years the most active of the four brothers. He bore the heaviest burdens, and bore them easily. He possessed a cheerful and buoyant temper, unfailing courage, and was always an admirable administrator. It was his thought which, in 1856, established *Harper's Weekly*, and in 1867, the *Bazar*, both which he made eminently successful. Though he had, of course, proper assistants, and trained one of his sons and one of his nephews in this department, he was for many years the active and chief editor of these publications, and especially of the *Magazine*. He always, with characteristic modesty, asserted himself to be without the qualifications necessary to enable him to judge of the literary merits of a book or an article, but his taste and judgment, and the quick tact with which he saw what would take with the public, were unerring.

In person Mr. Harper was tall, well formed, of light complexion, with blue eyes, and with a very noble head, full of intelligence and power. He was always, in business and socially, easily accessible to the humblest people, and his kind and winning manners set people quickly at ease. Like all the brothers, he took a kindly and affectionate interest in those who served him, and he will be missed and mourned by very many who have grown gray in the service of the house, and who always found in him a considerate friend ready to be helpful to them in distress and to show himself their friend as well as employer. In all the relations of life he was an eminently benevolent and humane man, whose pleasure was to make others happy, and who sought out by preference the friendless and lowly. His love of retirement and a modesty which amounted almost to shyness led him to keep himself from all public or conspicuous positions and to conceal his many deeds of charity from the world. He was most happy in his home, where he was surrounded by his children and grandchildren, and latterly his great grandchildren, and where his chosen friends were always welcome.

Mr. Harper's health began to fail several years ago. The death of his brother Wesley, to whom he was very fondly attached, was a great shock to him. As the brothers one after another died, he seemed to feel the growing loneliness of his position, and while he remained always cheerful, his health was evidently shaken. A great fondness for country life grew upon him in his later years, and he prolonged his stay at his country place on the Hudson each year, with greater satisfaction to himself and with evident benefit to his health. (*New York Herald.*)

Harper, James, was born at Newtown, Long Island, in this State, during the year 1795. His father being a respectable farmer of that place, he received as good an education as the locality afforded, remaining at the paternal home until he had reached his sixteenth year, when he, together with his brother John, was sent to this city and apprenticed to a printer. The trade was learned with great rapidity, the lad not being engaged many months in the business before he had become an excellent compositor. Sober, steady, economical, and hard-working, he contrived during his apprenticeship, by means principally of over-work, to save some few hundred dollars, as was also done by his brother John, who possessed all the excellent qualifications so marked in the deceased, and whose life has been so bound up with that of his brother that we can scarcely write an obituary of the one without giving a biographical sketch of the other. At about the same date, their obligations as apprentices ceased, and they became free to select their future life. With the money saved, to which we have already made reference, they opened a printing establishment in New York. Soon after, Wesley and Fletcher Harper, younger brothers of the deceased, were apprenticed to the firm, which was then and for some years after known by the name of J. & J. Harper. The business prospered exceedingly, and in a short time the proprietors began publishing books on their own account. In 1822, Wesley Harper was admitted to partnership, and from thenceforward to the present writing the firm has been known as that of Harper & Brothers. It is unnecessary to go into particulars of the high position which Mr. James Harper attained as the senior proprietor of one of the largest publishing houses in the world. The widespread reputation of the Harpers, the countless books they have published, and their pecuniary wealth, are subjects of common knowledge to the reader.

The deceased gentleman at one time took an active part in politics, and in 1844 was elected Mayor of the city of New York, but was defeated for the same position at the election held the year following. His administration, though devoid of any remarkable events, was, nevertheless, successful, and increased the respect and estimation in which he was held by the citizens generally. After 1845, he sought no political office, his extensive and constantly increasing business requiring his undivided care and attention. As a publisher, he was noted for the earnestness with which he endeavored to elevate the standard of American literature, and the encouragement he ever gave to native talent.

The fact, too, that his firm was the first in the United States that published a periodical composed almost entirely of American composition, and which has won a world reputation, is to no small extent attributable to his keen business sagacity and literary talent.

Although he had reached the ripe age of seventy-three, Mr. Harper remained in active business life until the day of the fatal accident which has ended his earthly career. It was remarked not long ago, that notwithstanding his age there was " no youth in the establishment more active than he."

He was always in hale, robust health, his mental faculties were as bright as those of a younger man, and it was often observed that, if personal appearances were to be judged by, he was likely to outlive his brothers who were younger than he. Personally he was a high-toned gentleman, generous, charitable, a firm friend and a warm-hearted, sociable man. He delighted in the society of the vivacious and entertaining, loved a good story and a good joke, and was as clever at relating as he was attentive in hearing. Whether as a public character, as a friend and patron of literature, or as a man of high social standing and domestic virtues, he was such a citizen as would necessarily and naturally gather around him the friendship and esteem of all. He died March 17th, 1869.

Harper, John, of the well-known publishing firm of Harper & Brothers, was a son of Joseph Harper, whose occupation was that of a builder, and was born and reared on a farm in the vicinity of what is now known as Newtown, Long Island. His father was a man of sound common sense, a pious member of the Methodist Episcopal Church, and to which the son has always adhered. John Harper was indentured apprentice to the printing business by his father when he was of proper age. Early in the summer of 1817, having just finished his term of apprenticeship at the printing trade, he, together with his brother, opened a modest printing-office in the second story of a small wooden house on the corner of Front and Dover streets, in New York City. When this little establishment was announced to the public, the business of printing books was in its infancy in this country, and the venture of these young men was looked upon as almost desperate. By great energy and industry, however, the firm prospered from the first. In a few years, they found their quarters too limited, and removed to another building in Fulton street, near Broadway. In 1823, a younger brother, Mr. Joseph Wesley Harper, who had learned his trade of them, was given an interest in the house. In 1825, they removed again to Pearl street, near Franklin Square, and shortly after to Cliff street, where they purchased two small buildings and materially extended their business. In 1826, another brother, Mr. Fletcher Harper, was admitted to partnership, and the style of the firm was changed from J. & J. Harper to Harper & Brothers. This was the origin of what is now the largest book publishing firm in the world. On the 10th of December, 1853, a fire occurred in the buildings occupied by Harper & Brothers, through the carelessness of a plumber, and property to the amount of $1,000,000 was destroyed. With their characteristic energy, they immediately determined upon rebuilding their establishment upon a scale which would have staggered the most prosperous commercial house. The new buildings were finished in 1855, and are the same which are now occupied by the firm. On the 25th of March, 1869, Mr. James Harper visited the store for the last time. On this occasion he was in his usual health and appeared to be possessed of unusually good spirits; he left the establishment at an early hour, and, as was his usual custom, went to ride in Central Park. By an accident he was thrown from his carriage, and received injuries from which he died two days afterward. His brother, Joseph Wesley Harper, became so afflicted at the demise of his elder brother, that he took sick and rapidly failed in health, and died on the 14th of February, 1870. After the death of his two brothers, John Harper withdrew from active business, and the firm was reorganized by the admission of several sons of the original partners. These, after receiving a careful education, several of them at Columbia College, entered the house, each serving a regular apprenticeship in some branch of the business. Mr. John Harper had been in very delicate health for upward of a year before his death, which occurred April 22d, 1875. The last occasion of his being seen in public was during the latter part of the month of May, 1874, when he indulged, at the advice of his physician, in a ride through Central Park.

Harper, Joseph Wesley, was born in Newtown, L. I., in 1801. Early in the century the firm, which now stands second to none in the United States, was founded. In 1822, the subject of this sketch was admitted to partnership. From the start he displayed great business capacity. His literary taste was pure and elevated; all the books selected by him for publication meeting, it is said, with marked success. And not only in choice of literature did he contribute to the advancement of his firm. When he became a partner, the establishment was by no means what it now is. At one time he performed the duties of foreman of the composing-room. In his intercourse with printers he met some disreputable characters on whom kindness would have been utterly lost. But excepting these, he always referred to his career as head of the composing-room, as being most pleasant. While maintaining strictest discipline, he succeeded in winning the friendship of all whose good opinion was worth having. At a later period than that referred to above, he took the position of proof-reader, but did not hold it a very long while. The firm had by this time increased its business greatly, and had already achieved an enviable reputation throughout the United States. On Mr. Wesley Harper devolved all the literary work of the establishment. Although he had not enjoyed the advantages of a collegiate education, his reading was extensive and varied He had cultivated a close acquaintance with English literature, and was conversant with all of continental literature that was of service to his business. His style of writing was finished though simple and unaffected; many of the prefaces in the works comprising the old Family Library were written by him, and are noteworthy for their compactness of expression. Mr. Harper, however, did not write much at any time, and as years passed on, he wrote less and less. A large number of the works submitted to the firm for publication were read by him, and his critical judgment was always found correct. To his credit be it said, neither prejudice for or against an author determined his decision. Every manuscript read by him was weighed according to its merits, and the rigid impartiality with which he acted, added to the soundness of his judgment, naturally enabled him to exercise a preponderating influence in the choice of books published by his house. For many years he was the real conductor of *Harper's Magazine*, but few articles appearing that had not been examined and approved by him. Mr. Harper also conducted the literary correspondence of the firm until his eldest son was admitted to the business, when he transferred this arduous duty to him. His letters to authors were always worded in a spirit of kindness that charmed the reader. To the unfortunate writer whose book had been declined, he even extended hearty sympathy, and did not fail, if the production exhibited marks of ability, to encourage him to persevere. Except as a publisher and literary gentleman, Mr. Wesley Harper was not known to the public. Indeed, his elder brother, the late James Harper, was and has been the only member of the firm that ever received the suffrages of his fellow-citizens, and even then the office was not sought after. Aside from his business character, there was much in Mr. Harper's private life to admire.

Personally he was modest to shyness. Quiet, unassuming, a model of gentlemanly courtesy, and ever mindful of the feelings of others, he was never known to utter language to others that could aggrieve or wound. He belonged to what is called the "old school" of gentlemen. His suavity of manners and thoughtful consideration for others, endeared him to all the employés of Harper & Brothers, as well as to his immediate relatives. To those in trouble he ever lent a ready ear, and was willing to aid the poor and unfortunate with his money and with personal attention, if this last was needed. He took a warm interest in the welfare and comfort of his subordinates, to whom he was always accessible, and who found in him a ready friend and adviser. For some years Mr. Harper had been suffering from the disease which ended his earthly career of usefulness. The physical sufferings that embitter some men's temper were endured by him with a calm and serene resignation. He had been, during the greater part of his life, a prominent member and officer of the Sands street Methodist church in Brooklyn, and was noted for his sincere devotion to the tenets of Christianity. Strong in his faith of a future full of light and love in a better world above, he met death undismayed.

Hart, Elizur, was born in Durham, Greene Co., N. Y., May 22d, 1803. His father, Deacon Joseph Hart, removed to Seneca County, N. Y., in 1806, and to Barre, Orleans Co., in October, 1812. It was several years after he removed to Barre, before any school was opened in his father's neighborhood, and he never had the benefit of much instruction in school. During his early life, he was employed mainly in clearing up land and in labor on the farm. About the year 1827, he was elected constable, an office he held two years. His business now called him to spend much of his time in Albion. He had some money, and his brother William had a like sum, which he put into Elizur's hands for their joint benefit. He then commenced a small brokerage business. About this time, his father deeded to his sons, William and Elizur, each 100 acres of land, for which they paid him $500. After some time, Elizur sold his interest to his brother William. As Mr. Hart found his means increasing, he began to invest in bonds and mortgages and in articles for land issued by the Holland Company.

On February 10th, 1860, in company with Mr. Joseph M. Cornell, he established the Orleans County Bank, at Albion, with a capital of $100,000. Of this bank he was president as long as it existed. It was changed to Orleans County National Bank August 9th, 1865, he being its president the remainder of his life.

Always attentive to business and never dilatory or impulsive, correct and exemplary in all his habits, beginning with comparatively nothing, without the aid or influence of wealthy connections, he became one of the opulent county bankers of the State, and at his death, which occurred August 13th, 1870, was master of a large fortune.

In his will he gave the Presbyterian church in Albion, of which he was a member, fifty thousand dollars to build a house of worship, and an endowment of five thousand dollars to the Sunday-school connected with his church. Mr. Hart married Miss Loraine Field in May, 1835, by whom he had three children. She died February 11th, 1847. He was again married to Miss Cornelia King October 16th, 1849.

Harvey, Charles W.—The subject of this sketch was born in Albany, N. Y., in

1810. In early life he received both academic and collegiate education in the Albany Academy, Lafayette and Union Colleges. He studied medicine in the office of the late Dr. Jonathan Eights, of Albany, and graduated in medicine in the Medical Department of the University of Buffalo. Later in life, he received the degree of Master of Arts from Lafayette College, and the honorary degree of Doctor of Dental Surgery from the Baltimore Dental College. He practised both medicine and dentistry in Albany until 1836, when he moved to Buffalo, N. Y., and there devoted himself exclusively to the latter profession until 1872, when he retired to private life. Among the eminent citizens of Buffalo who have for the past forty years been honored and esteemed both at home and abroad, no one is more sincerely beloved and respected in all the relations of life than Dr. C. W. Harvey. He is a man of firmness of character, though modest and unassuming in his manners, enjoying the confidence and respect of all who know him. He is both confiding and generous. One of the effective attributes of his popularity is the purity of his character. It is this which has given him the esteem of all men and the unbounded confidence of his patients.

Hayes, George E., D.D.S.—The subject of this sketch has been a practising dentist in the city of Buffalo for the last forty-eight years. When he settled there, it was but a village of 5000 inhabitants. He has witnessed its continuous growth in population, wealth, and refinement.

He is the son of Simeon Hayes and Betsey Gilbert, of Granby, Ct.; was born there, November 7th, 1804, in the family residence built by his great grandfather. The family trace descent from George Hayes, who emigrated to this country from Scotland, in 1650, and settled finally in the village of Salmon Brook, Granby, Hartford Co., Ct. In 1805, his parents removed to Prattsburg, N. Y., where they shared the labor of clearing the forests and laying the foundations of an intelligent Christian community. In those days it was deemed fortunate if settlers could secure the privilege of district-schools for their children, and with the exception, at a later period, of a few months' attendance at the Canandaigua Academy, they were his early aids in the way of education.

In 1820, he became a student in the office of Dr. Pliny Hayes, of Canandaigua, intending to prepare for the medical profession; but was induced in 1825 to accept the offer of a partnership with him, in the sale of drugs and medicines. In 1829, this establishment was removed to Buffalo, where, in the fall of that year, it was burned, on the site now occupied by Townsend Hall.

While a student with Dr. Hayes, he had learned what little was then known of dentistry; and it so happened that when he moved to Buffalo, there was then no one there who answered to that calling; and it also happened that the ex-sheriff of London, Parkinson, was there, and had the misfortune to break a front tooth. It happened also that a former resident of Canandaigua, who thought the Hayeses could do any thing, sent him over the way for relief. Thus it fell out, that the fire-fiend, aided by the gratitude and good-will of Parkinson, more than the foresight of the subject of this essay, caused a revolution in his business pursuits through life.

He was first married to Emily M. Hopkins, Dec. 27th, 1827, to whom were born sons and daughters, but one of whom survive, Harriet L., who married the Rev. Charles H.

Smith. He was again married Sept. 1st, 1858, to Catharine Bradt.

In 1834-35 and 1836, he engaged in real estate transactions, some of which shared the fate of the speculations of 1837; but others enabled him to weather the financial storm of that year and keep his escutcheon untarnished.

He was one of the founders of the Young Men's Association, and its second president. Also a life-member of the Society of Natural Sciences, and a member of the Buffalo Historical Society. While he had little leisure to spare from business pursuits, his tastes tended to scientific studies, and to gratify those fancies he spent the summer of 1837 at New Haven, in the study of geology, mineralogy, etc., under the direction of Professors Benjamin Silliman and Charles N. Shepard, with the privilege of attending their summer course of lectures on natural history.

He was the first to make and use the enamelled gum teeth, colored with oxide of gold, to resemble the natural gum, and was also the inventor of improvements in vulcanizers, and other instruments for dental use, which had a wide sale, not only here, but in Europe and South America, and which finally resulted in the organization known as the Buffalo Dental Manufacturing Company.

Heacock, W. J., was born at Kingsborough, Fulton County, N. Y., April 5th, 1821. In early life he received a common-school education, attending for a few winters only, being prevented by delicate health, which he did not overcome until twenty years of age. His first business experience was in the dry goods trade in his native village When twenty-four, he commenced the manufacture of gloves, which he continued successfully for several years, and was among the largest in the business. He was the founder of the Fonda, Johnstown, and Gloversville Railroad, its first and only president. It is mainly due to his exertions that the road was ever built. The same may be said in regard to the Gloversville and Northville Railroad, of which he is also president. He is also director in the Fulton County Coal Company. Twice he has served in the State Assembly. During the first term (1863), he was chairman of the Traders and Manufacturers' Committee, and in 1873 was chairman of the Railroad Committee. He was married February 11th, 1845, to Miss Minerva M. Avery, daughter of Rev. R. A. Avery, of Galway, Saratoga County, N. Y., by whom he has had four children, three of whom survive. At the breaking out of the war, Mr. W. J. Heacock was chairman of the county committee that raised the funds and troops for the Union. He also spent nearly two winters in Washington, looking after the interests of the glove manufacturers and adjusting properly the taxation which is applied in this country. We need scarcely say he was very successful and earned well the praise that the manufacturers bestowed upon him. Mr. Heacock lived at Kingsborough when the division in the old Congregational church took place, and the major part of the influential members left to form the present church at Gloversville. It was only by great efforts on the part of Mr. Heacock that the church was saved from financial ruin. In 1861, he moved his residence to Gloversville; and in 1864, there being no Presbyterian church in the village, Mr. Heacock, by his warm support and liberal subscription, was the main mover in having the new First Presbyterian church erected, one of the most beautiful edifices in this section. He has been one of the trustees since its erection, a member of the session

and superintendent of the Sabbath-school, excepting one year. He is at present actively engaged in managing the railroads of which he is the honored president, and which under his executive have proved successful from their commencement. Within the memory of Mr. Heacock, Gloversville has grown from a mere hamlet with the country school-house upon the main corner, surrounded with pine trees, to its present proportions and importance, through the development of the glove industry, which commenced in its primary state from the fact the woods in those days abounded in deer, and the first settlers being mostly peddlers of tinware, took the hides in exchange for goods. At first they knew not what to do with them. The ingenuity of the Yankees soon turned them into gloves. Though rude in construction, they have gradually advanced and improved until they now manufacture the finest dressed gent's glove made, which finds a market all over the United States.

Heath, Judge S. Pulver, was born at Minersville, Montgomery County, April 15th, 1820, and resided there till six years old, when, together with his parents, he removed to Troy. In two years they moved to Amsterdam, where he has since resided. His academic education was received at the hands of Horace Sprague, village of Amsterdam; then attended Union College, from which place he graduated 1840; when he studied law with Samuel Belding and Nicholas Hill, Jr., at Amsterdam, and was admitted to the bar in 1842. Subsequently he became a partner with Hon. Clark B. Cochrane, late of Albany, also Samuel Belding, Jr.; afterward Gerry W. Hazelton, of Wisconsin. In 1850, he was elected to the Legislature and served in 1851. From 1869 to 1871, he was the U. S. District Asssesor of Eighteenth district, New York. At the expiration of that term (1871), he was elected Judge of Montgomery County, a position he has since and now holds. He is also a director in the First National Bank of Amsterdam, and director in the Gas Company. He was married in 1847 to Miss Groat, of Amsterdam, by whom he has had six children. His eldest son is at present a partner in his law practice. Judge Heath is now in the fifty-eighth year of his age and the senior partner of the well-known law firm at Amsterdam. He has been a stirring, practical man, both in public and in private life, and his good constitution being still vigorous and unenfeebled and his intellect ripened by experience, he would do honor to any official function in the gift of his State.

Hedstrom, Eric L., was born in Stockholm, Sweden, August 21st, 1835. His father, Eric Hedstrom, came to this country in 1843, and settled in Lake County, Illinois, upon what was then government land.

The country was sparsely settled, and Mr. Hedstrom's advantages were necessarily limited.

At the age of sixteen, he was apprenticed to the trade of a blacksmith, at Waukegan, Ill., with the understanding that during the first year he should have six months' schooling. Failing to fulfil their agreement in this particular, he returned to the farm, remaining there for another two years, at which time he determined to go to Rochester with the purpose of taking a college course.

But straitened circumstances making it necessary for him to earn, to a large extent, his way through school, his health failed, and in the spring of 1856 he returned to Chicago.

He soon obtained employment with A. B. Meeker & Co., where he remained until 1864, when he was sent by that firm to Buffalo,

N. Y., to represent its interests there. He was at once given an interest in the business in Buffalo, the firm being known as E. L. Hedstrom until 1874, when a junior partner was admitted, the firm becoming known as E. L. Hedstrom & Co.

The principal business of the house is that of anthracite coal, being sole agents for the Lehigh Valley Coal Company, an interest identified with that of the Lehigh Valley Railroad Company. They also represent large interests connected with the Lake Superior iron regions.

Mr. Hedstrom was married in the summer of 1865 to Miss Anna M. Clampffer, daughter of Mr. G. M. Clampffer, of Reading, Pa., the issue of which has been two children.

One of the chief characteristics of this gentleman's success has been his untiring energy and indomitable will. With limited advantages he has surmounted many obstacles where others would have failed, and is to-day recognized as standing at the head of one of the leading houses in the line of his trade.

His business connections represent but a small part of his activities. For several years he was President of the Young Men's Christian Association of Buffalo, and is also actively engaged in church and Sunday-school work.

As one of his friends informs the writer of this sketch, "He is always to be found at the wheel when any public good is to be obtained."

Without doubt, Mr. Hedstrom is a self-made man, and one who has the esteem and confidence of the community in which he lives.

Hodge, John.—The subject of this sketch is in personal appearance robust physique, generous temperament, with bold and shrewd capacity, and in many respects a representative and typical business man.

He was born in Jefferson County, New York, during 1837, and in early life had many advantages of mental training and culture. His first tastes were formed for a professional career, and he studied for the law, which he afterward abandoned, determining to make himself useful and active as a business man. To this end he moved to Lockport, N. Y., where he commenced the manufacture of gargling oil. What success has attended his exertions and shrewd business management is apodictical to all; for there are few among our readers who do not know Mr. Hodge, personally or by reputation, as having built up a vast business, and the reputation of the goods he manufactures is as wide-spread as our vast country.

In 1872, he feeling an interest, and having faith in the future of Lockport, erected an elegant block known as the Hodge Opera-House Building, which contains the Post-Office, Western Union Telegraph Office, seven first-class stores, all the city and United States courts and offices, besides the opera-house proper with a capacity to hold 2000 people. He is also president of the Union Printing and Publishing Company, and president of the Firemen's Life Association of the State of New York. Mr. Hodge is worthy of more than the usual word in connection with his standing in the various grades of the fraternity of Freemasonry; but we forbear any further notice of him in these relations than to state that he has held many positions in both the York and Scottish rites, and in all his Masonic relations he discharges his duties with unswerving integrity and well-deserved honor. Mr. Hodge is an example to the young men of to-day. He is now in the prime of life and in the strength and activity of his manhood;

and the honors of well-doing shall gather round his steps when the days of his active toil shall be passed.

Hosmer, Gustavus P., was born August 2d, 1819, at Avon, Livingston County, N. Y. He moved to Batavia, Genesee County, N. Y., spring of 1827, and to Niagara County, N. Y., in 1836, with his father, who was one of the pioneers of Western New York (1793). The subject of this sketch received his early schooling at Avon and Batavia, finishing at the Canandaigua Academy in the spring of 1835. His early business experience was obtained while acting in the capacity of clerk in stores at Canandaigua, Rochester, and Buffalo, and T Forwarding House at Oswego. From the fall of 1839 till the spring of 1841, he was in the Bank of Western New York, at Rochester, as book-keeper and teller. In the spring of 1841, he moved to Albany, and occupied a responsible position in a stave and lumber house, and commenced business for himself in the same business in fall of 1841. This he has since continued with more than ordinary success, operating in Northern Ohio, Western Pennsylvania, and Michigan. In the last-named State, he has owned pine and oak lands, mills, and for many years was interested in vessel stock on the Western lakes. His goods have found their way all over the Northern States and as far south as Baltimore, and his business connections extended for many years to Portland, Me., with a firm who are largely engaged in sending shooks and cooperage stock to the West India markets, and he ships to many ports in Northern Europe, France, Spain, and California.

It was through his instrumentality that the manufacture of shooks was commenced in Western New York, and since its infancy it has developed into a very extensive business westward to Wisconsin. He has been successful in all of his business pursuits, from a rare combination of industry and judgment which has ever restrained him from embarking in visionary projects, and kept his energies properly directed, adding to and extending his business operations, which for many years have furnished a large number of persons with daily employment; and now, at the age of fifty-eight, after a successful result, he retires from *active* business to enjoy the comforts of a quiet home in Lockport, one of the most delightful cities in Western New York.

Howe, Elias, Jr.—This gentleman, well known in this country and Europe as the inventor of the sewing-machine, died at his residence in Brooklyn, October 3d, 1867. The deceased was a native of Spencer, Mass., where he was born during the year 1819, and was consequently forty-eight years of age at the time of his death. While a youth, he pursued the occupation of a farmer and miller; but as he approached manhood, learned the trade of a machinist. In the pursuit of this vocation he studied the science of machinery with marked success, the result of his studies being the invention of the sewing-machine, which brought him both fame and wealth, and proved one of the greatest benefits to the community. His first patent was secured in 1847, but it was not until 1854 that he finally succeeded in maintaining his claim as the inventor. He was awarded a gold medal at the Paris Exposition by the Emperor Napoleon in person for his invention, and was the recipient of other marks of favor from the ruler of the French. For some time before his death, Mr. Howe had been afflicted with a terrible disease, known as Bright's disease of the kidneys; and, although it was reported that he had been cured of it by a clairvoyant on his return from Europe, it is probable that was the cause of his death. The public in general regretted his loss, for his invention undoubtedly conferred a great blessing on mankind, and the poor working-woman in particular.

Hoysradt, J. W., was born in 1824, at Ancram, Columbia County, N. Y. During his early business experience, he clerked in the ordinary country stores until nineteen years of age, receiving his education in the district-schools. In 1845, after living at Hudson one year, he moved to Stockbridge, Mass., where he was engaged to Charles C. Alger in the manufacture of charcoal pig-iron. In 1850, Mr. Alger moved to Hudson, Mr. Hoysradt going with him, and where a stock company was formed, and the present works of the Hudson Iron Company were built. The subject of this sketch has been connected with these works from that time, and since 1864 he has held the position of president and general manager. He has been President of the Clapp & Jones Steam Fire-Engine Company since its organization; was President of the Columbia County Iron Company. At present he is President of the Farmers' National Bank of Hudson. He has always been a staunch friend to all improvements, and a liberal subscriber to stocks, and at present is connected with many institutions. When mayor of the city of Hudson, during 1859 and 1860, and again in 1867-8, he was ready to approve of every measure that would contribute to the growth and welfare of the city. He held the postmastership for eight years.

J. W. Hoysradt is a child of New York, and has been nursed amidst her institutions. He has, through a long course of successful life, shown himself worthy of all honor; and still in the meridian of his existence, the State in which he first drew his breath can hope all things from his talents, patriotism, and integrity.

Hughson, J. C.—The biography of such a man as J. C. Hughson is fraught not only with readable interest, but has a useful moral effect upon the present time and posterity. It teaches youth what industry and moral worth can achieve, and that they can hope for all things if they make honor their guide, and are prompted by honorable emulation.

The subject of this sketch was born in Schoharie County, N. Y., October 4th, 1820, where he continued to live until he was eighteen years old, receiving the best education the neighborhood afforded. In 1838, he moved to Catskill, where he worked in the capacity of clerk for five years. In 1845, he moved to Albany, and became a member of the firm of Higbee, Douglass & Co., who were large lumber dealers. Here he continued until 1857, when he sold out his interest in the Albany firm, and bought their entire manufacturing interest located in Canada, which he still continues to operate. After paying strict personal attention to his manufacturing business for eight or ten years, he returned to Albany, and started a lumber-yard on a large scale, since which time he has made Albany his permanent home, though he still retains large interests in Canada, besides having yards in Port Sarnia and New York City. In 1842, he was married in Catskill, N. Y., the issue of which has been eight children. Amid all the political agitation this country has passed through, Mr. Hughson was never allured from his business to take part in factional disputes, but has de-

voted himself most unremittingly to business, its extensive operations requiring all his time and most watchful attention. He is now in the prime of physical vigor and matured experience, though among the oldest dealers in the Albany lumber district.

Ives, Willard.—The subject of this sketch was born at Watertown, N. Y., July 7th, 1807. His father, Dr. Titus Ives, moved to that place from Connecticut, in 1801. In his early life, Willard Ives received such education as was afforded by the schools at that time and place—for he was brought up on his father's farm, which vocation he has followed all his life—so that the fortune Mr. Ives has amassed has been made legitimately in the business which he has followed, and the investments he has made in other channels. His motto in life was to excel in all he undertook, and his success in life shows how well he has lived up to the maxim which he set before him as a guide. As a citizen of Watertown, he has done more than his share to advance all her interests, and to-day he is president of the following companies and institutions: Merchants' Bank of Watertown, also trustee in National Trust Company of New York, Watertown Fire Insurance Company, Davis Sewing-Machine Company Ives Seminary at Antwerp, Jefferson County Orphan Asylum, and Jefferson County Bible Society. He is also president of the board of trustees of the Arsenal Methodist Episcopal Church. Probably the most eventful position he ever filled was as a delegate to the first Evangelical Alliance, held in London, England, in 1846; he was also a delegate to the meeting of 1873, held at New York City; and was delegate to the General Conference of the Methodist Episcopal Church, held in Brooklyn, in 1872. Mr. Ives was for many years a member of the board of managers of the Jefferson County Agricultural Society, filling the offices of secretary, treasurer, and president. In 1850, was elected representative of his district in the Thirty-second Congress.

He was one of the corporators and vice-president of the Thousand Island Camp-Meeting Association, organized in 1875, located upon Wellesley Island, in the St. Lawrence River, owning 1000 acres of land, and known as Thousand Island Park.

Mr. Willard Ives has been twice married; first, in December, 1827, to Miss Charlotte Winslow. His second marriage was to Miss Lucina M. Eddy, of Philadelphia, in Jefferson County, N. Y., which took place in 1862. One of the effective attributes of his popularity is the purity of his character. It is this which has given him the esteem of all men.

Jervis, John B., was born at Huntington, Long Island, N. Y., on the 14th of December, 1795, and moved to Rome with his father, Timothy Jervis, in 1798. He was educated in the common schools of Rome, N. Y., where he continued to reside until April 10th, 1818. In 1817, Benjamin Wright, the surveyor whom the State employed in constructing the canal, came to Rome for the purpose of breaking ground. An axeman was wanted to clear a way through the swamp, and Timothy Jervis said, "Take John." The offer was accepted, and the youth thus began the life of an engineer. At the end of a week, the task was done, but the axeman's ambition was aroused, and he solicited a place as rodman. It was promised by the next spring, and in 1818 he was thus employed at Syracuse on the salary of $12 a month. The principal engineer on the canal was Nathan S. Roberts.

During the season of 1818, the rodman learned with rapidity, and showed such energy in penetrating Montezuma swamp, that the year afterward found him at the head of a party as resident engineer, at $1.25 per day. Mr. Jervis continued in this service for seven years, until the entire canal was finished. His salary had been increased to $4 per day, and he had established a remarkable reputation for a young man only thirty years of age. At this time it was resolved to supply New York with coal directly from the Lackawanna mines, and the Delaware and Hudson Canal was projected. This canal was begun in 1825, when the Erie had just been finished. Benjamin Wright and John B. Jervis were the engineers, and in 1830 the works were opened for service. Mr. Jervis's salary had by this time been increased to $4000 per year, and he had won a name as the first engineer on this continent. The railroad above mentioned had a short level, on which was placed the first successful locomotive engine built in America, which was planned by Mr. Jervis. This locomotive is still in existence.

In 1830, the Mohawk and Hudson Railroad was projected. The construction of this road was committed to Mr. Jervis, who also built at the same time the road connecting Schenectady and Saratoga Springs. These works were finished in 1832, and were the objects of widespread admiration. The success of the Erie Canal led to a general desire to increase the system. In 1833, the Chenango Canal was begun, and the work was placed in Mr. Jervis's hands.

The Croton Aqueduct was begun in October, 1836, and the commissioners showed their sense of its importance by employing one who was justly considered the greatest of American engineers. Mr. Jervis was then more than forty years old, and in the fulness of manly vigor. The anxiety connected with so important a responsibility often reached intensity, and Mr. Jervis was at times threatened with utter prostration; but his natural vigor enabled him to overcome all difficulties, and he saw the waters of the Croton introduced to New York in the autumn of 1842. It required four additional years to bring the work to perfection. To carry the aqueduct across the Harlem River was an important as well as difficult task. Major Douglas had proposed inverted siphons as a permanent method, but Mr. Jervis determined to bridge the stream. The siphon system, however, was adopted for temporary use. The bridge was finished in 1846, and not a flaw can be detected in its entire extent. Mr. Jervis has lived to see New York enjoy the benefits of his genius for thirty years, and the work itself may last for ages.

Boston, following the example of New York, resolved to introduce the Cochituate stream, and Mr. Jervis accepted the work, which was finished in three years. The distance is twenty miles, and it cost about five millions. Considered by itself, it is a work of great importance; but comparison with the Croton diminishes it at least one half, both in expense and difficulty of construction.

Before the Boston water-works were in full operation, Mr. Jervis had been designated to a new enterprise. For twenty years, the need of railway transit between Albany and New York had been severely felt; hence the Hudson River road was planned, Mr. James Boorman being one of its chief patrons. In 1847, when the directors were ready to move, Mr. Jervis accepted the appointment of chief engineer. Although this road was very unprofitable for several years after completion, Mr. Jervis had confidence from the beginning in its success. Mr. Jervis built the road

to Poughkeepsie, and proceeded to locate the track to Albany, when failing health and other circumstances led him to make a trip to Europe. This enabled him to examine the finest works of engineering in England and on the continent, and he then returned and made New York his residence.

Mr. Jervis was subsequently engaged on the Michigan Southern, and also the Rock Island road, and passed six years in this new field. In 1858, being then sixty-three, he returned to Rome, and determined to spend his days amid the scenes of his boyhood. His natural activity, however, made a quiet life distasteful; hence he accepted, in 1861, the office of superintendent and engineer of the Pittsburg and Fort Wayne road. This concern had been running down so long that its stock sold at 8, and, indeed, it had gone into the hands of the bondholders. It had been ten years in operation, but its managers did not understand its needs and exigencies. They had no practical knowledge of railroading. After it had been two years under its new superintendent, a dividend of ten per cent was made. The value of Mr. Jervis's services to this road, for which he received $6000 a year, has been estimated at a million. In 1866, Mr. Jervis built his present stately mansion, and having passed so many years of hard labor, he felt the need of recruiting his health. The Fort Wayne road had been leased to the Pennsylvania Central, and the latter retained him as consulting engineer, an office which he still holds.

Johnson, Samuel, was born February 9th, 1835, in the town of Shelby, Orleans County, N. Y. His father was a farmer and a weaver of fancy linens, and his mother also a weaver. They came from the North of Ireland. His grandparents were Scotch. When the subject of this sketch was only seven years old, he lost his father. The first work done by him was binding bobbins; assisting his brothers, who were manufacturers of threshing-machines; and attending winter school; which occupied his time until about fourteen years of age. About this time, he assumed the management of his mother's farm. When twenty, he bought a farm adjoining his mother's, purchasing the most approved farming implements, and even these he found defective, but with his mechanical ingenuity made several improvements, besides inventing new labor-saving machinery. Among these was a "self-rake," which he attached to the Ketchum reaper, manufactured by R. L. Howard, of Buffalo. The success of this rake at once attracted the attention of Mr. Howard, who made Mr. Johnson an offer that induced him to sell his farm and enter the factory at Buffalo, where he was engaged making improvements on his machine, and inventing others that are now celebrated in all grain-growing countries. In 1864, he left Buffalo and commenced to license others to use his machines and "self-rake," moving to Syracuse, where two factories adopted his inventions. In 1867, he formed a copartnership with James S. Thayer, and commenced to manufacture the reapers and mowers of his invention, the firm being S. Johnson & Co. In 1868, he bought a factory at Brockport, N. Y., taking B. E. Huntley in as partner, when the firm changed to Johnson, Huntley & Co. Here the business increased so fast that, in 1870, they formed a stock company under the name of the Johnson Harvester Company, and the business continued to increase so rapidly that, at the close of the harvest season of 1874, the shop had grown in capacity to 10,000 machines per annum, from a capacity of 500 in 1868.

The business of licensing had also grown to 40,000 machines annually; when Mr. Johnson resigned the presidency of the company to give his sole attention to making improvements, collecting royalties, and studying the German and French languages to better enable him to converse with the users of his improvements in Europe, where the demand for his machines exceeded 12,000 annually. The result of his observation and inquiries in Europe induced him to invent two machines especially adapted to the wants of farmers in the different sections in Europe: these were eagerly adopted by European manufacturers; and the consequence is, that at the present writing eight tenths of the machines built in the United States, Canada, and Europe for self-raking use his improvements. This success is the result of well-directed energy, together with his fertile mechanical brain. By an industry that has never wavered, by an integrity that is unimpeachable, he has gained reputation, position, and wealth. If the youth of the rising generation would go and do likewise, they would in time achieve what he has done.

Judson, Edward B.—This well-known banker and financier was born January 11th, 1814, at Coxsackie, Greene County, N. Y. His father, William Judson, formerly from Woodbury, Ct., being an intelligent man of the old New England school, early inculcated in the minds of his children that love of industry, economy, and integrity which are still characteristics of New England training, and which qualities the son, E. B., inherited in a marked degree, his career and conduct being guided and governed by them in all the relations of life. His mother, Esther Barker, was a member of one of the old families of Branford, Ct., and a lady of intelligence and superior qualities. His earliest business training was in the banking office of his uncle at Coxsackie, Ralph Barker, who had been associated with Erastus Corning in the Albany City Bank. When twenty-two, he began the manufacture of lumber at Constantia, Oswego County, and soon afterwards engaged in the manufacture of iron. Twenty-five years ago, he became interested in the manufacture of salt, and in 1864–5, added to his business the manufacture of glass. In all these branches he is still interested. For a period of twenty years he was connected with his brother, William A., in the lumber commission business at Albany. In 1845, he was married to Miss Sarah Williams, daughter of Coddington B. Williams, of Syracuse. It was not to be supposed that a man of Mr. Judson's ability and popularity should not receive from the public some testimonial of respect and confidence. In 1839–41, he represented the county of Oswego in the State Legislature. As a member of that body, he served as chairman of the Committee on Cities and Villages, and as chairman of the select Committee on the State Lunatic Asylum. In 1868, he was appointed a presidential elector for the State of New York. As a banker and financier he is widely known and esteemed. He acted as chairman of the Executive Committee of the National Banking Association from 1864 to 1875. Associated with him in this position were Thomas Coleman, P. C. Calhoun, Charles B. Hall, George F. Baker, J. S. Norris, W. F. Coolbaugh, John W. Ellis, Fred W. Crownenbold, and F. B. Loomis. Mr. Judson took a leading part in organizing the Lake Ontario Bank of Oswego. This institution was appropriately styled a Bankers' Bank, as among its stockholders were John A. Stevenson, President, and C. H. Russell Vice-President of the Bank of Commerce,

New York; Erastus Corning, President, and H. H. Martin, Cashier of the Albany City Bank; Rufus H. King, President, and J. H. Van Antwerp, Cashier of the State Bank of Albany; J. B. Plumb, President of the Bank of the Interior, Albany; Hamilton White, President of the Onondaga County Bank; Horace White, President of the Bank of Syracuse; John D. Norton, President of the Merchants' Bank, and Thomas B. Fitch, President of the Mechanics' Bank, Syracuse; G. B. Rich, President of the Bank of Attica, Buffalo; and Luther Wright, President of Luther Wright's Bank, Oswego. Included in its list of stockholders were also Thurlow Weed, John L. Schoolcraft, David Hamilton, John Knower, John Crouse, F. T. Carrington, George Geddes, and William A. Judson. James Platt, one of the purest men in the State, was made President, and Mr. Judson was made the financial officer, remaining at Oswego until, at the request of Secretary Chase, he organized the First National Bank of Syracuse, of which institution he is still the president. This bank is the sixth in the list of our national banking institutions. Mr. Judson was at one period Vice-President of the Merchants' Bank of Syracuse; Cashier of the Salt Springs Bank of Syracuse, for over six years; a Director and Vice-President of the Trust and Deposit Company of Onondaga, and a director in the New York Central Railroad Company. He is now, and has been for many years, a director in the American Express Company; was one of the directors of the State Bank of Syracuse and the Syracuse National Bank, and is now President of the Syracuse Glass Company. He is also a member of the Board of Trustees of Wells College. Mr. Judson's business career has been a notably successful one, and presents a fine illustration of what well-directed energy, industry, resolution, and integrity may accomplish. To such men our country owes lasting obligations for their labors in developing its resources, and contributing to its prosperity and power.

Judson, J. D., was born in St. Lawrence County, N. Y., in 1811. His parents moved there when the place was a wilderness. They were among the earliest settlers of Northern New York, and doubtless had to endure the hardships incident to that early period, when the only ambition of the pioneer was to convert his new farm in the forest into a comfortable home, and to raise and educate his young family to habits of industry, economy, and integrity. Such a life, though full of hardship, is well calculated to rear up men and women able to fight the battle of life successfully. The subject of this sketch was raised on his father's farm, receiving during the winter season the advantages of the common schools of that locality by walking eight miles each way through the woods. While yet quite young he lost his father, after which he moved to Ogdensburg, where he continued schooling. Afterwards, through the kindness of his elder brother, David C. Judson, he went to the academy at Potsdam, where he finished his education, after which he returned to Ogdensburg and entered the store of G. N. Seymour as clerk, where he remained six years, and never lost but three days from business during the whole time. In June, 1831, he entered his brother's Ogdensburg Bank, organized the year before, and since that time he has been engaged in the banking business. Commencing as clerk, he has filled every position to that of president, which he now is, of Judson's Bank, started in 1853, though he has many other business interests, and owes his success to close attention to his own affairs, which have so claimed his whole time that we may say he has never been out of his native State. He has done much, and all honorably. In the community in which he lives he enjoys the confidence of all who know him.

Kelly, J. B., was born at Goshen, Litchfield County, Ct., August 6th, 1830. His father and grandfather were both born in New Haven County, Ct., and the latter was a soldier of distinction in the Revolutionary war. The subject of this sketch received his education in the common schools and academy of his native town, graduating from the last-named institution when seventeen. During this time, he worked most summers, helping his father, who was both tanner and farmer, though, when his schooling was finished, he commenced clerking in a country store. Here he continued eight years, when he commenced in a small way for himself. This lasted one year, when he received a proposition from William H. Imlay, of Hartford, to go to Michigan and take charge of his manufacturing interests, with an offer of an interest. This he declined until he had tried his adaptability. At the expiration of six months, he returned to Hartford, and consummated a partnership, dating from the beginning of their connection, and which continued until Mr. Imlay's death, which occurred in 1858. Since then Mr. Kelly has continued the same business, enlarging it yearly, until they now manufacture twenty-five million feet of lumber annually, which is cut from his own pine lands. In 1861, the requirements of his great and growing trade compelled him to find a location to dispose of his lumber, so he moved to Albany, N. Y., where he has since resided, and is now among the largest dealers in the district.

In manners he is affable and genial, and his disposition frank and generous. In business matters he has always been prompt, and has never allowed his engagements to be unfulfilled or postponed.

Kellogg, John.—Whoever achieves fortune and social position by his own efforts, and preserves at the same time an unblemished reputation, is a credit to any community, and is a safe example and guide to succeeding generations. John Kellogg was born at West Galway, Fulton County, N. Y., December 17th, 1826. He received a common-school education only, and at the early age of fifteen commenced working for his father, who was a manufacturer of linseed-oil. He continued in his employ, paying strict attention to the details of the business, until his father's death, which occurred in 1848, when he continued the business in partnership with his brother. In 1851, they bought their present works at Amsterdam. Two years later, his brother died. The business, however, was assuming such large proportions, Mr. Kellogg found it necessary to have a partner. He then received Mr. James H. Miller into the business, who is still associated with him. Their business has so increased that they now have a capacity to consume 1000 bushels of seed per diem, most of which they import from the East Indies. Their works are among the largest in this country. In 1850, Mr. Kellogg was married to Miss Olive Davis, of Galway, Saratoga County, N. Y., by whom he has had four children, his eldest son being a partner of the present firm of Kelloggs & Miller. In 1863, Mr. J. Kellogg was elected president of the village, and the succeeding year was elected member of the State Assembly, and served his term during the session of 1864. He is also a director of the Farmers'

National Bank of Amsterdam. Thus we see the business career of Mr. Kellogg has been most prosperous. His business talents, his industry and energy, would have made him successful in any sphere. Mr. Kellogg has reached a position in the business world which must satisfy all his aspirations. He is the senior partner of the well-known house of Kelloggs & Miller. His name has an influence in business, political, and social circles, the result of successful enterprise and exalted merit. Though he has amassed a fortune sufficient to supply all the luxuries which even a devotee of pleasure might require, he still pursues his usual routine of business habits, with nearly the same ardor which characterized him in early years, and his remarkable diligence furnishes a salutary example to the young members of his establishment.

Kelsey, George W., was born on Long Island, May 18th, 1808. His father, Daniel, was also born on the island. In the early days of George W. Kelsey, he received only a common-school education, which received attention partly at his birthplace and partly in New York City, to which place his parents moved when the subject of this sketch was nine years old. At the age of fourteen, he was apprenticed to the business of merchant tailoring. After serving faithfully for four years, he bought out his time. Until 1833, he was engaged in various occupations, but at this date he moved to Buffalo, and commenced mercantile business for himself, at which place he remained four years. In 1837, he returned to New York, remaining only a short time, when he moved to West Virginia. From there he moved to Muscatine, Iowa, where he bought a farm and attended closely to the details of this honorable pursuit for some time, leaving it in 1840, when the cholera made its appearance in that section, almost depopulating it. He therefore sold his farm, returned to New York, and engaged in the real estate business. In 1853, he moved to Williamsburg, now part of Brooklyn, where he has since continued in the same pursuit of real estate dealer. This, like all other ventures Mr. Kelsey has engaged in, proved prosperous from the fact it has had his personal attention. By his business capacity, his integrity and successful management, Mr. Kelsey has always held the respect of those whom he has encountered in his business operations; and his high moral worth connected with his business capacity, has given him influence and position in the place of his birth. As a fitting tribute to the confidence bestowed on him, he was in 1861 elected to the first vice-presidency of the Dime Savings Bank, a position he held and filled with distinction till 1874, when Mr. Dingey retiring, he was elected president, which office he still holds. In 1828, on the 20th of September, Mr. Kelsey was joined in wedlock to Miss Eliza, daughter of Edward Snow, Esq., of New York City, by whom he has had four children. At an age when most people retire from active business, Mr. Kelsey remains hale, vigorous, laborious, intelligent, and genial, the same benevolent friend to the poor and industrious he has been for the last forty years, still emphatically showing his faith by his works.

Leavenworth, Elias Warner, was born December 20th, 1803, at Canaan, Columbia County, N. Y. When three years of age, his father and family removed to Great Barrington, Mass. In early life, he received all the advantage of mental training, graduating from Yale College in 1824. This same year he began the study of law with

William Cullen Bryant, who was then practising at Great Barrington. One year later, he entered the law school at Litchfield, Ct. In January, 1827, he was there admitted to practise in all the courts in Connecticut. In November, 1827, he left Great Barrington, and moved to Syracuse, N. Y., where, in February, 1828, he was admitted in the Common Pleas as attorney and counsellor; two years later, in the Supreme Court at Albany, as an attorney, and, in 1833, as counsellor.

In 1850, he abandoned his profession entirely, on account of the loss of his voice by severe bronchitis. Rest and care for two or three years fully restored him. Other pursuits having in the mean time engaged his attention, he never again returned to the practice of law. In January, 1832, he was appointed lieutenant of artillery in the One Hundred and Forty-seventh Regiment of infantry, and promoted to captain the same year. In 1834, he was appointed lieutenant-colonel of the Twenty-ninth Regiment of artillery, and in 1835, received the appointment of colonel of the same regiment. In 1836, he was appointed brigadier-general of the Seventh Brigade of artillery. In 1837-8-9 and 1840, he was president of the village, going out in the spring of 1841. In 1839, he was elected supervisor of the old town of Salina, and was re-elected in 1840. In 1846-7, he was again president of the village. In the spring of 1849, he was elected mayor of the city, and in the fall of the same year, was elected a member of the Legislature to represent the city district.

In the fall of 1853, he was nominated for the office of Secretary of State almost without opposition, and elected. On the 4th day of January, 1855, he was elected a corresponding member of the American Historical and Geographical Society of the City of New York, and also the same year of the New England Historical and Genealogical Society of Boston. In the fall of 1856, he was again elected to the Legislature to represent the city district; he was chairman of the Committee on Canals and a member of the Committee on Banks, also chairman of the Select Committee of one from each judicial district, on the equalization of the State tax. In the spring of 1859, he was again elected mayor of the city. In the winter of 1860, by an act of the Legislature, he was appointed one of the Board of Quarantine Commissioners, was on its organization chosen its president, and spent most of the following summer in New York and on Staten Island, in the discharge of its duties. In the summer of the same year, he was chosen President of the Republican State Convention, assembled at Syracuse, to select delegates to the National Convention, then soon to assemble at Chicago. On the 5th of February, 1861, he was chosen by the Legislature, in joint ballot, one of the Regents of the University. In the month of March in the same year, he was nominated by the President of the United States, and confirmed by the Senate, as the Commissioner on the part of the United States, under the Convention with New Grenada, acting as such until the commission expired in 1862. In the spring of 1865, he was President of the Board of Commissioners appointed by the Governor, with consent of the Senate, to locate the State Asylum for the Blind, and in the fall of the same year, was appointed by the Governor a trustee of the State Asylum for Idiots, and in 1866, was reappointed. In 1867, he was appointed by the Legislature a member of a Board of Commissioners for the further improvement and repair of the State Armory at Syracuse, and in May, 1868, was appointed by the Legislature a member of a Board of Commissioners (of which he was the president) to establish a system of sewerage for the city of Syracuse.

At the annual commencement of Hamilton College in June, 1872, he received the honorary degree of Doctor of Laws.

On the 22d of November, 1872, he was appointed by the Governor and Senate one of the thirty-two commissioners selected to amend the Constitution of the State. In the fall of 1874, Mr. Leavenworth was elected by the Republican party to the Forty-fourth Congress, where he served on the Committee of Civil Service Reform, Committee of Expenses of Secretary of State's office, and on the special Select Committee to investigate the charges preferred against Judges Wylie and Humphreys.

When in the Legislature of 1850, he, as Chairman of a Select Committee appointed on his motion for that purpose, drew, reported, and carried the bill for the preservation of Washington's Headquarters at Newburg.

When Secretary of State, he also drew the Bill (Laws of 1867, chap. 951) for the appointment of a Board of Commissioners of Public Charities. On the 31st of January, 1855, it was introduced into the Senate by the Hon. Mark Spencer (Journal of 1855, p. 174). It resulted in appointing a Committee of Examination. For their report, see Senate Doc. 1857, vol. 1, No. 8.

On the recommendation of Governor Fenton, in his annual message in 1867, the subject was again brought before the Legislature. General L. furnished the House Committee, at their request, with a copy of his original bill, which is substantially the bill passed that year, and which he drew and furnished to Mr. Spencer in 1855.

In the Legislature of 1857, as Chairman of a Select Committee of one from each judicial district, on the equalization of the State tax, appointed on his motion, he drew and reported the bill, which was passed in 1859 (chap. 312, p. 702, etc.), entitled "An Act to Equalize the State Tax among the several counties of this State." The bill failed in 1857, only on account of his ill-health and absence.

He is now, and has been for many years, in the following positions: President of the Syracuse Savings Bank, Syracuse City Water Works, Syracuse Gas Light Company, Oakwood Cemetery, Historical Society of Central New York, New England Society of the City of Syracuse, Secretary and Treasurer of the Cape Cod Coarse Salt Company, Trustee of the Onondaga County Orphan Asylum, Syracuse Home Association, First Presbyterian Church, State Asylum for Idiots, Director in the Syracuse Northern Railroad, Syracuse, Phoenix and Oswego Railroad, and Regent of the University of the State of New York, a life position.

He was joined in wedlock June 21st, 1833, to Mary Elizabeth Forman, third child of Joshua Forman and Margaret P. Alexander. Mr. Leavenworth is now in the seventy-fourth year of his age. He has been a stirring, practical man, both in his public and private life, and his good constitution being still vigorous and unenfeebled, and his fine intellect ripened by experience, he would do honor to any official function in the gift of his country.

Lee, John A., was born at Tinmouth, Vermont, in 1804. When seven years of age, moved to Washington County, N. Y.; nine years later, he moved to Westport, Essex County, N. Y.; in 1824, was married to Miss

Cynthia Tarbell, of Chester, Vermont; in 1825, moved to Moriah; in 1856, moved to Port Henry; in 1869, moved to Saratoga Springs; the issue of marriage was six daughters, all of whom are living and married.

About 1844, Mr. Lee, together with George Sherman and E. Hall, bought the two mines of iron ore now owned and operated by Witherbee, Sherman & Co., from D. E. Sanford, for $4500, and began taking about 1000 tons of ore annually, increasing to about 100,000 tons in 1865; in 1862, Mr. Lee sold out his entire interest in this investment, and bought the Fisher mine, which he operated fourteen months; this he sold, and is still one half owner with the Bay State Iron Company, in the Dolleby ore-bed near Port Henry, N. Y. During his active life, he was member of the Legislature. He was one of the organizers of the Whitehall Transportation Company, Moriah Plank Road Company, stockholder in blast furnace in Westport, also in Fort Edward blast furnace, stockholder in Fisher Iron Company, stockholder in First National Bank of Troy, N. Y., First National Bank of Saratoga Springs. His principal interests, at present, are in the Union National Bank of Troy, N. Y., and First National Bank of Saratoga Springs. In 1865, Mr. Lee retired from active business life, and in 1869, moved to Saratoga Springs, N. Y., where all of his daughters reside, excepting one, who still lives at Port Henry.

Mr. John A. Lee has passed through many phases of business life without reproach, and now all the elements of happiness are within his reach, and they are of his own creation.

McCammon, William, was born in the city of Albany, Feb. 26th, 1811. He received the greater part of his education at the old Albany Academy, under Theodore Romeyn Beck, until 1828, when he left school to learn the trade of pattern-making, for the purpose of becoming a practical civil and mechanical engineer, working at it until twenty-one years of age. During this time, he studied mathematics under Prof. Joseph Henry, now Secretary of the Smithsonian Institute. While learning his trade and studying with Prof. Henry, he was freely admitted to his experimental rooms, in the Albany Academy. At that time, 1830, Prof. Henry had coils of wire around the room and a machine which vibrated by electricity, and was the incipient electrical telegraph. He heard Prof. Henry often say, that with it communication *could be had* any distance. In 1855, he was resident engineer on the Erie Canal enlargement. After finishing the trade alluded to, he returned to the Albany Academy, continuing his studies with Prof. Henry. In the fall of 1832, he removed with Prof. Henry to Princeton College, and there continued the studies of civil and mechanical engineering for six months. He returned to Albany after six months, and took charge of the pattern-shop of Townsend Furnace, where he superintended the building of every description of machinery. In one year from this time, he had full charge of the whole establishment. During 1836, he built the first locomotive ever built north of New York City, which was then the largest in the country. In 1838, he built the horizontal low-pressure engine, original design, for the steamship Simeon De Witt, which plied on Cayuga Lake. In 1848, he built a low-pressure beam engine for Smith, Patton & Co.'s flour-mill, at Albany. This piece of machinery is still running, and capable of competing with many of more modern construction. During his connection with Townsend Furnace, he built the Rensselaer

Yours Truly
Wm M Cammon

Wm McDonald

Iron-Works, in the city of Troy. This was the third mill ever built in the United States for rolling railroad iron. In 1852, Mr. McCammon was appointed Superintendent of the Albany Water-Works, a position he held two years. He was then called to Chicago, as engineer for the Chicago Water-Works, but soon after left, predicting for the whole works a failure, which ultimately proved true. In 1854, he returned to Albany, and commenced the manufacture of draining tile, which he continued until 1862, increasing the products of the yard from 250,000 to 1,250,000 tile per annum. In 1862, he bought out the piano-forte manufacturing establishment from Boardman, Grey & Co. From that time until now he has continually improved the mechanical construction and tone of his instruments, until they have no superior. He has proved successful in all of his business pursuits from a rare combination of industry and judgment, which has enabled him to undertake many enterprises, proving himself successful under all circumstances. On Jan. 1st, 1877, Mr. McCammon virtually retired from active business life, and his business is now conducted by his son Edward.

McCarthy, Hon. Dennis, was born March 19th, 1814, in the village of Salina, now Syracuse, N. Y. He is of Irish and American descent. His father was born in Ireland, and his mother in Massachusetts. After a few years of common school and academic education, he commenced business for his father, whom he ultimately succeeded as a manufacturer of salt, and merchant, and to-day his partners in the mercantile business comprise his sons, making the third generation conducting the same business, which has now been established over sixty years. Their business now occupies two immense establishments, devoted to their wholesale and retail business, which in point of size and architecture have no superiors in the interior of New York State. Besides having at all times conducted a large business, the Hon. D. McCarthy was elected Supervisor of the town of Syracuse, in 1842. He, however, entered political life in 1845 as a warm supporter of the policy of Silas Wright, A. C. Flagg, and John Van Buren, and was originally a Free-Soil Democrat. He was elected to the State Assembly in 1846, Mayor of Syracuse in 1853, was elected to the 40th and 41st Congress, and served as a member on the Committee of Ways and Means in the 41st Congress. In 1875, he was elected to the State Senate, and in these high official positions he has served his constituents without causing one reproach to be cast upon his character which, politically, is spotless. He has also been largely associated with different manufacturing industries, has been trustee of the Syracuse Savings Bank mostly since its organization, is a director in the First National Bank, also president and director in the Syracuse and Chenango Railroad.

McDonald, William, was born the 29th of February, 1784, in New Milford, Litchfield Co., Ct., a locality which has furnished many of the earlier settlers of the town of Queensbury, among the number being the large and influential families of Pecks and Sanfords. His paternal grandfather emigrated from Scotland during the old French war. His father was a physician of considerable eminence, and as a surgeon served in the American army during the Revolutionary struggle. After the war was ended, he resumed the practice of his profession, at New Rochelle, Westchester Co., N. Y., where he died at the advanced age of eighty-five. His mother's name was Mary, the sister of David Sanford, who removed to the town of Queensbury about the year 1785, and was one of the first settlers at the Ridge, where he established a large and very successful mercantile business. Mr. McDonald first moved to that place when he was only eight years old, but returned to New Milford shortly afterward, where he received what was considered in those days a good education. In 1799, having become an accomplished penman and accountant, he returned to Queensbury, and immediately received employment from his uncle Sanford as clerk in the management of his extended business. By his assiduity and attention to his employer's interest, he very shortly became the trusted manager of the store, Mr. Sanford's time being engrossed by outside pursuits. His fair, even, and bold chirography appears on the town records for the years 1802 and 1803, when Mr. Sanford held the office of town clerk. At the time of the institution of the Hamilton Lodge F. and A. M., in 1805, he was made a Mason, a large delegation of high officials in that organization, from Albany and vicinity, visiting for the purpose of conferring the degrees. About the same time, he bought out his uncle's interest in the store, and continued the business until 1808, when he removed to the thriving village of Waterford. Here he embarked in a large and successful trade, which he continued until the year 1820, when he returned to the Ridge, and resumed the mercantile business in the old place.

Three years later, he disposed of his stock and moved to Glen's Falls, where he soon afterward bought the old Wing farm, and enlarged, rebuilt, and completed the half-finished dwelling to a spacious and elegant mansion, the home he continued to occupy up to the time of his death. Prior to the erection of Warren County, and until after the year 1822, the district embraced by Warren and Washington counties sent from three to six members to the legislature, according to the ratio of representation. In 1821, Mr. McDonald was placed in nomination for the Assembly, in opposition to Asahel Clark, a Clintonian of distinguished abilities and extended influence. Notwithstanding the numerical ascendency of the Clintonian party, the Bucktail ticket was successful in this district, chiefly through Mr. McDonald's popularity and instrumentality in bringing about one of those political revulsions which, like a whirlwind, triumphantly sweeps away all opposition. It was during this session of the legislature that a survey and appropriation was obtained through his personal efforts, for the construction of the Glen's Falls Feeder. He was re-elected to the Assembly the following year, and such was his popularity that there were only 17 votes cast against him in town. He was again elected to the Assembly in 1828. To him, more than any other man, is the credit due for opening up the resources of the place and preparing the way for that healthy development and growth, which makes it to-day one of the great business centres of Northern New York. As is shown by the record, Mr. McDonald was chosen one of the vestrymen of the Episcopal Church at its first organization. At the formation of the old Commercial Bank, he was elected its president, which position he held with great acceptance for a term of years. From that time forth he kept retired from the toils and cares of public life, devoting his leisure to the management of his estate, and the remainder of his days was passed in serene tranquillity. He died on Sunday, the eleventh of Sep-

tember, 1870, and his remains were deposited in the new cemetery, where a large and costly monument marks the place of his earthly rest.

McGraw, John.—Among the most active and useful forces of a nation's life is a large class of the higher ranges of business men, those who originate the enterprises of the period, and direct and control the industries pertaining to them. From these result a nation's prosperity, and the foundation of its growth in wealth, commerce, and the elevation and refinement which accompany them. Eminent among this class of men was the subject of this notice, John McGraw, who died at Ithaca, May 4th, 1877, aged 62 years. Born in Dryden, Tompkins County, in 1815, a period when the country was new, and wealth and its surroundings almost unknown, he was educated to business as a merchant's clerk, and from his early manhood, when he entered business for himself, with the hard-earned savings from a small salary, he began to develop especially those intellectual forces which characterize the man of superior ability in the management of affairs. When first launching in business for himself, it was in copartnership with his brother Thomas, who died in 1837. The subject of this sketch continued this business alone until 1840, when he moved to New Hudson, Alleghany County, and entered the lumber trade. About the year 1850, he moved to New York, and became largely interested in business. In 1861, he moved to Ithaca, where he resided until his death. Always in feeble health, he was physically unable to attend to the minor details of business, and remitted them wholly to others. He dealt with principles and ideas, boldly grasping the outlines of important projects which commanded his attention, and his judgment, once convinced of their soundness and utility, followed up with all the force of his character any enterprise once entered upon. As he was ripened by years and experience, the results of his great industry were represented by a large accumulation of wealth, no inconsiderable portion of which has been devoted to the benefit of mankind. He was an early and life-long friend of the late Ezra Cornell, and in full sympathy with his ideas in the founding of Cornell University, and was one of its earliest trustees. His clear, practical head has always been a power in the management of its interests, and his noble gift of the Library Building, at a cost of $150,000, is an enduring monument to his generosity and desire to promote the interests of education. In all his relations with men, he was kind, affable, and sympathetic. In his business he combined great force and boldness with great caution and sagacity. He was upright, prompt, true, and sensitive to the nicest shade of honor. His friendships were based upon what he deemed deserving qualities, and were not lightly awarded ; but the man who had his confidence always had a friend, warm, true, and if in need, sufficient for any service that friendship could ask or command. He made few professions, few verbal demonstrations of his interior life. But his active, practical life was a living exponent of that within which abounded with faith, hope, courage, and fidelity—the qualities which make up and stamp the noble man. With these for his guidance, he has worked faithfully and with rare ability in the sphere wherein God was pleased to place him. Few men, now that his days are ended, have better title to the award—" Well done, thou good and faithful."

Merrick, Moses, was born November 17th, 1811, in Chenango County, N. Y., where he resided until eleven years old, during which time he received a common-school education. He afterward lived in St. Lawrence County three years, then moved to Jefferson County, and for a short time was in the employ of Jesse Smith. While with him he attended Belleville Academy part of the time. His next move was at Clayton, when he commenced clerking for Jesse Smith & Co., his brother, Eldridge G. Merrick, being the company: here he remained several years. In course of time he was admitted a partner to the business, when the firm style changed to E. G. Merrick & Co., and continued until 1867, when it was discontinued. During that period, they established a forwarding and commission house at Cleveland, Ohio, under the firm name of D. N. Barney & Co., where the subject of this sketch spent three years, attending to the business duties of the establishment. In the spring of 1845, Moses Merrick opened another business at Oswego, under the firm name of Merrick, Davis & Co., transacting general forwarding and commission business. He also owned one third interest in the Ontario warehouse at Oswego, where he also owns real estate, besides pine lands in Michigan. In 1850, Mr. Davis died, when the firm became M. Merrick & Co., which style still continues.

The firm bought their present mills, "Columbia," in 1860. These mills have a storage capacity of 200,000 bushels, and are furnished with five run of stone. The firm are also largely interested in the "Genesee" Mills, water-lots, saw-mill and barrel factory, at Fulton, N. Y. During the present firm's existence, they also built the "Seneca" Mills, with fifteen run of stone, which was burned to the ground in 1864. Mr. Merrick stands high in the community as a Christian gentleman, a philanthropist, and, in every way, beyond the imputation of ever designing wrong to any one with whom he has transacted business during long years of a useful life. The writer has known him long; and most truly can it be said he is an honest man, upright and fair in all his dealings and associations in life. He is of sanguine temperament, pleasant, affable address, and is one of the actual pioneers of Northern New York.

Lockwood, D. N.—This distinguished and promising jurist was born in East Hamburg, N. Y., June 1st, 1844. In his younger days he received the usual advantages afforded by the common schools. But at the age of fourteen he came to Buffalo, and attended the Central School. At the age of seventeen, he entered Union College, from which institution he graduated with honors, July 27th, 1865, his class being the last that ever did so under the celebrated Dr. Nott. In November, 1865, he commenced reading law with Messrs. Humphrey & Parsons; was admitted to the bar May 19th, 1866, and became a partner with his former preceptor, Mr. Humphrey, taking the place of Mr. Parsons, who moved to the West. Filled with an honorable emulation, it was not long before he became known as a rising man in his profession. In 1871, he was nominated for district-attorney, and, though defeated, ran 1500 ahead of his ticket. In 1874, he was renominated, and elected by a majority of 1500. In 1876, he received the nomination for Congress, and was elected over a very strong opponent. In the community in which he lives, he enjoys the confidence of all who know him, regardless of party or condition. Being still young, he can enjoy the fruit of the seed he has sown, while his nature is susceptible of enjoyment, and the stamina of life have not weakened and de-

Yours &c.
A Loomis

cayed. He has all the elements of happiness within his reach, and they are of his own creation.

Loomis, Hon. Arphaxed, was born April 9th, 1798, at Winchester, Ct. His parents, Thaddeus and Lois Loomis, moved to Salisbury, Herkimer County, N. Y., when the subject of this sketch was only three years old.

He had all the advantages of the good common schools of his adopted home, and became well versed in the common branches, including arithmetic and grammar, and made some progress in Latin. At the age of fifteen years, he commenced to teach school. The next year he entered Fairfield Academy, and continued to teach and study alternately for four years, and acquired a fair classical education. He then commenced the study of law in the office of William I. Dodge, of Johnstown, Montgomery County, N. Y. Shortly after, he moved to Jefferson County, where he taught a short time, and then pursued his legal studies in several offices, last and mainly with Justin Butterfield, of Sackett's Harbor. He was admitted to the bar in January, 1822, and at once became a partner of his late preceptor, with whom he continued two years, when he moved to Little Falls, where he has since resided. Here he soon acquired a fair and successful practice. He has filled the positions of Surrogate of Herkimer County, First Judge of the Common Pleas Court, member of Congress 1838-9, member New York Assembly, 1841, 1842, and again in 1853; was a member of the Constitutional Convention, 1846; and was one of the Commissioners on New York Code of Legal Procedure, 1847-50. In every place he has held, his influence has been marked and useful and he has especially left his impress in legislation, in the constitution of 1846, and in the Code of Procedure.

Lorillard, Peter.—Mr. Lorillard was a native of New York City and was one of the oldest of her merchants. His father, Peter Lorillard, Senior, who died many years ago, was, with his brothers, one of the many men whose energy and hard labor resulted not only in gaining them wealth, but in promoting the prosperity which the metropolis of the United States now enjoys. Descended from an ancient Huguenot family, the three brothers, Jacob, Peter, and George, commenced life in humble circumstances, but by dint of hard labor amassed a competency which their heirs have greatly added to. The mother of deceased subject of this sketch was a daughter of Nathaniel Griswold, long since dead, but during his lifetime was one of the most prominent merchants. His parents being possessed of ample means, Mr. Lorillard received an excellent education, and after leaving school connected himself with his father and uncle, Peter and George, in the tobacco business; possessing uncommon business capacity, he soon materially aided his firm in its progress to prosperity, and upon the death of his uncle, who was a bachelor, he found himself left the heir to a fortune valued at some $200,000. Upon the death of his father, Mr. Lorillard succeeded to the business, which prospered so well that it brought to its proprietor millions of dollars, and made it, what it now is, one of the largest tobacco houses in this city.

The deceased married many years ago and survived his widow, by whom he had a large family of children. For many years past, he had ceased to concern himself personally in the affairs of his business, these being attended to by his sons, who were the virtual proprietors. To the poor of New York and elsewhere, his death was greatly regretted, for they found in him a most liberal and kind-hearted benefactor, and the possession of this charitable disposition he inherited from his father and uncles, who were noted for their unquestioning liberalities and for the prompt manner in which they responded to all demands made upon their benevolence.

In the circle in which he moved, deceased was greatly esteemed and respected, as one of the old men of standing in the community and the remains of another and past generation. His departure will be lamented by all who knew him, although his ripe age has rendered his death a looked-for event for some time past.

He died October 6th, 1867.

Newman, E. J., was born May 3d, 1817, at Pompey, Onondaga County, N. Y. His father's name was Amos Newman, who came from Vermont at an early date, and had to clear the woods away for his farm. Mr. Newman attended school at Pompey Centre till he was nineteen, when he left and commenced farming; this he continued till he was thirty-six years old. He then moved to Akron, Erie County, N. Y., where he built a flour-mill and cement works, the capacity of the former being fifty barrels of flour per day, and the latter five hundred barrels of cement annually. These same works he continues to operate, in company with his brother, Leroy Newman; W. C. & H. L., sons of the above, being partners. The capacity of the flour-mills has been doubled, and the cement works have facilities for turning out seventy-five thousand barrels per annum; they find a market for their cement all over the Western country. Eight years ago, the subject of this sketch moved to Buffalo, where he has since resided and proved himself to be a valuable citizen and a sterling business man.

Newman, John, son of Thomas B. Newman, born in Saratoga County, near Ballston, N. Y., October 16th, 1796. When quite young, removed to Oneida County, near Rome. Resided there until twenty-one years of age, when he removed to New York City.

Was married January 1st, 1823, to Elizabeth, daughter of Joseph and Esther Miller, then residing in New York. The birthplace and early residence of Mrs. Newman were at Mamaroneck, Westchester County, N. Y.

After removal to New York, Mr. Newman became early identified with the then new business of constructing machinery for steamboats. He was at different times connected with most of the larger New York establishments in this business at that day.

In 1828, the firm of Hall & Newman (of which he was a member) built the beam-engine and boilers for the steamboat De Witt Clinton, a large Hudson River boat. This was one of the largest, perhaps the largest steamboat engine that had been constructed at that time. The drawings, still preserved in the family, are of interest, showing the progress made at that early day, the arrangement and construction being but little different from that of the engines now in use on the Hudson River and Sound.

In the autumn of 1832, immediately after the first visit of the Asiatic cholera to this country—by which the business of New York was nearly paralyzed—at the solicitation of Oliver Newberry, of Detroit, Mich., he left the Novelty Works, New York, with which he had been associated since its organization, and spent the winter at Detroit, assisting in the construction of the steamboat Michigan

(No. 1). This boat was of the largest class of that day, and was propelled by two low-pressure beam-engines. The following spring, the steamboat owners of Buffalo, N. Y., urged him to locate in business in their city. He removed from New York to Buffalo, where he continued to reside from June 30th, 1833, until the time of his death. He became prominently identified with the construction of machinery for lake steamers, making a specialty of steam boilers. With fortune varying with the vicissitudes of the times, he continued in the business until a few years before his death, when he retired from active life, with an ample competence. He died August 28th, 1867, universally respected and esteemed for his high integrity, unassuming worth, and many generous and genial qualities.

Newman, William H. H., second son of John Newman, was born in New York City, February 8th, 1826. Removed thence to Buffalo, N. Y., where he has resided since June 30th, 1833. Early in life he entered the office of his father's iron-works, soon became prominent in the business, and continued associated with it while his father remained in active life, a portion of the time having an interest in the business. Was married October 2d, 1849, to Jerusha A., daughter of Hon. Latham A. Burrows, of same city.

Having some time previously secured favorable connections for supplying some leading goods, in the year 1858 he opened a store on Main street, corner of Dayton, for the sale of iron, metals, belting, etc., supplying railroads, machine-shops, engineers, and others, with goods required by them; a business to which his experience as to the wants of such customers had fitted him.

With energy, by close attention to business, and strict adherence to a few plain but pointed rules or maxims, which marked and characterized all his business life, with rigid promptness, accuracy, and thoroughness, he was enabled to build up a business of goodly proportions, of value to the interests of the city, and ultimately attain to a position of independence and prominence among the merchants and business men of Buffalo.

He has been successful in all of his business pursuits, from a rare combination of industry and judgment, and has gained the confidence and respect of the whole community, by at all times exhibiting a rectitude of character which never wavered from a proper direction. He has done much, and all honorably; and now, dwelling in the affluence and honor gained by his industry and talents, he can look upon the past unsullied career with conscious pride and satisfaction.

Noxon, B. Davis, the subject of this sketch, son of Dr. Robert Noxon, of Poughkeepsie, N. Y., was born in that city April 21st, 1788, of a family highly respected in itself and in its numerous connections, long settled in the eastern part of the State. He received a good academic education, and afterward pursued the study of the law in the office of Philo Ruggles, a lawyer of reputation. Having been admitted to the bar, he commenced practice at Marcellus, in Onondaga County. He soon after married Miss Sully Ann Van Kleeck, daughter of Teunis Van Kleeck, Esq., of Poughkeepsie, who became the mother of twelve children, eight of whom still survive. After a few years' residence at Marcellus, Mr. Noxon removed to Onondaga Hill, then the county-seat. Though the bar of Onondaga County then embraced among its members not a few lawyers of uncommon ability and learning, Mr. Noxon early acquired a prominent position. In 1829, he removed to Syracuse. Here he resided until his death, May 13th, 1869.

Mr. Noxon possessed legal talents of the highest order. He was quick to seize the points of a case, and bold and fearless in presenting them to the court or jury. In the examination of witnesses, his skill was unsurpassed. His mind was logical, and he reasoned clearly and closely. Before he settled in Syracuse, he had already achieved a high reputation throughout Central New York, and for thirty or forty years he stood at the head of its bar, the peer of the most brilliant lawyers in the State. No name of the time is oftener found on the pages of the law reports. His integrity, moderation, and liberality are attested by the fact that, although for many years enjoying the most extensive and important practice in Central New York, he retired with a competence only.

For many years, he wielded great public influence in the central part of the State, and his name was influential in State and national politics. He was attached to the Whig party, and, from conviction, acted with it as long as it existed. After its dissolution, he voted with the Democratic party. He was a member of the Protestant Episcopal Church. In his family relations he was most happy, a kind husband and father. Being widely known and greatly respected, the announcement of his death elicited marked expressions of sorrow. The bar of Onondaga County appointed one of the most distinguished of their number, the Honorable Charles B. Sedgwick, to prepare and deliver before them, and a large concourse of citizens which the occasion brought together, a eulogy of the deceased. Many other eminent jurists and judges in all parts of the State were invited to, and did unite in testifying to his extraordinary qualities as a lawyer and a man. We cannot better close this brief sketch of Mr. Noxon's character, than by quoting from one or two of these addresses.

Said Mr. Sedgwick, in his oration, after referring to Mr. Noxon's earlier career:

"The nisi prius courts were held by the judges of the Supreme Court—the giants of the profession—the elder Spencer, Kent, Platt, Van Ness, Livingston, Tompkins, and Yates. Lawyers of the highest reputation, from all parts of the State—Van Vechten, Elisha Williams, Emmett, Daniel Cady, Martin Van Buren—were constant attendants upon our courts. These were the men with whom the young lawyers of that day were to measure their strength, and such the tribunals which were to decide where victory was to be awarded; and among such lawyers, Mr. Noxon was conspicuous. In knowledge of this branch of the law, in careful preparation, in the acumen necessary to mark every nice distinction, in the skill requisite to detect and expose fraud and perjury, in boldness, tact, pertinacity, in his hard logic for the court, and his skilful appeals to juries, he was in the front rank of his profession." . . . .

The Honorable William F. Allen, of the Court of Appeals, writing to the same public meeting, said of Mr. Noxon:

"He was a great man, and worthy of all admiration. He was strong in his native good sense and sound judgment; strong in the knowledge of the law, in the rudiments and principles of which he was 'thoroughly rooted and grounded;' strong in his knowledge of human nature, and his ability and tact in the use of that knowledge; strong in his self-reliance, strong in his affections and

social ties, drawing to himself, with cords of love, respect, and affection, all who came to know him; strong in his love of right and justice, truth and equity."

Many like estimates of him are contained in the letters and addresses of other eminent men, in the memorial published by the bar of Onondaga County, intended to perpetuate the memory of the honored dead.

Osgood, Hon. Jason C., was born in the town of Nassau, Rensselaer County, N.Y., November 16th, 1804. At an early age, his father moved to Madison County, where he purchased a mill, and here Mr. Osgood's mechanical ingenuity was first developed in the many little improvements he devised, and added to the machinery in the mill. His ambition was to be a mechanic and an inventor, and it was during the year 1833 that he obtained his first patent for a horse-hair picking and curling machine which produced a revolution in that branch of industry. About this time, he moved to Virginia, and engaged in the performance of contract work on public improvements. In 1838, he obtained the patent for a dumping and tilting wagon; the invention was afterward applied to freight cars. In 1846, Mr. Osgood moved to Troy, N. Y., where he afterward resided until his death, which occurred April 27th, 1875. Previous to his removal there, he, in connection with Daniel Carmichael, of Brooklyn, obtained a contract for deepening some of the State canals, during which time his fertile mechanical brain invented the celebrated Osgood dredging-machine, by which his name became famous and world-wide. In 1855, he constructed the "double-dredger," with a well-hole for depositing its excavations.

The "rock-breaker" was invented and patened by him in 1851, while dredging the Mississippi River at Des Moines Rapids. As there were many rocks to break, necessity for its work prompted and suggested the invention. One of these machines moved 10,000 yards of rock on that river, and made his name almost as famous as the dredger. In 1862, Mr. Osgood invented the canal dredger with an endless chain, so constructed that it was very easy to regulate the depth the dredge should work. His last invention of note was the "ditcher," perfected in 1870, and could be worked either by horse or steam power. As intimated, he was connected with many public works and improvements, in which employment many of the ideas of his invention were perfected. Among the most important works in which he was engaged were deepening the State canals, dredging the Chesapeake Bay, dredging Charleston harbor, S. C., digging the canal through the Dismal Swamp, dredging the Mississippi, Missouri, and San Juan Rivers, and improving the Hudson River. Mr. Osgood was interested in politics, only so far as to desire the furtherance of the best interests of the city of his adoption. In 1852, he was elected a member of the State Assembly. In 1857, he was again elected; also in 1871. He was a member of the Board of Fire Commissioners of Troy, serving from May 1st, 1861, until December 31st, 1868. He refused all other honors, though tendered him many times. He was a shrewd, careful, and successful business manager, and possessed a powerful brain and active mind. He was truly a self-made man—one of that class who not only gave us a country, but assured its wonderful progress and prosperity. Mr. J. C. Osgood not only possessed genius for mechanical achievement, but the qualities of noble manhood. He felt kindly to all; cherished no revenges. His judgment was anchored to the rock of integrity; genial in companionship, loving and liberal. A true representative of American nobility, he went to his grave crowned with the honor of a well-spent life.

Ovens, Robert, was born August 12th, 1815, in the village of Stow, Scotland, twenty-four miles distant from Edinburgh, and early in life learnt his trade in the vicinity of his birthplace. On the first of January, 1833, he was joined in wedlock to Miss Jeanet Dickson, and in the following April left with his wife for America. He having faith in the future of Western New York, came immediately to Buffalo, and after one year's stay in that locality moved to Dunkirk, though only to stay eighteen months, and, finding he had a preference for the first city of his adoption, returned to Buffalo and took charge of the bakery and confectioner shop of Mr. Atkins, remaining with him until Mr. A. sold out his business, when he accepted the same position under Mr. Spencer, where he continued till 1848, when his ambition for promoting himself prompted him to commence in a small way for himself, which he did on Seneca street, just below the present site of the post-office, which he occupied twenty-four years. In 1866, he, in company with his son, W. S. Ovens, bought out their present location and business, Nos. 55 and 57 Ellicott street, from D. B. Fuller, together with his entire aërated bread machinery, continuing to operate his old store on Seneca street as a branch till 1872, when they concentrated all their business under the present roof. This move was necessitated by the fact that their business had so steadily increased the old place was much too small, which indeed proved their new quarters—for they have built and enlarged till the factory now occupies from Nos. 59 to 67 Ellicott street, and is one of the best bakeries and cracker manufactories extant, fitted up with all the latest and best improved machinery, including one of Vicker's celebrated mixing, breaking, and cutting machines. From a small beginning the business gradually increased till they consumed as high as eighty barrels of flour daily, and the goods they make find a market in most of the larger cities of the country. This has been accomplished by strict personal attention to business, which for some years was shared by his wife, who daily attended to the wants of their customers by personally attending to the Seneca street store. At the age when most men retire from active business, Mr. Ovens remains hale, vigorous, laborious, intelligent, and genial, the same benevolent friend to the needy and industrious he has been for the last forty years, still emphatically showing his faith by his works.

Park, Paul, was born in Canada, in 1814, and is the son of S. and H. Park, and is one of a family of nine. At the age of twelve he lost his father. Had the benefit of common-schools only. After finishing his education, and until 1840, was in the employ of various houses as clerk, etc., at which time he joined in partnership with two others and built a gang-mill on Grand River, Ontario, which business and partnership proved an unhappy one, the result being that Mr. Park was left with but little means.

But he bought another mill, mostly on credit, fitted it up and operated it till 1855, when he moved to Buffalo, where he engaged in the lumber business, which he has carried on successfully for more than twenty-one years. Though now well along in years, he is still engaged in active business, and enjoys the respect of the community in which he lives.

Yours truly,
R.V. Pierce

Parks, Salmon A., was born at Moreau, Saratoga County, N. Y., February 22d, 1827. His father's ancestry, back to his great grandfather, were settlers in this county before the Revolution, and his mother was formerly from Great Barrington, Mass. His parents moved to Sandy Hill, Washington County, when the subject of this sketch was only six years old, where he remained twenty years. In early life he was engaged rafting and sawing lumber, at which he continued three or four years, receiving his education during the winter months. In April, 1846, he first entered a paper-mill at Baker's Falls, and commenced to work at the bottom rung of the ladder. By close attention to business, he soon found promotion, and gradually did he pass through every department in the manufacture of paper, till he thoroughly and practically mastered every branch. In 1852, he was married to Miss Harriet A. Hewitt, of Saratoga County, by whom he has had seven children. For one year after this eventful step, he continued to work as journeyman, when, being ambitious and desiring to better his and his family's position, he, in 1853, moved to West Milton, where he associated his knowledge with the capital of others, and commenced manufacturing news paper. In 1860, the firm changed to the Pioneer Paper Company, where he remained interested until 1865, when he sold his interest and joined hands with Hon. George West at Rock City Falls. This partnership continued until 1872, when he moved to Glen's Falls, where he has since resided. Here he became interested in the Glen's Falls Paper Company, assuming the sole superintendency of the works, which turn out about one hundred tons of news paper per month, shipped principally to New York and Brooklyn papers. As a man and citizen he stands deservedly high, and at present he has the honor to be president of the village of Glen's Falls.

Perry, John Strong, of Albany, N. Y., was born at Farmington, Ct., December 17th, 1815. His paternal ancestors were Perrys, Lords, and Leavenworths; maternal ancestors, the Treadwells and Pomeroys.

Mr. Perry had only the advantages of a common-school education till the age of fourteen; afterward he was a clerk in Hartford, Ct., for one year, and subsequently for thirteen years in the old house of the Webbs in Albany.

He embarked in the manufacture of stoves, under the firm of Treadwell & Perry, in 1843, and has been indefatigable in the improvement of stoves and furnaces to an extent not surpassed by any others. Industry, system, order, and exactness are among his leading traits. He strives to act upon the principle that "what is worth doing at all is worth doing well."

He was one of the founders of the National Stove Association, and for several years its first President; also the first President of the National Patent Association.

The firm of Perry & Co., of which he is the senior partner, are largely engaged in the manufacture of stoves, which find a market in nearly every State and Territory of the Union, as well as in many foreign countries. This firm have three large foundries in Albany, and have lately contracted for the labor of 900 convicts in the State Prison at Sing Sing, N. Y.

Pierce, R. V., M.D.—Every nation owes its peculiar character, its prosperity—in brief, every thing that distinguishes it as an individual nation—to the few men belonging to it who have the courage to step beyond the boundaries prescribed by partisanship, professional tradition, or social customs. In professional no less than in political life, there occasionally arise men who burst the fetters of conventionalism, indignantly rejecting the arbitrary limits imposed upon their activity, and step boldly forward into new fields of enterprise. We call these men *self-made*. The nation claims them as her proudest ornaments—the men upon whom she can rely, in peace for her glory, in war for her succor. Of this class of men the medical profession has furnished a distinguished example in the successful and justly celebrated physician, Dr. R. V. Pierce, of Buffalo, N. Y., and any history treating of the industries of the Empire State would be incomplete without a sketch of his useful life and earnest work. We regret that space will not permit a more detailed account of his early history and parentage, our limits allowing only a brief survey of his life and the herculean labors which his indefatigable industry has enabled him to accomplish. His ancestors were among the early settlers of Massachusetts, but soon after the Revolution they removed to Central New York. Ray Vaughn Pierce was born August 6th, 1840, at Stark, Herkimer County. While an infant, his parents removed to Venango County, Pa. He early developed a marked aptitude and love for study and scientific research, which foreshadowed his useful and active life. Selecting the medical profession for his life-work, at the age of eighteen he entered into the diligent study of the healing art. Four years later, he graduated with the highest honors, having ranked as one of the most brilliant and earnest students. Thus specially educated for the profession which he so eminently adorns, he early supplemented his studies by extensive and original research in its several departments. He brought to his chosen work acute perceptive and reflective powers, and that indomitable energy that neither shrinks at obstacles nor yields to circumstance.

As indicated by the accompanying steel portrait, in physique Dr. Pierce is an ideal type of American manhood. Of medium stature, robust, his appearance is characterized by a healthful, vigorous vitality, while the full, lofty brow, and handsomely-cut features, are indicative of that comprehensive mental power and remarkable business sagacity which have combined to place him among the distinguished men of the age.

Whoever is, to a great extent, dependent upon others for the execution of labor, must possess, in no ordinary degree, the power of reading character, that he may be enabled to select as his agents men of sound integrity as well as ability. Whether this faculty be intuitive, or acquired by experience and the study of physiognomy and phrenology, or partly intuitive and partly acquired, to those who know him the fact is obvious that Dr. Pierce possesses it in an extraordinary degree, reading character at a glance, and seldom erring in his first impression. This faculty is a rare endowment, and cannot be too highly prized. It has been said, and we think not unwisely, that the greatest blemish on President Grant's administration was due to the non-possession of this faculty by the chief magistrate. On the contrary, the princely Stewart possessed it in an eminent degree. Like the latter, the exercise of this invaluable faculty has enabled Dr. Pierce to secure the most efficient and honorable men as his assistants and subordinates. He is thus enabled to labor thoroughly and successfully in several departments, while his reputation is fully and honorably sustained by the excellence of the work accomplished.

Another characteristic prominently displayed by the subject of this sketch is an intensely energetic disposition, which he has reduced by rigid practice to a firm habit of thoroughly accomplishing every undertaking. He believes, and his practice is in strict conformity with his conviction, that whatever is worth doing is worth doing well. Although enjoying an extensive and lucrative practice at Titusville, Pa., the inherent energy and honesty of the man would not permit him to pursue the narrow routine of practice prescribed by the "school." If there were errors in its methods of practice, he desired to abandon them. If the other schools possessed advantages over his own, he wished to introduce them into his own practice, regardless of the proscription of his "school." He carefully investigated foreign methods of practice, and by original researches in *materia medica*, discovered the remedies which have made his name a cherished household word in American homes. Assured of their unparalleled efficacy in the diseases for which he compounded them, he naturally conceived the idea of extending his practice—of making it world-wide. To realize this ambitious project, Dr. Pierce removed, in 1867, to Buffalo, N. Y., and there established the World's Dispensary, for the treatment of chronic diseases—the greatest institution of its kind in the world, and, in many respects, the only one.

Dr. Pierce possesses, in an eminent degree, that rare executive talent which can thoroughly systematize and reduce the most extensive and complex business, even in its minutest details, to perfect order. This fact is apparent to every person who visits the World's Dispensary, passes through its several departments, and observes the great diversity of duties being performed by more than two hundred employés, yet every thing being done with the regularity of clockwork. He cannot fail to perceive that its manager is richly endowed with that comprehensive executive talent which enables him to conduct with ease and success those vast branches of industry which are almost infinite in detail. This fact can only be fully appreciated after a visit to his far-famed Dispensary. Entering the printing department, the visitor will see twelve large steam presses, which are kept constantly running throughout the entire year on pamphlet literature for gratuitous distribution. These pamphlets are issued in many languages, and scattered broadcast throughout the civilized world. In the bindery department, are four folding-machines, doing the work of a hundred expert hand-folders; and also machinery for stitching, trimming, and otherwise facilitating the work. In the publishing department, we find an extensive and complicated business carried on through a thousand agents, by whom Dr. Pierce's large and popular work, "The People's Common Sense Medical Adviser," is represented throughout the United States. The successful conduct of the agency department alone requires thorough organization and careful management. In the advertising department, the visitor sees a large number of clerks busily engaged in receiving and assorting the four thousand newspapers, magazines, and other periodicals, in which the proprietor advertises, carefully recording each insertion as well as omission of the notices. All advertisements are contracted for through written and special agreement with publishers. All publishers failing to insert the notices according to the terms of the contract are promptly notified and required to make good such omissions. In the pharmaceutical department, where the proprietary or Family Medicines are prepared, every process is conducted in a strictly scientific manner. The laboratory is neat and cleanly, and its appurtenances are arranged in the most perfect order. The drug-mills, stills, percolating and filtering apparatus, are all of the latest and most approved kind. In the department for the special examination and treatment of the patients (soon to be removed to the Invalids' Hotel), the same thorough and systematic organization prevails.

Dr. Pierce's Medical and Surgical Faculty, at present embracing nine physicians and surgeons, is thoroughly organized according to the several departments of medical and surgical practice—each member being an expert specialist. Commenting on Dr. Pierce's Medical Faculty, the Buffalo *Express* says: "By associating with himself only those physicians and surgeons who possess the most thorough qualifications and varied, extensive experience, Dr. Pierce is entitled to the utmost confidence of his patients, whose best interests he seems ever anxious to subserve."

The medical and surgical practice may be considered under three general divisions.

1. The first division includes all cases treated without personal consultation. The original and ingenious system of diagnosis devised by Dr. Pierce to determine the character and extent of disease in these cases, is fully explained in his popular work, entitled "The People's Common Sense Medical Adviser." He perceived that in each of the natural sciences the investigator proceeds according to a *system of signs*. The geologist in his cabinet accurately determines and describes the cleft of rock, which he has never seen, from the minute specimen on his table, and the chemist in his laboratory notes the constituents of the sun with the same precision that he analyzes a crystal of rock salt. The analogous system developed by Dr. Pierce in medical science is worthy of his genius, and has made his name justly celebrated.

2. The second division embraces those more complicated cases which require a personal examination, after which they are allowed to return to their homes to pursue the prescribed treatment.

3. In a practice so extensive there would necessarily be many obstinate and complicated cases, as well as those requiring surgical operations and careful nursing, which would demand the immediate and personal attention of the physician. To provide a real *home* for this class of patients, Dr. Pierce has erected that magnificent edifice known as the Invalids' Hotel, at a cost of nearly a quarter of a million dollars. The same energetic spirit that prompted him to lay so substantial a foundation for his professional life, and subsequently to preface every undertaking by careful preparation for its thorough and detailed execution, he has manifested in the construction of this elegant and commodious hotel. Note its architectural features, its unusually strong and massive walls, its graceful and lofty towers and pavilions, and its spacious verandas. Observe, too, its substantially-constructed passenger elevator, its exquisitely-wrought furniture, especially designed and adapted to the architecture. Walk upon the tiled floors, or luxuriate in its health-giving baths, which rival in elegance of construction the far-famed baths of the Orient. In each and every detail, the thoughtful observer sees the reflection of the founder's dominant characteristic trait, viz., *thoroughness*. In the conduct of the hotel, the same systematic organization is observed as at the Dispensary.

For effective execution, the general divides his army into corps, subdividing the corps

into divisions, the divisions into brigades, the brigades into regiments, and the regiments into companies, each order and sub-order having its responsible leader. In a similar manner has Dr. Pierce subdivided his large corps of professional and other assistants, thus obtaining thorough efficiency in each department. His original methods of practice are fully explicated in his work on Domestic Medicine, which we have already mentioned. It well deserves the popularity it has won, by its terse, practical explanations and illustrations of physiological and hygienic laws. As a manual of Domestic Medicine, it is pronounced by professional critics to be the best work which has ever appeared. A volume of over nine hundred pages, handsomely bound in cloth, and selling at $1.50, obviously its compilation was no labor for self-interest, the proceeds barely defraying the expense of publication alone. We can therefore well believe the author's prefatory assertion that it was a work undertaken solely in the interests of humanity. His labor, however, has not been unrewarded. The day has passed when the benefactors of humanity were allowed to live in ignominious poverty, their sacrifices, their labors unrecompensed. To-day, the benefactors of the people—the men who devote their lives and energies to the interests of humanity—these are the men whom the world delights to honor, and whom it rewards with princely fortunes. As an earnest worker for the welfare of his fellow-men, Dr. Pierce has won their warmest sympathy and esteem. While seeking to be their servant only, he has become a prince among them. Yet the immense fortune lavished upon him by a generous people he hoards not, but invests in the erection and establishment of institutions directly contributive to the public good, the people thus realizing, in their liberal patronage, a new meaning of that beautiful Oriental custom of casting bread upon the waters. Noted in both public and private life for his unswerving integrity, and all those sterling virtues which ennoble manhood, Dr. Pierce ranks high among those few men whose names the Empire State is justly proud to inscribe upon her roll of honor. Ambitious, yet moved by an ambition strictly amenable to the most discriminating and well-balanced judgment, his future career promises to be one of unparalleled activity and usefulness, ably supplementing the work he has already accomplished by a life at once noble in effort, enviable in its grand results.

Powers, D. W.—The subject of this sketch was born at Batavia, Genesee Co., N. Y., June 14th, 1818; his parents being among the early settlers of that county. Mr. Powers was of an aspiring disposition, and at the age of twenty he determined to leave the precincts of his old home to seek his fortunes in a clime where the business current was not so stagnant and his efforts for future distinction more certain of accomplishment. So he moved to Rochester, N. Y., and accepted a humble position in a hardware store, where he remained twelve years, during which time he received marked promotion. Having formed a taste for banking, he in 1850 issued the following card:

"NEW EXCHANGE OFFICE.

"The subscriber has located himself in the Eagle Block, Rochester, one door west of the Monroe Bank, on Buffalo street, for the purpose of doing the Exchange Business in all its branches. ☞ Uncurrent monies bought and sold. Exchange on New York and the eastern cities, bought and sold. Certificates of

Deposits in banks, and notes payable at distant points collected. Canada and western bank notes discounted at the lowest rates. Drafts on Buffalo can be had at all times. Foreign and American gold and silver coins, bought and sold. ☞ Deposits received and interest allowed. Monies remitted to England, Ireland, and Scotland, and other portions of the old world.

"By prompt attention to business I hope to merit a share of public patronage.

"I am authorized to refer to Ebenezer Watts, Esq.; George R. Clark, Esq., Cashier; Ralph Lester, Esq., Cashier; Thomas H. Rochester, President; C. T. Amsden, Cashier; Everard Peck, Esq., President; Isaac Hills, Esq.   DANIEL W. POWERS.

"ROCHESTER, Monroe Co., N. Y., March 1, 1850."

and started in business on a small scale. The very place that Mr. Powers commenced business he does his business now, but the aspect of the concern is quite different. The small office is replaced by the most elegant business block west of New York City, having a frontage of 176 feet on State, and 175 feet on Main street with 150 on Pindell alley. The main centre is faced with Ohio freestone elaborately carved, the blocks being alternately vermiculated and cut in panel, and is seven stories in height exclusive of the basement, which is of New Hampshire granite. The great wings present uniform fronts. The ground floor contains one bank and fifteen stores; the upper stories, 220 rooms, all of them occupied for almost every conceivable kind of business, which are communicated with from the ground floor by means of elegant stairways and two elevators which are continually in operation. The whole is absolutely fire-proof, and contains one of the finest art collections in America, the property of Mr. Powers. Among them are to be found the best copies extant from such of the old masters as Giotto, Michael Angelo, Raphael, Correggio, Paul Veronese, Murillo, Titian, Carlo Dolci, Sassoferrato, Bassano, Annibali Caracci, and others, made especially for Mr. Powers, by artists of international reputation, each selected for his special aptitude to copy from certain masters, who, in many cases, rival the originals in excellence, and perhaps surpass them in freshness and beauty of coloring. In the main room of this department of art, can be seen and heard the most perfect orchestrion ever made in America, and which is a continual source of delight to all visitors. In addition, there has been made lately a contribution of the highest value, viz., an extensive series of double photographic views exhibited by means of stereoscopic apparatus, representing scenes and localities from all sections of the universe. The whole collection proves Mr. Powers to be one of the great art connoisseurs of our country, and who has spared no pains to lavish his princely fortune for his taste in art. Mr. D. W. Powers has been ever adverse to the turbulent currents incident to political life. He has amassed a fortune that would content the extravagant requirements of royalty, by attending wholly to one business, until he has become honored for his integrity and known as one of the most influential citizens of Rochester.

Pratt, Daniel, was born in Greenwich, Washington County, N. Y., in 1806. In 1833, he graduated at Union College, and in the same year moved to Onondaga County, where he read law with David D. Hillis at Camillus. In the fall of 1836, he

moved to Syracuse, where he has since resided. He was admitted to the bar in July, 1837, with Judge George F. Comstock and Hon. Charles B. Sedgwick, and commenced the practice of his profession with David D. Hillis, Esq. In February, 1843, he was appointed by Governor Bouck First Judge of Onondaga County. Four years later he was elected Judge of the Supreme Court, and re-elected in 1851. At the close of the term for which he had been re-elected, he returned from the bench enjoying the unreserved confidence of the people he had so long served, both as to his unquestioned integrity, and his great judicial ability. While upon the bench, both Hamilton and Union Colleges conferred upon him the degree of LL.D., a fitting tribute to his private and public worth. He resumed the practice of law January 1st, 1860, forming a partnership with the late lamented David J. Mitchell, an advocate of surpassing persuasive power. Two years later, Mr. Wilbur M. Brown was admitted to the partnership, and the firm, as thus constituted, for fifteen years ranked among the first in the State, having an unusually lucrative and successful practice. Judge Pratt was elected as one of the counsel to prosecute Judge Barnard in the impeachment trial, and the same year received the appointment from Governor Hoffman as one of the Commissioners to revise the Constitution. In 1873, he was elected Attorney-General, a position he filled with distinction and honor. It is often asserted, but without reasonable support, that if a man have genius and talent he will become eminent in the sphere in which he moves, even if he has not the advantage of proper previous training. Examples are not often given of men who, by the mere force of intellect, without its being strengthened by proper training and preparation, become lights in the various avocations and professions of life. Fortunately for Judge Pratt, he had received all the adventitious assistance of thorough training in mental exercise previous to commencing the study of the law, and when he had mastered his profession he possessed an untold advantage over those who had been deprived of a suitable preparatory education. His genial disposition, his strong intellectuality, his direct and positive argumentative power, strengthened and enforced by a fund of knowledge which he could draw from a thousand sources, soon won for him hosts of friends, and made him eminent in the community. It was not to be supposed that a man of Judge Pratt's ability and popularity should not receive some demonstration of confidence and esteem, hence his appointment and election to the positions above-mentioned.

Pratt, Samuel F., was born May 28th, 1807, in Windham County, Vt. He was the son of Samuel Pratt, Jr., who was the son of Captain Pratt.

In 1801, Captain Samuel Pratt made a long expedition into the almost savage wilderness of the far West, returning by the way of Buffalo, then but a cluster of log cabins. Comprehending the advantages of this little village, and his observations in his explorations on the lakes west, convinced him that this was to be the future outlet of a large commerce. He therefore determined to cast his lot here; this was in 1803.

In 1804, the following year, he closed up his affairs in Westminster, and set out with his family on their tedious journey for

Buffalo, which he reached in September of the same year.

Captain Pratt, eldest son of Samuel, and father of Samuel F. Pratt, did not emigrate with his parents, but joined them in August, 1807, bringing with him his wife and Samuel F. Pratt, who was then about three months old.

He led an active life, and was closely engaged in business or public duties until the time of the burning of the village. This severe blow so embarrassed him that he soon found himself without the means to carry on his business, but an unforeseen source was near at hand. Meeting a former friend, William Bigelow, who chanced to be passing through Buffalo, and knowing of his embarrassed condition, proposed to Mr. Pratt that he should assume management of his business interests at St. Thomas, Canada, and he left for that place in May, 1818, leaving Samuel F. Pratt, who was then only eleven years old, in charge of his mother. In about one year Samuel F. joined his father, where he remained about one year and a half, when he returned to Buffalo, his health being so poor, and he died in August, 1822.

Samuel F. Pratt remained in Canada in the employ of the same firm his father had been connected with three years. On the death of his father, he returned to Buffalo, when he entered the employ of G. & T. Weed in 1822, who conducted a hardware business. In 1826, a small interest was allowed him in the business, although he was then but nineteen years old. In 1828, a partnership was formed which included Samuel F. Pratt. In 1836, he bought out the entire Weed interest, and the firm became S. F. Pratt. In 1842, his brother, Pascal P. Pratt, who had formerly clerked for him, became a partner, and in 1846, Edward P. Beals became a general partner in the firm of Pratt & Co., which has since remained unchanged. In 1852, Messrs. Pratt & Co., finding the space which they had occupied entirely inadequate to accommodate their largely-increasing business, removed to the Terrace, where they had built commodious warehouses. The firm of Pratt & Seitchworth was established in 1848. Few partnerships ever existed with so uniformly pleasant relations, says one of his partners. There seemed to be a wellspring of kindness and charity in his breast sufficient to sweeten all the cares of business life. He was inclined to look hopefully into the future; any thing unpleasant and annoying he put aside. At the age of twenty-eight, in the fall of 1835, he married Miss Mary Jane Strong. The marriage was the consequence of a long acquaintance and mutual attachment, and resulted in a well-ordered home, their offspring being two daughters. From the time Samuel F. Pratt entered the Weed hardware store upon a salary of eight dollars a month, he made it a conscientious duty to contribute according to his means to all works of benevolence that came to his notice, and after joining the church (which he did at the age of eighteen), he gave liberally, not only to the church itself, but to all the various objects under its fostering care. He always recognized in a liberal degree the claims society advanced for its well-being and protection, and gave with no stinted hand.

Samuel F. Pratt died on the 28th of April, 1872, after a very successful career, and was most deeply mourned, not only by his immediate family, but by all who knew him. His life was an eventful one. He was successful in all of his business pur-

Sincerely Yours,
J. H. Redfield

suits from a rare combination of industry and judgment, and at all times exhibiting a rectitude of character which never wavered from the proper direction.

Redfield, Lewis H.—The subject of this sketch was born at Farmington, Ct., in 1793, and has therefore lived under the administrations of all our Presidents, and is nearly as aged as the government itself.

The nineteenth century has been eminently an era of invention and progress. Mr. R. remembers when steamboats were a novelty and a fireside wonder, when railroads were unknown, and the electric telegraph was not dreamed of. The cotton gin, the mowing and threshing machines, are all the product of this century, and have been brought into use under the observation of Mr. R. In 1799, dropping into the tide of emigration then largely setting westward, the family moved to the "Genesee Country," where they began pioneer life in the primeval forests by clearing away the timber and making a farm. When fifteen, with no educational advantages except those obtained from reading and study at evening by the light of the winter's fire, he entered the office of the *Ontario Repository*, edited by James D. Bemis, at Canandaigua, as printer's apprentice. Here he was engaged six years, first as office boy, then compositor, pressman, and editor. Besides mastering his trade, he learned industry, frugality, and self-reliance—three lessons of inestimable value to the architect of fortune. When Mr. R. was scarcely twenty-one, Mr. Bemis loaned him $1400 with which to start business, and on the 27th of September, 1814, the first number of the *Onondaga Register* made its appearance under his proprietorship, and at once sprung into favor. During this period, the subject of building the Erie Canal engaged public attention very largely, and the *Register* took a leading position in favor of that important State enterprise. In 1828, Mr. R. concluded to move his home and business to Syracuse, that place having become the foremost business town of the county. In the following year, having previously purchased Mr. Durnford's paper, the *Gazette*, he united the two under the name of the *Onondaga Register and Syracuse Gazette*. Here a greater measure of prosperity than before followed his labors. In 1832, owing to ill-health, he was forced to abandon the journalistic work to which he was strongly attached, and to which he had devoted the best years of his life. There were then, as now, strong men connected with the newspaper press of New York, and among his contemporaries were William Coleman, Colonel Stone, M. M. Noah, A. C. Flagg, Solomon Southwick, Thurlow Weed, Edwin Croswell, William H. Maynard, H. and E. Phinney, J. D. Bemis, A. G. Dauby, V. W. Smith, E. Mack, Orrin Follett, and S. H. Salisbury.

After this period, he spent several years mostly in travel, seeking health, which, when obtained, he settled down again with just work enough to render life enjoyable, giving attention to his private affairs. Mr. R. is the oldest representative of the press in N. Y. State now living, he having entered the field sixty-three years ago. He is, therefore, entitled to the appellation of "Father of the Press of New York." In politics he is a Democrat, and has served his party manfully through many a heated campaign; but he never sought office or aspired to public distinction. In 1872, however, he was prevailed upon to accept the nomination for Presidential Elector on the ticket of his party. He also held for many years the office of postmaster at Onondaga Valley, and likewise filled important offices in the village government of Syracuse, having been one year the President of its Board of Trustees. He was also one of the projectors of the Bank of Salina, and always a director in that institution. He is now, and for many years has been, a director in the Salt Springs Bank, and is connected with several of the street railway companies of Syracuse. Although Mr. R. long since passed the age allotted to man, he is still vigorous and active, attending to business affairs with as much regularity and strictness as ever, and, from all indications, is not unlikely to be able to do so for many years to come. While mindful of the obligation to devote what time may be necessary to the management of his pecuniary affairs, he finds frequent occasions for relief from business engagements, for travel and relaxation, and no one relishes more keenly the companionship of nature. Generous and ever ready to aid the deserving, he is passing the evening of his days in such activities as tend to the promotion of physical and mental enjoyment, and prolong the years of a useful and well-spent life.

Ricard, George, was born in the city of New York, December 25th, 1798, and was the son of John and Catharine Ricard. His father went to New Orleans from Bordeaux, France, in 1792. And, on account of the proclamation issued by the Spanish government that all Frenchmen who would not swear allegiance to their government must leave the country in twenty-four hours, he took passage to Philadelphia; but before the ship had fairly got to sea, they were captured by a Spanish privateer, plundered of every thing they possessed, put aboard of a cartel, and taken to where the French fleet were lying off San Domingo, and there exchanged as prisoners of war. While aboard the fleet, Mr. R. offered his services, which were accepted, the fleet coming to New York for repairs and supplies in 1794. While lying in the harbor, the British frigate Boston made her appearance, and sent a challenge to the officers of the French fleet, which was accepted. The Ambuscade whipped the Boston, but could not catch her, on account of the shattered condition of her masts and rigging. When the fleet were again ready for sea, Mr. R. decided to leave the service, and so remained in New York.

The subject of this sketch received a limited education only, attending the minor schools only till his thirteenth year, when he was engaged with the house of Fisher & Sethbridge, with whom he remained eighteen months. He then worked in a cotton factory for six months. In 1814, he became a substitute for one Joseph Conkling in the N. Y. Militia, and, after three months of active service, he volunteered for six months longer, and was stationed at Harlem Heights until the following March (peace having been declared in February). He then received his discharge, was for a few months after a clerk, and was then apprenticed to Christian Bergh, the shipbuilder, for whom he worked three years. He continued at his trade till 1819, when he went to Ossabaw Island, Ga., and commenced cutting live-oak timber for the U. S. Government under Lieut. Thomas Newell, of the Navy. After six months, he returned to New York, and worked at his trade, and in the winter of 1820–1 he

was employed in Savannah, Ga. In July, 1820, he lost his father, who died from yellow fever in Savannah. In the spring of 1822, he worked in New York for a few months, when he shipped as carpenter on the Superior, Captain George R. Dowdal, engaged in the East India (Canton) trade. In this capacity he made two voyages, which occupied about two years. On his return to New York, with his hard-earned savings he opened a small retail grocery store on the corner of Chrystie and Bayard streets; here he remained seven years. In 1827, he engaged in the cooperage business, and continued the grocery business until 1832. In 1833, the failure of Hinton & Moore, white lead manufacturers, caused him considerable loss, they owing him for work done. In 1834, he was given a position in the Custom House as inspector of the customs; he remained in the Government employ until 1841, part of which time he held the position of U. S. Boarding Officer. In 1842, he moved to Williamsburg, now part of Brooklyn, where he has ever since resided as a private citizen. In 1851, he was called upon for the use of his name in getting up a savings bank, which resulted in the formation of the Williamsburg Savings Bank in April of that year. He was elected its first vice-president, and held the position thirteen years, when, at the resignation of William Wall, the president, he was elected to fill the executive, a position he still holds. The building they now occupy was finished at an expense of $500,000, and first entered by them May 31st, 1875. Mr. Ricard is a man of great intelligence, his reputation for honor and integrity is unimpeachable, and he is one of those men of whom it is safe to say, he never wronged a man out of a cent, and his friends know him as such when they are in trouble. He is loved, honored, and respected by a large circle of admiring friends and acquaintances. In 1864, he was Presidential Elector for A. Lincoln and A. Johnson.

He was joined in wedlock to Abigail Hendrickson Roberts, of New York City, April 20th, 1834, and she lived to brighten the comforts of his domestic happiness until January 27th, 1866.

Schoellkopf, J. F., was born on the 15th of November, 1819, in a small town of 5000 inhabitants, named Kirchheim U Teck, in the Kingdom of Würtemberg, Germany. His father was a tanner, and his grandfather also. After going to school till his fourteenth year, he was apprenticed to his father's trade, and after staying with him five years, he went to a mercantile house, and from there went to the United States aged twenty-two years, arriving here December 10th, 1841.

After working for a living for about two years in currier shops and tanneries, he came to Buffalo in the spring of 1844, and started, with a capital of $800—which he received from his father—a small leather store on Mohawk street.

The same fall he bought a small tannery at White's Corner for $1200, payable in six years. In the spring of 1846, he started a sheep-skin tannery, and after successfully running those concerns, he started, in the spring of 1848, with some friends, a tannery in Milwaukee, Wis, under the name of G. Pfister & Co., where he remained partner until 1857. In 1851, he started a tannery in Chicago under the firm of C. T. Grey & Co., and went out of this last-named firm in 1856. Both were successful concerns, and at present rank with the largest in the West. In 1853, he bought a tannery at North Evans, N. Y., which he ran for about twenty years. In 1856, he built the North Buffalo Mills, and in 1857 bought a small tannery in this city, which in time he enlarged, so that to-day it is one of the largest in Buffalo. In 1864, he purchased a site for a tannery in Sheffield township, Warren County, Pa., and built a tannery, which is to-day in full operation. The "Frontier Mills" he bought in 1871. Besides aforesaid establishments, he interested himself largely in the building up of the Buffalo, N. Y., and P. R.R., also in the Citizens' Gas Works of this city, of which he is at present president, besides being a director of the Buffalo, N. Y., and Philadelphia R.R., "Citizens' Gas Co.," "German Insurance Co.," and of the German Bank, and senior partner in the firm of J. F. Schoellkopf & Son, proprietors of the "City Tannery" at Buffalo, the "Sheffield Tannery" at Sheffield, Pa., also of the firm Schoellkopf & Mathews, running the "Frontier," and "North Buffalo Flour Mills," located at Black Rock, and has always been identified with various enterprises for the good of the city of Buffalo.

The fortune Mr. Schoellkopf has amassed has been made legitimately in the business enterprises he has organized and developed. His motto in life was to excel in all he undertook, and his success in life shows how well he has lived up to the maxim which he set before him as a guide.

Seabury, James M.—The subject of this sketch was born at Hempstead, Queens County, N. Y., January 29th, 1810, and was the son of Samuel and Catharine Seabury. His great grandfather was the well-known Bishop Seabury, the first bishop of the Episcopal Church in this country.

James M. Seabury received only a common school education, part of which he received in his native town, and part in Brooklyn, to which place he moved with his parents when nine years old. When fourteen he left school and moved to New York City, where he learned the trade of a baker, his term expiring when twenty-one. In 1821, he commenced the business for himself in Brooklyn, which he was engaged in for a period of twenty years, the result proving very successful during his business career. He was appointed a member of the Board of Education, and in 1853 was elected by the Democratic party to fill the important office of County Treasurer. In this capacity he served nine years, being elected three successive terms. During his first term as Treasurer, finding the position required his undivided attention to properly fulfil the duties imposed upon him, he disposed of his business, and though the position of Treasurer was offered him for the fourth term, he respectfully declined the nomination. How well he filled the position of Treasurer is best acknowledged from the fact that Kings County never had a better one. In 1866, or about two years after retiring from the County Treasurership, he was elected president of the Long Island Savings Bank, which position he has held ever since. Mr. James M. Seabury has been successful in all of his business pursuits, from a rare combination of industry and judgment, and has gained the confidence and respect of the community by at all times exhibiting a rectitude of character which has never wavered from the proper direction.

Selden, G. V., was born at Williamstown, Oswego County, N. Y., April 9th, 1816, to which place his father, Asa B. Selden, emigrated from Connecticut when fifteen years old. The subject of this sketch remained in his native town until 1851, receiving a very limited course of study. His first business experience was work on a farm, though since eighteen years of age he has been engaged in the lumber business.

In 1851, he moved to Rome, where he opened a grocery store in connection with his former business; this he continued for eight years. Since that time he has devoted himself wholly to the lumbering and manufacturing business. In 1867, it became necessary to enlarge the business and include manufacturing, and, to consummate his object, he bought out the firm of H. S. Armstrong & Co. Continuing to grow, the business soon demanded larger premises, and during 1868-9 he built his present factory and mill, a fine three-story brick building fitted up with all the latest and best-improved machinery for facilitating and economizing labor, and the successful production of doors, sashes, blinds, mouldings, etc.

Besides his large business cares, Mr. Selden is a director in the Fort Stanwix National Bank, also a stockholder in the Merchants' Iron Mill, and the Rome and Clinton Railroad, and has probably done more to build up Rome than any other single individual. He is well known to the citizens of Rome, and, in connection with his acknowledged business qualifications, he is highly esteemed for his moral attributes. He is now in the full vigor of manhood, and has long since accomplished what most men lay out as the work of a protracted life—wealth, honor, and the good-will of all men.

Seymour, Horatio, LL.D., nephew of Senator Horatio, was born at Pompey, Onondaga Co., N. Y., May 31st, 1810; removed in childhood to Utica; studied at Oxford and Geneva Academies, N. Y., and at Partridge's Military Institute, Middletown, Ct.; was admitted to the bar at Utica, 1832, but soon withdrew from its practice to devote himself to the management of the large estate he inherited by the death of his father; was a member of the staff of Governor Marcy, 1833-39; was elected to the State Assembly as a Democrat, and three times re-elected, serving as speaker in 1845; was chosen Mayor of Utica, 1842; was an unsuccessful candidate for Governor, 1850; was Governor, 1853-55; vetoed a prohibitory liquor law March, 1854; was defeated in the election of that year by the prohibitionist candidate, Myron H. Clark; was again elected Governor as a War Democrat, 1862; aided in suppressing the riots in New York City, and forwarded efficient co-operation to the national Government in the war of the Union; was defeated in the election of 1864, in which year he presided over the national Democratic Convention at Chicago, as he did again at New York, 1868, when he was himself nominated for the Presidency much against his will, and received eighty electoral votes. He resides at Deerfield, near Utica, and is president (1876) of the National Dairyman's Association and of the American Prison Association.

Shapley, M. W., was born June, 1817, at Cazenovia, Madison County, N. Y. He lived there until eighteen years of age, receiving the advantages of a good schooling. At the age of sixteen he taught school, and when eighteen he moved to Skaneateles,

N. Y., and learnt his trade with Hannum & Delano, with whom he stayed three years. He then returned to his home, where, with his father's aid, he immediately started in business, together with a partner (Mr. Backus). This continued about two years, when Mr. Backus retired, and Mr. Shapley's brother John became his partner. This continued nine years, during which time they were principally building machinery for woolen mills. In about 1850, the firm was dissolved, Mr. M. W. Shapley taking the foundry as his share, and his brother the machine shop. Six months after that time, the subject of this sketch sold out his entire business, and moved to Binghamton, where he has since resided. At first he took charge of the Empire Works, where he continued about eight months. After that he took charge of the Binghamton foundry and machine shop; here he remained fifteen months, when he commenced business for himself, under the firm style of M. W. Shapley, doing general machine work until 1855, when he associated himself with A. Dunk, the firm style changing to M. W. Shapley & Co. This continued until 1858, when Mr. P. A. Hopkins was admitted, and the firm became Shapley, Dunk & Co. It did not change again until 1863, when Mr. Dunk retired, and the firm changed to Shapley, Hopkins & Robbins. In 1867, Mr. Robbins retired, and the firm became Shapley & Hopkins. In 1870, Mr. J. S. Wells bought Mr. Hopkins' interest; the firm changed to Shapley & Wells, which still continues. They are now chiefly engaged in the manufacture of the Shapley Engine, which they sell all over the United States. They have a warehouse in Philadelphia, where they dispose of their goods. The works at Binghamton cover three quarters of an acre of ground, fitted up with all the modern improvements for expediting and facilitating work and labor. When busy they employ over one hundred hands.

Mr. S. was married to Miss Jane E. Berthrong, of Cazenovia, in January, 1843, by whom he has had three children, two of whom survive, both in the works with their father.

He has given the whole of his time to the details of his business, never mixing with politics, and through a long and successful business career never had to succumb to financial embarrassment. The fortune Mr. Shapely has amassed has been made legitimately in the business he has followed, and he has never strayed into other channels. His motto in life was to excel in all he undertook, and his success shows how well he has lived up to the old maxim set before him as a guide.

Sherman, Augustus, one of the remarkable men of his day, was born in the town of Arlington, Vt., on the 11th day of February, 1801. He was the fifth child, and third son, of Ware Darwin and Anna D. (Canfield) Sherman, the latter of Arlington, Vt., the former of Conway, Mass. When he was five years of age, his parents removed, first to Kingsbury, N. Y., and the following spring to the then frontier settlement of Fairfield (now Luzerne), on the Hudson River. Mr. Sherman's opportunities for acquiring an education were exceedingly limited, and only derived from an occasional winter attendance upon such schools as the wilderness districts then afforded. The father followed both lumbering and farming. To lighten his labor by sharing his toils, and to have his father relieved from debts

which had accumulated, was to his young son Augustus sufficient inducement for hard and exhaustive labor, for his father was to him the great and the good man. In December, 1823, the family sought a new home in Pennsylvania, where the father had purchased a farm, making the journey to Buffalo in a covered wagon, young Sherman driving the horses. Having seen them thus far on their way, he returned to Luzerne, and now, with a right good will, went to work for himself. His first venture was the purchase of one fourth of a saw mill, whose running gear consisted of two saws. He also had the running of a small grist mill near by, besides drawing and rafting his lumber to market. At this laborious double task he laid the foundation for the princely fortune he has since acquired. On the 4th of March, 1824, he was married to Miss Nancy Weed, of Luzerne. Of this marriage there were nine children, six of whom are now living. Having disposed of his interest in Luzerne, he removed to the Feeder Dam, where he resumed the manufacture of lumber, with increased facilities, and on a larger scale. Two years later, he took up his residence in Glen's Falls, which has since been his home, and about this time made has first investment in timbered lands by the purchase of half of the sixteenth township. His wife died June 12th, 1848. He was married again September 1st, 1856, to Charlotte H., daughter of the Rev. S. L. Conkling, of Martinsburg, Lewis County, N. Y. Of this marriage four children have been born, though none now survive. Steadily but surely his business increased, until it assumed vast proportions. He is founder and senior member of the old established firm of L. Thomson & Co., lumber dealers in Albany, N. Y., and still manages his extensive lumber business with its numerous branches and establishments. (Mr. Sherman is the oldest lumberman now doing business on the Hudson River, put the first loom in that river for catching logs, and was one of the first to send a boat out of the Feeder.) When Mr. Sherman moved to Glen's Falls, it had no bank, and credit is due him for first agitating the subject, when, in 1853, he was instrumental in organizing the "Commercial," now First National Bank of Glens Falls, himself one of the directors, and now the only original director remaining in the board. In 1855, he was made vice-president of the bank, and president in 1858, still holding the office. His skilful and successful management of this bank is well known and appreciated, as in all his business affairs proceeding carefully and cautiously at first with his newly-adopted measures, whilst legal proceedings against delinquent customers were rarely resorted to. The stock of the bank soon rose from 70 to 100 per cent, and for a number of years has paid eight per cent semi-annually. He is the senior partner of the private banking house of Sherman & Johnson, proprietor of the Sherman Lime Works of Glen's Falls, president of the Glen's Falls Paper Mill Co., vice-president of the Glen's Falls Insurance Co., and was made first president of the Bald Mountain Lime Co. (which position he resigned), besides owning moneyed interests in other industries which have developed Glen's Falls into an important business centre. Never venturing into the uncertain depths of speculation, but conducting his business into legitimate channels, he did not commence grasping at once for immediate returns, but allowed it to fully develop and secure a foundation strong enough to guarantee permanent results. Neither does he owe his fortune to having been born under the auspicious star, for he started at the bottom round, without wealth or influence, but, possessed of rare good judgment and strong common sense, he has by degrees crept forward through a checkered life until he has attained a fortune greater than that of any other person in the county, and owes his present position to his indomitable perseverance. Though he is seventy-six years old, he is still vigorous and active, giving his personal attention to his business affairs, while the purity of his character and the frankness of his disposition have endeared him to a large circle of friends.

Sherman, George.—The subject of this sketch was born October, 22d, 1801, in Rutland County, Vt. When one and a half years old, he, in company with his parents, moved to Moriah, Essex County, N. Y. During his early life he received a limited education, and when only seven years old commenced to work on a farm in the woods, which he continued until thirty-six years of age, when he became the possessor of a farm himself, which he sold four years later. About 1846, he, in company with John A. Lee and E. Hall, bought two iron ore beds of David E. Sanford, and commenced digging ore and disposing of it to the furnaces. They then exhumed about 1000 tons annually. He has ever since been in this business, and has increased their production to so great an extent that the firms he has been a member of have produced as much as 150,000 tons of iron ore in one year. In 1873, the Cedar Point Furnace, one of the finest and best extant, was built, and Mr. Sherman is a large stockholder and director, besides being interested in other furnaces, and for many years he has been a director in the First National Bank of Port Henry. In 1822, Mr. Sherman was married to Miss Theda Tarbell, of Chester, Vt. The issue of this marriage was two sons, one of whom (Kinsly Sherman) died January 28th, 1873. The other, G. R., is now president of the First National Bank of Port Henry, president of the Lake Champlain and Moriah R. R., and director in the Furnace Co. Mr. George Sherman lived at Moriah until two years ago, when he virtually retired from active business life, and, together with his wife, moved to Saratoga Springs. In 1870, he endowed the "Sherman Academy" at Moriah with $30,000, besides fitting the building for school purposes, and giving them new additions of land. Thus he has liberally dispensed his charities while living, and thousands of young hearts who are and will be educated by his bounty, breathe his name with gratitude.

Sherman, Kinsly, was born at Moriah, Essex County, N. Y., June 19th, 1825, and was the eldest son of George Sherman, also of Essex County. In early life, the subject of this sketch received a common-school education, and at the age of sixteen was clerk in a general store in his native town, where he continued until 1844. At this time, his father became identified with the iron industry, and Kinsly Sherman took a similar position with him, that of managing the general store attached to the iron ore mines. Here he remained until 1852, when, seized with the California excitement, he left for San Francisco to seek his fortune in the gold-fields, only remaining about seven months, when he returned to his native place.

In 1853, he went into Wisconsin and pur-

chased considerable farming lands, and in the fall of the same year, after spending some little time at home, he moved to Cleveland, Ohio, and became resident agent of Witherbee, Sherman & Co. Soon after, he commenced operating for himself, buying his ores mostly from Witherbee, Sherman & Co. In this business he remained until his death, which occurred January 28th, 1873. He was joined in wedlock during 1862 to Miss Sarah J. Holcomb, who died less than a month before him.

In early life, the subject of this sketch developed remarkable talent for business pursuits, which was followed by untiring energy and undoubted ability, which enabled him in subsequent years to plan and execute large and important business operations. He was a man of the most delicate tenderness of feeling, and, in his intercourse with others, was gentle and unassuming. His death caused a deep gloom to be spread among all who knew him.

Shumway, Horatio, was born at Belchertown, Mass., in 1788. Descended from Huguenot and Puritan ancestry, he inherited the distinguishing virtues of both peoples. Belonging to a family of twelve children, he was noted, even in childhood, for truthfulness and reliability, qualities which strengthened with his youth, and became prominent characteristics of his manhood.

His thoughtful disposition inclined him to a student life, and his own persevering efforts enabled him to prepare himself for admission to college. After his graduation at Middlebury, he entered the office of the Hon. Luther Bradish, in New York City. Becoming, at Mr. Bradish's urgent request, a member of his family, he was ever regarded by him with true interest and affection.

In 1817, he commenced the practice of his profession in Watertown, and was soon appointed District-Attorney for Jefferson County, the duties of which office he fulfilled with fidelity and honor.

In the year 1824, the attention of Mr. Shumway was drawn to Buffalo, and with many others he established himself in that city when it was just commencing that development of its natural advantages which resulted in the creation of a great city during his lifetime. At that time, Buffalo was but a village of twenty-five hundred inhabitants, and though the ranks of its legal profession were adequately filled in number, by his studious habits, integrity of action, and continuous industry, Mr. Shumway soon acquired a reputation and practice which placed him among the more eminent of the Buffalo bar— even then taking a decided rank for ability with older and larger towns of Western New York.

In the year 1847, he was elected one of the members of the State Legislature, in which he bore a distinguished part in introducing and advocating the rights of married women in the protection and possession of their property.

One of the most important acts of Mr. Shumway's professional life was the settlement of the estate of the late Jabez Goodell, a well-known citizen of Buffalo, who bequeathed to various benevolent and religious societies property estimated at $200,000. This was mostly in real estate in the city and county, and somewhat embarrassed by debts; but so skilfully was it managed that the sum of $400,000, or nearly double the amount bequeathed, was realized and paid to the various beneficiaries of Mr. Goodell. Owing to his careful attention to details, his watchful interest and scrupulous honor, the American Bible Society and the Board of Foreign Missions, as residuary legatees, were placed in possession of a sum much larger than they could have possibly anticipated. These societies marked their grateful appreciation of his services by presenting him the highest testimonials in their power to bestow. It is worth while to mention here, that not a cent of the assets did he appropriate to his own use during the settlement of the estate, voluntarily accepting at its close a small sum, totally inadequate to the arduous labor of years.

Through the influence of Mr. Shumway, the large donation of land was secured from Mr. Goodell, so essential to the establishment of the female academy, whose name, "Goodell Hall," perpetuates his memory. He was deeply interested in the prosperity of that institution, was the first President of the Board of Trustees, and its life-long friend.

In 1861, Mr. Shumway retired from the active duties of his profession, with the consciousness that every duty had been discharged faithfully and well.

Ten years later, at the age of eighty-three, this long career of usefulness and honor closed, amid the sincere regrets of his fellow-citizens, leaving no enemy to reproach an act of his life. In his own family, Mr. Shumway was the true gentleman; all his actions indicated kindness and refinement. In him the profession lost an able member, society an example of integrity and honor, the world a noble living example of a proper life.

(See portrait page 365.)

Smith, Elijah F., was born in Groton, New London County, Connecticut, December 13th, 1792. He left his home and removed to Petersburg, Virginia, where he was engaged in mercantile pursuits until the year 1825, when he was married and removed to Rochester, N. Y. Here he was engaged in the wholesale grocery business until about 1860, doing a very heavy and successful business. He has been trustee of the Rochester Savings Bank since 1840, and president of said bank the greater part of the time. Mr. Smith was twice elected mayor of the city of Rochester, in the years 1839 and 1840.

Mr. Smith was not born to affluence, but began from a humble commencement, and owes alone to his efforts and industry his present position and fortune. What he has done can be done again if the same method be used for its accomplishment. Any young man who will copy his perseverance, economy, and industry, and like him be sedulous in preserving his reputation and credit, must attain affluence and reach a reputable position. Who properly sows in spring, must reap a harvest; and he who in youth commences life with the practice of temperance, industry, and economy, must gather bountifully of the fruit they naturally produce.

Smith, H. P.—The biography of such a man as H. P. Smith is fraught not only with readable interest, but has a useful moral effect upon the present time and posterity. It teaches youth what industry and moral worth can achieve, and that they can hope for all things if they make honor their guide and are prompted by honorable emulation.

The subject of this memoir was born April 24th, 1811, in Warren County, N. Y., and he emigrated to Western New York with his father, Isaac Smith, when only eight years old. His first commencement in life was teaching school; afterward he became a clerk in a mercantile store at Niagara Falls; this he continued for some time, when he moved to Tonawanda, and clerked in the grocery store of Uriah Driggs. In 1833, in company

with his brother Daniel, he commenced for himself in the general store and stave business. Though not being entirely satisfied, he moved to Chippewa, Canada, in 1836, and commenced merchandising. Money in those days was a very scarce commodity, so he took in exchange for his wares timber, which in return he brought to Tonawanda to sell and pay for his goods. This he continued till 1840, when he moved to Lockport, N. Y., and commenced the lumber business with his brother Philo; this partnership lasted till 1844, when he gave his entire business interests to his brother and moved to Township of Walsingham, Canada. With his former good credit in Buffalo, he had no trouble to obtain a stock of goods, which he took to his newly-adopted home in Canada, and commenced exchanging them for saw-logs. This proved eminently successful, and he took in a partner and commenced operations on a large scale. They soon became the possessors of a fine lot of pine saw-logs, which were stored away in the creek, and their next move was to transport them to market. The fertile brain of H. P. Smith conceived a plan to make a large raft and tow them across the lake. (This was the first experiment ever made in this direction, and his plan of making the first one is the same now in use on all the lakes.) After six years spent this way in Canada, he moved to Tonawanda, continuing as heretofore to ship logs, which he sold to the mills at Tonawanda. In the winter of 1855-6, he went up Sable River on Lake Huron, and put up two large rafts of black-walnut and oak, which he towed to Buffalo. These were the first rafts ever towed on that lake. In 1861, he commenced towing logs on Saginaw Bay, in company with Luther Westover, of Bay City, Mich., and continued this business till his death, which occurred July 14th, 1874.

To Mr. Smith more than any other man belongs the honor of inaugurating a business which led to the development of the vast lumber interests of Tonawanda, by supplying them with timber, and which was a very hazardous and risky business. Besides having the weighty cares of a wide-spread business, he was vice-president of the Niagara County National Bank of Lockport, and a stockholder from its organization; a director in the National Exchange Bank of Lockport. In 1860-61, he represented the First district of Niagara County in the State Assembly; and though this position was offered him a second time, he declined, preferring to devote all his valuable time to business, not caring for political honors. He also turned his attention to agricultural pursuits, which proved, as did his business, successful. He was married to Miss Christianna Long, daughter of Benjamin Long, of Marietta, Pa., by which marriage he had nine children, six of whom, with his wife, survive him; his business interest still being continued by three of his sons.

The life of H. P. Smith was an eventful one. He always directed his conduct by principles based on the soundest morality. There was not a word of reproach against his character, nothing to sully his fair name, nothing to dull the lustre of his life, still left shining as a bright example to be followed.

Mr. Smith liberally dispensed his charities, and saw and enjoyed the fruits of them while living. His good works live after him; and now the sands of life are all spent and he has been gathered into his "narrow house," he will be mourned as a public benefactor, and his name will not be forgotten.

Smith, Moses, the subject of this sketch, was born August 12th, 1824, at Springfield, then Essex, now Union County, New Jersey, and came from the old settled stock of that State. His father, Samuel C. Smith, his grandfather, great grandfather, and great great grandfather on his father's side, were all born and lived at the same place. He attended the schools of his native town, after which he clerked in the village of his birth for two years, when he emigrated to Oswego with his uncle, N. Robins, and was engaged clerking in the dry goods and forwarding business for eleven years. In 1852, he moved to New York City, where he remained one year, during which time he clerked in a large produce house. In 1853, he moved to Buffalo, and commenced the lumber business for himself, and in this business he continued for twenty years, when, having a desire to start in the more dignified calling of banker, he in July, 1874, opened a private banking house at 179 Main Street, and in this business he still continues, which proves successful under his management.

In February, 1854, Mr. Smith was joined in wedlock to Miss Esther M. Davis of Buffalo.

Amid all the political agitation this country has passed through, Mr. Smith has never been allured from his business to take part in factional disputes, but has devoted himself most unremittingly to business, its operations requiring all his time and watchful attention. He is still comparatively young, and in the prime of physical vigor and matured experience.

Spaulding, Hon. Elbridge Gerry, was born Feb. 24th, 1809, at Summer Hill, Cayuga County, N. Y., being fifth son of Edward Spaulding and Mehitable Goodrich. He came to Buffalo in 1834 and has resided in this city ever since. He has served the people ably and satisfactorily in many positions of trust and responsibility. He has been Mayor of Buffalo, Treasurer of the State of New York, Member of the Canal Board, and Member of Congress. He filled the latter position six years, four of which he was a member of the Committee on Ways and Means, the most important and responsible committee in the House, on which he rendered valuable service to the entire country. During the early months of the war, when the greatest need of the nation, next to men, was money, Mr. Spaulding's practical knowledge of financial matters was brought into requisition. In framing the legal-tender law he achieved a world-wide reputation as a financier and legislator. The following particulars of his active life are taken from the "Spalding Memorial: A Genealogical History of Edward Spalding of Massachusetts Bay and his descendants, by Samuel J. Spalding," printed at Boston in 1872:

"He is a descendant in the seventh generation from Edward Spaulding, who emigrated from Lincolnshire, England, and settled in Massachusetts about the year 1630. This early pioneer had five sons, and the Spaulding family in this country has increased greatly in numbers during the last two hundred and forty years. His father served four years in the war for American Independence, and his grandfather, Capt. Levi Spaulding, was in the memorable battle of Bunker Hill, with eight others of the same family. He has erected a granite monument (cenotaph) in Forest Lawn Cemetery, at Buffalo, in filial regard to their memory. The dedication ceremony was largely attended on the 17th of June, 1875, which was the centennial anniversary of that great battle. Among other inscriptions on the monument is the following:—" One hundred years of Progress," " In

Memory of the New England Fathers, who fought for Civil and Religious Liberty, American Independence, resulting in National Union."

When about twenty years of age, he commenced the study of law in the office of Fitch & Dibble, at Batavia, Genesee County, N. Y. He taught school in the winter and other portions of the year, and also acted as recording clerk in the County Clerk's office, during the first two years of his law studies, in order to pay his board and other expenses. In 1832, he entered the law office of Hon. Harvey Putnam, at Attica, in the same county, where he pursued his law studies until admitted to practise in the Court of Common Pleas of Genesee County.

In 1834, he removed to Buffalo, and continued the study and practice of the law in the office of Potter & Babcock. At the May term of the Supreme Court in 1836, he was admitted to practise law as an Attorney of the Supreme Court of the State of New York, and as a solicitor in the Court of Chancery; and in 1839, as a counsellor of the Supreme Court, and in the Court of Chancery. After his admission to practise as an attorney in the Supreme Court, he entered into partnership, first with George R. Babcock, and afterward with Heman B. Potter, and continued to practise law until 1844, when the partnership was dissolved. He afterward received into partnership the Hon. John Ganson, with whom he continued until 1848. From the time he entered the profession of the law until he retired from it, he was laborious and unremitting in his exertions, and enjoyed an extensive and lucrative practice.

In 1836, he was appointed City Clerk of Buffalo, and in 1841, was elected Alderman, and served as Chairman of the Finance Committee. In 1847, he was elected Mayor of Buffalo, and during his term many important measures were inaugurated. Among these, he took a very active part in the adoption by the State of the Erie and Ohio basins for enlarging the facilities of lake and canal commerce at Buffalo; the organization of the Buffalo Gas Light Company for lighting the city; and the adoption of an extensive system of sewerage. In 1848, he served one term as a member of the New York Legislature, and was Chairman of the Canal Committee. In the fall of the same year, he was elected a member of the Thirty-first Congress, which assembled in December, 1849. In the long contest for the Speaker, he voted on every balloting for Robert C. Winthrop, but owing to some defection among the Whig members, Howell Cobb was finally elected. He was placed on the Committee on Foreign Relations. He opposed the extension of slavery on all occasions; supported the policy of General Taylor for admitting California and New Mexico as free States, and opposed the Fugitive Slave Law and the compromise measures adopted at the very long session in 1850, and which received the approval of Mr. Fillmore after the death of General Taylor.

In 1853, he was elected Treasurer of the State of New York, and *ex-officio* a member of the Canal Board, serving two years from January 1st, 1854. During this term, he performed important service as a member of the Canal Board, in adopting the plans and contracting for the work of enlarging the Erie and Oswego Canals, involving an expenditure of $9,000,000, which was borrowed on the credit of the State of New York.

He opposed the repeal of the Missouri compromise in 1854; took an active part in organizing the Republican party; was for several years a member of the State Central Committee; and in 1860 he was an active member of the Congressional Executive Committee in conducting the political campaign which resulted in the election of Abraham Lincoln for President.

In 1858, he was elected to the Thirty-sixth Congress, and in 1860 re-elected to the Thirty-seventh Congress, and served four years on the important Committee on Ways and Means. He was one of the most active members of this committee during a most eventful period in the history of the country. As Chairman of the Sub-Committee of Ways and Means, he drafted the National Currency Bank Bill, and originated the Legal Tender Act for the issue of treasury fundable notes to circulate as money, which he introduced in the House of Representatives, December 30th, 1861. He advocated it as a war measure, and opened the debate upon it in an exhaustive speech, showing the imperative necessity of the measure to sustain the army and navy.

This speech was the first official exposition of the *necessity* of the legal tender notes as a war measure, the constitutionality of that measure, and a full statement of the grounds on which it should be supported, in order to provide the means for carrying on the war. It received very general comment from the press, as well as from individuals. The opponents of the measure criticised it in severe terms, but the positions he took in the speech, legally and otherwise, have never been successfully controverted, and it stands to-day as one of the best arguments in favor of legal tender fundable notes, as a war measure, that has ever been presented. It had great influence in carrying the bill through Congress. Nearly all the most important loan laws for carrying on the war originated under the supervision of the Sub-Committee of Ways and Means, of which he was chairman. In a letter to him, dated Aug. 3d, 1869, Hon. Charles Sumner says: " In all our early financial trials, while the war was most menacing; you held a position of great trust, giving you opportunity and knowledge. The first you used at the time most patriotically, and the second you use now (in preparing a financial history of the war) for the instruction of the country." The history alluded to by Mr. Sumner, as having been prepared by Mr. Spaulding, was published at Buffalo, N. Y., 1869, entitled, " History of the Legal Tender Paper Money issued during the Great Rebellion."

Mr. Spaulding has been engaged in banking since 1852. He organized the Farmers and Mechanics' National Bank of Buffalo in 1864, and he owns more than three fourths of its stock, and is its President. By industry, frugality, and economy, he has accumulated a handsome fortune.

Starbuck, Senator James F., was born in Cayuga County. In his early infancy his parents removed to Niagara County, where he continued to reside till after he was twenty-one years of age. He is of English and New England parentage, being one of the descendants of the ancient family of that name, who at an early day located on Nantucket Island, and were for many years extensively engaged in the whale fishery. During his minority, when not in school, he was occupied in assisting in the cultivation of his father's farm, in Niagara County. He was elected to the Senate in November, 1875, to represent the Eighteenth district, composed of the counties of Jefferson and Lewis. He entered upon the performance of his duties as Senator in January, 1876, that being his first experience in any legislative body.

After he attained his majority, he soon

determined to abandon agricultural pursuits and to acquire and practise the legal profession; and, persevering in this purpose, he earned and paid the expenses of his education, and was admitted to the bar of his State in 1844.

In 1846, he was elected to the office of Secretary of the Convention which framed our present Constitution. The duties of this office brought him into intimate relations with such men as Governor Wright, Comptroller Flagg, Robert H. Morris, Michael Hoffman, Samuel Nelson, William Cassidy, Edwin Croswell, Samuel J. Tilden, Charles O'Conor, and, in fact, with many of the public men in all parts of the State.

This experience proved of great service. Since then he has kept up an extensive acquaintance with the public men of the country; and has long been regarded as one of the closest observers of public events, and as a specially sagacious politician in estimating political forces and calculating probable results.

In the political struggle of 1848, he acted with that large and influential organization of Democrats who then formally interposed their protest against the making of further concessions to what was then known as the "slave power." His position on this and kindred questions brought him into intimate and confidential relations with the friends of Governor Wright, and he uniformly acted with them on most political questions up to and including the presidential election of 1860. In that campaign he supported Stephen A. Douglas for President, and was himself the Democratic candidate for Congress in his district, and, like all other Democratic candidates in that locality, he failed to be elected.

In all his connection with public affairs, Mr. Starbuck has never allowed himself to be diverted from the duties of his profession. For several years after 1850, he held the office of public prosecutor for his county, and performed its duties in such a manner as prominently to call the public attention to his professional ability, and especially to his powers as an advocate. From that time he has occupied a conspicuous place in the front rank of his profession, and has probably tried more cases in the Supreme and Circuit Courts in his county, than any other man living. In these courts he was always present, actively engaged in the performance of his duties, and, when elected to the Senate, he had attended and tried causes at every Circuit Court held in his county for more than twenty years.

No one who has observed Mr. Starbuck's action in his present office can fail to be impressed with the apparent extent of his education in the political doctrines of Jefferson and Madison, and with his fidelity on all occasions to those principles.

Any attempted invasion of the reserved rights of the States, any departure from the principle of home rule, any extravagance in the public expense, any interference with the freedom of religion or of the press, any invasion of the right of election by the people, any of these or kindred measures are always sure to encounter in Senator Starbuck a ready and inflexible adversary. His views were well epitomized in one of his speeches in the Senate, from which we make a brief extract:

"One hundred years ago, our fathers found themselves the victims of that same kind of intermeddling legislation, interference with private rights, and denial of the principle of home rule, to which I have averted. They had seen the long arm of power stretch out from governmental centres and interfere with all the domestic and private affairs of the people. In their own case, they had seen it reach three thousand miles, across the ocean, levy enormous taxes, and even exact that stamp duties should be paid in order to validate any contract or agreement. They wisely determined that all that kind of abuse should cease—and that self-government and home rule should be established. To that end they ordained the American system of government, founding it upon the wise maxim that 'That government is best which governs least.' They therefore organized government upon the principle of the greatest possible power in the individual citizen and in his local government, and the least possible authority in the general government; and they took great care that the powers delegated to that government should be clearly defined and strictly limited, and that all powers not so expressly delegated should be 'reserved to the States respectively, or to the people.'"

Early in the session of 1876, Mr. Starbuck made his first speech in the Senate. It was on the bill which became widely known as The "Gray Nun" bill. Senator Starbuck regarded the measure as a deliberate attempt to create an excitement against one of the religious organizations of the country, and to revive and intensify sectarian hate and religious intolerance. It was based upon the idea of supposed danger to our institutions, and especially to our school system, to arise from the action of a few charitable Catholic women, who were known as "Gray Nuns." His speech was regarded at the time as a masterly exercise of the power of satire and ridicule, combined with good sense and strong argument. It commanded the closest attention of all who heard it, and had a wider publication and more extensive reading than any speech delivered in the Senate for many years.

The speech was also productive of great good. It proved, for the time being, the death-blow to that spirit of religious intolerance and sectarian hate which it was intended to rebuke; and since then, the words "Gray Nuns" have proved a sufficient answer to any and all attempts to revive any undue excitement on the subject of sectarian appropriations for educational purposes, or the exhibition of religious intolerance in political affairs. From that time its author, by universal consent, assumed that position in the Senate which he has since maintained, and which entitles him to be regarded as one of the ablest members of that body.

Mr. Starbuck is always ready and able in debate, and has taken a prominent part in the discussion of nearly all the important questions that have come before the Senate. He is never tedious or prolix—generally brief—always pointed and clear; and high evidence of his ability as a debater is found in the fact that he is always listened to with marked attention.

In the session of 1877 he was conspicuous in the debates on the numerous bills affecting the local government of the city of New York. Finding an adverse political majority determined to force upon the people of that city offensive measures, without their consent, and against their protest, he interposed a determined opposition, condemning them as invasions of the right of home rule and local self-government. He also made strenuous opposition to that feature of the scheme for the government of cities, which sought to establish a board of finance founded on a property qualification; and he was chiefly instrumental in defeating the proposition to take the appointment of presidential electors from the State, and confer it upon the several congressional districts.

Senator Starbuck has always believed that the great error in American politics was committed in 1848, and in the years following, up to 1860. In those years, the advice of Governor Wright's political friends was rejected, and the majority of the Democratic party undertook the experiment of reversing the teachings of Jefferson on the subject of negro slavery and its relations to the Constitution. Then, for the first time, the doctrine was boldly avowed that slavery must be accepted, not as a temporary evil, but as a positive good, and that it ought to be cherished, encouraged, and extended, by the active support and favor of the general government. This error was seized upon by the fanatical men of the Northern States as the foundation on which to build up that great party, bounded on the South by Mason and Dixon's line, whose central idea was intolerance and hate; and to the existence of which the country traces, as Mr. Starbuck believes, its enormous public debt, its oppressive taxation, its depreciated paper currency, the destruction of its commerce, the creation of a multitude of banking corporations of more than doubtful constitutionality, and most of the other disastrous results of the departure from the wise principles on which our government was founded. Believing that such a party must necessarily be destructive to the best interests of the people, and that it was conceived in hostility to the warnings of Washington against the spirit of disunion, and against the formation of sectional parties, it encountered his determined opposition. Though zealously opposed to the unwarrantable aggressions of the slave power, and believing firmly in the principles of Jefferson, Benton, and Wright, on the whole question of the relations of slavery to the government, he denied the right to violate the Constitution to make war upon any of the rights secured by that instrument to any of our people, and always maintained that persistence in such unwise action was likely, as Washington warned us, to result in a bloody war between the Northern and Southern portions of the country.

The result of the election of 1860 subjected these views to the crucial test of experience. The party of the North succeeded in electing their candidate for the presidency—he was inaugurated in March, 1861—and, in April following, the anticipated war was begun by the firing upon Fort Sumter. This was regarded by Mr. Starbuck, in common with the great mass of right-thinking Democrats, as an act, not only of extreme folly, but as a great crime; they insisting that the commission of one error or one crime ought never to be pleaded as the justification for another. They insisted that the wrong done by sectional organization and action should be corrected by peaceful methods, and that the unity of our government must be preserved and perpetuated.

The crisis was one well calculated to test a man's fidelity to principle. As a candidate for Congress at the then late election, Mr. Starbuck had fully discussed the questions at issue—had pointed out the danger of the situation, and had earnestly appealed to the people to stay the tide of sectional agitation which he believed so likely, if persevered in, to culminate in armed collision. The appeal had been contemptuously disregarded, and now the predicted results were upon us in all their fearful proportions. This calamity had been predicted—the people had been warned against it—the adversary had been deaf to the warning—the crisis had been precipitated, and the new administration stood powerless before the storm they had evoked, and, trembling for their own safety, they appealed to their opponents to save them. To such an appeal, every thing short of patriotism and the most inflexible fidelity to principle might be expected to turn a deaf ear. The ready answer would be, "We told you so, you disregarded our warning, now take care of yourselves." Had such been the answer, the Union of these States would now be a thing of the past, and the party then invoking aid would have been swept out of existence by the sword. Unfortunately, such was the answer of a few of our people, and, from this misguided and mistaken action of these few persons, more evil has befallen the Democratic party and the country, as he believes, than *they* will ever be able to repair.

Senator Starbuck was not one of these. Strong as was the temptation to leave his political adversaries to the fate they had invited, he saw that to do so was to consent to the dismemberment of the country, and to the erection of two rival and antagonistic governments in our present territorial jurisdiction, to be in perpetual hostility to each other. To this he would never assent. Like the great body of right-thinking Democrats, he recognized the legality of Mr. Lincoln's election, and recognized him as the only constitutional head of the government.

Steele, Oliver G.—There are some men whose characters are so nobly planned by nature, and so plentifully adorned with those virtues which ennoble humanity, that it is a duty and a pleasure to write their biographies and hand them down to posterity for its benefit and instruction. The subject of this sketch was born in New Haven, Ct., December 16th, 1805, and is the son of Oliver and Sarah Steele. One of the forefathers of Mr. Steele was the first secretary of the colony.

Mr. Steele received only a common-school education, and though his attendance was very regular, he left at the age of twelve, at which time he was sent to New York as a message boy in a store of a relative, where he remained over two years, when he returned home. At the age of fifteen he was apprenticed to the book-binding trade, which he finished at Norwalk, Ct.

Early in the spring of 1827, or when a little over twenty one years of age, he went to New York in search of employment. Finding times very dull, and no opportunity of engaging himself, and when about discouraged with his misfortunes, he received an offer to come to Buffalo, then a small village (though the terminus of the Erie Canal, recently completed), where he arrived in May, 1827, engaging himself with a Mr. R. W. Haskins, with whom he remained about three years at a salary of $5 a week and his board.

In 1830, Mr. Steele went into business as bookseller and bookbinder. Soon after, in 1831, he was married to Miss Sarah E. Hull, granddaughter of Judge Zenas Barker, one of our earliest settlers of Buffalo. In 1837, Mr. Steele was called to the office of superintendent of city schools, which were then in a very low state. In the winter of 1837-8, he, in connection with Judge N. K. Hall, prepared the school law paper, continuing in office three years, during which time the school system was thoroughly organized, and which since that time has been very little changed. And to-day we may safely say the system is one of the most complete in the country. In 1841-2, Mr.

G. was one of the city council, and was again elected in 1847.

In 1848, he became very much interested in the organization of the Buffalo Gas Light Co., became its secretary, and has been connected with it as director, manager, or officer ever since. He was an active mover in the organization of the Water Co., in 1852, and was its first secretary, holding the office for several years, and was one of its directors during its existence as a Company. Mr. Steele was one of the originators of the Buffalo Lyceum, and was one of its officers till the organization of the Y. M. Association, into which the old Lyceum was merged. For several years Mr. Steele was president of the old Mechanics' Society, and the first Mechanics' fairs were organized during his administration. He was also one of the originators of the Historical Society, and since its organization has been an officer, and was for some years its president, besides being the principal mover of the Normal School, of which he is now the president.

By looking over old records, and conversing with many of this gentleman's associates, we find he has been an active mover in every thing that has been for the public good.

We also find he has been an officer in every literary society for public improvement, and we should think one in Mr. Steele's position can look upon the past unsullied career of his useful life with conscious pride and satisfaction. In the community in which he lives he enjoys the entire confidence of all who know him, regardless of party or condition, as one of the purest of men, reliable in every respect, though modest and retiring, a man of great attainments, which are sound and substantial.

Steinway, Henry.—Mr. Henry Steinway, founder of the well-known piano firm of Steinway & Sons, died at his residence February 7th, 1871. He was born in the Duchy of Brunswick, Germany, on the 15th of February 1797. An inherent talent for music, combined with positive inclination induced him in early boyhood to make his own musical instruments, on which he played with marked predilection and taste. These were the cythera and the guitar. In a short time his efforts in the direction he had selected received a further impetus. He first learned cabinet-making at Gosiar, and there also worked in an organ factory. After having thoroughly studied the art of piano-making, he found it an independent business, and becoming dissatisfied with the narrow sphere of a German State, he came to America with his family in 1850, and settled in New York. Three years after, with the assistance of his four sons—Charles, Henry, William, and Albert—Mr. Steinway founded the present firm. The commencement was made in a small rear building in Varick street, and the extent of the business did not average more than one piano per week. It is unnecessary to speak of the change which eighteen years have brought forth, and how the firm of Steinway & Sons grew to its present colossal proportions. Mr. Steinway was universally respected, and a host of friends mourned has loss.

Stewart, A. T., was born near Belfast, Ireland, October 27th, 1802. Left an orphan at an early age, he was cared for by his maternal grandfather. Distinguished himself at school, and was entered at Trinity College, Dublin, where he did not graduate. Upon the death of his grandfather, a distant relative—a member of the Society of Friends—became his guardian. He emigrated to New York about 1818, bringing with him a few hundred pounds, a small part of which he inherited, and for a time taught mathematics and the classics in a private school. Having invested his ready money in a small mercantile venture, he found himself unexpectedly left alone in the business with the rent of the shop on his hands, and forced to become a trader. Returning to Ireland, he sold his other property, invested the proceeds in Irish laces and similar goods, and in 1823 opened a small store on Broadway, and commenced the business which has since grown to be the most extensive dry goods establishment in the world, with branches in England, France, Scotland, Ireland, and Germany, besides large manufactories of woolens, carpets, and hosiery in the United States, England, and Scotland, the whole employing about 8000 persons. In addition to this manufacturing and mercantile business, he came to be a large holder and improver of real estate in New York and vicinity, Saratoga, and other places, and at the time of his death was reputed to be one of the three wealthiest men in the United States, the other two being John Jacob Astor, who had a few weeks before inherited the bulk of the great Astor estate, and Cornelius Vanderbilt, who acquired the greater part of his property in railway operations. He retained all through his life his early fondness for classical literature, and was a munificent patron of art in certain departments, his picture-gallery containing some of the finest examples of modern art, while he had a little appreciation for the works of the old masters. Among his enterprises was the establishment of a town called Garden City, on Long Island, a few miles from Brooklyn. Here he purchased a tract of 10,000 acres, upon which he built more than one hundred dwellings, adapted for persons in moderate or comfortable circumstances, none of which were to be sold, but all of which would be rented, furnished, if desired, he himself defraying all the expenses of grading, lighting, and watering the streets, and building a railway to connect Garden City with Brooklyn. Some years before, he had commenced the erection of a large and costly building in New York designed as a home for working girls, and he had also made preparations for the erection of a similar building for young working men, each structure being designed to afford accommodation for 1500 inmates. He took no prominent part in public affairs, except that during the civil war he was an earnest upholder of the national government, and in 1869 accepted from President Grant the nomination as Secretary of the Treasury. The nomination was withdrawn, it being found that he was rendered legally ineligible for that position on account of his being engaged in the importation of foreign merchandise. He was president of the honorary commission sent by the United States Government to the Paris Exposition of 1867. During the Irish famine of 1864, he chartered a vessel which he freighted with breadstuffs at his own expense, for gratuitous distribution among the sufferers, and brought back, free of charge, as many emigrants as the vessel would carry, stipulating that all should be of good character, and taking care that situations should be

ready for them upon their arrival. He made considerable donations to the sufferers of the Chicago fire of 1871, and in the Franco-German War; but apart from these, his benefactions, public or private, were not considerable, either during his life or by his will. Died in New York, April 10th, 1876, leaving no children. By his will his entire estate, with the exception of certain legacies, was devised to his wife, who, with Henry J. Hilton, his confidential friend and legal adviser, and William Libbey, his sole surviving business partner, were appointed executors. To Mr. Hilton was left a legacy of $1,000,000, and to several of his principal employés sums amounting in the aggregate to something more than $100,000, his wife also being requested in a codicil to make provision for others who had been long employed by him in such amounts as she could think proper. She appropriated for this purpose a further sum of a little more than $200,000, making the entire amount of his legacies, exclusive of that to Mr. Hilton, about $1,325,000.

Stewart, James T., was born at Dalkeith, near Edinburgh, Scotland, in 1824. He came to this country in 1837, and first settled in Tompkins County, New York, where he worked on the farms of his relatives for seven years, attending the common schools of the neighborhood each winter. While here he conceived the idea of being ambitious, and to satisfy his aspirations he started out alone for Rochester, with very little capital, which he put into the grocery business with a partner. At the end of two and a half years, Mr. Stewart bought his partner's interest, and continued the business alone for five years. This having proved successful, he determined to put his capital in a business susceptible of larger development, and concluded to start the manufacture of boots and shoes, in which he was engaged many years. In 1874, he gave up leather, and embarked in rubber, the commodity being the same—boots and shoes, which he still continues on a larger scale. He is also president of the Rochester Hydraulic Co., a large stock concern, owning much of the real estate and water power of the Genesee Falls. In 1849, Mr. Stewart was married to Miss Minerva Hildreth, of Tompkins County, by whom he had three children. One son only survives, who is associated with his father in business. He was again married in 1859 to Miss Elizabeth M. Smith, of Fairfield, Herkimer County, N. Y., by whom he has had four children; two only survive.

James T. Stewart possesses all the frankness of manner, cordiality of feeling, hospitable disposition so characteristic of the true Scotchman. He necessarily has become popular in Rochester, and can number as his friends many of the most influential citizens.

Story, Albert G., was born at Cherry Valley, Otsego County, N. Y., October, 1813. Here he continued to live until 1833, receiving his early mental training in the village of his birth, and Union College. At the age of eighteen he was appointed teller of the Central Bank of Cherry Valley, which position he kept till his removal to Little Falls in 1833, where he accepted a similar position in the Herkimer County Bank. In 1835, he was appointed cashier, and in 1866 became president of the institution, a position he still occupies. He was married in 1835 to the only daughter of Judge Morse, of Cherry Valley, by whom he has had five children, three of whom survive. During his whole life he has been a stirring practical business man, and his constitution being still vigorous and unenfeebled, and his fine intellect ripened by experience, he does honor to the official position he has so long held. Through life he has accomplished much, and now, dwelling in the affluence and honor gained by his industry and talents, he can look upon his past unsullied career with conscious pride and satisfaction.

Squier, George L., was born in Lanesboro, Berkshire County, Mass., May 29th, 1824. His great grandfather, lieutenant Andrew Squier, was one of the pioneers of Western Massachussetts, having moved from Connecticut to Lanesboro in 1734.

Socrates Squier, the father of George L., was reared on the old homestead, and was for many years a prominent citizen of the town, holding many offices of trust and honor. George L. Squier, the subject of this sketch, received all the advantages of a New England education, and was graduated at Williams College in 1845. After graduating, Mr. Squier entered upon the study of law, and was admitted to the bar at Springfield, Mass., in 1848. He practised law in Holyoke for a short time, but his taste for mechanics soon drew him into manufacturing, and he became a member of the firm of Whittemore, Squier & Co., engaged in manufacturing agricultural implements, at Chicopee Falls, Mass. He remained in this connection until 1857, when he removed to Buffalo to take the position of president and manager of the Buffalo Agricultural Machine Works (a corporation engaged in the manufacture of agricultural implements), which position he held during the existence of the company.

Mr. Squier then formed a partnership with his youngest brother, Henry, and commenced the manufacture of plantation machinery for tropical countries, in which business he is still engaged.

Mr. Squier is a member of the Lafayette Street Presbyterian Church, and has held the offices of trustee, elder, and superintendent of the Sunday-school in that church.

In February, 1857, he was married to Frances C. Pierce, of Waverly, N. Y., and has had five children, of whom four sons are now living.

Tallman Charles, was born in Tully, Onondaga County, N. Y., in the year 1810. His parents, who were of Dutch and Danish descent, emigrated to that section from New England in the early part of the present century. His father, Easton Tallman, a man of unusual energy, died at the early age of thirty-eight years, leaving six children, Charles, next to the oldest, being but nine years of age.

The mother located upon a small farm, held her family together, and by strictest economy and industry reared them to manhood and womanhood.

Charles, being of slender constitution, did not take kindly to the labors of the farm, and was early on the look-out for some other occupation. He confesses that the early advantages afforded by the district school near him, scanty at the best, were not well improved, but later realizing more fully his need, he did apply himself at the Homer Academy, running in debt for board and tuition, an obligation afterward discharged by means obtained by teaching a district-school.

In 1833, he emigrated to Ohio, the "West" of those earlier days, but was unsuccessful in obtaining business, and soon returned to Tully.

After gaining some little experience in the store of his uncle, the late Jedediah Barber, of Homer, in 1837 he commenced his career as a merchant in the village of Vesper, in his native town, where he remained for nine years, demonstrating his ability to succeed, and gaining a respectable financial standing. In the spring of 1846, he removed to Syracuse, a village at that time of about 11,000 inhabitants, and engaged in the drug trade with William H. Williams, under the firm name of Tallman & Williams.

From this time his activities were not confined to any one sphere, but he became identified with many interests of importance in Syracuse and elsewhere, among which was the business of distilling, the provision trade, extensive farming in the West, cattle growing and wool raising, the mining of coal, the handling of real estate, and more recently he has lent his experience and means to extensive wholesale trade in his own city, being at present senior partner in the firms of A. N. Palmer & Co., W. L. Ross & Co., and Tallman, Giddings & Co. His business has made him familiar with various sections of our country, and his natural desire for travel has taken him to nearly all parts of it, visiting the Pacific coast in 1875.

Being an interested observer, he has become conversant with the topography and resources of the United States. He is largely identified with the growth of his own city, to which he has contributed by the erection of buildings and warehouses, and by the employment of his means in home industries. He has had the satisfaction of seeing it grow from 11,000 to nearly 60,000 inhabitants, and he may feel that he has done his part towards its material growth and prosperity. He has gained from his varied enterprises not only an ample fortune, but experience and a correctness of judgment which commands the respect of his associates, and makes his counsel valuable to younger men. He has never sought or held political office.

He lives in the southern section of the city, in a valuable residence, surrounded by extensive grounds, to the improvement of which he devotes more of his leisure, as he feels less and less the necessity for the close application to business which has distinguished him, and when surrounded by his children and children's children, he enjoys the comforts of a busy life.

Tifft, George W., was born Jan. 31st, 1805, in the town of Nassau, Rensselaer County, N. Y., and was the youngest son of a family of twelve, of John and Annie Valette Tifft, who migrated from Rhode Island some years before his birth.

Mr. Tifft spent most of his time on the farm with his mother till he was sixteen years old; the only schooling he received was about two months each year. At the age of sixteen, the farm was sold to his older brothers, and an arrangement was made by which he should work on it till he was of age, he to have three months' schooling and four dollars a year, and on becoming of age a yoke of oxen and a horse for his service; but owing to a disagreement, he left at the end of one year and went to work for his brother David for ten dollars a month, where he remained only a short time; at the end of which time, he went to work with his brother John. They together cleared some new land and divided the profits on the sale of the wood. At this he did well. When through, he went to New Lebanon, Columbia County, and attended school for four months At the age of eighteen, he returned to his former home, and bought a five-acre lot of timber and an axe, and went to work clearing, doing the work himself; the wood finding a ready market, he made quite a nice little sum. He afterward bought considerable land for clearing; but instead of doing the work himself, he engaged laborers, he measuring and selling the wood. This lasted till between the age of twenty-one and twenty-two, when with $1000 he had received from his father's estate, and $1200 he had saved, he went to Orleans County and bought a farm. After settling up the business part of this transaction, he returned to his former field of labor and resumed the wood-cutting business, and speculated considerably in lands. On the 14th of March, 1827, Mr. Tifft was espoused to Miss Lucy, daughter of Joseph and Thankful Enos. They have had seven children, three of whom are living. In 1830, Mr. Tifft closed up his affairs in Nassau, and went out to his farm in Orleans County, which he worked himself till 1832; at which time, though continuing to live on his farm, he gave his whole attention to operating in grain and the milling business, which proved very successful. In 1842, he went to Buffalo, and went into the milling business with Dean Richmond, Esq. At the end of one year, however, he made an arrangement with Gordon Grant, of Troy, who was owner of the Troy and Michigan Line, to open a branch of the Troy house in the forwarding business, the firm being G. W. Tifft & Co. At the end of a year, Mr. Grant sold out the line of boats, and Mr. Tifft formed a partnership with Henry H. Sizer in the produce commission business, the firm being Sizer & Tifft. After one year, Mr. Tifft sold out his interest to his partner. In 1845, he again went into business with his former partner Dean Richmond, when they bought the Erie Mills, which they ran in conjunction with three others. Mr. Tifft was fully identified with the milling business till the starting of the International Bank in July, 1854, when he became its first president, continuing such until 1857, that being the year of the financial crash. Mr. Tifft being a heavy stockholder and indorser of the Buffalo Steam-Engine Company, for whom he had to pay $94,000, was compelled to suspend. He took the charge and responsibility of the said company in his own hands, the creditors allowing him an extension of four years, and by his superior financiering and management paid his whole indebtedness in one half the time. In 1857, he invested in coal-mines in Mercer County, Pa., which came into his hands as did the Engine Company, where he built two blast furnaces. While operating these, he made the experiment of melting Lake Superior ore with mineral coal, which proved a grand success.

In 1858, Mr. Tifft was elected president of the Buffalo, New York and Erie R.R. In 1863, he built in the city of Buffalo seventy-four dwelling-houses, the Tifft House, and an elevator, which latter he afterward sold to the Erie R.R. Co. The business occupying his attention now is the Buffalo Steam-Engine Works, owned by G. W. Tifft, Sons & Co., and a private stock company, the shareholders being members of his own family, including his daughters, though the premises are owned by Mr. Tifft personally. They also own the Tifft Fire-Proof Elevator, which cost about $600,000. Mr. Tifft also owns one half interest in the Evans Elevator.

The subject of this sketch has been a member of the Presbyterian Church for forty years, and may always be found taking an active part in all benevolent and charitable enterprises. Among the many things he has done was the donation of the Ingleside Home, which cost between forty and fifty thousand dollars. Thus he has liberally dispensed his charities, and seen and enjoyed the fruits of them while living. He has the love and respect of zealous, admiring friends, and many business men who have been helped on in life by him breathe his name with gratitude.

Thompson, J. L.—The subject of this sketch was born December 1st, 1797, at Amenia, Dutchess County, N. Y. He can trace his ancestry to Anthony Thompson, of Coventry, England, who arrived in Boston, on board the ship Hector, in company with Gov. Eaton and the Rev. Mr. Davenport, June 20th, 1637. Anthony Thompson had two children. Then comes John Thompson, three children; Samuel Thompson, who married a daughter of Gov. Bishop of Connecticut, eight children; Samuel Thompson, three children; Ezra Thompson, nine children; Ezra Thompson, Jr., nine children; John L. Thompson, of Troy, who was married in August, 1829, to Mary P. Thompson, of New London, Ct., and by whom he has had eight children, all living. Mr. John L. Thompson moved to Troy in 1817, and entered the drug-store, on the same spot he now is engaged in business, as clerk for Dr. Samuel Gale. Five years later, he became a partner, the firm style changing to Gale & Thompson. Subsequently Mr. Thompson bought Mr. Gale's interest. In 1841, Mr. D. Cowes, formerly a clerk, was admitted to the firm, and in 1855 his sons John I. and William A. became partners, and the firm changed to J. L. Thompson, Sons & Co., the present style. The present head of the firm has pursued sedulously his trade, never wavering from the paths of legitimate business, and giving it that attention which insures success. There are some men whose judgment appears almost infallible. The ambition of Mr. Thompson has been to become a thorough business man; and his well-known and enviable reputation is a testimony that he has succeeded in the accomplishment of his wishes; and though in his eightieth year, he still pursues his daily business routine with that zeal and ardor that would characterize the ambition of youth.

Trowbridge, Dr. Josiah, was born in Framingham, Mass., September 28th, 1785. He was a descendant from a highly respected English family, and his American ancestry occupied an elevated position among the early colonists, his direct lineage being Thomas Trowbridge, a gentleman of means, who emigrated to this country in 1636. The father of Dr. Trowbridge was no ordinary man, as the records of his life show. He served in the Revolutionary army, first at the battle of Bunker Hill, and afterward orderly sergeant with Washington, in New Jersey and Pennsylvania.

Dr. Trowbridge remained at home, somewhat advanced in years, assisting his father on the farm. This proving too laborious, he, in 1799, took the position of clerk with an elder brother, in Boston. Tiring of this, and seized with a desire to see more of the world, he shipped for Holland in 1800. After his return, he undertook a course of preparatory studies, with a view to the adoption of the medical profession. During this time, he taught school two winters, the first in Southboro', and the next in his native town. He first began to read with Dr. Willard, of Uxbridge, and finished with Dr. Kittridge. His first professional efforts were put forth in Weathersfield, Vermont, where he remained for a brief time. In 1811, in company with a young lawyer, he came to Buffalo on horseback. Buffalo not offering sufficient encouragement, he took up his residence in Fort Erie, and there remained till the declaration of war, when he returned to Buffalo. During his residence in Canada, he formed an attachment and was married to Miss Margaret Wintermute, September 22d, 1813. He continued his practice in Buffalo till 1836, when he had accumulated a handsome property, and retired from his profession and gave his time entirely to the management of his private affairs. In 1837, when the crash came, he was among the unfortunates, losing his all.

It was in this year he was elected mayor. In 1839, he was appointed commissioner to represent certain rights possessed by the State of Massachusetts, in the lands owned by the Seneca Indians, and about to be ceded to the Ogden Land Company, by treaty and purchase. In 1838, he resumed his profession with Dr. Winnie and so continued till 1842. He, however, did a large private and consulting practice till 1856, and died on the 27th of September, 1862, deeply mourned by all who knew him, as a man whose like was seldom to be met with.

(See portrait page 365.)

Urban, George, was born in Alsace, France, August 19th, 1820. His early education received attention in his native country, and when fifteen years old, he emigrated to this country with his parents, who settled in the town of Black Rock. The first seven years spent here, he was engaged at various kinds of laborious duties, though in 1842, he received the appointment to a clerkship, which he filled for four years; being industrious and ambitious, he confined himself closely to business, and in 1846, started in the flour, feed, grocery, and provision business for himself, on the same spot he now occupies, at No. 144 Genesee street, Buffalo. Ten years ago, he became purely a flour merchant, which business he still continues in the full tide of success. He was married August 15th, 1846, to Miss Mary Kern, formerly of Alsace, the issue of which has been two sons and one daughter, his eldest son, George Urban, Jr., being a partner with his father in business. Mr. Urban is also one of the Park Commissioners of Buffalo, besides being a director in the Western Savings Bank. Thus we see the biography of such a man as George Urban is fraught not only with readable interest, but has a useful moral effect upon the present time and posterity. Commencing at the bottom rung, he has steadily progressed till he is ranked with the soundest and most substantial business men of Buffalo. It is such subjects that teach youth what industry and moral worth can achieve, and that they can hope for all things if they make honor their guide and are prompted by honorable emulation.

Vanderbilt, Cornelius, was born on Staten Island, N. Y., May 27th, 1794. His parents emigrated from Holland, and were among the early settlers of New York. He had a meagre education, and at an early age devoted himself to sailing boats in New York Bay. At the age of sixteen, he purchased a boat of his own, and ran it as a ferry

between New York and Staten Island. During the war of 1812, he carried some officers from Fort Richmond during a perilous storm, being the only boatman in the harbor who would undertake the task—carrying them, as he said, "part way under water." In 1814, he carried government supplies to various posts about New York, and that year he built a small schooner for his increased business; in the year following, he built a larger schooner for the coast trade. In 1817, having accumulated $9000 from his harbor trade, he entered the employ of Thomas Gibbons, and became captain of a small steamboat running between New York and New Brunswick, N. J., on the road to Philadelphia. He also took charge of a hotel at New Brunswick, where the passengers remained over night. He remained with Mr. Gibbons for twelve years, during which time the line of steamboats had grown to be one of great importance; at the end of that time, he resigned his position and started out for himself; he built several small steamboats; and ran them to points on the Hudson River, and other places near New York. In 1851, he established the route of steamships between New York and California, by way of Nicaragua, which he managed for two years, when he sold out and acted as agent for a short time; subsequently he was chosen president of the company. In May, 1853, having amassed immense wealth, he built the steamship North Star, and taking his family on board, made a tour of Europe in it at his private expense. In April, 1855, he established an independent line of steamships between New York and Havre. In the spring of 1862, he presented the government with the finest steamship, the Vanderbilt, for which Congress passed a resolution of thanks to him. Subsequently, he withdrew his money from vessels and invested it in railroads. He was President of the New York Central and Hudson River Railroad, the Harlem Railroad, and was a Director in the Western Union Telegraph Company. In 1870, he purchased the building known as the Mercer Street Presbyterian Church, in New York City, and presented it to the Rev. Charles Force Deems, pastor of a free and independent church of Jesus Christ, organized in 1868 under the name of the Church of the Strangers, to be used by that society as a place of public worship. On March 27th, 1873, Mr. Vanderbilt presented the Methodist Episcopal Church, South, with $500,000, afterward increasing the amount to about $1,000,000, to be used in founding a university at Nashville, Tenn., for the education of the youth of the church. The board of trustees of the proposed institution voted to call it Vanderbilt University, after its chief founder, and it was opened October 4th, 1875. Mr. Vanderbilt had been twice married, and had thirteen children. He died at New York, January 4th, 1877. His son William Henry, born in New Brunswick, N. J., May 8th, 1821, was in 1873 elected Vice-President of the Hudson River Railroad Company.

Verplanck, J. A., was born in the town of Coeymans, Albany County, N. Y., on the 16th of October, 1812. He received a good academical education. He entered Union College at the age of fourteen, and graduated at the age of twenty-two. In 1831, he moved to Batavia, Genesee County, and began the study of law with Allen & Chandler. He was admitted to the bar in 1834, and speedily attained a very respectable position. Upon the retirement of Mr. Allen, his preceptor and father-in-law, he became a partner of Daniel H. Chandler. He subsequently practised in partnership with John H. Martindale, now of Rochester. During his residence in Batavia, he served two terms as District-Attorney of Genesee County, was a brigadier-general of the militia, and was appointed United States agent to negotiate treaties with the Indians in the Lake Superior country. He came to this city in 1847, and entered into partnership with H. K. Smith; was one of the justices of the Superior Court in 1854. Since then was twice elected to the same office, once without opposition, and occupied the position at the time of his death, which occurred April 15th, 1873. He was a member of the Constitutional Convention in 1867-68. Judge Verplanck was a remarkable man, we scarcely need hesitate to say, a great man. He reached accurate decisions with lightning speed, as if by inspiration. He was a man of great mental resources, an able lawyer, a true-born gentleman and a noble-hearted, generous citizen.

Vick, James, was born in the suburbs of Portsmouth, England, November 23d, 1818. At an early day he exhibited a passion for every thing pertaining to horticulture. At the age of fifteen, he came to this country, with his father's family. On his arrival, he engaged himself with a printing-house in New York, for the purpose of learning the trade; and for three years he applied himself so thoroughly that he moved to Rochester, and was engaged by various offices as a compositor. But as his taste was in the agricultural line, he was drawn toward the office of the *Genesee Farmer*, published in this city by Luther Tucker. So much attraction had floriculture for him that about this time he secured a small garden, cultivated flowers, and wrote on their beauty and habits.

When the *Genesee Farmer* passed out of Mr. Tucker's hands, Mr. Vick assumed its publication, though it was owned by others. As a publisher and editor he proved himself a most decided success. By the untimely death of Andrew J. Downing, Mr. Vick became the owner and publisher of the *Horticulturist*—he moving it from New York to Rochester, Mr. Patrick Barry being its editor. Mr. Vick published this valuable paper for about four years, when he disposed of it, in order that he might devote his whole time to seed-growing, to which he had always given much of his attention. He, however, found it difficult to give up journalism altogether; and in 1857 he became the horticultural editor of *Moore's Rural New Yorker*, continuing to give a portion of his time as such till 1862, when his seed business demanded his sole attention.

In the ten years intervening, his business had increased to a surprising extent; so much so, indeed, that his name had become a "household word." His "Floral Guide" had found willing readers all over the land. The number of these books now annually published is about one quarter of a million. The business of which he is the head is one of vast importance, not only in the city in which it is carried on, but over the whole land. The number of hands employed is about one hundred and fifty. As much of his business is done through the mail, he has a post-office in his establishment; so that the mail is all put up in the bags, and taken directly to the railroad, without going through the city post-office, one of his employés acting as deputy postmaster for the government. To give the reader an idea of the vastness of this department of the business, it is only necessary to say that the number of letters received and dispatched in a day

often aggregates 4000, the year's postage amounting nearly to $35,000. In connection with the house is a printing-office, bookbindery, and box-factory. Perfect system prevails in every department, Mr. Vick overseeing the entire business himself. It is very easy to understand that the control of such an establishment demands no small amount of executive ability. Want of space only compels us to withhold much of interest in connection with the sketch of this gentleman. His knowledge of horticulture has won him an enviable reputation in not only this country, but in all parts of the world. He was for a long time secretary of the American Pomological Society—a position, though involving much labor, at the same time bringing him into intimate relations with all the ablest horticulturists in this country. In 1871, he was paid the high compliment of an election as "corresponding member" of the Royal Horticultural Society of England —a compliment more marked, because rarely tendered any one outside of England or English domain. In all parts of Europe where he has travelled, he has received considerate attention and the most hearty welcome.

We can safely say, in conclusion, that Mr. Vick is one among a thousand, a truly self-made man; one who has given much of his time and labor for the benefit of his fellow-man. And well may the citizens of Rochester be justly proud in being able to claim him as one of them.

Vilas, Samuel Flint, was born at Sterling, Lamoille County, Vermont, January 9th, 1807.

When in his twentieth year, Mr. Vilas commenced, without means and wholly upon credit, to wholesale Yankee notions through the northern portion of New York.

To this business in this then very thinly settled country, where dwellings were miles apart, he devoted the first ten years of his business life, enlarging his business with his steadily increasing means.

These early years of patient labor and of close, calculating economy, laid the foundation, broad and firm, for that remarkable success which has attended him in every thing he has undertaken.

The property acquired during this period was not so large; but the business character, principles, and habits which he formed; the thorough knowledge of mankind which he acquired; and the extended acquaintance which he made with business men, have been of incalculable advantage to him.

Settling at Plattsburg, N. Y., in 1836, he there commenced and continued for over thirty years the first and only wholesale business carried on in Clinton County. This embraced not only dry goods and Yankee notions, also the manufacture and sale of tinware upon a large scale.

He personally superintended and directed its management for about eleven years, when he gave up its chief care to a partner, and devoted his own time, with characteristic energy, sagacity, and success, to the business of a private banker.

In 1864, he organized "The Vilas National Bank of Plattsburg," of which he has ever since been the president. So large and prosperous was the business of this bank, that Mr. Vilas in 1868 gave up entirely the wholesale business.

He has dealt quite extensively in wool, lumber, iron, and timber lands. Regarding Plattsburg as his permanent home, he has always taken a lively interest in whatever his well-balanced judgment assured him would promote its welfare.

The older residents recall with interest how the dulness of the times and the great difficulties of doing business in Plattsburg and Clinton County were relieved by the building of the Saranac River Plank Road, and the P. & M. R.R.; they also recall the material and efficient aid given to these public enterprises by Mr. Vilas; indeed, it is no injustice to others to say that he, more than any one individual, was instrumental in organizing and prosperously maintaining, during his connection with them, both of these roads.

The existence, high standing, and prosperity of the Northern New York Insurance Company, which, after paying or securing all its policy-holders, was dissolved a few years since, were chiefly due to his management as its president.

To the churches, academy, and schools of Plattsburg, he has been a liberal supporter, both by his means and his counsel, while a member of their several boards of trustees.

He was joined in wedlock, August 6th, 1836, to Miss Harriet E., daughter of James Hunt, Esq., of Pinckney, Lewis County, N. Y.

By his own personal efforts and by strict application to business, he has reached his present assured condition of prosperity, and he has reason to feel at least satisfied with his life's work and success.

Walker, William H., was born August 20th, 1825, at Utica, N. Y., a son of Stephen and Sally Walker. His father moved from Utica to Buffalo in 1832, and the subject of this sketch was educated at the Buffalo Academy, Silas Kingsley principal, and also at the well-known private school of Mr. Fay and Mr. Chambers. At the age of nineteen, he entered the boot and shoe store of O. P. Ramsdell, and became his partner in 1851. In 1853, he went to Albany, studied law, and took the gold medal for the best essay in equity jurisprudence at the close of the term at the Albany Law School. He returned to Buffalo in 1854, again became associated with O. P. Ramsdell, and continued in business with him till February 1st 1876, when his present business was established.

He was married October 21st, 1869, to Edith Kimberly, daughter of John L. Kimberly, Esq., of Buffalo, the issue of which has been two children.

Weaver, George S.—Among the many who have attained prominence through industry and unwearied application, few are entitled to more respect and consideration than George S. Weaver. Reared amid rural opportunities, his early training was unfavorable to the development of his mental powers; but with the native force of his mind, enriched by reading and observation, he soon overcame the obstacles of early life. Without the advantages of inherited aid or consequence, he worked the problem of his own fortune, and lives to enjoy the fruition of a successful business career.

Mr Weaver was born July 9th, 1826, in Yates County, N. Y., where he received a limited common-school education, working summers upon a farm, and attending school in winter. The benefit derived from manual labor was to invigorate and strengthen a constitution naturally frail. At the age of seventeen, he engaged as clerk in a general store, in which capacity he served until his twentieth year, when he was admitted as junior partner with John H. Lapham, a successful druggist at Penn Yan. It was

JARED S. WEED

here he acquired habits of industry, economy, and perseverance, traits of character peculiarly prominent in Mr. Lapham. His duties in this connection were arduous, working from five o'clock in the morning until eleven at night, it being the custom of Mr. L. to sit in the store evenings until very late. This laborious life proved too much for his slender constitution, and, to his reluctance and the regret of his partner, he was forced to quit the business he had fairly entered with flattering prospects of success. For three months he struggled against disease, caused by over-work and the unwholesome atmosphere of the drug store.

Mr. Weaver passed the following winter in a rude lumbering shanty in Pennsylvania with his father and brother, who were engaged in manufacturing square timber for the eastern market. By close attention to the laws of health, with plenty of pure air and plain food, he came out of his forest quarters improved in physical condition. What appeared a misfortune at the time he severed his connection with the drug store, turned to his advantage in after life. The knowledge he obtained of the lumbering business, in this effort to regain his health, proved of great value in enabling him to extend his business operations. His health restored, he was not long waiting for something to do. With a small capital, and fair credit, he invested with his father in the lumbering business. He also operated with his brother until the year 1861, when a co-partnership was entered into with Elish Mors, of Waterford. The new firm dealt largely in all varieties of lumber. This enterprise proving successful, the business was afterwards extended to West Troy and Greenbush. The war commencing about this period, found the firm of Mors & Weaver fully able and prepared to enter the field in competition with any company in the country for government work and supplies. To them was awarded the contract to furnish timber for the five Monitors built by Messrs. Corning & Griswold, of Albany and Troy. With three large saw mills in operation, and the constant employment of about fifty men in the city of New York, the work was vigorously pushed forward. Time was important, and to the promptness and energy of this firm much credit must be given for meeting the necessities of the hour in a critical period of the rebellion.

Mr. Weaver remained in business with Mr. Mors until the year 1871, when he retired from the co-partnership. Since the dissolution of the firm he has continued to deal extensively in lumber, and for several years furnished all the timber used by the N. Y. Central and Hudson River Railroads.

He never sought official position, but confined himself exclusively to his legitimate pursuits. By industry, sagacity, and good judgment, he has accumulated a substantial fortune. He is endowed with a heart of unstudied and disinterested generosity, of liberal impulses, and of a sympathetic nature. In manners he is polished and graceful, with a geniality that makes him agreeable in every circle.

Weed, Jared S.—The subject of this sketch was the eldest son of the late Alsop Weed, one of Troy's oldest and most prominent merchants, and was born in the town of Greenfield, Saratoga County, N. Y., May 3d, 1808. When five years of age, he moved with his parents to Troy, where he resided until his death, which occurred in 1876. Having completed his education, he became one of the firm of A. Weed & Sons.

With his superior education, and all his keen business talent, he soon discovered that he could learn much from the practical sagacity of his father, and he doubtless drew from that source much that in after years gave him such a ready and thorough insight into all the various bearings of a great business enterprise.

In 1835, Mr. Weed was joined in wedlock to a daughter of the late Sylvanus Norton, long identified with the business interests of Troy. The issue of this marriage was one daughter. Mr. Weed, though not an office-seeker, held several offices of trust and responsibility. From 1842 to 1845 he was a member of the Aldermanic Board; from 1846 to 1849 he was Chamberlain of the city. He was the second president of the Troy and Boston R. R. From 1850 to 1870 he was president of the Troy Savings Bank, and for many years an active member of the Second Street Presbyterian Church. In every position in life he was the same; modest, unassuming, he performed all his labors in a dignified, noiseless manner, and those who knew him well know what a vast amount of labor he disposed of. Of all his business enterprises, the Troy and Boston R. R. was the most successful, and will live long as a proud monument to his fair name and reputation.

Weller, Jacob J.—The subject of this sketch was born in Buffalo, N. Y., April 27th, 1839. At the age of fourteen years, he came to the determination to do something for himself, and engaged as an apprentice to Hersee & Timmerman to learn the cabinet business. He readily mastered it, and showed such marked ability that before the expiration of his apprenticeship he was made foreman over a number of men in his department. He was afterward promoted to a clerkship; he mastered the detail of the business, and in course of time became the leading salesman, also doing all the buying for their large establishment, which annually sold some hundreds of thousands of dollars' worth of their manufacture. He being prudent and careful, and with a view to his future interests, saved his earnings, and was thus enabled to purchase a quarter interest in the business, which he retained for four years, at the end of which time the partnership was dissolved. In less than three months, such was the influence he possessed, and great the esteem in which he was held by the business men of the city, he was enabled to induce some capitalists to join him in the purchase of the business; he negotiated the business successfully, and became the senior member of the firm, under the style and title of Weller, Brown & Mesmer.

The house has sustained an enviable reputation, which is not confined alone to Buffalo, and is owing to the business tact and experience of its head, who is destined to become one of the foremost business men of Buffalo.

Wells, John E.—There are men whose characters are so nobly planned by nature, and so plentifully adorned with those virtues which ennoble humanity, that it is a duty and a pleasure to write their biographies, and place them on record as memorials to posterity for its benefit and instruction. The subject of this sketch was born at Johnstown, N. Y., August 7th, 1822. During his youth he received a thorough training in the common school and academy at Johnstown, and at an early age he had charge of his father's business. In 1843,

he opened a flouring mill, and since that date he has been most actively engaged in milling, farming, and building, and to his credit, be it said, he has in the latter branch of industry done more to build the town of his birth, and furnish it with beautiful homes, than any other man who ever lived there. In 1845, he was married to Miss Sabra M. Steel, by whom he had one daughter, now living at Kingsboro. In 1848, he was married the second time to Miss Margaret E. Burton, of Johnstown, and they now live in their beautiful homestead which has been in the family possession for eighty-four years. This house was originally built by Sir William Johnson, in 1762, and is one of the few landmarks remaining of that celebrated English lord. The halls on both floors are fifteen by forty feet, and the staircase is still provided with the original banisters which Brandt, the Indian chief, hacked with his tomahawk as a signal to the incoming tribes not to destroy the mansion. (See Stone's History of Brandt).

John E. Wells has liberally dispensed his charities, and seen and enjoyed the fruits of them while living. His good works live around him, and he can enjoy them, for there is no one more deeply respected by zealous, admiring friends than is J. E. Wells.

Wheeler, William A., was born June 30th, 1819, in Malone, Franklin County, N. Y. Entered the University of Vermont in the class which graduated in 1842, but was compelled by adverse pecuniary circumstances to leave at the middle of the course. He pursued the study of law at Malone with the Hon. Asa Hascall, and was admitted to the bar in 1845. He was for several years District-Attorney for the county of Franklin. He represented that county in the Assembly of New York in the years 1850 and 1851; in the latter year he engaged in the business of banking at Malone, which was continued until 1865. From 1854 to 1865 he was president of the board of trustees of the second mortgage bondholders of the Northern New York Railroad Company, and as such managed the railroad of that company. He was a member of the Senate of the State of New York for the years 1858 and 1859, and for that time president, pro. tem., of the same. He was a member of Congress during the first two years of the war of the rebellion. Was a member and president of the New York Constitutional Convention in 1867-8. He was again elected to Congress in 1868, where he remained continuously until March 4th, 1877. On the 5th day of March, 1877, he was inaugurated Vice-President of the United States. Mr. Wheeler was a member of the House Committee, raised in the 43d Congress, upon Southern affairs, and in that capacity united the State of Louisiana, and was the author of the plan for composing the political difficulties in that State, which was finally accepted, and is known as the "Wheeler Adjustment."

White, John G., was born on board the Ship Fair America, Captain Duplex, on the Atlantic Ocean, on the 22d day of July, 1801, his parents, Matthew White and Elizabeth Given White, emigrating from the County Tyrone, north of Ireland, for America, and landing at the city of New York. The years of his childhood were spent mostly in the western part of Pennsylvania, and until 1813, when his parents moved to the city of Albany, where, in 1814, his father died at the age of forty-five, leaving a family of seven children—four boys and three girls—in humble circumstances, so that the boys were obliged to put on the harness for the journey of life at a very early age, and with but little advantages of education. John G., the subject of this article, was, in 1814, at the age of thirteen years, indentured as an apprentice to the publishers and printers of the *Albany Gazette*, with whom he served the full length of his apprenticeship. During the first year of his apprenticeship, Thurlow Weed, Esq., worked in the office, type-setting as a journeyman printer, and the subsequent year J. G. assisted Tom Tillman to make the first *patent roller* that was ever made outside New York City, which very soon took the place of the old-fashioned balls. Before he had reached his twenty-first year, he purchased from Solomon Southwick, Esq., the printing office and *Albany Register*, a semi-weekly paper, Israel W. Clark being editor, which in a few years was given up and the printing office sold to John C. Johnson. In 1823, J. G. W., in connection with his brother William, was for a year or two engaged in the wholesale grocery business, during which time they, in connection with some of the principal merchants of the city, got up a West India Company, with the view of opening a direct West India trade with this city. The schooner Enterprise was chartered from Davis & Center, and loaded with flour and provisions, together with twenty horses, leaving Albany in the month of November, and did not return until next spring, with a cargo of sugar and St. Croix rum, proving a very profitable trip for the owner of the vessel, but unfortunate for the stockholders. In 1824, J. G. White was one of the committee appointed by the city authorities to make suitable arrangements for the celebration of the completion of the Erie Canal, there now being only three of that committee living, viz., Thomas W. Alcott, Samuel Morgan, and John G. White. In 1825, J. G. W. and his brother William entered into the brewing and malting business, and, in connection with Samuel Puyn, it was continued several years. On the 25th of March of that year, Mr. J. G. White was married to Hannah J., the third daughter of Elisha Putnam, Esq. Subsequently withdrew from the brewing business, but has continued that of malting up to the present time in connection with his sons Matthew and Andrew G. The latter is personally interested, being one of the firm of John G. White & Son. The senior of this firm has, during his long experience in the business, built and rebuilt nineteen malt-houses, and introduced many improvements; among them is one universally adopted in building malt-houses, where real estate is valuable, and embodies the construction of a number of kilns, one over the other, and the use of superheated steam in drying malt.

On the 25th of March, 1875, the subject of this article, with his partner in life, had the pleasure and satisfaction of meeting a great number of their friends on the fiftieth anniversary of their wedding, their union having been blessed with eleven children—seven boys and four girls, three of the former dying in childhood, and one at the age of twenty-four, of malarial fever, while serving in the defence of his country on the Island of Roanoke.

The parents' children and grandchildren now number thirty-three in all, and for many years they have been in the habit of meeting regularly on every Thanksgiving

JOHN D. WILLARD

day around the parental table with thankful hearts to an overruling Providence for a liberal portion of health, happiness, and prosperity.

Willard, John D., was a native of Lancaster, N. H., where he was born November 4th, 1799, and was the son of a clergyman. He was a descendant of Major Simon Willard, who emigrated to this country from the County of Kent, England, in 1643.

Senator Willard was educated at Dartmouth College, where he graduated at the early age of nineteen. He commenced the study of law in Chenango County, N. Y., completed it in Troy, and was admitted to the bar in 1826. He immediately opened an office in that city, where he had already made many warm friends. The next year he was nominated by DeWitt Clinton for Surrogate of the County of Rensselaer. In 1834, he was appointed Judge of the County Courts of Rensselaer County, on the nomination of William L. Marcy. This office he held six years. In the mean time his business as a lawyer had been constantly increasing, and was now very extensive. He then determined to devote himself entirely to his profession, and after this time steadily refused all nominations for election to public office. In 1850, accompanied by his wife, he carried out a plan he had long cherished of visiting Europe. He spent two months in Great Britain, and two months in Paris; in the autumn he visited Belgium, Western Germany, and Switzerland, and passed the winter in Italy, dividing his time chiefly between Florence, Rome, and Naples. In the following spring and summer he extended his tour through Austria, Hungary, Prussia, and Poland, going as far east as Warsaw. He afterward visited Holland, and returned to America after an absence of more than a year. In 1855, he again embarked for Europe, partly for the benefit of his health, and partly to accompany a son. He was absent from the country on this visit about fifteen months.

In the fall of 1857, Judge Willard yielded to the earnest request of his Democratic friends, and accepted the nomination of that party for Senator from the Twelfth district, and was elected, although the district gave at the previous election a majority for Fremont over Buchanan of nearly five thousand.

Judge Willard, though not a church member, attended the services of the Presbyterian Church, and for several years was chairman of the board of trustees of the Second Presbyterian congregation in Troy —the Rev. Dr. Smalley's. He was a director in the Commercial Bank of Troy, and a member of various literary and scientific societies. In 1839, he married Miss Laura Barnes. He had a taste for literary pursuits, and found time amid the engrossing cares of a laborious profession to give much attention to general literature. In public, as in private life, he was straightforward, upright, decided, and reliable; a sound, successful lawyer, always occupying the front rank in his profession; an able legislator, and a representative of whom the people of the Twelfth Senatorial district may well feel proud.

He died at Troy, October 9th, 1864, deeply mourned by all who knew him, and his loss was felt by the whole community in which he lived.

Wotkyns, Dr. Alfred, was born at Walpole, N. H., September 7th, 1798.

His father was a farmer. He was mainly educated by a private tutor, under whose charge he was put at the age of thirteen. At the age of nineteen, he came to Troy, and entered the office of the late Dr. Morris Hale. In 1821, he was admitted to the practice of medicine, and became a partner of Dr. Hale; but not long afterward, wishing to perfect himself in his profession, he removed to Philadelphia, where he read medicine one year under the tuition of Dr. Nathaniel Chapman, and attended the lectures of the University of Pennsylvania, of which institution he is a graduate. He returned to Troy in 1822, and applied for the appointment of surgeon in the United States army, and received the appointment, though there were some three hundred applications for the position, and was soon ordered to Natchitoches, La., on the Red River, about two hundred miles above New Orleans, an extreme frontier post. A subsequent order changed his destination to Pensacola, Fla., at which post there were then stationed some two thousand men. Here he remained two years as surgeon, when he resigned. Returning to Troy, he reopened a physician's office, and for a long period of nearly fifty years was a practising physician of that city. He has been president of the County Medical Society. He was many times a delegate to the State Society, of which organization he was a permanent member. In 1838, when Troy had but three supervisors, Dr. Watkyns represented the Second district. He was one of the originators of the Marshall Infirmary, and a governor of the institution from its commencement, and a member of the medical board. When the State Bank went into operation in 1852, Dr. Watkyns was chosen its president, and continued as such until January, 1868. The prosperity of this banking institution is well known, and it is conceded that its success has been largely due to the striking financial abilities and great business sagacity of its president. In 1857-58, Dr. Watkyns was mayor of Troy. It will be recalled as the panic year for the whole country. City finances were somewhat embarrassed throughout, and the aid of Mayor Watkyns, furnished in enabling the city to meet all of its obligations on the one hand, and to escape the extortion of money-lenders on the other, was very considerable as well as very timely. In the discharge of his official duties, he exhibited his characteristic business promptness. Dr. Alfred Watkyns died on the 23d of December, 1876, deeply mourned by his family and friends. The life of Dr. Watkyns was an eventful one. There was not a word of reproach against his character, nothing to sully his fair name, nothing to dim the lustre of his life, still left shining as a bright example to be followed; and now that his spirit hath calmly glided from this earth, his honored name will not be forgotten.

Wilcox, Captain Timothy Dwight, was born at Simsbury, Hartford County Ct., on the 1st day of February, 1803. The early years of his life, and until he was fifteen, were mostly spent on a farm. During this period, he obtained all the education he ever had, attending the country district-school a few weeks each winter. In February, 1818, his parents left Connecticut for Ohio, taking with them their whole family. When they reached Albany, both were taken sick, and compelled to stop their journey. The subject of this sketch was obliged to obtain work, and on the opening of navigation

on the Hudson River, in April, he was employed on Fulton's steamboat, the Paragon. From that time to the present writing (September, 1877), a period of fifty-nine years, he has been engaged constantly and actively in the steamboat interests, and to-day is one of the oldest, if not the oldest, steamboat man living. During this remarkably long period of active life, he was for a number of years steamboating on the Hudson River, Long Island Sound, between Boston and points on the Penobscot and Kennebec. In the fall of 1841, he removed his home from New York City to Ithaca, N. Y., where he has since lived, excepting five years, from 1850 to 1855, in the steamboat business on Cayuga Lake. For many years, he has been the sole owner and proprietor of the steamers on that lake, and at present he owns and runs five boats. Captain Wilcox has been twice married, and now has three children living.

Wright, Luther, was born at Nelson, N. H., September 13th, 1799. In 1806, his father moved to the town of Rodman, Jefferson County, N. Y., and followed the occupation of farmer. The subject of this sketch was brought up on his father's farm until seventeen years of age, during which time he received a common and academic education. He then taught school for two years, after which he clerked in a store six or seven years. In 1825, he moved to Tompkins County, became a merchant, and continued there until 1832, when he removed to Oswego, then a very small village, where he engaged in the milling and forwarding business until 1842, when he was burned out. In 1843, he commenced banking, a calling he has been more or less engaged in ever since. In 1828, he was married to Miss Lucinda Smith, daughter of his former employer. In 1840, he was married a second time, to Miss L. Baily, formerly from Adams, Jefferson County, New York, by whom he has had four children, two of whom survive. In the course of his long and useful business career, he has held several directorships in banks, and otherwise interested largely in business operations. He is now President of the Oswego City Savings Bank, and Oswego Gas Light Company. He was also Treasurer of the Oswego and Syracuse Railroad from its organization until leased to the Delaware, Lackawanna, and Western Railroad.

A brief sketch of Mr. Wright's life is useful for its practical instruction. He has amassed a large fortune. Yet he has never risked a dollar in the precarious investments of speculation, but gradually added to his little commencement till its present proportions have been reached; and nothing exists to dim the lustre of his life, now so near its setting, in the sear of which hosts of friends and family gather round him; and when his spirit will calmly and hopefully glide away, his honored name will not be forgotten.

Wright, William, was born in Wayne County, N. Y., in 1818. He belongs to the number of our self-made men, as his success in life is due to his mechanical genius and his continual exertion to improve on his own works, and excel others by his own labor. He received in early life only a common-school education, until, at the age of eighteen, he commenced to learn his trade as a mechanic with one John Daggett, of Newark, N. Y. He had shown his natural genius for steam engineering by building a small engine, alone, in the cellar of his father's house, doing all work by hand, after having seen only one small engine before. After contin uing with Mr. Daggett for two and a half years, being part of this time foreman of the shop, he moved to Niagara Falls, engaging in the repair-shops of the Buffalo and Niagara Falls Railroad, with the intention to become an engineer of that railroad, but was compelled to desist on account of ill-health. A few months' stay at home enabled him to engage in building steam-engines, with a Mr. Williams, in Palmyra, until he removed to Rochester, in 1842, where he built engines, with a Mr. John Bush, until 1845. It was while here that Mr. Wright took unto himself a life-partner by being married to Miss Elizabeth G. Taft. In that same year Mr. W. invented a rotary steam-engine, and went to Providence with one F. Church, with whom he formed a partnership, to build these engines; but he continued with him only one year, after which he was for a short time with a Providence Tool Company, until he engaged with Corliss, Nightingale & Co., manufacturers of steam-engines, with whom he was employed until 1850. At that time, Mr. W. engaged to build a large condensing engine for Brown Brothers, of Waterbury, Ct., which engine is still in use by the above firm. After this, Mr. W. was employed as general superintendent, with a salary, by Messrs. Woodruff & Beach, of Hartford, Ct., and superintended the designing, building, and erection of several large engines, similar to the one built for Brown Brothers, besides the large pumping-engines for the Brooklyn Water-works, which he patented, with another automatic cut-off engine, extensively built and used in all parts of this country. This cut-off engine was one of the first of that kind made. During that time, Mr. W. also superintended the building and erection of the machinery of the Kearsarge, and many other gunboats used in the late war. In 1863, Mr. Wright resigned his position with the above house, and became one of the firm of the New York Steam-Engine Company, remaining as such until 1866, building during that time many engines for the government boats. In 1866, he connected himself with Homer Ramsdell, Esq., of Newburg, N. Y., for the purpose of building his patented steam-engines, Mr. W. receiving a salary and royalty on his patents; as, in 1867, the firm changed hands, Mr. W. made the same arrangements with the new firm; and again, when the Washington Iron-Works became an incorporated company, remaining such until 1870, when Mr. Wright himself formed, with several partners, the house of William Wright & Co., doing business in the same shop formerly occupied by the Washington Iron-Works. Mr. Wright is at present the only surviving member of that firm; he is engaged in manufacturing his greatly improved automatic cut-off engines, which are extensively used in all parts of our country; and has lately built some more of his patented pumping engines, greatly improved by applying the system of compound engines, which attain a duty of work heretofore unknown, and which are a credit to his mechanical genius. Mr. Wright, through his long experience and his application to the improvement of steam-engines, stands now at the head of his profession as an engine-builder. He has made as many inventions and improvements in steam-engines as any one we can now call to mind, and he has through a long course of successful life proved worthy of the highest esteem for honor and integrity; and now, in his sixtieth year, still living at Newburg, has promise of many years in which to enjoy the fruits of his labor. His motto in life has been and is to excel in all he undertook, and his success in life shows how well he has lived

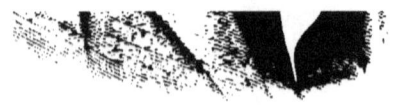

up to this maxim, which he set before him as a guide.

Wyckoff, Arcalous, was born in Asbury, N. J., on the 10th of April, 1816. He was the fifth son of Peter Wyckoff, a farmer, who, when the subject of this sketch was one year old, moved to Tompkins County, N. Y., and had the misfortune to lose all his property. He then commenced to make fanning-mills, by which he earned his living some time, his son Arcalous learning the trade of his father, which he afterward put to good use.

Mr. Wyckoff attended the common schools of his home until sixteen years old, when he gave his time to making what he could in different ways till he was about twenty-four. Being ambitious to make money, he left his home, going to Wellsburg, Chemung County, N. Y., where he commenced to manufacture fanning-mills. This he continued about two years, when he went into the manufacturing of potash, and mercantile business, with a brother, continuing it three years. Thinking the field not large enough, he moved to Elmira, and engaged in the manufacturing and sale of fanning-mills. Here he remained one year. At this time, the chain-pump came largely into use, and he engaged in the manufacture of the wood work and the sale of the pump in the place of his adoption, Ulysses, Tompkins County, N. Y. At the expiration of one year, he returned to Elmira, where, in company with D. B. Wheeler, he commenced the manufacture of the chain. The next year, they moved to Tompkins County, took in another partner, and continued to manufacture on a larger scale. Soon after this, Mr. Wyckoff sold out his interest, and moved to Dayton, Ohio, where, in company with a partner, he engaged in the sale of the chain-pump. He afterward manufactured the pump chain at Springfield, Ohio, then at Cincinnati. While here, his partner's behavior caused financial embarrassment, which, after Mr. W. had adjusted properly, he moved to Columbus, and was in business with Abner Cooper, formerly of Elmira. While here, he lost his wife, in 1855, who was the daughter of Dr. Hopkins, of Wellsburg, and by whom he had four children, two only surviving. After this sad loss referred to, Mr. Wyckoff returned to Elmira, where he has since resided, proving himself one of her most active and useful citizens, useful not only to the city of his residence, but to the country at large; for he is the inventor of both the Wyckoff pavement and the Wyckoff boring-machine, both widely known. He is also largely interested in real estate and building operations, having erected in one continuous block eleven stores, the whole being fire-proof excepting four. In 1860, he, in connection with three gentlemen from Rochester, built the water-works at Elmira, all the pipe used being constructed by the machinery of his invention. To these enterprising gentlemen, who were losers by the operation, is the city of Elmira indebted for its present water supply.

Thus we give a short sketch of a useful and somewhat eventful life of one of Elmira's most enterprising citizens, who still lives to enjoy the benefit of his arduous labors, much respected by the community of which he is a member.

Wyckoff, Nicholas, was born in the town of Bushwick, now Brooklyn, Kings County, N. Y., on the 30th of October, 1799. His parents were Peter and Gertrude Wyckoff, and his father's ancestry emigrated to this country from Holland in 1635. During his youth, the subject of this sketch attended the common-schools, then very poor. At the age of twelve, he finished his education by attending for two years a private school in Connecticut; after which, he returned home and helped his father on the farm, attending school during the winter months. From this time until 1842, he worked the farm with his father, producing market supplies, at which they proved very successful. In 1842, his father died and left his son Nicholas the sole possessor of the homestead farm. This he continued to work until 1860, when he was elected to fill the vacancy in the presidency of the Williamsburg City Bank (now First National), caused by the death of its former president, Noah Waterbury, Esq. This office he still holds, and, since the commencement of his banking career, his son has had charge of the farm, though Mr. Wyckoff continues to reside at the old homestead, situated about two miles from the bank. In 1826, he was married to Sarah A., daughter of Gen. Jeremiah Johnson, by whom he has had four children, only one of whom (Peter) survives. Throughout his successful career, Mr. Wyckoff has been a hard worker, and believes that energy and industry will accomplish almost any thing. It is this that has gained for him esteem, position, and wealth, and if the youth of the rising generation would go and do likewise, they would in time achieve what he has done.